TRAVELERS' TALES

ONE HAND DOES NOT CATCH A BUFFALO

50 YEARS OF AMAZING PEACE CORPS STORIES

VOLUME ONE: AFRICA

Edited by

AARON BARLOW

Series Editor
JANE ALBRITTON

D1323273

Travelers' Tales
An Imprint of Solas House, Inc.
Palo Alto

Copyright © 2011 Jane Albritton. All rights reserved.

Travelers' Tales and *Solas House* are trademarks of Solas House, Inc. 853 Alma Street, Palo Alto, California 94301. www.travelerstales.com

Cover Design: Chris Richardson
Interior Layout: Howie Severson
Production Director: Susan Brady

Library of Congress Cataloging-in-Publication Data

One hand does not catch a buffalo : 50 years of amazing Peace Corps stories : volume one, Africa / edited by Aaron Barlow ; series editor, Jane Albritton. -- 1st ed.
      p. cm.
   Includes bibliographical references and index.
   ISBN 978-1-60952-000-7 (pbk. : alk. paper)
   1. Peace Corps (U.S.)--Anecdotes. 2. Volunteers--Africa--Anecdotes. 3. Volunteers--Developing countries--Anecdotes. I. Barlow, Aaron, 1951- II. Albritton, Jane.
   HC60.5.O54 2011
   361.6--dc22

                                    2010054339

First Edition
Printed in the United States
10 9 8 7 6 5 4 3 2 1

To all who served in Africa

*and to all of those in Africa who welcomed them,
worked with them, and taught them.*

Table of Contents

Part Three
GETTING THROUGH THE DAYS

Part Four
CLOSE ENCOUNTERS

Part Five
SUSTAINABLE PEACE

Series Preface

THERE ARE SOME BABY IDEAS THAT SEEM TO FLY IN BY STORK, without incubation between conception and birth. These magical bundles smile and say: "Want me?" And well before the head can weigh the merits of taking in the unsummoned arrival, the heart leaps forward and answers, "Yes!"

The idea for Peace Corps @ 50—the anniversary media project for which this series of books are the centerpiece—arrived on my mental doorstep in just this way in 2007. Four books of stories, divided by regions of the world, written by the Peace Corps Volunteers who have lived and worked there. There was time to solicit the stories, launch the website, and locate editors for each book. By 2011, the 50th anniversary of the founding of the Peace Corps, the books would be released.

The website had no sooner gone live when the stories started rolling in. And now, after four years and with a publisher able to see the promise and value of this project, here we are, ready to share more than 200 stories of our encounters with people and places far from home.

In the beginning, I had no idea what to expect from a call for stories. Now, at the other end of this journey, I have read every story, and I know what makes our big collection such a fitting tribute to the Peace Corps experience.

Peace Corps Volunteers write. We write a lot. Most of us need to, because writing is the only chance we have to say things in our native language. Functioning every day in another language takes work, and it isn't just about grammar. It's everything that isn't taught—like when to say what depending on the context, like the intricate system of body language, and like knowing how to shift your tone depending on the company you are in. These struggles and linguistic mishaps can be frustrating and often provoke laughter, even if people are forgiving and appreciate the effort. It takes a long time to earn a sense of belonging.

And so in our quiet moments—when we slip into a private space away from the worlds where we are guests—we write. And in these moments where we treat ourselves to our own language, thoughts flow freely. We once wrote only journals and letters; today we also text, email, and blog.

Writing helps us work through the frustrations of everyday living in cultures where—at first—we do not know the rules or understand the values. In our own language we write out our loneliness, our fury, our joy, and our revelations. Every volunteer who has ever served writes as a personal exercise in coming to terms with an awakening ignorance. And then we write our way through it, making our new worlds part of ourselves in our own language, in our own words.

The stories in these books are the best contribution we can make to the permanent record of Peace Corps on the occasion of its 50th anniversary. And because a Volunteer's attempt to explain the experience has always contained the hope that folks at home will "get it," these stories are also a gift to anyone eager and curious to learn what we learned about living in places that always exceeded what we imagined them to be.

It has been an honor to receive and read these stories. Taken together, they provide a kaleidoscopic view of world cultures—beautiful and strange—that shift and rattle when held up to the light.

I would like to acknowledge personally the more than 200 Return Volunteers who contributed to these four volumes. Without their voices, this project could not have been possible. Additionally, editors Pat and Bernie Alter, Aaron Barlow, and Jay Chen have been tireless in shepherding their stories through the publishing process and in helping me make my way through some vexing terrain along the way. Special thanks to John Coyne whose introduction sets the stage for each volume. Thanks also to Dennis Cordell for his early work on the project.

There are two people critical to the success of this project who were never Peace Corps volunteers, but who instantly grasped the significance of the project: Chris Richardson and Susan Brady.

Chris and his PushIQ team, created a visually lush, technically elegant website that was up and ready to invite contributors to join the project and to herald both the project and the anniversary itself. He took on the creative challenge of designing four distinct covers for the four volumes in this set. His work first invited our contributors and now invites our readers.

Susan Brady brought it all home. It is one thing to collect, edit, and admire four books' worth of stories; it is another to get them organized, to the typesetter, the printer, and the team of marketers on time and looking good. Susan's good sense, extensive publishing experience, and belief in the worthiness

of this project sealed the publishing deal with Travelers' Tales/
Solas House.

Finally, there are the two others, one at each elbow, who
kept me upright when the making of books made me weary.
My mother—intrepid traveler and keeper of stories—died
four months after the project launched, but she has been kind
enough to hang around to see me through. My partner, cultural anthropologist Kate Browne, never let me forget that if
Americans are ever going to have an honored place in this
world, we need to have some clue about how the rest of it
works. "So get with it," they said. "The 50th anniversary happens only once."

—JANE ALBRITTON
FORT COLLINS, COLORADO

Thirty Days That Built the Peace Corps

BY JOHN COYNE

*In 1961 John F. Kennedy took two risky and conflicting initiatives
in the Third World. One was to send 500 additional military
advisers into South Vietnam. The other was to send 500 young
Americans to teach in the schools and work in the fields of eight
developing countries. These were Peace Corps Volunteers. By 1963
there would be 7,000 of them in forty-four countries.*

—Garard T. Rice, The Bold Experiment: JFK's Peace Corps

KENNEDY'S SECOND INITIATIVE INSPIRED, AND CONTINUES TO
inspire, hope and understanding among Americans and the rest
of the world. In a very real sense, the Peace Corps is Kennedy's
most affirmative and enduring legacy that belongs to a particularly American yearning: the search for a new frontier.

Two key people in Congress, Henry Reuss (D-Wisconsin)
and Hubert Humphrey (D-Minnesota), both proposed the idea
of the Peace Corps in the late 1950s.

In January of 1960, Reuss introduced the first Peace
Corps-type legislation. It sought a study of "the advisability

and practicability to the establishment of a Point Four Youth Corps," which would send young Americans willing to serve their country in public and private technical assistance missions in far-off countries, and at a soldier's pay.

The government contract was won by Maurice (Maury) L. Albertson of Colorado State University who with one extraordinary assistant, Pauline Birky-Kreutzer, did the early groundwork for Congress on the whole idea of young Americans going overseas, not to win wars, but help build societies.

In June of 1960, Hubert Humphrey introduced in the Senate a bill to send "young men to assist the peoples of the underdeveloped areas of the world to combat poverty, disease, illiteracy, and hunger."

Also in 1960, several other people were expressing support for such a concept: General James Gavin; Chester Bowles, former governor of Connecticut, and later ambassador to India; William Douglas, associate justice of the Supreme Count; James Reston of *The New York Times;* Milton Shapp, from Philadelphia; Walt Rostow of MIT; and Senator Jacob Javits of New York, who urged Republican presidential candidate Richard Nixon to adopt the idea. Nixon refused. He saw the Peace Corps as just another form of "draft evasion."

What Nixon could not have foreseen was that a "day of destiny" waited for the world on October 14, 1960. On the steps of the Student Union at the University of Michigan, in the darkness of the night, the Peace Corps became more than a dream. Ten thousand students waited for presidential candidate Kennedy until 2 A.M., and they chanted his name as he climbed those steps.

Kennedy launched into an extemporaneous address. He challenged them, asking how many would be prepared to give years of their lives working in Asia, Africa, and Latin America?

The audience went wild. (I know this, because at the time I was a new graduate student over in Kalamazoo. I was working part-time as a news reporter for WKLZ and had gone to cover the event.)

Six days before the 1960 election, on November 2nd, Kennedy gave a speech at the Cow Palace in San Francisco. He pointed out that 70 percent of all new Foreign Service officers had no foreign language skills whatsoever; only three of the forty-four Americans in the embassy in Belgrade spoke Yugoslavian; not a single American in New Delhi could speak Indian dialects, and only two of the nine ambassadors in the Middle East spoke Arabic. Kennedy also pointed out that there were only twenty-six black officers in the entire Foreign Service corps, less than 1 percent.

Kennedy's confidence in proposing a "peace corps" at the end of his campaign was bolstered by news that students in the Big Ten universities and other colleges throughout Michigan had circulated a petition urging the founding of such an organization. The idea had caught fire in something like spontaneous combustion.

The day after his inauguration, President Kennedy telephoned his brother-in-law Sargent Shriver and asked him to form a presidential task force to report how the Peace Corps should be organized and then to organize it. When he heard from Kennedy, Shriver immediately called Harris Wofford.

At the time, Shriver was 44; Wofford was 34. Initially, the Task Force consisted solely of the two men, sitting in a suite of two rooms that they had rented at the Mayflower Hotel in Washington, D.C. They spent most of their time making calls to personal friends they thought might be helpful.

One name led to another: Gordon Boyce, president of the Experiment in International Living; Albert Sims of the Institute of International Education; Adam Yarmolinsky, a foundation executive; Father Theodore Hesburgh, president of the University of Notre Dame; George Carter, a campaign worker on civil rights issues and former member of the American Society for African Culture; Louis Martin, a newspaper editor; Franklin Williams, an organizer of the campaign for black voter registration, and a student of Africa; and Maury Albertson, out at Colorado State University.

Unbeknownst to Shriver and Wofford, two officials in the Far Eastern division of the International Cooperation Administration (ICA) were working on their own Peace Corps plan. Warren Wiggins, who was the deputy director of Far Eastern operations in ICA, was still in his thirties but had already helped administer the Marshall Plan in Western Europe. He was totally dissatisfied with the manner in which American overseas programs were run; he called them "golden ghettos." With Wiggins was Bill Josephson, just 26, and a lawyer at ICA.

They started developing an idea that would be limited to sending young Americans overseas to teach English. But as they worked on it, their vision broadened. The paper detailing their recommendations was titled "A Towering Task." They sent copies to Wofford, Richard Goodwin at the White House, and to Shriver, who thought it was brilliant and immediately sent a telegram to Wiggins inviting him to attend the Task Force meeting the next morning. It was Wiggins who advocated initiating the Peace Corps with "several thousand Americans participating in the first twelve to eighteen months." A slow and cautious beginning was not an option.

Three times in February, Kennedy would telephone Shriver to ask about progress on the Peace Corps. The final draft of the report was created with Charles Nelson sitting in one room writing basic copy, Josephson sitting in another room rewriting it, Wofford sitting in yet another room doing the final rewrite, and Wiggins running back and forth carrying pieces of paper.

Shriver held the position that Peace—not Development, it might be noted—was the overriding purpose, and the process of promoting it was necessarily complex. So the Peace Corps should learn to live with complexity that could not be summed up in a single proposition. Finally, the Task Force agreed on three.

- Goal One: It can contribute to the development of critical countries and regions.
- Goal Two: It can promote international cooperation and goodwill toward this country.
- Goal Three: It can also contribute to the education of America and to more intelligent American participation in the world.

On the morning of Friday, February 24, 1961, Shriver delivered the report—the Peace Corps Magna Carta—to Kennedy and told him: "If you decide to go ahead, we can be in business Monday morning."

It had taken Shriver, Wofford, Wiggins, Josephson, and the other members of the Mayflower Task Force, less than a month to create what *TIME Magazine* would call that year "the greatest single success the Kennedy administration had produced." On March 1, 1961, President Kennedy issued an Executive Order establishing the Peace Corps.

And today, fifty years later, we are still debating what the Peace Corps is all about. As Sarge Shriver thought all those years ago, "the tension between competing purposes is creative, and it should continue."

Well, it has!

John Coyne, who is considered an authority on the history of the Peace Corps, has written or edited over twenty-five books. In 1987 he started the newsletter RPCV Writers & Readers that is for and about Peace Corps writers. This newsletter, now a website, can be found today at PeaceCorpsWorldwide.org.

Introduction

LEARNING WORKS BOTH WAYS. YOU CAN'T HELP PEOPLE UNLESS you allow them to help *you*. Idealistic? Yes. But this is also the virtue and value of the amateur, the person learning along the way instead of bringing along prior expertise. Rarely vested in personal advancement, the amateur is a discoverer and a doer, concentrating on the thing-at-hand.

This, of course, is the idea behind the Peace Corps. Though PCVs do take expertise with them, it is hardly ever in development. They learn as they go and even when they return. And their learning helps others.

At about the time the Peace Corps was founded, a project called Airlift Africa, set up by Tom Mboya soon after Kenyan independence, brought students to the United States. Among these was the father of Barack Obama. Another was Mboya's younger brother, Alphonse Okuku. While studying at Antioch College in Ohio, Alphonse stayed with the family of my teachers Ernest and Elizabeth Morgan, rooming with their son Lee.

I met Alphonse in the fall of 1963 and was enchanted by this serious and slender young man. Because of him, my seventh-grade self began reading about Africa, learning of a far, distant place. Though I would drift away from my interest in Africa until drawn back to it over twenty years later, the fascination sparked by Alphonse was always there.

Over the next few years, I remember reading *Jambo, African Balloon Safari* by Anthony Smith, *Congo Kitabu* by Jean-Pierre Hallet, *Things Fall Apart* by Chinua Achebe, and *Cry, the Beloved Country* by Alan Paton—and more. Just by his presence, and in the course of his own education, Alphonse had opened a new world to me. Just as the presence of PCVs does, all over the globe.

After the close of my Peace Corps service, I visited Alphonse, whom I had written from Togo. He did not remember me, but kindly showed me around a bit of the Luo areas of Kenya and even arranged for a balloon ride over the Masai Mara, something I'd wanted to do ever since reading Anthony Smith's book as a kid. It was a fitting end to my service. Now, I had seen the world Alphonse had opened for me, making a vast intellectual broadening possible.

These stories, today, are continuing the same process. The process of editing this volume has taught me more than I had ever thought to learn, now, about Americans in Africa.

For the better part of a year, I've lived with the essays, going through them, sorting them, cutting them down so they could all fit in this volume. They've provided me with recognition, with joy, sadness, hope, disillusionment, and memory. They've taught me. They've re-opened a world I long ago left behind, and have helped me understand the nature of the Peace Corps beyond my own small experience. Ultimately, they have convinced me that, whatever its legacy in development, the Peace Corps will always be known world-wide as one of the United States' most significant contributions to human kind.

Each perspective presented here is distinct. Though we who served in Africa will often nod in recognition as we read these essays, our experiences were never lock step, but were diverse and often extraordinary. This volume reflects that, as much as I could make it do so. Some of the stories deal with the small, daily events that came to be commonplace. Others present astonishing once-in-a-lifetime events. Together, they present a picture as true to the Peace Corps experience in Africa as I could make it.

The Peace Corps may not change the world in grand ways, but it does change individuals—and not just the volunteers. Like that seventh-grader awed by an African, there are thousands and thousands of people world-wide whose views of the world were expanded by naïve and idealistic PCVs who came to rest in their villages and towns, even if just for a short time.

That is one great success.

—AARON BARLOW

PART ONE

ON OUR WAY...
AND BACK AGAIN

ROBERT KLEIN

✳
✳　✳

Why I Joined the Peace Corps

Going, at first, was much more mysterious,
much more romantic, than now it may seem!

I<small>T ALL HAD TO DO WITH THE</small> 1930<small>S MOVIE</small> *B<small>EAU</small> G<small>ESTE</small>*: <small>BRAVE</small> young men, faced with incredibly complicated personal lives, joined the French Foreign Legion, making their way to remotest North Africa, there to become involved in legendary exploits. This image sustained me as I settled into being a junior high school teacher in New York City in the late 1950s. When I had to deal with an impossible class or wanted to untangle from a romantic involvement, I would think to myself, "They can't do this to me; I'll go and join the French Foreign Legion!" By 1961, I had carried the fantasy out only so far as to grow a beard. In dim light, at a distance of thirty to forty feet, I did look mysterious.

That it was a different era is illustrated by what happened after I first attempted that goatee, over the summer vacation in 1960. It was the first day of class and my students, amidst a lot of giggling, good-naturedly commented about the change in my appearance:

"Hey, Mr. Klein, are you a beatnik?"

"I think that's cool. Tell the principal to grow one too."

"Are they going to let you keep that thing?"

I was pleased; I liked the beard and intended to keep it. Before reporting to school that September, being the Union representative in my building, I had checked Board regulations. They stated that teachers must be neatly attired (men wore jackets and ties, women skirts or dresses) and well groomed. But it did not say anything about beards.

Then I heard a rapid knocking at the classroom door. The principal waved me out of the classroom. I stepped into the hall.

"You can't teach wearing a beard!" he said.

He wore horn-rimmed glasses, had a scholarly and distant look, and was, at all times—except this one—calm and cerebral. His receding hairline emphasized his shiny forehead and his quizzical eyes; it made him look like a cross between Adlai Stevenson and Woody Allen. In ordinary conversations, he seemed to be reading from prepared remarks. But now he was apoplectic. I tried to respond quietly.

"Sir, I feel that I'm properly dressed and my students seem to like the change."

"But it isn't right; it will upset the class. How can you teach like that?"

"Certainly if my appearance causes a noisy classroom, I would immediately shave off the beard. But that doesn't seem to be the case, does it? May I return to my class?"

He turned and slowly walked down the hall.

So began my fifth year of teaching. Along with it were pressures toward responsible domesticity. My mom and pop kept saying, "You're old enough to get married now; you're thirty-two. Come home next weekend and meet Maxine. Her folks think you are wonderful. She's such a nice girl."

In my head, I was hearing the drums of the Legion.

My first attempt to answer those drums did not turn out well. I applied for a Fulbright Teaching Fellowship at a secondary school in Northern Rhodesia. With an M.A. in History from the University of Chicago and five years teaching experience, on paper I was a highly qualified candidate. Within weeks of applying, I was called for an interview at Columbia University.

I had done nothing to prepare for the interview.

The first question was: "Why do you want to teach in Rhodesia?"

Although it was mid-February, I immediately began to feel cold sweat uncomfortably tickling my armpits and, in a panic, realized that these interviewers might not be impressed with my *Beau Geste* story.

"Well, I really enjoy teaching...um...um."

"Do you have any special interest in or knowledge of Rhodesia?"

I could find it on a map, but I felt that this was not the kind of answer that they were looking for.

"No, I am interested in a new challenge and would like to teach overseas."

"Are you at all familiar with Northern Rhodesia's current status?"

"Uh...no...uh."

"Can you name the major colonial powers in Africa and discuss their influence?"

"Uh...England! No, the British; uh...Great Britain."

"Yes?"

Silence and then, trying to be helpful, the African professor: "Of course, you've heard of Timbuktu."

Of course, I had. Mom always used to tell me that if I didn't do my share of the household chores, she'd run away to Timbuktu. I didn't think that was the reference the Professor had in mind. The interview ended shortly thereafter, and the Fulbright Fellows lost a good, though ill-informed, prospect to the Peace Corps.

Much of my motivation to join the Peace Corps actually came from my experiences when I served in the U.S. Army in Korea from 1952 to 1954. Having completed my master's degree in History, I was drafted. Within six months, I was assigned as Company Clerk in a Forward Ordnance Depot about ten miles behind the front lines in Korea. I worked with First Sergeant Burl Grant, a black man who had worked his way up through the ranks during this period when the armed forces were being integrated, a process that was far from complete in 1953. Sergeant Grant dealt with the world through brown, deep-set eyes full of life, but sometimes cold and unblinking. They seemed flecked with fire when he dealt with diehard racists in our company. He would never raise his voice, but his eyes signaled the anger and contempt he felt. That, and his rank, forced men to accept and follow his orders.

We shared a tent and, in the evenings, listening to jazz and be-bop (Errol Garner, Shorty Rogers, Dizzy Gillespie). I'd look at Grant, and his eyes would now be soft and mellow.

Our own houseboy was Yoo Yung Shik, whom we called Pak. He was fifteen with black hair and eyes, broad-faced, and with a very expressive mouth. In anger or in joy, his lips always parted broadly into a smile, giving him a pleasant appearance. When he was upset, the smile would freeze into a grimace, but when he was happy it would be accompanied by a slight giggle. Pak came from a small farming community in central Korea that had been fought through several times. He had attached himself to a U.S. Army unit as a means of survival. When we paid him, he would take off to his village, buying whatever he could with the MPC [military payment certificates] that we all, Koreans and Americans, used as currency.

Grant and I treated Pak decently, and he became a friend, taking us to his village to meet some of his family. This kind of relationship was discouraged officially and scorned by many of the Americans in the company who could only deal with the Koreans by thinking of them as "gooks" and treating them as inferiors.

About six months after I had arrived in Korea, Pak came to me one day in the orderly room tent where I worked. For the first time since I had known him, his face was dark and somber. I even noticed tears in his eyes. He told me about what had been happening in the company mess hall.

Our mess hall was typically American with a superabundance of whatever ill-prepared food we were being served. There were no shortages, and much food was wasted. Sergeant Grant had started the practice of allowing the local-hire Koreans to either eat or take home the surplus of prepared food from each meal. The Mess Sergeant, Pak told us one day, had become verbally and physically abusive to the Koreans as he reluctantly gave them the table surplus. He had even gone so far, now, as to throw the food into the trash cans before allowing the Koreans to take any. Grant stormed out of the orderly room to find the Mess Sergeant. I was not witness to their encounter, but Pak happily reported to me within a few days that all was *"Dai jobi"* [O.K.] in the mess hall.

Pak said that he and some of the other houseboys wanted to learn to speak and read English; knowing that I was approachable, they wanted me to be their teacher. As Company Clerk I did have a lot of free time, which I could devote to teaching rather than drinking at the enlisted men's club. With no training or preparation other than the fact that I had used the language for twenty-five years of my life, I became a teacher of English. It felt good to be doing something creative, rather than pushing mounds of meaningless forms and reports through my typewriter or spending vapid hours at the club, sharing alcohol-fueled inanities with my fellow drinkers. I also found that I enjoyed being a teacher. When I finished my military service in 1954 and could find no want ads in *The New York Times* for "Historians," I changed careers and became a teacher of Social Studies.

Korea and Pak and that Mess Sergeant (and *Beau Geste*) were on my mind as I went to the post office on Broadway and 68th Street in Manhattan to pick up a Peace Corps Questionnaire in April 1961. I remember filling it out. It included a lengthy list of personal and professional skills to be checked on a scale from "highly skilled" to "unskilled." With five years' experience, I hoped to become a Peace Corps teacher, but I wasn't sure of what Peace Corps was looking for (they weren't either). I pondered how best to mark:

"Milk a cow."

"Drive a tractor."

"Service an automobile transmission."

"Use a welding torch to repair equipment."

Where, I thought to myself, were the items I was totally confident about? Such as:

"Interpret a New York City Subway map."

"Control a class of 8th grade students on Friday afternoon."

"Read the Sunday edition of *The New York Times*."

Even though I wasn't ready to announce to the world that I was "joining the Legion," I went ahead with it and mailed the form to Washington. In responding to the item in the questionnaire that asked, "Why do you want to serve with the Peace Corps?" I had written the following:

"My experience as a teacher in New York City and in the Army in Korea both convince me that it is important to reach out to people. We Americans are a privileged people and too many of us go overseas and become 'Ugly Americans,' arrogant and insensitive. I would like to teach in another country because I am an experienced teacher and I would like to live in another country so I can learn more about it."

On June 24th I was accepted to train to become a Peace Corps Volunteer teacher in Ghana.

Robert Klein served in Ghana from 1961-63. He retired in 1994 after careers as a teacher and a supervisor in special education. For the past several years he has been involved in developing the RPCV Archival Project in cooperation with the Kennedy Library. He lives in Tucson, Arizona.

TOM KATUS, GEORGE JOHNSON,
ALEX VEECH, AND L. GILBERT GRIFFIS

There at the Beginning

The first Peace Corps Volunteers were guinea pigs
as well as tough young Americans.

JULIUS NYERERE, LEADER OF THE TANGANYIKA AFRICAN National Union (TANU) and pending first Prime Minister and later President of Tanzania, was the first Head of State to request the Peace Corps in April 1961. Following Neyerere's request, Sargent Shriver, Franklin Williams, and Ed Bayley, Public Relations Officer, visited eleven countries in twenty-six days beginning April 22nd.

According to the biography *Sarge: The Life and Times of Sargent Shriver,* "Shriver...stayed up all night on the flight from New York, playing cards and drinking gin martinis with Thurgood Marshall who happened to be on the same plane." Their first stop in Ghana resulted in a commitment from President Kwame Nkrumah to be the second Head of State to request the Peace Corps providing, "you get them here by August?"

Williams, a former NAACP lawyer and protégé of Marshall's, had gone to college with Nkrumah at Lincoln University in Pennsylvania. Williams was the first African American executive hired by Shriver. He was former California Assistant Attorney General, later to become Ambassador to Ghana and still later, my boss as President of the Phelps Stokes Fund. I was commissioned by Williams to conduct a Self-Study of the Phelps Stokes Fund—so I got to learn much of the behind-the-scenes history.

All three—Marshall, Nkrumah, and Williams—had large and frequently clashing egos. Franklin was upper-class Harlem, and Kwame was a poor African student who worked in the Lincoln University cafeteria. Kwame resented Franklin's airs and initially refused him when President Johnson nominated Williams as Ambassador to Ghana. Nkrumah told Johnson, as the first African Head of State, he deserved the best top-flight ambassador. However, Nkrumah relented when Johnson told him that Williams, the first African American ambassador to be assigned to an African nation, had to be better qualified than the "white boys." (Ralph Bunche was already a U.S. ambassador assigned to the U.N.)

Williams was ambassador when Nkrumah was deposed by the CIA. As a consequence many Ghanaians and other African heads of state turned on Williams. A close friend of Williams and a fellow ambassador later confided in me that CIA had set up Williams and he was unaware of the coup until after it had occurred.

—Tom Katus

As I remember it, Tanganyika went into training at Texas Western on a Saturday, Ghana went into training on a Sunday, and Columbia went into training on a Monday. So, really, there were three groups that can claim to be first. Our group got the first Peace Corps Volunteer Numbers. Jake Feldman from our group, now a professor of civil engineering at Cal Poly San Luis Obispo, is Peace Corps #001. I'm #014.

Ghana didn't have to do the Puerto Rican training program (lucky them), so they got to Ghana first. Every once in awhile, I see a picture of their group getting off the plane in Accra, captioned as the "nation's first Peace Corps group." More power to them, although I will continue to tell my relatives that I was in the first Peace Corps group.

—George Johnson

Despite Nyerere being the first head of state to request Peace Corps, Tanganyika would not achieve independence until December 9, 1961. It would have been embarrassing to have Peace Corps serving under Colonial rule. Thus, we were placed in a holding pattern. After seven or eight weeks of training at Texas Western College and the Rose Garden meeting, we were sent for four weeks to Arecibo, Puerto Rico, to open Peace Corps' Outward Bound Training Camp. The camp was run by Bill Coffin, civil rights activist with Martin Luther King and former OSS (CIA predecessor) officer, and ably assisted by Freddie Fuller, former head of commando training for the Brits during World War II.

—Tom Katus

Tom says that our training director in Puerto Rico was Bill Coffin, "ably assisted" by Freddie Fuller. Rather than "able," I would describe the direction given the group by the Coffin-Fuller duo as a combination of prep school rah-rah, sophomoric anti-Communism (a reaction to a novel called *The Ugly American*, very current at that time, which held that the Communists were winning the battle for hearts and minds in the Third World because they spoke the local languages flawlessly, ate the local foods, and never got malaria or dysentery), and something which Jerry Green (the NBC producer of our one-hour Peace Corps special) once described as "muscular Christianity."

The muscular Christianity was Bill Coffin's special addition to the program. He used to call the group together for three-minute oral prayers, which included references to Christ our Lord and Master, despite the fact that there were several Jews and at least one atheist in our group. (Guess who the atheist was.)

The Arecibo program was equal parts both silly and objectionable. Nobody could argue that it wasn't a complete waste of time. It was certainly the low point of my Peace Corps experience, and my vocal objections to it nearly got me fired from the Peace Corps before I started.

Coffin recommended to headquarters that I be fired at the end of the Arecibo training program because I was the kind of guy who, if ordered to hold a machine gun position to the death in order to save the others in my platoon, would eventually break and run. He was probably right, but other higher-ups who knew me at the El Paso training saved my neck. Maybe they appreciated my "intangibles," as Eddie Stanky would have said.

I have since struck up a better relationship with Bill Coffin and continue to admire him a lot. Maybe we've both grown older, and maybe I at least have gotten a little bit wiser and more tolerant (not less atheistic, however). Thank goodness I never got the chance to test my machine gun resolve. All I was ever called upon to do was quietly build a road in far southern Tanganyika.

All that having been said, I did want the record to reflect this dissent to Tom's opinion about the Arecibo training. No one should hark back to it as something to be remembered fondly or repeated. It's best chalked up as one of the Peace

Corps' many youthful errors, one which it has hopefully grown out of.

—George Johnson

It is good that George has finally explained for me his animus toward the Arecibo experience. This was all lost on naive old me. I thought the training in Puerto Rico was very easy, mostly boring, just part of the adventure I'd opened myself to, and all in all rather silly. My main recollections of training there were playing volleyball, drinking raw sugar cane rum with McPhee in a field on our overnight test, seeing the most magnificent sunset I'd ever seen, and learning that the rifles issued to the geologists for fighting off lions had been confiscated because the State Department was afraid we'd appear to Cuba as an armed group just off their shore at the very time our relations with Cuba were on the run up to the Bay of Pigs. The objections to Coffin weren't even on my radar, and I have only the vaguest impression of the man. Actually I have no impression, on second thought, he's just a name I recognize. Looking back, the time we spent in Arecibo was sufficiently forgettable that it is essentially gone from memory. I recall training at Texas Western and Tengeru much more vividly.

—Alex Veech

Bingo!!

I thought my reference to Freddie Fuller's "able assisting" might generate some fire. George "ably" demonstrates why he remains our chief iconoclast.

I believe the vast majority of us would agree with George's view—though some of us ex-military and young jocks for a while got off on the camp's challenge to our masochism. I remember Jerry Parson (JP), ex-paratrooper that he was, jumping onto the Tarzan rope, grasping it firmly, graciously gliding high above the ground, sailing into the cargo net and scrambling over the top. PC always encouraged the press to be present to boost the PC image. Little did they know that one of the Puerto Rican news photographers was stringing for Cuba. The next day, in the Cuban press appears my future sidekick swinging into the net, with the caption: "Peace Corps Prepares for Next Invasion of Cuba."

The cocky green kid from the Dakotas followed JP, grabbed the Tarzan rope and started to swing toward the net. My grip slipped and my *matako* scraped along the entire ground, leaving me ingloriously at the base of the net with considerable road rash, and I still had to scramble to the top. If the Cuban photographer had colored film, he would have found my face as red as my ass.

As you may recall, the "Able Fuller" had one set of clothes, a net shirt and shorts he washed every night and jumped back into at 5 A.M., complete with drill sergeant whistle to jolt us out of our soggy sleep—it rained continuously in the Arecibo forest. We groggily ran down wet rocky paths in the dark. This nonsense continued until ex-paratrooper Jerry severely sprained his ankle—or was it a hairline fracture?

While I couldn't give a damn one way or the other about the prayers—I thought they were silent—but maybe that was after George's initial protest. I do know Coffin threatened to remove George. My recall was that many of us admired our self-appointed leader and threatened to go down with him.

George's moment of silence or prayer protest, together with the engineers' *Bridge on the River Kwai* were symbolic of the group's tweaking PC's nose. I recall that Shriver visited us late in training to reassure us that our beloved George would indeed remain in the Corps and admired the engineer's bridge.

Despite the Mickey Mouse nature of the training, like the Combat Engineering training I had taken straight out of high school, I did enjoy the rappelling from cliffs and dams. One day, I was anchoring Bob Milhous at the top of a cliff as he was rappelling below. He lost his footing and was spinning in the air. The rope temporarily burned around my back and Bob's dead weight nearly pulled this 155-pound kid off the cliff. Fortunately for both Bob and yours truly, the anchoring technique worked.

In spite of personally enjoying some aspects of Arecibo's physical fitness routine and the four-day "live-in" with community families, I agree with George that it was totally irrelevant to our service in Tanganyika. I think PC just needed something to delay our entrance into Colonial Tanganyika and we were the guinea pigs.

Arecibo continued as an aspect of Peace Corps Latin American training for a number of years. Jerry Parson, Rodgers Stewart, Gil Griffis and I later used the community "live-ins" as an aspect of our Volunteer Training Specialists Inc. (VTSI) training of other PCVs for Kenya, Ghana, Malawi, and Swaziland. We even trained "Talking Head Chris Matthews" for the first Swaziland project in Louisiana—including a two-week live-in with small-scale Black American farmers. Rednecks harassed our farmer partners and trainees by cutting pickup cookies on their homesteads and firing shotguns to scare us all.

—Tom Katus

Tom and George certainly have better memories than do I re: the names of some of the characters who managed our fate in Arecibo. My memories of the training in Arecibo and examples of what they included are:

* *Terrifying*: The event planned for the next day when I was to be tossed into the swimming pool with hands and feet

tied behind my back, with the objective of learning how to overcome fear and adversity. And not drown.

- *Really Annoying*: When the event was called off due to rain, and after I had spent the entire previous night mentally preparing myself for the challenge.
- *Pointless*: Shaving with cold water.
- *Of Dubious Value*: The early morning runs in the woods. The afternoon hike on a trail along which we were individually dropped off to spend the night by ourselves. I remember it being very dark and rather boring, especially after my jungle hammock fell and I had to sleep on the ground. I remember being surprised that some of the guys found the experience to be very frightening.
- *Of Some Value But a Lot of Fun*: Learning to rappel.
- *Really Neat*: The three-day, two-night hike through the Puerto Rican countryside. Taking the old USAF truck with the leaky muffler (The Rolling Gas Chamber) down to a local beach to swim and canoe. Visiting the dam below our campsite, especially now that it is the site of the SETI project. The great meals. The library. The group discussions
- *Something to Pass the Time*: Bill Coffins' daily homilies were of little bother in that I was at that time a born-again Southern Baptist and was used to sermons.

Overall, I remember wondering what was the point of the entire program, but having had a good time participating in it.

—L. Gilbert Griffis

Tom Katus was South Dakota's first Peace Corps Volunteer, serving in Tanganyika (now Tanzania) from 1961-63. After graduating from the School of Mines and serving in the National Guard, he volunteered as a suveyor, building roads in what was that country's first year of independence. He went on to found Volunteer Training Specialists, Inc. (VTSI), a private company that trained over 2,000 PCVs. He has served as a South Dakota Legislator and is now that state's Treasurer.

George Johnson, PCV #14, served in the first group in Columbia.

Alex Veech served in Mtwarra, Tanzania from 1961-63, who was able to climb Mt. Kilimanjaro during his time abroad.

L. Gilbert Griffis also served in Tanzania from 1961-63.

TOM WELLER

✦
✦ ✦

Learning to Speak

*Sometimes triage on the subject tongue is
the only way to learn a language.*

DURING THE FIRST DAYS OF IN-COUNTRY TRAINING, THE NEW
Volunteers took oral French exams. One by one we sat
under a baobab tree with the head language trainers, all of
whom were Chadian, and did our best to carry on conversations in French. I spent most of my conversation trying
to explain, using hand gestures and three-word sentences,
why I liked using the drive-through at fast food restaurants.
How I got on this topic I don't remember. Perhaps I was
asked what I liked to do on the weekends. Or perhaps I had
been asked what I liked to eat, and when I groped for food
words all I managed to conjure up was the image of Madame
Doering, my tenth grade French teacher. Perhaps I saw her
horned-rimmed glasses hanging from the chain around her
neck, swaying and bumping against her chest as she floated
around the room, pointing at objects, rattling through a
series of nouns: "*Le bureau*, the desk, *le bureau*. *La fenêtre*, the
window, *la fenêtre*." Yes, good, the window, go with that, I
might have thought.

After all of the new Volunteers had been interviewed and scored, the trainers divided us into small groups, five or six people, to begin our language classes. Some of my compatriots arrived in Chad already conjugating French verbs, mentally sifting through lists of French adjectives in a flash, understanding when to use the subjunctive as instinctually as understanding when to exhale. These people took classes together.

I sat in a class with four virtual mutes. We would arrange our chairs in a half circle around a blackboard resting on an easel in the center of a *boukarou*, a type of round hut that dotted the training center's grounds like giant mushrooms. Our French teacher, a woman named Nemerci, would always jounce into class bedecked in one of her traditional Chadian dresses: several layers of vibrant wrap-around skirts circling her legs, intricate gold embroidery surrounding her plunging neckline, short sleeves that poofed up like pastries rising off her shoulders. She would stop next to the chalkboard, her wide hips shimmying slightly as if some faint music tempted her to dance. Then she would chime, "*Bonjour.*"

We mutes all liked *bonjour*, *bonjour* made sense. We'd almost shout over one another demonstrating our comprehension. "*Bonjour, bonjour,*" we'd all squawk back like a nest of baby birds exercising their chirps.

But class would get difficult. Nemerci would lean in toward us, her head pivoting slowly so she could look each one of us in the eye. I'd watch her dark lips undulate, narrow and thicken as her tongue pushed syllables out of her mouth, linking one sound to the next to the next until she had constructed a complete French sentence. Often, Nemerci would pause, straighten her back, raise one finger in the air and instruct us to, "*Écoutez.*" I quickly recognized that *écoutez* was a command to listen closely, a prompt I didn't need. Nemerci couldn't have stopped me from listening closely. I craved the ability to understand and control the French language. Unlike much of my formal education, the benefits of my Peace Corps French classes were obvious and immediate. Any word or phrase learned might illuminate some tiny corner of my new life and allow my own voice to develop.

After *écoutez*, Nemerci would lean toward the class again and repeat the exact same syllables, building the same sentence in the same measured, careful way. All of us mutes would nod to the rhythm of the growing chain of syllables. I'd rub my chin with my thumb and forefinger, stroking the beard I'd started to grow, a gesture meant to look thoughtful. "Yes, so there it is, indeed. A sentence. How interesting." But the slight shuffle of our feet in the sand under our ladder-back chairs betrayed growing tension, for we all knew that, after Nemerci had laid the sentence in our laps twice, it would be our turn. We would be expected to do something with it.

Sometimes, after giving us the sentence a second time, Nemerci would straighten up, give the command, "*Répétez*," and point at an unlucky mute. I was not a good repeater. I always listened intently to Nemerci, let her syllables float up my auditory canal. I tried to clear a spot in my brain where the melodious French sounds could sink in and become my own. But something terrible happened to those sounds when forced to travel from my brain to my lips. My syllables moved slowly. Clearly, whatever they had gone through on their trip between my brain and my mouth had exhausted them. Where Nemerci's syllables floated and glided, mine herked and jerked, as if their trip had made them paranoid or punch drunk or both. My syllables became shape-shifting tricksters. I recognized the moment they escaped my lips that they didn't flow the way that Nemerci's did. Still, as I listened to the sounds of my words, the shy, muffled *h*; the wild, rolling *r*, they seemed spot-on to me, the kinds of sounds that must hover in the air over outdoor cafés in Paris. But, by the time they reached Nemerci, they must have transformed themselves into something very different. As I spoke, Nemerci would twist up her face as if she were listening to me pound away at the keyboard of a piano while wearing boxing gloves.

Other times, instead of repeating, class members would have to respond to Nemerci's sentence with a sentence of their own creation. Nemerci would stand before us and say something like "*Comment tu t'appelle? Comment tu t'appelle?*" Even without vocabulary we could always tell when Nemerci expected an answer. When she pronounced the final word of a question, her voice would suddenly jump an octave, as if she had been poked with something sharp, and she would raise her eyebrows until they nearly crawled under her head-scarf. When she finished speaking, she would cock her head to the side and point an ear toward our group as if anxious to capture the brilliant sounds about to erupt from us. Then she would point.

The first mute called upon faced special challenges. I had to go through Nemerci's questions word by word, skimming through my sparse French vocabulary, hoping to find the alchemy that would transform the French words into English words. Some transformed easily. *Comment* for example, became *how* as soon as it entered my consciousness. *Comment* I retained from high school. I had heard Madame Doering speak it a thousand times. I also recalled *comment* easily because I liked the word, admired its versatility. In addition to starting questions, in casual conversation *comment* could become a sentence all by itself. Stretch out the middle *o* sound, raise the pitch of your voice slightly as you bit off the silent *t* clinging to its end and it became *cooommen*, an expression of surprise and awe, a kind of Chadian equivalent of "holy cow." Just as quickly, I could transform *tu* into *you*. Pronouns were almost impossible not to learn. They forced themselves into nearly every communication, buzzing through the air of the training center like swarms of gnats.

How and *you* provided an entryway into Nemerci's sentence, but the bulk of the hard work of making meaning still remained. Anything might follow *how* and *you*. How are you feeling today? How would you like your eggs? How far are you from home? How do you plan to survive in Chad without understanding French? The most important elements of Nemerci's questions always lay at the end, and these most important elements tended to be the most cryptic, for example *t'appelle*.

From high school French class I remembered *t'appelle* as an awkward-looking contraction. The apostrophe appeared much too early, jumping up out of nowhere at the beginning of the word like someone barging into a conversation, interrupting the beginning of a story. The construction of *t'appelle* struck me as tenuous and ugly. The word lacked balance, all the weight resting at the end. The *t* seemed like a kind of tumor growing off the front end of the word, disfiguring it, obscuring its meaning.

I developed a strategy for dealing with the unfamiliar and confusing elements of the language, letters blooming in unexpected places, slashes and dots perching atop letters. I ignored them. When confronted by *t'appelle*, I performed mental surgery on the word, cutting away what looked problematic and ugly, leaving me with a mutt of a sentence: How you appelle?

To transform a word like *appelle* into English, I first scoured the already converted words for clues. Even mundane words like *how* and *you* provided some help. While the meaning of *appelle* remained wide open, *how* and *you* hinted at the function of *appelle*. In order to form a coherent question, *how* and *you* needed the aid of a verb.

Once I could make an educated guess as to the part of speech a French word might be, I started looking for English cognates. The one redeeming quality all of us mutes recognized in the French language was that it is filled with English cognates, words that share common origins with English words. The cognates were like cousins of the English words I knew so well, cousins that had grown up in Europe and acquired exotic mannerisms and habits, but retained a familiar essence. The French *taxi*, stripped of its lilting pronunciation, became the earthy English *taxi*. *Banane* affected some sophistication, but so strongly resembled *banana* that their relationship could not go unnoticed.

The cognates usually revealed themselves right away or not at all. I'd let a word like *appelle* bang around in my head, try to visualize the word, investigate the letters that made it up, try to feel the sounds tripping across the bones of my inner ear, listening for the English heartbeat that I hoped pumped somewhere in the background. And when my search came up empty, I'd get desperate. *Appelle. Appelle.* It seemed to have a lot in common with *apple.* Could *apple* be a verb? Maybe. Maybe in agriculture circles one could apple something, maybe apple a new orchard. But would Nemerci ask me how I apple? Is this the kind of thing that would prove handy in a Chadian village? Did apples even exist in Chad? I had to admit that I had hit a dead end.

Once a cognate search proved fruitless, I had only rote memory to turn to. For years, I thought of the bits of high school French classes I retained the way that other people might think of the recalled flashes of car accidents. Infrequently, I'd dust off my memories and examine them, but only to cringe, to feel the chill run up my spine, to feel the muscles in my shoulders contract, to feel the wave of relief, like a sudden blast of cool air, when I reassured myself I would never have to sit through a Madame Doering lecture again.

For the most part, I was a quiet and pleasant high school student. I got along with most teachers, and though I found some classes to be misdirected or boring, I never found any of my teachers offensive. Except for Madame Doering. Every snap of her pointy-toed shoes against the tile floor, every word that came out of her puckered mouth plucked at my nerves. If she would have walked into class and announced, "Instead of teaching today, I'm just going to run my fingernails up and down the blackboard for the next forty-five minutes," I would have been relieved. I can't say exactly what bothered me so much, but her French accent, the way her voice became twittery and birdlike when she spoke, was part of the problem. And I hated the clucking she made in the back of her throat when students gave poor answers, the way she would slowly shake her head from side to side as if dumbfounded that children from northern Indiana spoke French badly.

But my irritation with her went deeper, deeper than I could understand. It seemed almost innate, a kind of allergic reaction. Pollen caused my eyes to burn and my nose to run. Madame Doering caused the muscles of my back and jaw to tense. But, sitting in a *boukarou* surrounded by Nemerci and my fellow mutes, all eyes on me, waiting for some response, I had no one else to turn to but Madame Doering.

Every chapter of my high school French textbook opened with a dialogue, a script presented under a crude cartoon drawing of teenagers. Madame Doering gave these dialogues the weight and import that the English teachers gave *Hamlet* and *Huckleberry Finn*. We'd spend days on every new dialogue. First Madame Doering would read them to us, walking around the classroom, using her one free hand to pantomime, as best she could, the action of the dialogue, the pitch of her voice rising or falling to indicate a change of character. Then the students would read the dialogue aloud, first all together,

like a chorus of first graders recounting the adventures of Dick
and Jane in unison. Then Madame Doering would call on
individuals to read. Eventually, parts would be assigned. Tom,
you be Jean-Paul and Mary, you can be Stéphanie. Over and
over I'd read and hear the dialogue until the characters' conversations bored into my memory like a commercial jingle I
couldn't shake.

Finally, in Chad, I found a use for the French small talk
Madame Doering had pounded into me. I discovered that I
could still recall large portions of those dialogues. Over the
years they had became an amalgam, rather than a series of
distinct conversations; all the greetings, the obvious questions,
the flat answers had jumbled together in no particular order.
When I needed to decode a word like *appelle*, I'd start digging
through the hodgepodge, hoping to find something useful. It
was like listening to a series of whispered non-sequiturs.

"*Comment ča va?*"
"*Fermez la porte.*"
"*Où vas-tu?*"
"*Il fait chaud.*"
"*Quelle huere est-il?*"

Surprisingly often, I would stumble across something useful: "*Oui, ča va. Et toi?*" "*Je m'appelle Philippe.*" I'd found
it. *Appelle*. The '*m*' troubled me though. Nemerci's *appelle*
sprouted a '*t*'. There is a big difference between an '*m*' and
a '*t*' and I worried that maybe I had wandered down a blind
alley, fallen into a trap. I searched the dialogue fragments one
more time.

"*J'ai soif.*"
"*Pas mal.*"

Nothing. "*Je m'appelle Philippe*" was my best option.

I'd lurch back into decoding mode. *Je* was easy, another
one of the omnipresent pronouns. I could see the conversion

going on in my head, variables shaken out of their disguises like working on an algebra test. *Je* = I. Philippe was also easy. *Philippe* = Phil. I liked translating proper names, liked to strip them of their Frenchness, break them down to something that felt more blue-collar. I could close my eyes and see the new sentence, glowing like neon: I *m'appelle* Phil. I'd conjure up Nemerci's question that I had partly translated, make comparisons, get my equation in order.

If *Comment tu t'appelle?* = How you *t'appelle?* and *Je m'appelle Philippe* = I *m'appelle* Phil, what does the variable *appelle* equal? I'd start lining up the like terms in my head while rubbing my chin and looking at the straw ceiling of the *boukarou*. Nemerci would repeat the question. "*Comment tu t'appelle.*" I could feel the drops of sweat blooming on the back of my neck, hear the fabric of my fellow mutes' pants and skirts rubbing against their chairs as they shifted in their seats.

How you *t'appelle?* I *m'appelle* Phil. I knew Nemerci had asked a question. The scrap from the high school dialogue seemed more like a statement...maybe an answer. How you something. I something Phil. I started to recall other lines from the dialogue.

Philippe: Je m'appelle Philippe.

Alice: Bonjour Philippe. Je m'appelle Alice.

Philippe and Alice traded names, probably paving the way for future discussions about what time they got up in the morning and things they enjoyed buying in the market. More importantly, they had provided me with an answer for Nemerci. Finally.

I'd lower my head as if I had lost interest in the *boukarou* ceiling and make eye contact with Nemerci. Her dark eyes grew to the size of fifty-cent pieces, imploring me to take a shot, to say *anything* French.

"*Je...*" I would start.

The other mutes would always lean slightly toward any mute starting to speak, listening carefully, knowing that they soon would have to give a similar response.

"*...m'appelle...*"

Nemerci's hands would come together palm to palm in front of her chest, almost like prayer.

I'd end with a flourish, a nod toward cultural sensitivity and an attempt to hang a big, flashing sign in the air that said Look How Frenchified I Am: "*...Toe-ma.*"

I'd feel the French syllables in my mouth as I spoke them, each one slippery and alive with erratic tremors, like Jell-O sliding across my tongue. And as I'd launch them into the air, I'd grip the seat of my chair and watch Nemerci's face and listen, hoping that the wobble of life I felt in the syllables as they formed in my mouth could sustain them in the real world, but fearing they would simply splat against Chad's parched, bronze soil, absorbed into the dust, drowned out by the braying of nearby donkeys, ignored by the women and men and children I'd been sent to help.

Tom Weller, who served in Chad from 1993–95, is a former factory worker, substitute teacher, and Planned Parenthood sexuality educator, in addition to being an RPCV. He currently teaches at Indiana State University, where he is the Student Support Services writing specialist. He eats at least one pound of peanuts per week, a bad habit he picked up while serving in Chad. "Learning to Speak" appeared previously in Americans Do Their Business Abroad: Stories by People Who Should Have Known Better but Are Glad They Didn't.

BOB POWERS

*
*   *

First and Last Days

Who gains the most? A simple recounting provides the answer.

IN 1964, TEMBWE WAS A SMALL VILLAGE IN CENTRAL MALAWI composed of seven or eight mostly Indian-run mom-and-pop stores, a church, and one bar open three months (the growing season) out of every year.

I woke up, that first sunny morning, to find half the village standing in a line outside my front door. I'm not sure who organized it, my Malawian counterpart or the village chief. Along with my roommate Dick, I was asked to take a seat in one of the two chairs placed directly in the path of the front doorway.

Over the next three or four hours, one by one, five hundred or so Malawians entered our new home.

Always respectful, they placed one hand over their right arm and, bowing slightly shook our hands. Then, most asked if they could touch our hair, which they did, giggling hysterically.

I sat there and grinned from ear to ear.

Two years later Dick, who worked the agricultural end of the newly formed Tembwe Cooperative Society, and I, who helped with the consumer end, were quickly evacuated from the small village that we had learned to love.

Unbeknownst to us, a similar evacuation among co-op Volunteers was taking place throughout the country. "Politics" had reared its ugly head and, along with our Malawian counterparts, we were forced to leave.

"It's for your own safety," we were told, though after forty years I don't recall feeling unsafe.

What I do recall is that I went to Malawi thinking that I would "change the world." I left knowing that the world, in this case Malawi and its people, had changed me.

And, for that I have been ever grateful.

Bob Powers served in Malawi from 1964-66. He was a member of the Co-op Project. He became head of training at AT&T and later a management consultant to some of the world's largest corporations. He has written several books on business and gay and lesbian issues. Bob lives with his husband, Donald Clement in Portland, Oregon and Lucca, Italy.

AMANDA WONSON

* *
*

Hena Kisoa Kely and Blue Nail Polish

*When we leave, we certainly leave something behind,
if nothing but a piece of ourselves.*

WHEN I THINK OF VAVATENINA, I TRY NOT TO REMEMBER THE things that made me uncomfortable, like the slightly creepy man who lived next door or the taxi-brousse driver who couldn't understand why I didn't want to sleep with him and have the *café au lait* babies he was offering. I try not to think of the reasons why I left, even though I'm convinced they were valid for me at that time in my life. Instead, I mostly remember the children, the ones I taught. The five-year-old girls who used to dance and sing in front of my house, the ones I taught to play Frisbee, and the others who became hooked on Go Fish. The children of Vavatenina welcomed me and brought joy to my heart.

The one with the biggest hold on my heart was a four-year-old named Tino who lived next door to me. It was love at first sight between us, from the first shy smile he gave me, and it is impossible to separate him from my memories of Vavatenina.

Tino's big sister Clara was one of my first friends in Vavatenina, a *troisième* student desperate to learn English and who was always ready to lend a helping hand in my transition to the town. It wasn't long before all of Clara's and Tino's siblings were frequent visitors at my house: the oldest brother and Clara to practice English, the middle brother to do a little helping out and to look after the younger ones, and the two youngest to play and watch whatever I was up to. The two brothers above Tino loved teaching him one of the few English words they knew and daring him to run up and say it to me. Gradually these brief encounters gave way to something of a friendship between me and the little boy.

Tino would show up accompanied by an older sibling or occasionally by his father, and often became shy as soon as he got close to me. Yet Clara told me that it was to my house Tino threatened to run when he didn't like things at home; there was a bond that developed between us.

I've always enjoyed the company of little kids, and Tino was the sweetest of them all in my little neighborhood of Bemasoandro. Some of the others were loud. Some of them were annoying. One of them used to hit me. Tino liked to watch whatever I did. He was fascinated by my Walkman with the little speakers I had bought back home. When I brought out nail polish to a gathering of kids on my front porch, he insisted on wearing the color I chose for myself, a color that I still think of as "Tino blue."

While I played with all of the neighborhood children and loved sharing time and games with them, there were a few special rituals that only Tino and I shared. We couldn't communicate well in words, as I spoke very little Malagasy and he didn't speak French or English. All the same, I began to teach him English. If I held up my hand and pointed to my fingers, he would recite: "One, two, three, four, feeve!" He also picked up quickly on "Give me five" and "Give me ten." And then there was *"Hena Kisoa Kely."*

Most Americans remember "This Little Piggy" fondly from childhood, I think. And who can resist playing with the toes of a barefooted child sitting in front of them? But what do you do when the child in question can't possibly understand "This little piggy went to market...?" I don't know about other PCVs, but I created *"Hena Kisoa Kely"* for Tino.

After only two and a half months in country, my Malagasy was extremely limited. I spoke French fluently and, because that was a much more efficient way for me to communicate, I relied on it much more heavily than Malagasy. I couldn't speak to the woman I paid to do my laundry, but we managed. I did the same with Tino, asking *"Inona vaovao?"* over and over, because it was about all I had to say to him. But I took what little I knew and worked out a translation of that favorite children's game.

I didn't know if there was a Malagasy word for "piglet" or "piggy" so I used the words for "little pig." That's *"hena kisoa kely."* And I knew how to say "go to market"; that's a pretty basic phrase to learn in training. So the first part of the translation was easy: *"Hena kisoa kely miantsena."* It got a little trickier after that, but I decided on *"Hena kisoa kely mipetrapetraka"* for the little piggy staying home and *"Hena kisoa kely mihinana henan'omby"* for the little piggy eating roast beef. In reality the two mean, respectively, something closer to "The little pig made himself at home" and "The little pig ate cow's meat," but I was doing the best I could. "This little piggy had none" was pretty easy, as I knew how to say "didn't eat." Hence, *"Hena kisoa kely tsy mihinana."* Finally, though, I was completely stumped as to how to say "all the way home." So that last part of the rhyme got dropped and my *hena kisoa kely* merely said "wee wee wee."

It didn't matter if the translation was exact. It didn't matter if there was any cultural context behind it. It didn't matter if

I looked foolish. All that mattered was the big grin on Tino's face when I'd play the game with him.

One look at that sweet little boy's face, and I couldn't help but feel happier. On the tough days, that meant a lot. On the days when it's hard to believe I left, I wonder how Tino looks now, as an eleven-year-old who I hope is doing well in school. I wonder how he has changed, and I feel guilty for leaving without a true explanation to him and all the rest. I left for myself, telling a story that I thought would make sense to the people of Vavatenina, something that wouldn't prejudice them against the Peace Corps. All the same, I left a little piece of my heart there in Vavatenina, where I hope a little boy still remembers how an American woman once painted his toenails blue, taught him to count in English, and told a silly story while playing with those toes.

Amanda Wonson served in Madagascar from 1999-2000, after receiving her BA in International Studies. She returned to school in 2001, obtaining her master's in Social Studies Education.

SARAH MOFFETT-GUICE

Coming to Sierra Leone

*Africa can quickly become a part of one, its
future a signal to our own, all of our own.*

THE PEACE CORPS TRUCK PULLED AWAY, DISAPPEARING DOWN
the hill. I was finally here, in Taiama, my assigned village, starting my new life in Africa.

For many years I had a fine career at home, as a nurse and
health educator, and could have continued beyond retirement
age. But, for reasons I couldn't fully explain, I wanted to go to
Africa; the Peace Corps offered me the chance.

However, they had high expectations.

The year-long application process required eight references,
the more prestigious, the better. But how could the Chief of
Surgery, who knew me only from my work in the medical
center, be expected to know if I could function effectively in
an African village? I had to submit essays also, explaining where
I wanted to go, and why, and what I expected to do once I
got there.

As a female applicant over the age of fifty, I also needed
advance medical clearance. I asserted that I could lift fifty
pounds, although I was unable to take it anywhere, and that I

could walk wherever I needed to go, and keep walking for as long as would be required. I submitted my fingerprints, and assured the National Security Agency that I had no criminal record or vile habits.

After ten months of preparation, the letter finally arrived. Twenty-nine of us, all eager trainees, gathered in Philadelphia for the four-day ritual called staging, then flew to Sierra Leone for eight weeks of cross-cultural and language instruction.

We lived together in dormitory-style lodging, sharing rooms, meals, recreation, day-long classes and a constant flood of new experiences. It was an intense time of developing friendships and a few animosities. I was eager to do everything and try everything, to speak the pidgin dialect called Krio, to eat the hot, spicy rice dishes, and even to ride a bicycle, something I had never learned to do as a child. In spite of falls and many bruises, I persisted with the bicycle until our medical officer finally told me that if I broke a hip it would be the end of my Peace Corps experience. In the end I didn't need the bicycle in Taiama. Everything, including the bus stop, was within walking distance.

A Sierra Leonean staff member, who could negotiate the primitive roads to the villages, had operated the Land Rover; there was room for a few new Volunteers and their gear. Only essentials were allowed, a plastic water filter, mosquito net, pillow and mattress, a medical kit with emergency drugs, and the prophylactic malaria medicines we had to take every week. We didn't need a lot of clothes, only lightweight cottons for the year-round tropical heat.

Sashi was the only other nurse in our trainee group, and our sites were less than thirty kilometers apart, so we rode in the same truck.

She was young, with the petite stature, almond-colored skin, and delicate features of her native India. As a U.S.

resident and naturalized citizen since the age of twelve, she had assimilated American behavior and styles of dress, but still enjoyed the foods of her native land. On occasional visits to Freetown we sometimes would go to a restaurant serving Indian cuisine. But for this day, en route to our villages, we settled for a roadside "chophouse," a collection of three or four oilcloth-covered wooden tables with straight-backed wooden chairs placed in the cleared space in front of the cook's house.

The woman of the house boiled white rice over a ground fire in the dirt-floored kitchen, then added a spicy sauce of peanut paste, tomatoes, eggplant, okra, and hot peppers. Her husband collected the money, served customers and kept the tables cleared, and there were chores for all the children. We all ate heartily.

The two male Volunteers in our van, Tom and Matt, were tall and athletic and not long out of college; they had healthy appetites. Harry, the driver, was short and wiry, but he had learned never to let a good meal pass him by. Food was a serious matter in Sierra Leone, especially for travelers, who might encounter only one chophouse in a whole day's journey and would need to fill up or go hungry.

None of us talked much during the trip. My site was in the south, just fifty miles from the Liberian border where armed conflict had broken out the previous year and all the Americans had left. But I wasn't worried about that. I was here at last, in Africa. The villagers would be happy to see me and anxious to help. What could go wrong? How could anything go wrong, after all the planning and preparation?

By mid-afternoon we were driving down the soft dusty road, passing smiling faces and waving hands. Crimson hibiscus blossoms on the sloping hillside flanked the health center gate. Harry skillfully backed the Land Rover up to the door of my assigned apartment and helped unload my belongings.

My new home was a two-bedroom apartment, within the compound gates and 100 yards up a gentle slope from the health post. It had been built and furnished by missionaries and was luxurious by village standards. The large living room was furnished with a worn green leatherette sofa, two matching chairs, and a long wooden table. A solar panel in the roof provided enough electricity for lights a couple of hours each evening, so my apartment became the locus for meetings of the health commission.

There was also a tiny kitchenette, with shelves and a kerosene-operated refrigerator. But kerosene was expensive and often unavailable; I learned how to function without it by salting fish and buying fresh produce every day, just as the villagers did.

The bathroom served a dual function, as it was the only source of water. There was no kitchen sink, but an elevated tank just outside the bathroom wall held a week's worth of water, pumped from the underground cistern by solar power, which then flowed by gravity into the bathroom sink, commode, and bathtub. Because of gravity and the placement of the tank, it was impossible to have an overhead shower.

Of course, the water in the cistern came from the heavy downpours of the rainy season. A few months into the dry season, I began to contemplate the exhaustion of the supply, and how I would function without running water. The village women walked to the Taia River each morning and carried their daily supply home in buckets on their heads. I supposed I would have to hire someone to carry water for me, since I lacked the balancing skills and the neck muscles for the task.

My favorite feature of my new home was the small screened porch with a view of the hillside behind the health post. Tiny fragrant white flowers on lush deep-green bushes bloomed beside my porch, and stately date palms lined the path below. Many evenings, I would sit on my porch contemplating life and how I had come to Africa with such high hopes.

I sincerely believed that these people, whose lives and experiences were so very different from mine, would be better off for my coming to stay with them, even if only in some small way. I was eager and optimistic, and tried to push apprehension down into the deepest recesses of my mind. Fear of the unknown, the unfamiliar, was not allowed here.

It was late afternoon. The clinic had closed and the workers had gone home to their families. I stood in my doorway and watched the Peace Corps truck drive away, and wished it would not leave just yet.

One evening I sat on my small screened porch, gazing at the hillside beyond the health center, and thinking about life:

And when my time is done, will I cry for Africa the rest of my days? The sun is burning on the western slope, the first candle is lit. On the road fisherwomen trudge home carrying their hoop-shaped nets, balancing baskets of fresh caught fish on their heads. In the field of dry leaves below the hospital, circles of fire glow and send pale gray smoke drifting toward the river.

I go to see what is happening, the pastor comes from his house also, probably to reassure me. He speaks of what he thinks I want to hear—wild animals which used to live in the forest on the edge of town, of trees cut down and hopes for replanting, of times of his youth and times of the future.

Dusk has settled in, murmuring shadows drift by, the evening breeze floats on the treetops, and the leaf fires have gone out. It is cooler now, the time for relaxation and contemplation. And when my days are done, will I cry for Africa?

Sarah Moffett-Guice was a Peace Corps Youth Development Volunteer in Sierra Leone from 2004-06. She now teachers Tamna University in Korea.

SUSAN L. SCHWARTZ

Shattering and Using
Book Learning

Learning, and walking away, in the real world,
from what we've thought we've learned!

I SHOULD HAVE KNOWN THAT PEACE CORPS WOULDN'T BE QUITE
what I expected. The recruiter interviewing me had said that,
with my strong science background, I could easily get a position teaching math or science. Huh?! I had never taken even
one math course in college and the only science courses I'd
taken were a beginning astronomy course and a geology course
popularly known as "rocks for jocks." The resume she was
looking at was for a person with the same name as me.

Once that was straightened out, I was told that maybe I'd be
offered a position teaching English. That did not appeal to me;
I was an anthropology major, focusing on Africa and development, and felt it was much more important for people to be
able to grow their own food and have enough to eat than to
be able to speak English as a foreign language.

The recruiter said there weren't many generalist positions
available and didn't have much hope.

So I was thrilled when I received the invitation to go to
Sierra Leone as an agricultural extension agent. I'd gotten
exactly the type of job I'd wanted.

Most importantly, I wanted to live like the local people. Wasn't that what anthropology was all about? Blending in, being as unobtrusive as possible. Becoming a part of the community, but not influencing or changing it with foreign ideas or products which would damage the culture. Waiting for the people to ask for my help instead of me proselytizing about the benefits of irrigated-swamp rice production. Who was I, a twenty-two-year-old college graduate from New Jersey, to tell these people they needed to change farming practices that must have been centuries old? They first needed to want to change; I couldn't force them into it.

Oh, I so wanted to be culturally sensitive!

That's why I hadn't brought a Frisbee with me, although I had seen other Volunteers throwing them to kids during training, and the kids seemed to have lots of fun playing with the toy. What would happen when the Volunteers left and took their Frisbees with them or, if they gave them to some kids, they got lost or damaged? That's why I didn't want to have a motorcycle like the other PCVs: I didn't want to have something that the people in the village I went to had no way of owning. I just didn't think it was right if I could ride in and out whenever I wanted, and the villagers had to walk and depend on public transportation to get anywhere.

I was so naïve!

When I arrived in "my" village, two and a half miles from a main road—which I'd have to walk from now on any time I wanted to go to town for supplies or to attend Ministry meetings—the first thing I saw was a motorcycle leaning against the wall of a mud-brick house! How could it be? What was going on here? I'd been told that this village had really wanted a Peace Corps Volunteer because they didn't grow enough food for themselves and didn't have the money to buy food during the "hungry season." So how was it that someone had had enough money to buy a motorcycle?

All my grandiose ideas were shattered.

I realized that all the anthropological theory I'd read and accepted in college did not necessarily apply out here in the real world. That was reinforced when Sierra Leoneans found out I didn't have a motorcycle, because they thought that foreigners who were richer than they should have one. Without that status symbol, I think I was somehow less respected by some people. On the other hand, being forced to use taxis and minivans gave me the opportunity to meet and talk with far more Sierra Leoneans than I would have if I had had a motorcycle.

After the initial shock of feeling betrayed by my anthropology background, I never seriously regretted not having a motorcycle. Once I reconciled myself to the fact that academia wasn't a totally reliable guide to life in the bush, my knowledge of African history and my awareness of issues in development, gained during my coursework, made it easier for me to adjust and adapt to living in Sierra Leone.

Later, I learned that the bike I'd seen was broken and the owner didn't have the money to repair it.

Susan L. Schwartz has been a teacher and teacher trainer in the field of English Language Learner education since 1990. After Peace Corps and graduate school, she worked in China and Indonesia before taking a teaching position at a public school in Massachusetts. Susan has traveled widely in Asia and received a Fulbright-Hays Seminar Abroad grant to India in 2007.

LARRY W. HARMS

* *

The Adventures Overseas

What does one find in a rainforest or in an airplane over it?

ONE STARTS PEACE CORPS BY STUDYING A MAP.

In May 1963, at the end of my senior year of college, the Peace Corps sent a letter indicating that I was accepted, pending final clearances, as a Volunteer for assignment to Guinea, Africa.

Early June was wheat-harvest time in western Oklahoma. So, first things first—I had to help family and other farmers until there was clearance.

One event confirmed that the Peace Corps was working on it.

I was working for a neighbor, tilling fields immediately following the harvest. I took a mid-afternoon break for sandwiches and ice tea, and the owner and a neighbor stopped by to talk. They had been over at a rebuilt bridge, checking it out. The person checking *me* out found them there. They told me about the guy, how he was dressed, where he might be from, and what kind of car he was driving, then jokingly said, "We didn't tell him anything." They also said he would always remember the interview. Standing on the bridge, he had leaned against one of the railings. The black wood treatment was not completely dry; he left with some on both his clothes and hands.

Guinea was the first independent French colony in Africa, and it set the stage for all others. President Sekou Toure was the key person in gaining its independence. His reputation with Africans was (and still is) that of a hero. With France, his situation was very difficult: France had both commercial and political interests that it wanted to continue after independence. President Toure turned to Russia for assistance. That was against the interests of France.

Politics aside, the economic, social, educational, and other developmental progress expected by the people could not be realized. President Toure had a very good reputation within Guinea when we arrived, but a lot was rapidly lost during our two years there. Toure was known for strong opinions, and he was instrumental in putting in the Peace Corps, ousting it after about four years, and then inviting back in after an additional number of years.

We were Guinea I, 1963-65, the first group of Volunteers. I was assigned to Macenta, a town in the southeastern rainforest. The primary elements of my Peace Corps Volunteer experience, from the technical standpoint, were to introduce an improved chicken breed and meet the nutritional and other needs for higher levels of production, to teach students using direct field training to improve vegetable and poultry production, and improve production of high-quality vegetables for the town market. The details seem a little lost at this point (forty year later). We certainly didn't create the revolution that we had envisioned!

It is the people, the experiences, and the adventures that stay with me.

At the operational and social level in Macenta, there was a small, diverse, international group of interesting people. There was a team of Chinese who were introducing cultivation, harvesting and processing of tea, some Russians working in forestry and the educational system, several Lebanese merchants, a U.S. missionary couple, and some French of various professions. The working-class Guineans didn't initially make distinctions as to who we all were.

We were leaving the Regional Agricultural Office one day and a young Guinean rushed out of the building to catch us, indicating that we had some mail. He gave it to us, and it was all in Chinese. We must have looked a little confused, and he said with some confusion, "You are Chinese, aren't you?"

Islam and Christianity were both present, especially in the cities and towns. The traditional practices and beliefs were strong, especially in rural villages. Talk about it always brought up witchcraft. Some of the PCVs, including me, were prone toward ridiculing it. One day, I fell into that with the American missionary, and he interrupted me. He said that I should always respect it. I asked what that meant. Did he have any details about it being real? He simply stated again what he had said. Always respect it.

In Macenta, the rainy season was ten months long with several rains even in the two-month dry season. The height of the rainy season was constant showers throughout the day and night.

The rainforest is a paradise of nature. I lived several kilometers outside of Macenta on an old French farm/research station in the rainforest. We lived with nature. Mosquitoes, lizards, and sometimes army ants were a given. Seeing the army ants was impressive. Their march was not an hour or even a half-day affair. It went on for several days. In difficult spots, some of the ants would hold their bodies together to form a bridge that the others could walk over.

Shortly after my arrival in Macenta, a hunter showed up at the door. He wanted to sell me a python skin. It was fresh and bloody. Did I need a python skin? Maybe I'll never see another one. Maybe, the hunter is right—they are hardly ever to be found. So, I bought it. I cured it over time by salting and washing. It stank. Finally I rolled it up and put it in a box. I unpacked it a few years ago. It looks good, but what do I do with it?

Once, a fellow PCV excused himself from the evening conversation, indicating that he was headed for a shower and bed. A few moments later he came back in, saying there was a snake in the shower. I would have thought it a practical joke, except his voice was quivering. His face was absolutely white. Yes, there was a snake in the shower.

The drain from the shower was a pipe through the floor and then through the foundation wall. Water then spilled onto the ground and the hillside. We must have taken covers off both the shower drain and the outside drainpipe. The snake had come in through the pipe. Many of the snakes are poisonous, so we normally minimized our risks. Rather than getting it back to nature, we did it in.

A Peace Corps Volunteer (a teacher) in Macenta decided to get a monkey as a pet. It wasn't that nice a pet, but he liked the monkey. He kept it outside in a hut off the ground in which it could spend the night. It was also on a long cord so that it could move about. At one point the monkey and a dog got into a fight. The monkey had some wounds. The Volunteer cared for his pet as a dedicated owner does. But the monkey's health deteriorated. After several weeks, the monkey was in bad shape. We took a blood sample and sent it off for testing. The monkey had rabies from the fight with the dog. We, especially the other Volunteer, were fearful about our exposure to the rabies. All went O.K. for us. But the monkey was put to sleep.

There were also chimpanzees in Guinea. A PCV teacher decided that her pet should be a chimp. One day another Volunteer and I were traveling through her town and saw the little beast. Being with that thing for an hour or so was eerie. It was not in a cage or on a leash; it lived in the house. It seemed clear to me that, for the chimp, we were all one family. For me, it was an uneasy feeling. The Peace Corps staff learned of her pet and immediately insisted that for health reasons, she find a new home for the chimp.

A few weeks after a staff visit and collection of samples for medical tests, I got a telegraph message that I was to come to Conakry. A preliminary test for a water-borne disease was positive. I protested a bit. They were insistent. I was to come by plane.

I made arrangements. On departure day, a rainstorm was in the making. At the airport, the pilot ordered us immediately on the plane so he could take off before the storm hit. We got to the end of the runway, but a wind gust blew the plane sideways. He straightened it out; another gust hit and again blew us sideways. He taxied back, and we sat in the plane, hot and humid, until we could finally take off. It was still stormy. He stayed below the clouds, which meant that he also had to do some maneuvering to get through the mountains.

We had flown for a while, and then we turned left for a few minutes, then right, and then left again. A man in traditional dress looked out the window and then started seriously studying things. Talking out loud to himself, he said in frustration and disbelief, "We're in Mali, we're in Mali!" A co-pilot came walking through the plane and got a map. Soon after that, we turned a hard right and flew until we hit the Niger River. We were in Mali. We then flew up the river to Kankan. The medical tests were negative.

Larry W. Harms is a retired Foreign Service Officer, United States Agency for International Development (USAID) with extensive experience in Africa and Haiti. He served in the Peace Corps in Guinea from 1963-65, where he and other PCVs introduced an improved poultry breed, upgraded poultry feed for increased production, reinvigorated a large government-run vegetable garden, and carried out field training of students in the regional secondary school.

E. T. STAFNE

A *Toubac* in the Gloaming

Sometimes the cultural barriers just do not
get broken, no matter what we do.

MY EXPERIENCES IN NORTHERN SENEGAL VARIED FROM THE sublime to the insane, often within the same day. Quite often I think of those times that seemed impossibly embarrassing and try to make sense of them, even many years later. Most of the strangest events occurred early in my Peace Corps service, when I spoke little Toucoulor and understood even less of Senegalese culture. Some of these still haunt me; I know I will never fully understand what happened.

I kept a daily journal during my service, as many Volunteers did. Most of it was mundane, but what I really wanted was a memory-jogging device for later in life. Sometimes I will send a certain meaningful passage to another RPCV that served with me, but that is becoming less frequent as time marches on. Since my return to the States in 1996, the only other person to read the entire journal was my wife; the majority of it just isn't that interesting. However, some days, like Tuesday, June 14, 1994, are.

My village was Nguidjilogne, not too large, but it had a market that made it a crossroads right on the banks of the

Senegal River. Numerous small villages lined the river and
considered Nguidjilogne a center of commerce, so there were,
in essence, no strangers from Nguidjilogne. Every village, no
matter how small, knew of Nguidjilogne and its residents.
Occasionally, soccer matches between Nguidjilogne and
another village would be coordinated, and surprisingly large
numbers of villagers would attend. It was in the gloaming of
that June day when I attended a soccer match that turned into
one of those inexplicable, memorable events.

In my early days, I had gotten to know the schoolteachers
in the village. They spoke varying degrees of English and my
French was tolerable, so we could communicate easily. It was
after 5 P.M. when they invited me to attend the soccer match
at a neighboring village. We walked, en masse, to the soccer
pitch behind the mud-brick schoolhouse. The gathered crowd
numbered in the hundreds. It was still very hot, but the sun
was slowly setting, making it bearable. I took my place on
the sidelines to watch the match with all the interest I could
muster. At that time everything was still new to me: the swirling sand, the smell of dead animal carcasses, and the shared
existence of people who lived in that desolation.

Not long after the match started, it became apparent that
our team was overmatched, but it was all played out in fun.

When the match ended, players from both sides gathered
on the pitch, as did the observers. Among them was a horde of
children, who seemed in be in a state of agitation. They were
loud and boisterous.

And, like the colors on a soccer ball, the interface between
black and white was about to become razor thin.

I, of course, was the only white face for miles, and judging
by the reaction of the children, the only one they had seen
in quite some time. As a group, they gathered behind me and
began to chant in unison the obligatory white man descriptor,

"*Toubac, Toubac.*" The school teachers did little to quash the chanting, although later they claimed to be embarrassed by it.

We marched to the edge of town with darkness encroaching, followed by almost one hundred children chanting for the white man. In retrospect, I believe it provided some entertainment for the villagers and, in that sense it is hard to begrudge them that. So, if it had ended there as I walked off toward Nguidjilogne, I probably would never have given it a second thought.

But it didn't end there.

I turned to the crowd one last time, in a daze, to soak it all in. The black faces with white pearls for teeth, all moving in slow motion shouting and pointing at me. While I stood there captivated and unable to process that strangeness before me, the horde of children slowly parted and a girl came toward me, urged on by the masses. She lacked the usual dark pigmentation in her skin and had white hair. She wasn't completely white, but that mattered little to the vocal group behind her. They pushed her up in front of me, all along relentlessly chanting, "*Toubac, Toubac.*" She uncomfortably stuck out her hand to me and said, "*Toubac.*"

At that point nothing made sense anymore. What was I doing here in the middle of the Sahel surrounded by an African mob? I did the only thing I could—I shook her hand and tried to put on a smile. When our hands parted she turned around and was swallowed up by the crowd. It was then they all broke out into hysterical laughter. I turned my back to them and started walking back to my village.

I couldn't make any sense of it then and still can't today. Sometimes things get a little bizarre in the gloaming.

E.T. Stafne served in Senegal from 1994-1996. He wrote a novel shaped from his experiences in Senegal called The Wretch Unsung. *He considers his Peace Corps service one of the most formative, and odd, experiences of his life.*

ARNE VANDERBURG

* *
*

Family Affair

Peace Corps all in the family? It certainly can bring one together.

AT LAST COUNT THERE WERE SEVEN: SEVEN OF US BROTHERS, sisters, sisters-in-law, brothers-in-law, nephews, sons, wives, ex-wives, ex-husbands who, gathered at any one time in a room, usually find old and even new Peace Corps experiences from Ghana, Nigeria, Turkmenistan, Malawi, El Salvador, Paraguay, and Belize dropping into our extended family ramblings.

Some of us couldn't get enough. We came back for a second dose of whatever version of Peace Corps was playing in the next forty years...some for a third, fourth...even a fifth dose. As PCVs we were teachers, archaeologists, photographers, school builders, community organizers, department chairs, librarians, TV performers, beekeepers, farmers, tree planters, public speakers and a myriad other things that, had we stayed home we would never have been, smelled, tasted, or learned in those two or three short years. We learned what it meant to be outsiders and honored and not-so-honored guests as collectively we brushed up against dozens of cultures and hundreds...

thousands...of different beliefs, traditions, and subtle little behaviors to which we were totally oblivious, but that could make or break a friendship—like when you casually waved at someone on the other side of the street carrying a huge load and they dropped everything and came running to see why you had called them, or you held up your thumb to hitch a ride and found out you'd just flipped someone off, or you smelled a bowl of soup and offended the cook.

We learned that when offered a drink on some special occasion, don't forget to dribble a bit of it onto the ground, and make sure you never offer someone food with your left hand, and when people come to visit give them something to drink as they come in or they will think you don't want them to visit, and if you are the only person with a radio or tape recorder in the village, play it loud enough for everyone to hear or they will think that you think you are better than they if you play it just loud enough so that only you could hear it.

An easy answer might be that four of us joined Peace Corps because, once the first one did in 1964, it just seemed natural that the next would and then the next. But the simplicity of that belies the streak of independence that seemed to be the one thing we all had in common. So, in trying to put reason to our opting to leave friends, family, and familiarity for two or more years, five of us might say it had to do with a young President who gave an idealistic speech and got us wondering what we could do for our country or even if our country would actually let us do something for it. Some of us had already been asked to do something else for our country and though we were young and filled with a spirit of adventure... nightly network news photos of body bags or our trusted allies blowing the brains out of suspected enemies at point blank range encouraged us to seek our tropical adventures elsewhere...perhaps even in places where we would be tolerated if not down right welcomed.

In a pre-draft lottery age, Peace Corps promised at least a deferred tour of military duty. Still, even without that hanging over the male heads amongst us in those early years, my guess is we still would have been caught in the centrifugal pull that so many of us felt...a sense of adventure fulfilling youthful dreams of far-off lands and unknown places, made doubly seductive by the hope we would actually be doing something useful for ourselves, our country, and the people with whom we'd be living.

Once there—wherever there was—most of us found out that much more was expected of us than we had planned on... or hoped for. The teachers of us became the chairs of our science or English or math or whatever departments. If you had performed in a high school play, you ended up directing your schools' dramatic presentations. One of us who dabbled in amateur archaeology was dropped altogether as a teacher at the end of his three months of training and spent three years cataloging priceless artifacts, publishing in a respected journal. Another, who had a passion for photography, spent a summer crawling around in the West African bush taking wildlife photos for a fledgling wildlife preserve hoping to tap into a growing tourist market. Nearly all of us found ourselves writing grants to access monies and organizing labor for the construction of schools and community latrines, while others built beehives and ran trainings on apiculture or having healthy babies or performed American folk songs on national TV, which admittedly at the time amounted to some 200 televisions.

And while at times it actually felt like the hardest job you'll ever love, one of the hardest parts of the job at first seemed to be the best...filling in the downtime in our jobs...

the excessive surprise, unscheduled, day upon day upon week of unplanned time off due to holidays and celebrations. We learned quickly what it meant to be an honorific society, where independence day was followed by Liberation Day and by Christmas and New Year's and Hero's Day and the start, and end, of Ramadan and if in a former British colony, Boxing Day.

Having left the comfort of living amongst family and friends who naturally occupied the spaces of our lives, we were now confronted with the necessity of contriving ways to fill those gaps. Many of us learned that, while we humans are a curious lot, always searching out the new, we like to do this from a familiar perspective, surrounded by or at least able to be surrounded by ideas, images and experiences with which we can touch base if we so feel the need.

The reality of our new lives was in fact an ideal many of us strived for: to be in an isolated, rural setting solely dependent on our wits and the good will of locals for whatever satisfaction the experience could provide. Those of us who arrived in the first few years of Peace Corps did so not only amidst high hopes and expectations, but also with a large trunk filled with what seemed like more books than were in my high school library. What felt at the time like manna falling from heaven, in retrospect should have been viewed as a warning…something to the effect that we were hereby being put on notice that we will have huge amounts of time when we will have absolutely nothing planned and or needing to be done and therefore will be left with the only alternatives available which are…do nothing, find something to do…or read. So we read, and when we had finished the books in our own book locker we traded books with those who had book lockers different from ours.

We visited neighbors, studied languages, started clubs, made gardens and tapped in as deeply as possible to local culture...some of us spending long nights recording the sounds of traditional dances and ceremonies while partaking freely in the festivities. And after that...we read for days and for weekends at times.

Peace Corps, even in the confused wisdom of its early years did its best to prepare us for these realities...for a job for which some government couldn't find a local warm body and for a lifestyle that had nothing in common with the one we had left...nothing. We wondered how Peace Corps came up with the idea of sending us to classes up on West Broadway, at Barnard College where bizarre psychiatrists ran group sessions that reduced hopeful PCVs to tears by beating into us how emotionally unprepared we were for life in Nigeria or Ghana or wherever, as Peace Corps Volunteers. And we questioned the wisdom of the weekly posting, after dinner on Thursday evenings, of those who were not being invited to do the hardest job they would ever love or the large group sessions where we were told to complete questionnaires asking us to name those amongst our group whom we thought might be the best or the worst PCVs. (This last activity we eventually gleefully walked out on, en masse.)

We did avoid what others were going through in training programs from Puerto Rico to New Mexico, boot-camp-like physical endurance training, thinking maybe that was the best way to get future PCVs up to the task. But the good news is that it was only us early kids that were subjected to personal humiliation or extreme physical challenge as the method of choice for preparing PCVs to be successful at living and working in unfamiliar places around the world.

Early on, Peace Corps worked hard to recruit childless, married couples...maybe thinking that two people would be able to rely upon and support each other in the hard times. What they didn't count on was that most Americans have so many distractions in their lives that they may spend only a few hours a day with each other, one on one. A married couple going to their PC site often discovered that living with each other for 24 hours a day, 7 days a week, 12 months a year... elevated them to a whole new level of togetherness...either tightening bonds to where only death would do them part or stretching the limits of familiarity and secret knowledge beyond anything humanly possible. Married couples got to know each other in the most detailed ways, and if the high percentage of PCV separations is any indication, a lot of us didn't like what we found out.

Eventually we all came home, not realizing just how much we had been changed by what we had been doing day in and day out for two, three, or four years. At times we felt like we had stepped onto a train and traveled to unexpected places and exposed to unimaginable people and events while everything we came back to was as we had left it. There were differences...more houses, more or bigger kids, older friends, newer cars...but as the anthropologist E. T. Hall has said, the most important parts of any culture are the invisible ones. It was those once unseen things that our travels had now made visible. The attitudes, beliefs, perceptions about us and the places we had been, the people who lived in those places and even the places we were coming back to were the same, while everything in our own world had been completely altered by stepping onto that train.

We had seen a world where people with so little to spare still put hospitality and friendship before their own needs, where people who were in a day-to-day struggle to survive were still cheerful and welcoming to strangers. We saw the depth of extended families and the values inherent in tradi-tional communities. We also saw how the introduction of religions and belief systems from the outside were corrupting those values and destroying the families. I think we were surprised when the questions we were asked on our return were seldom about what we had learned or what it was that had changed us.

Home now, our family with deep PC connections has a special bond that doesn't require explanation. Quietly, we believe...we hope...the collective experiences have had a positive impact on us, helping us to give more emphasis to the people side of our lives, to the interactions we have in our jobs and communities, to the perspectives we bring on how we should deal with each other; whether that be the people next door or a wider international community. Individually, we've turned into public health professionals and development workers in other international organizations and NGOs, college professors, businessmen and women, teachers and artists trying to contribute something back to the country from which we'd started but always with one foot planted in that thing we had done in a moment of idealistic fervor...or in a haze induced youthful confusion...five, ten....and now forty-plus years ago. I think most of us have felt we were deep down changed but it isn't easy to say what that means: except to maybe six other members of a rather deep Peace Corps family.

Arne Vanderburg is currently a history teacher at a private school in Albuquerque, New Mexico. He took his first plane flight ever from rural Ohio to New York City preparing to be a Peace Corps Volunteer. Over the next forty years he was to become divorced from the woman who first joined him on that adventure and married to another whom he met in Peace Corps. One of his best Peace Corps friends married his brother, a former PCV, his nephew decided to head off to Peace Corps in Eastern Europe, and most recently his youngest son spent three years as a PCV.

S O L V E I G   N I L S E N

*　*　*

Your Parents Visited
You in Africa?

Accident and death: never far away, or far from mind.
But home and our families aren't, either.

MY PARENTS ARRIVED IN SAN FRANCISCO FOR THE UNVEILING OF
their first grandchild exactly one month after she'd made her
debut in the Kaiser Permanente delivery room. My mother of
immaculate house fame would get her first glimpse of my skills
as a housekeeper. She and my father would be sleeping under
their married daughter's roof for the first time.

Fortunately, they'd never considered a trip to see us in
Africa; going abroad was not much done in their circles in
the sixties, an unimaginable extravagance for someone with
kids in college whose vacation traditions tended toward visits
with the relatives and camping in national parks. Besides, if
international travel could be contemplated at all, Africa would
not have been on the list. First things first—they'd fantasized
about someday making a trip to Norway, the "old country"
of their mothers.

It was inconceivable to imagine them making the trip to
Addis Ababa. When our plane had landed in Beirut for refuel-
ing, in September 1967, it was in the aftermath of a Middle

East war. The airport was full of soldiers with machine guns, two accompanying me back into the bathroom to retrieve the purse I'd somehow managed to leave behind.

Yet getting to Addis Ababa was the easy part. The three-day journey to our village in the upper reaches of the Simian Mountains started out with a flight to the Eritrean city of Asmara, where we spent a day loading up on provisions: three-kilo tins of powdered milk, five-pound cans of Danish butter. Local dairy products were proscribed; tuberculosis was prevalent.

Next morning, we boarded an overloaded bus for the two-day journey to the village in the mountains that would be home for the next two years. On the second day, we began the climb high into the Simians, a range of mythic proportions replete with bottomless crevices and spectacular fissures. Located between the valley of the Blue Nile to the west, the Rift Valley to the east, this drama-queen region of the world was created by an ancient volcanic cataclysm resulting in one of the planet's most precipitous drop-offs, down to 400 feet below sea level. All I had to do was look out the bus window, and there it was, a view in the direction of one of the lowest points on earth, the Danakil Desert. Our bus driver navigated the edge of the abyss to the accompaniment of Ethiopian pop blasting at top volume from speakers directly above our heads.

The bus crawled up the steep grade, the driver downshifting, then downshifting again until we were almost at a halt, engine grinding and roaring. The hairpin turns required the skilled (we hoped) bus driver to navigate them inch-by-inch, pulling to the very edge of the chasm, backing up, inching forward again, backing up again until we could proceed along the narrow road carved into the side of the mountain. Until we got to the next switchback. And the next.

I tried to distract myself by imagining the moment I longed for, of disembarking in Maychew, of opening the door to the house that awaited us. Rented on our behalf by a Peace Corps staffer who'd been sent to reconnoiter, it was—we were assured—in decent repair and appropriate to our station in life. The University of Utah dorm room that had been our honeymoon quarters during the three months of training was about to be superseded by our first home. Trying to fill in any of the details of the picture, however, was useless. I had no idea what awaited us. Besides which the view out the bus window demanded my vigilance, crucial (I was certain) to the driver's efforts to keep us on the road.

We had fabulous front-row seats for this thrilling show, the place of honor directly behind the driver, who had cleared them of the previous occupants in a mini-drama of shout and gesture. When the unfortunates who'd been occupying the seats didn't go willingly, they were dragged out and shoved down the aisle. Our protestations were ignored. We acquiesced in this humiliating situation; our rudimentary language skills were apparently insufficient to communicate our preferences. There was, of course, the real possibility that our driver understood us perfectly, but held to his own beliefs about the proper order of seating on his bus.

The front row seats were not such a wonderful advantage; they began to feel more like a curse with their unobstructed down-views of deep gorges, at the bottom of which we saw the twisted skeleton of a crumpled vehicle far below. My own personal curses, tendencies towards vertigo and anxiety, were super-activated. Closing my eyes didn't help.

Peace Corps training staff had warned us about dangers we would encounter, including a list of diseases so long and entertaining that we couldn't take it seriously: elephantiasis, leprosy, schistosomiasis, cholera, malaria, tuberculosis, Rift Valley Fever, rabies, multiple varieties of dysentery. They concluded by telling us that, statistically, the greatest danger to life and limb for PCVs "in country" was motor vehicle accident.

A bus top-heavy with cargo might have triple the allotted weight riding on its axles; the brakes might not be up to the load. Or the taxi driver in Addis Ababa might have been invited in for drinks when he dropped off his last fare, and be all over the road on his way home. You might be in a questionable place at a drastically wrong time—or you might be in a perfectly appropriate place, except the taxi driver might hit the accelerator instead of the brakes, plowing into a couple on a sidewalk in front of a hotel, hitting one of them with such force that she went flying through the air before landing in the street a distance away.

That was the night we arrived in Addis. We were just barely on the ground, having landed at Haile Selassie International Airport two hours before.

On the bus ride into the city, we inhaled our first amazed breaths of African air, thick with smoke from cooking fires, the pungency of eucalyptus. The ride was punctuated with frequent stops, our bus driver slamming on the brakes, honking his horn, leaning out the side window to shout and shake his arm at shepherds with their flocks of goats or sheep blocking the road. The darkness, at 6 P.M. in this part of the world close to the equator, was part of the unfamiliar territory. We were Northerners, used to long summer nights and, once night came, there were always streetlights.

The bus delivered us to the hotel where we were to check in and have a first formal welcome to the country. But there weren't rooms enough for everyone; it would be necessary to send a few of us to another hotel. Three of the married couples, Erik and I among them, volunteered. We piled into a Peace Corps Land Rover along with Susan and Charlie, Gwen and Nile. After we'd checked in, the driver drove us back to join the rest of the group, pulling into a parking space just off the street, directly in front of the hotel. Susan and Charlie got out of the back seat first. I followed. Somehow, they must have lingered, for they were behind me when I heard Erik shout: "WATCH OUT! RUN!"

Maybe Susan and Charlie weren't behind me. Maybe I ran faster, my husband's peremptory order being so urgent. When a person you trust, someone whose vocal modulations you know intimately, screams out an order in a tone of voice you've never heard him use before, instinct kicks in; you obey without thinking. You run, expecting a screech of brakes, the crash of metal on metal.

But there were no dramatic sounds. Just the single thud of impact, the muffled chilling sound of a soft object, a person being hit by a car. Turning back to look, I saw a body, airborne.

It was already over, too late to replay the scene, to cut and start over, to retract our offer to go to the other hotel, to take a few minutes longer to settle in at the hotel instead of rushing.

Someone appeared and took me by the arm, leading me away from the scene of the accident. I remember hearing a disembodied keening sound before I realized that it was my body making that sound.

"Try to calm down," they said. "Everything is going to be all right; an ambulance is on the way. Don't worry," they said, "there's a decent hospital in this part of town, not that far away."

When they took us back to the hotel they promised to keep us informed. As soon as there was any news about Susan and Charlie they'd let us know.

They kept their promise.

We were awakened before dawn by a knock on our door. I remember sitting up in bed next to Erik, after the Peace Corps rep had expressed his regret at having to bring us the terrible news, leaving us to go down the hall to knock on Gwen and Nile's door. Susan had died during the night. Charlie's injuries, he assured us, were relatively minor. He had a broken arm; he was going to be O.K.

Less than twenty-four hours before, I'd been sitting next to Susan on a bench in the airport in Amsterdam when Charlie came over and dropped a small glossy package in her lap. I watched her open the tiny bottle of French perfume he'd just bought her in the duty-free shop, teasing her about wearing it on the job in their village. But Susan never made it to her village, never opened that bottle of French perfume, never woke up to even one African morning, nor to any morning anywhere.

Our heavily curtained hotel room was dark when I awoke, but there was a narrow strip of light on the floor from a gap at the corner of the window. Had we overslept? I got up to find my watch and draw the curtains. I looked down on a broad avenue, across from which a high-walled compound stretched the entire length of the block.

Sitting atop the wall were two full-maned motionless creatures. I stared, blinking. We were in the city, traffic moving on the street below. They couldn't be actual lions. Then one of them turned its head, and stretched a leg.

"Erik," I said. "Wake up."

Our hotel, as we soon found out, was across the street from the palace of the Emperor.

I remember virtually nothing else of the week in Addis, of the schedule of events that were to orient us to life "in country." I have no memory of any other details of the hotel across the street from the compound of His Excellency, Haile Selassie, also known as the Lion of Judah, Elect of God, and Negusa Negast, King of Kings. We were fully *dis*-oriented; we wanted to get out of there, to get on with it, to get to our village in the mountains.

A week later, on the last leg of our journey, a turn in the road gave unto a view of a town below. The driver gestured towards the scene ahead, speaking to us in Italian (*ferengi* in northern Ethiopia were assumed to be Italian, or at least be able to speak the language). *"Scusi!"* he said, and then, in English this time, "We are soon to arrive, Maichew. You see? Is visible, your town!"

We were about to set foot in our village, on a high plateau in the mountains of Tigre Province, Ethiopia, the Horn of Africa. We were to be the first *ferengi* in residence. We'd volunteered for this. Peace Corps didn't send people to outpost locations if they didn't want to go.

We were so relieved to be getting off the bus that we were primed to view *whatever* awaited us as a marvel and a refuge. The living quarters they'd rented for us were of typical *chico* construction, sticks and mud, the Ethiopian version of adobe. Bright green shutters opened to let in the light, the flies, and the occasional chicken. The amenities: a tin roof, cement floors in the living room and bedroom, a light bulb that dangled by a cord from the living room ceiling, providing electricity for two or three hours in the evening. In the kitchen, a packed earthen floor, a table, three chairs. A small gas stove was, for the time being, a tantalizing but useless convenience, since the propane tank which would fuel it hadn't arrived. The two fifty-gallon drums in the corner, our water system, were empty, the water itself not part of the onsite package.

The women we hired to carry water from the river delivered it to our door in large earthenware jugs balanced on their heads. They poured the water from the jugs into one of the drums in an every-other-day system dictated by the Peace Corps Health Officer so that any water we touched would have "sat" for forty-eight hours, after which the flukes of the schistosomiasis snail would no longer pose a danger. At that point we were free to boil the cloudy water for the twenty-minute minimum, after which we poured it into a filter apparatus so that it would resemble drinking water, the flotsam and worse from the river strained into the quickly clogged filter.

The intricacies of navigating daily life required a whole new set of routines. A trip to the WC entailed a mini-trek through the compound, past the landlord's house, past the goats, the chickens, the donkey, out the back gate into the field behind us to the *shintebet,* newly constructed as a pre-condition of the rental agreement. Should the need to make this journey occur in the middle of the night, it was made to the accompaniment of the nocturnal song of the hyena, whose laughing howl we heard every single night.

No, it never occurred to me to invite my parents to visit us in Africa. But entertaining them in our San Francisco flat would be a piece of cake. The *shintebet* was down the hall. No hyenas in the alley. Electricity flowed through our wires tweny-four hours a day. We had a stove *and* a refrigerator. I missed our bright green shutters, but with glass in each and every window we didn't need them.

My parents in our village in Africa? They've now been there via the stories embedded forever in my memory, that I've loved to relive, over and over again, so they've been there in a way, as have all of you who sit and open yourselves to the witness we brought home, letting yourselves be taken all the way to our village in Africa.

Solveig Nilsen was a Peace Corps Volunteer in Ethiopia from 1967–1969 to 1969. After some post-Peace Corps years in New York, San Francisco, and New Hampshire, she settled down in Minneapolis, Minnesota as librarian with Hennepin County Library for thirty years. She has been organizer and chief steward of AFSCME Local 2864 and was given the Berman Award for Social Responsibility in Library Services.

WILLIAM G. MOSELEY

What I Tell My Students

Don't underestimate the Africans...or yourself, either!

I AM A GEOGRAPHY PROFESSOR AT A SMALL LIBERAL ARTS COLLEGE
in the Upper Midwest. The college, which prides itself on
internationalism, tends to attract a lot of students with an interest in faraway lands. It is also a somewhat left-leaning campus
where students have a deep interest in making the world a better place. The courses I teach are international in scope, focusing on environment, development, and Africa. Slides from my
Peace Corps days and other international development experiences often feature prominently in my lectures. That's why,
clearly, a number of students walk into my office every semes-
ter asking about my experiences as a Peace Corps Volunteer.
Most of them also want to know what I think of this as a
possible opportunity. While I have all sorts of responses, I try
to be honest, sharing both positive and negative aspects of that
time in my life.

I don't think I was ever out to save the world. I was pretty
cynical about development in general, having read many of
the classic development critiques in my anthropology, history,

and economics courses. No, I think I joined Peace Corps to experience the world in some remote part of that global South. I wanted to be as far away from the "West" as I could. If I am to be brutally honest, I believe this desire to be "away from the West" probably had something to do with my mixed feelings about where I grew up, in the suburbs outside of Chicago. Clearly I had benefited from the good schooling this environment had provided me. Yet my college education and experiences abroad made me increasingly uncomfortable with the blatant materialism, homogeneity, and pro-business orientation of the suburbs. Perhaps Peace Corps was the logical antidote for my suburban American upbringing.

So where did I go, how did I live and what did I do? I learned in the spring of 1987 that I would be sent to Mali two weeks after I graduated from college in June. Of course, I had no idea where Mali was when I received my appointment letter—having to look it up in the world atlas just like all of the other non-sophisticates. Some members of my extended family thought I was going to Bali (Indonesia) or Maui (Hawaii), tropical states which were quite different from the semi-arid, land-locked, West Africa nation which is probably best known for a town many people are not sure really exists, that legendary city at the end of the world—Timbuktu.

Why I was sent to Mali I am not sure. I had told the Peace Corps recruiter I would go anywhere, and my French language skills are probably the best explanation for this appointment. Mali was also recovering from a major drought in 1984–85 which had struck much of Sahelian Africa. As a result, Mali and a number of other countries in the region were targets for expanding Peace Corps initiatives, all under an umbrella program known as the African Food Systems Initiative (AFSI).

I underwent four months of training in a small town outside of the capital city, Bamako. I perfected my French, learned a local language known as Bamanan or Bambara, studied community development approaches, and learned country-specific skills related to my chosen technical sector of agriculture and community gardening. To say that I was an agricultural expert would be a huge misnomer. I had studied history as an undergraduate and played around in the garden growing up. About the only other qualification I could claim was a high school career test which indicated, to the horror of the school guidance counselor, that I should be a farmer.

Training was amazing in terms of quality, as well as in the opportunity to bond with fifty other Volunteers who formed my training group; I was ready to begin my service when the training period was over.

Having listened to my request for a remote, rural site, I was sent to small Bamanan village of 200 people about fifty kilometers from the nearest paved road. There were two other French speakers in my village, the grade school teacher and the government agricultural agent who was my counterpart. I distinctly remember the Peace Corps truck driving away that first day, feeling like I was really, really on my own.

Over the next six months, I would live in temporary homes while the village and I built my house. It was a basic adobe structure with three non-standard (for the area) improvements: a cement floor, a tin roof, and a pit latrine. While I had my own home, I took my meals with a family in the village that had been assigned to look after me.

During those initial months, my only real job was to perfect my Bamanan language skills and to get to know the place. I spent a lot of time hanging out. One of the main ways males pass their time is to do tea in the evening. (This is, of course, while women are doing all of the work.) Over several hours, one will prepare and serve three rounds of strong, sweet tea to their friends. During the long dry season, this is typically done

under the stars. It is here that I perfected my Bamanan, discussing everything under the sun with my new-found Malian
friends.

Hanging out is a difficult task for many workaholic
Americans. Getting things done is so engrained in us that this
initial phase is challenging for most Volunteers. Even after my
initial start-up, there were often slow times, especially during
the rainy season when all of the villagers were busy at work
in their fields. I did work with people in their fields during
this time, and even farmed my own peanuts, but there were
real physical limits to how much I could do. This meant lots
of time reading during the rainy season. I remember becoming totally engrossed in Tolkien's *Trilogy of the Rings* and then
emerging from my hut to rejoin village life. It could be surreal,
very surreal.

While I was trained to be a gardening volunteer, I quickly
learned that I had little in the way of agricultural insight to
offer to members of this community. In fact, the more I
observed, the more I became impressed with the agricultural
and natural resource management practices of this and surrounding villages. These farmers' tillage techniques, their way
of mixing different crops in the same field (known as inter-
cropping), their knowledge of different soils, and their fallow-
ing schedules were all fascinating to me. I became increasingly
skeptical of the government's attempts to promote "modern
agriculture," which tended to emphasize cotton production
and the use of pesticides and fertilizers.

While I eventually did work with community gardeners, I
did many other things in response to village interests. I helped
form a beekeepers co-op which sold honey in the capital city;
built an improved, cement-lined well; offered basic nutrition
training; grafted fruit trees; and experimented with different agro-forestry approaches. Had I been a formally trained

agronomist, I am not sure if I would have been as flexible as I was. Being a broadly trained liberal arts college graduate, I never positioned myself as the expert, but rather as someone who could work with the community to address certain problems. I also did not have large sums of project money with which I could purchase local cooperation. If people didn't like my ideas, they eventually let me know their disapproval by dragging their feet, or just telling me.

It is at about this point in my conversation with a student that I pause, and let them know that I am very biased in my assessment of Peace Corps. It may sound corny, but it was a transformative experience for me. I found my calling—so to speak—which was to study, write, and teach about agriculture and natural resource management approaches in Africa. This was a rare moment in my life where I could just "be" and it taught me lasting lessons about how people think and live in a small rural farming community. Had I been hell bent on writing a dissertation at the time, or bound and determined to mount some huge development project, I am not sure I would have learned half of what I did.

Mine being well-trained, critical students, it is usually at about this time that I get two to three somewhat inter-related questions.

First, isn't the whole development process a flawed, neo-imperialist project? (I told you I have left-leaning students.) Yes, mainstream approaches to development are highly flawed. Nonetheless, I argue that our job is to re-invent development and to begin to think about this process in very different ways. I further assert that places like Mali are increasingly connected to us, whether we like it or not. Our job is to figure out how to engage positively with the Malis of the world.

Once we acknowledge that Africans are already in contact with the Western world (whether we like it or not), I believe we open a new space for development. With its Frierian inspired, bottom-up approach to development, I believe Peace Corps is closer to a sound development approach than almost any other group active in this arena.

Second, students often ask if they are only serving U.S. interests abroad by joining the Peace Corps, becoming "an agent of the U.S. Government." In my experience, today's students are very skeptical of any good that could be delivered by a government organization. Perhaps this is a triumph of Reaganism, or Republicanism more broadly—but I suppose the right should take pride in knowing how skeptical left-leaning students are of government in general. While Peace Corps will not serve where the U.S. has no diplomatic rela-tions, the reality is that most Peace Corps countries are of little strategic importance to the U.S. I never felt like an agent of the U.S. government in Mali. I know some of my village friends thought I might be CIA at first. But, as far as I know, they came to realize that this was not what I was about.

Third, there is the American workaholic question: Do Peace Corps Volunteers really achieve anything meaningful in terms of development? I certainly knew some Volunteers who did not accomplish much in the way of work, but these were the exception. Some of these individuals were suffering from culture shock and/or depression; others eventually went home early. However, by and large, most of the Volunteers were hard work-ing. I also remind my students that Peace Corps is more than just a development organization, but serves as a vehicle for cross-cultural exchange. While what we actually did as Volunteers may be difficult to quantify, the understanding we brought back home is just as important. God knows, the lumbering giant we call America can always use a more informed citizenry.

In other cases, Volunteers often plant seeds that take years to bloom. I remember being frustrated that a large community

garden was never established in my village when I was there—
despite numerous suggestions that this be considered. I went
back several years later to discover that one had been established and they thanked me for initiating the idea.

There are loads of other questions I am often asked. For
example, isn't two years too long of a commitment, or isn't
it better to work on these issues at home rather than abroad?
I left Peace Corps ready to leave (two years and four months
was just about right for me), but anything less than this would
have been unfair to the people I was with. I laud those who
work on development issues at home, but I think there is
something very important to be gained from living outside of
your culture and country. It also allows one to appreciate the
immense power that the U.S. exerts on the rest of the world.
Peace Corps isn't for everyone, and that my positive tenure
may not be the norm. But I also want my students to make an
informed choice, and I hope that they are open to considering
what was for me a life-altering experience.

*William G. Moseley is an associate professor of geography at
Macalester College in Saint Paul, Minnesota. He was an agricultural
volunteer in Mali from 1987–89. He is married to another Mali
RPCV, Julia Earl, and they have two children, Ben and Sophie.*

KELLY McCORKENDALE

*
* *

Slash and Burn

Giving thanks thousands of miles from home—making "there" home.

THE MALAGASY HAD TAKEN ME FOR CRAZY WHEN THEY HEARD the deep breath of defeat I exhaled in the face of freshly butchered cow. Yet, now, as I glanced out of my hut to see Michelle holding two chickens—their necks weeping red—I breathed with ease. This dinner would be special, and recent death no longer hindered me. We planned an ambitious meal; considering we had no oven, only a broken two-burner hot plate and a scrappy tin cooker that burned charred rainforest, my excitement heightened.

We'd be cooking on ravinala, I thought, or eucalyptus. I hoped not. Even with sanctions, Madagascar was being stripped of its beauty. My village on the east coast of *"L'ille de passion,"* or, Mad Land, as I lovingly called this African island, heeded little conservation warning. Survival defined a person's life, and survival was sometimes "slash and burn." That understood and partially accepted, my friends and I anticipated the feast for which we had gathered, that Saturday after the holiday exalting the gift of survival: Thanksgiving.

We gathered Saturday because all of us had worked Thursday: teaching, weighing babies or farming, but this Thanksgiving would resemble most. I imagined those first few that the Pilgrims had shared with Native Americans despite not feasting on November's third Thursday. Though no Malagasy joined us, we bowed, in our way, to those who, in our years there, had ever lit a fire for us, stripped a litchi of its shell, or had taken us to market and taught us to barter.

The Malagasy, like the Indians to our Pilgrim ancestors, noticed our distinct whiteness. "*Monaohona vazaha.*" *Vazaha* implied paleness. Meant foreignness. And insinuated igno- rance—an ignorance we unwittingly accepted.

At first, we were lost without comfort—electricity, toilet, faucet. I asked questions from dawn until dusk: What's this? Are you sure I can eat that? You want me to sit where? Prior experience certainly did not apply to cooking in my brave, new world. I now had to assemble an oven, pluck chickens and soften plantains, but I was still a *vazaha*—rejecting cooking lessons because I had gone to Madagascar to save the world, not to eat.

A man named Gaby had tried to teach us basic skills during training—a ten-week period after we first arrived in Mad Land. I had imagined there would be wild fruits at copious markets, but I never contemplated the art of baking in the developing world or the edibility of meat colored ruby. Gaby, our official cook, invited us into his kitchen and tried to teach us how to make our favorites with limited tools. His delicious and warm brownies softened in my mouth while I reasoned that I would be too busy teaching, studying Malagasy and develop- ing life-skills projects to dream of baking sweets. Besides, I was sure that cooking would be instinctual. I could, after all, boil noodles, slice an onion, and sauté tomatoes. God knew, I had little desire to stray from these safe staples after the *famadihina*.

A *famadihina* is a celebration held every few years where-upon Malagasy families remove their relatives' bones from tombs and re-wrap them in new *lambahoany*, or cloth. There is moonshine and dancing and a traditional fatty pork meal of whole pig. My group had attended one such event.

We sat at a long wooden table—hands folded in our laps, underneath a wet weather tarp—and practiced our language. Bowls of *vary mena*—red rice—and plates of pork steamed with oil. The Malagasy, always gracious to guests—especially the "exotic"—sought to please us. We received a second plate of fresh pig to share. I asked a friend to dish out more. He plunged in and pulled up an entire jaw—complete with teeth—and grimaced, a stout laugh escaping from mid-throat. I declined.

As soon as I got to go to the capital, I gorged myself at Hotel De France on the familiar—hamburgers.

Nearly eighteen months later, it seemed another girl had consumed both meals.

In Vatomandry, I awaited my five closest American friends, just as eager to see them as they were to make the trek to my beach. The ocean roared me awake each morning, and a sea breeze often shook me to sleep—that and the sound of pigs making sweet love beyond my yard.

Litchis, papaya, *ampalibe, zaty,* mangoes, oranges, passion fruit, *corresol,* and even watermelon abounded; I lived a dream friends envied. My markets' generous offerings in mind, we had planned our meal via letters: coconut chicken, garlic mashed potatoes, sautéed carrots and green beans, stuffing, banana bread and as much beer as we could afford. We would pool our resources to purchase these extravagances—spare no expense—butter, flour, coconut, and rum.

Stephanie had arrived a day early. When the pigs' play awoke me, a familiar hollow feeling had invaded my belly: the hungry/

full symptom of giardia. In America, we see doctors for this. In Madagascar, I co-existed with it for two years. It lay latent, waiting to strike once every month. Still, I followed Stephanie to market where we bartered for six kilos of vegetables and fruit. On our walk home, we stopped at a *hotely*—a crude restaurant similar in appearance to a Depression-era shanty—and ordered fish for lunch. As we dug in, my stomach imploded. I rushed to the *kabone*, or hole-in-the-ground. Once. Twice. Three times in fifteen minutes. Stephanie looked up at me from her food. I was flushed, sweaty and doubled over.

She couldn't help me; by then I had accepted giardia as my companion—a forbidden lover to whom I abandoned reason with every rendezvous. Minute bacteria slunk in and rooted deeper into my intestines every month, for I no longer feared what I ate, how I cleaned it or where I bought it.

During training, after the pig jaw incident, I had refused to eat in a "hotely." By Thanksgiving, I had fallen in love with these reminders of bar-food-gone-bad at a hole-in-the-wall.

When I had first arrived in my village, I had tiptoed around most foods like one circles an elephant—peculiar, obvious and maybe even deadly—at the front door. My first meal in Vatomandry had been Quaker Oats—a gift I pulled from a care package after I waved my Jeep/escort goodbye.

My shoulders had curled as my chest sunk and spine condensed around my abdomen: instant apprehension. I went inside my house for the first time alone. In my concrete hut, I eyed the skeletal kitchen and approached the stove. It was hooked to a gas bottle, so I turned the knob and heard a faint click. Fire flared. I reveled in joy.

And then flames shot out. The metal on top blackened and caved. I panicked, flinging a dirty towel at the fire before fumbling the switch off. A lone tear slid over my cheek as I wondered how I would ever eat.

Fortunately, the other burner worked, and later, as I sat on my back stoop, the sun setting beyond the banana tree, my tiny lips struggled around the wide brim of a wooden spoon piled high with brown sugar and cinnamon. I still ached inside from fear of death by starvation; the elephant still sat at the door, and would for a while.

On Thanksgiving Saturday, despite my illness, we started cooking early. We soaked the veggies in filtered, chlorinated water. Cubed potatoes. Sliced carrots. Chopped onions. Pounded garlic.

Amber, Michelle, and I sat over plastic buckets enjoying the vegetables' thud with our knives' every slip. Stephanie and Sara perused the market chickens and picked up a bag full of coconut shavings while we awaited the arrival of Becky. The over-feathered chickens were scrappy with little meat, but we settled on four decent ones. Michelle and Becky conquered them while Amber and I sifted flour and sugar into creamed eggs and bananas. We filled the bottom two inches of a ten-gallon pot with sand, placed a tin can in the center and topped it with a smaller buttered pot. We poured in the batter. Outside, Michelle and Becky slit the chickens' throats. The blood drained. They steeped the headless creatures in boiled water before plucking, and afterwards, Becky grabbed a knife and divided them at their joints. We would even fry the back, neck and tailbone.

Michelle lived in a town near me. During our first few weeks, we had thought only of food, often feeling as if we were starving. A tomato and a cup of pasta washed through our bowels like sand from shore. We needed sustenance— heavy and thick, doughy and greasy, chunky and chewy. We prepared oil-logged spaghetti and fried eggplant by the subtle glow of candlelight. We next endeavored to produce shrimp scampi and French fries. The shrimp were little larger than maggots. By our third meal together, we realized we needed meat—the land-dwelling kind.

When we bought the chicken, we turned from each other to the bird. And then back again. Michelle was willing to kill. I consented to assist. We took it to Michelle's room. I diced vegetables and boiled rice as Michelle placed one foot on its wings and the other on its feet. Its head in her left hand: knife in the right. Back turned, I knew when she slit its throat; it smelled like I imagined birth, or war, might—a rush of blood, shit and piss piercing the air all at once, orchestrated to the bawling decrescendo of death.

By Thanksgiving our second year there, neither Michelle nor I minded the process. We had managed to create hamburgers, chili, honey roasted nuts, refried beans, nachos and tacos, tuna and salmon—even brownies. On daily jaunts to market, we faced cow and pig, just dead and splayed out. I had learned to recognize stomach by it almost furry appearance and to appreciate that hooves could be boiled into a gelatinous soup.

Michelle and I worked swiftly on Turkey Day, a well-oiled machine. I seasoned flour for frying while she mixed tomatoes, garlic, ginger and onion with coconut milk for sauce. I strained the shavings with hot water twice to keep the milk rich. Becky sat on the back step at the *fanta peara*—the tiny charcoal cooker lit by that rare wood—and sautéed the green beans and carrots. Sara pulled the finished banana bread out of the ten-gallon pot while wearing leather garden gloves and poured in the second batch. Stephanie ran to the store for more butter and refilled the water buckets. We drank Three Horses Beer and continuously cleaned my two knives, five spoons, and three bowls in a clothes-washing bin. We played Christmas tunes and wiped sweat from our necks, cheeks, and chests with pocket scarves.

My first day at site—after the stove incident—a tiny girl had popped into the frame of my open window. Florence. I noted her rank odor. Still, she became my teacher and best friend. Prideful, she behaved differently from the typically timid Malagasy; whenever I whined loneliness she would try to send me on a blind date with an eligible, clean man. Together, we de-shelled, roasted, and pounded peanuts with sugar, salt, and honey until they were creamy paste. She taught me to round my *mofo gasy*—a cake-like, sweet bread. I showed her how to stew tomatoes. We ate meals together and talked politics, boys, hopes and dreams. We communicated best in the kitchen—my hands kneading, mixing, chopping.

Sitting there grading papers or entertaining neighbor kids, I realized how misguided I had been, thinking I wouldn't invest time in food. When I needed a break from speaking Malagasy, being a liaison to the world and teaching English, cooking replaced TV, theater, personal vehicle, and nightlife.

I spent hours hunting down yeast. Melting chocolate for brownies. Marinating beef. Pasteurizing milk and mixing it with butter for Alfredo sauce. Snapping the heads off shrimp. Scaling fish. Mixing ketchup, mayonnaise and sweet and sour or schezuan sauces. Frying crepes. And I did all this, often, wrapped in nothing but the thin *lambahoany* of the dead, as if I too had been sent to heaven anew.

The colorful wrap kept me about as cool as an ape in a greenhouse when I stood over a flame during the hot season, but I still invited my students to cook with me. They loved that I adopted their dress. That I enjoyed Malagasy "compose" and sugared avocadoes. Ate plates heaped with "*vary mena.*" We sang and talked life. Listened to the Black Eyed Peas. They perused my magazines and flipped through pictures of my family.

The green beans sautéed, banana bread baked, potatoes mashed, stuffing soggy but tasty, two chickens fried and two simmered in coconut sauce, my friends and I sat down at 4 o'clock—beers in hand—to a warm Thanksgiving dinner. We ate from the only pots and plates not filled with food. Sara and Becky sat on the *tsi*—a woven grass mat. Michelle and Stephanie took the wooden chairs. Amber and I sat on raffia stools and placed our food on our laps. We all said our silent thank you and ate.

My kitchen floor, a gray plane of cracked concrete dappled blue, resounded with crunch from the sand beneath our feet and bottoms. The room was hot, but my peach-colored curtains billowed with a breeze. The sun shone in, pawing at our skin like cactus thumbs. We laughed about my bubble-blue walls and defective stove. We grazed well into dark, and, when Florence came by, we gave her family the leftovers.

I noticed, during my first Thanksgiving back in the States, that everything in the green bean casserole came from a can. The turkey arrived at our door as cold and white as a snowflake. The bread just appeared, wrapped in plastic. Cooking started at 9:00, and we feasted at 11:30. Around the oval oak table, we couldn't agree on music or politics or even funny stories.

And then it was as if I had flipped the channel on a lazy Sunday, suddenly, back to Madagascar. I even felt a fissure of heartache crack inside for my old beau—giardia. I wanted the scent of coconut chicken tickling my tongue and coconut-rum punch slurring my speech.

During Thanksgiving in Madagascar, tired and frazzled, I had not silently thanked the inventor of ovens. I had not wished for the ease of frozen, skinless chicken breast and a refrigerator. I had not praised the ingenuity of sinks. Instead, I had marveled with a new appreciation of all things truly culinary—from raw to ripe and overcooked.

I had been thankful for a warm kitchen where sixteen-year-old girls shed their cultural inhibitions. I had slashed and burned both expectation and ego for survival. I learned that it took stripping ideologies—and food—bare, beyond beauty, to appreciate progress.

But I knew, despite it all, sitting there and singing along to "Silent Night," that I would still always be innately American.

Even so, now having transitioned back to that overfed and under-appreciative American, with every spoonful of Quaker Oats or a microwave meal—too busy to eat and drink with joy—I yearn for something more. The smell of raw ginger and garlic. Perhaps a bucket of cool water and one knife as I stand at a lone table in an azure-blue kitchen, demanding more butter for bread. My friends laughing beside me, drunk on gratitude for the skills we had acquired that enabled us not to just survive, but do so with joy. Filled with immense love, not just for each other, but also a big, red island—drifting, almost, unnoticed in the Indian Ocean.

After serving in Madagascar from 2004–2006, Kelly McCorkendale learned the other side of development as an admin assistant in the Europe and Central Asia Region at the World Bank. Life ordering office supplies and booking plane tickets was quite dull compared to teaching in a Malagasy village, so she went back to school—completing her master's degree in International Training and Education in 2010 from American University in D.C., where she resides.

SALLY CYTRON GATI

Two Years Lasts a Lifetime

We teach best when we are also learning.
And the teaching we do can return to us.

"ASK NOT WHAT YOUR COUNTRY CAN DO FOR YOU—ASK WHAT you can do for your country." When I was about to graduate from UCLA in 1963, I thought about Peace Corps. My anthro professor, Council Taylor, talked about fascinating experiences in Guinea on the west coast of Africa. It was also the time of the civil rights movement, and I was ready and interested to learn more about Africa firsthand. Going straight to graduate school did not inspire me.

What did was a chance happening on campus. One of the first groups going to Ghana was training there, so I sat in on a lecture; that was the spark I needed, and I knew this was to be my next move. I filled out the extremely long application form and was invited to train for a program in Brazil. That would have been fine but, since I knew that there would be a training session for Nigeria at Columbia University, I asked to be considered for that instead.

Nothing seems to be easy; in those days, this was also true. Peace Corps Washington held me up until I had lost weight.

Besides that, they didn't let me go to Nigeria with my group because the FBI hadn't finished my background check. I had to wait and go by myself, arriving in Nigeria about a month later.

When I finally got there, I was assigned to a high school in the capital city, Lagos; this caused raised eyebrows in my group from those who believed that the reason I came late, alone, and didn't get a "bush" assignment was that I was really working for the CIA.

My assignment was to teach English literature, grammar, and writing in a boys' high school—United Christian Secondary Commercial School. I was given a one-bedroom, air-conditioned apartment that had a kitchen, bathroom, and living room. It was in a six-unit building about twenty minutes walk from the school in a very nice area of Lagos called Apapa. From my front window, I could view an undeveloped field with a small community center recreation building behind which was a big Kingsway supermarket. There were shops that sold fruit and vegetables, a beauty parlor, a bakery, a butcher shop, a clothing store, and a place to buy gas containers for heating water.

Down the block from my place, separated by a parking lot, was the fancy Excelsior Hotel and the famous Moroccan Room with a band and bar and nightly dancing. I, of course, was a good girl, and only visited to see what was going on there. I lived on the corner lot. The *"ashewos"* (Yoruba word for prostitutes) used to stand in front of my apartment. When the headlights of cars came down the road, they'd shine on these ladies before making the turn, and I'd watch them from my third-floor balcony.

It wasn't easy being green, never having had a class of my own. The school was organized into Five Forms, the first, corresponding to Freshman; the second, Sophomores; the third, Juniors, the fourth, Seniors, and the fifth, those who were in school for an extra year to prepare and take advanced placement tests. I was lucky in one sense, though, because another Peace Corps teacher was at my school, and he was already there when I arrived.

Duane was a math teacher from Seattle. How nice for both of us to be able to commiserate and to talk about our situation, especially when things weren't going well. I had a shoulder to lean on when the headmaster caned my P.E. class for not coming in on time because I had not insisted that they stop their soccer game. Duane helped me when I had uncomfortable encounters with an British English teacher, who told me, "Sorry, Sally, we can't have an American in charge of the English Department." When my monthly allowance (about $150) was stolen by my "houseboy," Duane was there to help me through the month. When Duane's girlfriend came as a PCV, I was pleased to be a witness at their wedding, attended by Peace Corps Director Bill Saltonstall and his wife Kathy.

Both Duane and I were active at our school and in the community. Duane organized projects for the Lagos Work Camp, getting volunteers to build a concrete receptacle for garbage. I had a music club, in which I had students playing traditional Nigerian instruments. We met once a week, and the kids practiced and got so good, we were asked to be on Nigerian TV. I also organized a swimming club.

The one project outside of school that I feel most proud of was a sleepover camp that I organized that gave twenty-four boys from my school a chance to have a terrific "scoutlike" experience, swimming in the lagoon, canoeing, fishing, cooking, building a campfire and cutting logs for seats surrounding it. I worked with a wonderful man from the Ministry of Social Welfare, got the Chief of Police to release one policeman who was a fine swimmer to be one of my counselors, had an Olympic swimmer as swimming coach, had two PCVs help as counselors, and a Mariner Scout to do the canoeing classes. We had some publicity in Nigeria because of an article in the *Nigerian Daily Times*, but more fun was to hear from my mom in the States that there was a report on one of the major American TV news programs on Christmas Eve telling about my boys' camp.

What I learned about myself was that whatever my interests, experience, and abilities were before I went to Nigeria, I expanded on. I was interested in music, folk instruments, and folk art and found Nigeria the perfect place for all of these. I collected many traditional instruments and loved to "jam" with the students. I often went highlife dancing with Nigerian friends. Having been a Scout counselor for years in California, I brought an innocence coupled with enthusiasm that helped me move forward to organize the camp in Nigeria. I was good at sports and loved the idea that when our school became co-ed, I could introduce volleyball to the girls in my P.E. class. I love Shakespeare and enjoyed the opportunity to teach some of his plays in my classes. I learned to cook Nigerian stew with cayenne peppers and okra and eat it with cassava with my fingers. I fried plantain and made it regularly. I rode on my motorized Solex bicycle with my crazy monkey Ukhekhe, and we watched the goings on from our balcony.

I saw a country in turmoil: coups, killings, corruption, cultural clashes, and political instability. I marveled at the many living languages spoken by divergent tribes, fell in love with the folk art, came away with new perspectives, and made many meaningful friendships.

When I returned from the Peace Corps, I went back to graduate school, got an M.A. in Comparative Folklore and Mythology at UCLA with an emphasis on African Studies and did a master's thesis on Yoruba folklore. My first job was in Los Angeles as an A.B.E (adult basic education) teacher and later I began teaching ESL (English as a Second Language). When I moved with my husband and son to San Francisco, I began teaching ESL for the Community College (now City College of San Francisco), and I'm still happy in the classroom.

Besides my full-time ESL job, I also teach a Seniors' class in World Cultures in Oakland once a week. I can immediately recognize when a Nigerian is speaking English. One day, not so long ago, as I was doing my attendance sheets at the Pleasant Valley Adult School Office in Oakland, I heard someone speaking with a distinct and recognizable Nigerian accent. It was another teacher, a new hire. When he acknowledged that he *was* from Nigeria, I told him that I had spent two years at UCSCS high school in Apapa, Lagos, Nigeria.

He then told me that school was where he had been a student. Now that was something! Out of 55 million people in 1964 and 180 million today, how unlikely would it be to find someone who not only knew of my Nigerian high school but had been a student there?

As we talked, he started telling me about various people in his class, about his math teacher, Duane, and about other teachers and students we both knew. He asked me what my name had been when I was in Nigeria. I told him, "Sally Cytron." He spelled my last name correctly and said, "Believe it or not, *you* were my English teacher."

'Dapo, Duane, and I got together in Oakland and had a mini-reunion in April of 2008. My Peace Corps experience came full circle.

A Yoruba proverb says, "One does not easily or casually take the child from the palm-nut." Mr. Oyekan Omomoyela (in *The Good Person: Excerpts from the Yoruba Proverb Treasury*) explains: "It takes effort to accomplish a good end." I never knew if the effort I made as a Peace Corps Volunteer really brought about anything good, but the benefits and good memories for me have definitely been long lasting and have spread over my lifetime.

Sally (Cytron) Gati was a Peace Corps high school teacher in Lagos, Nigeria from 1964-66. She's been teaching for over forty years and still teaches ESL at City College of San Francisco. She's also a teacher/trainer, textbook writer, and documentary filmmaker. Her web site is HTTP://FOG.CCSF.EDU~SGATI.

STARLEY TALBOTT ANDERSON

✦

Sister Stella Seams Serene

Though things don't always work out, the experiences—
and the places—stay with us.

IT WAS A LONG WAY FROM A WYOMING RANCH CORRAL TO A
Setswana chief's *kraal* in a rural village of South Africa. The
cultural distance may have been even further for this ranch-
raised sixty-year-old woman traveling to Africa with the
United States Peace Corps.

The sights and sounds of the July day I began my journey
are burned in my mind like a brand on a calf. High trill voices
rang out in greeting over the rocky, red hills, echoing back
to the chief's *kraal*. Black pots bubbled over open cook fires
watched by black faces eager to meet the Americans arriving
on a big bus from Pretoria. The chief's *kraal* harkens back
hundreds of years to when it was actually a corral to hold
livestock or a cluster of buildings to hold the chief's family
and their possessions. The modern *kraal*, however, is a cluster
of buildings housing offices similar to a city hall in any city in
the United States.

South African television cameras whirred, recording the
news that the Peace Corps had arrived for the first time in the

Northwest Province. Volunteers had been serving in two other provinces in South Africa for only a few years. Our mission as school and community resource volunteers and for a new project on AIDS education was eagerly anticipated in the Province. Although we would only remain in the village of Moruleng for ten weeks during training, the villagers were quite excited.

Dancing, singing, eating, and speeches filled the middle of a sunny winter day (the seasons are opposite those in the northern hemisphere). Then, it was off to our host homes to get acquainted with those who would be our families for the next few weeks. The village had conducted meetings long before our arrival to seek those who would like to have a Volunteer as a guest. Hosts would not receive compensation for hospitality, but instead a small biweekly box of food.

I greeted my diminutive hostess, Stella, a fifty-three-year-old widow, mother of four grown children and grandmother of four. One grandchild lived with Stella while his mother attended college.

I was to learn of the life of this amazing woman over the weeks to come.

"We didn't think you would really come," Stella told me. "And, we didn't think you would really live with us. It is truly a miracle, to have white people actually staying in our village."

After a ride on public transport, a fifteen-passenger van, I toured Stella's rather surprisingly large home built of brick and cement. The home contained three bedrooms, living room, kitchen, and a sewing room. It also had space for two bathrooms, which lacked any plumbing whatsoever. But it did boast electricity, an electric range, refrigerator, television, and telephone. Most of the rooms had not been finished on the inside and there was no insulation or central heat.

The house was surrounded by an expansive yard of dirt that was swept clean each day. In the back yard was a spotlessly clean cement outhouse divided into two separate cubicles. The yard also had a covered area used for outdoor cooking and laundry.

The home had piped cold water into the kitchen, although the pipe was broken throughout my stay. We carried water from a tap in the back yard to be stored in a large plastic barrel in the kitchen. Water was usually heated with the use of an electric hot pot. Bath, dish, and laundry water was recycled to water the fruit and decorative trees bordering the yard. I soon learned to take a bucket bath and deal with the inconvenience of no indoor toilet.

The first evening with Stella and her grandson, Kele, was delightful. Stella and I bonded immediately and found we had the love of sewing in common. Stella earned her living from sewing, mostly clothing for other women in the village. She received no pension or social security.

Most of the younger Peace Corps Volunteers came to fondly refer to their host women as "Mom." Stella and I felt that we were more like sisters, so she became Sister Stella. And I became Sister Starley, or Ausi Naledi. (*Ausi* is the Setswana name for sister and *naledi* the Setswana word for Star.) I also became Kele's granny or *koko* in Setswana. Kele proudly told all his classmates at preschool that he "has a white granny now."

Stella's youngest daughter, Tsolofelo, mother of Kele, was home for a few days before she had to return to college, so she cooked dinner my first night there. We all huddled in the living roomed wrapped in wool blankets and ate our meal in front of the television, which came to be our custom during my stay. The meal consisted of chicken, beets, squash, cabbage slaw, and the staple food of most natives, a cornmeal mush called *pap*. I never learned to like *pap*, but I learned to cook it and occasionally ate some.

Our Peace Corps literature had warned us that it might be cold, but I hadn't realized how bone-chilling it really would be. As a soon as the sun set, the cold began to creep into every corner of the unheated cement house. By bedtime, my fingers and toes were numb. I dressed in every layer of sleepwear I had brought, including socks. Then I snuggled underneath four layers of warm wool blankets.

I was up at 6:00 A.M., because I found it took me twice as long as it did at home to perform my morning chores. The Peace Corps van arrived at 7:30 to pick up the three of us in our neighborhood; we joined eleven others already packed into the van for a ten-mile trip to the college. Thirteen other Volunteers staying in a different village met us there for our joint training held one day each week. Other days during training were spent on language lessons and technical training at various locations.

Stella and I treasured our evenings getting acquainted and teaching each other of our unique cultures, fulfilling one of the goals of the Peace Corps. Stella spoke excellent English, sometimes to my detriment. We were so anxious to share our life experiences that we spoke mostly in English; I was not learning the Setswana language very quickly.

"Why did you want a Volunteer to stay with you?" I asked.

"I wanted to learn about Americans and I wanted to know more about white people. Our people have worked for white people, but we have never had the chance to really become acquainted with them. I'm interested in learning whatever I can about people and the world, and I just wanted to have an American live with me," she said.

It seemed that nearly all of the people of the village were keenly interested in learning about Americans. Shortly after my arrival I walked to the post office during a workshop break. A young man tapped me on the back and then came around to face me.

"Don't be afraid," he said. "I just want to look at you. I want to look into your eyes."

The man gently touched my gray hair, then my face, my earrings, and back to my hair.

"Very old, very wise," he commented.

Then, apparently satisfied to have seen a white person up close, he walked away.

I found that people were often totally fascinated with my gray, curly hair. The children, especially, seemed to enjoy touching it.

I usually arrived home exhausted after a day of language classes, workshops, and guest speakers. Some days I walked the two miles home, scuffing my feet in the red dirt pathway beside the only paved two-lane highway running through the village. By late afternoon the brilliant sun in a cloudless blue sky had warmed the winter day. I brewed two cups of *rooibos* (red bush) tea, which Stella and I sipped as we visited in her sunny sewing room. She nearly always stitched busily until darkness enfolded us.

As a chill invaded the house, I gathered the teacups and returned to the kitchen to make dinner, the chore I inherited when Stella's daughter returned to college. Stella delighted in eating such creations as tuna casserole and spaghetti with tomato sauce, which she had never tasted before. Our conversations continued during mealtime; then I washed the dishes and prepared each of us a two-liter glass coke bottle filled with hot water to warm our beds.

Throughout the next several weeks, Stella wove the threads of her life as serenely as she stitched the beautiful blue-and-white cloth symbolizing village traditions. By the time she completed a traditional cloth skirt for me to wear to a wedding celebration in the village, she had seamed together many stories of her life as a black woman in South Africa.

She had come as a bride to the village. They had met in Johannesburg, where Stella was reared in a family of seven children. As a young adult, Stella had lived in fairly comfortable surroundings, and she found married life in the village to be a challenge. "I had to carry wood from the mountain and cook on an outdoor fire. I had to carry water from the river for cooking, bathing, and laundry. And I had to learn the many customs of the village and how to fit into a family that really didn't want me."

The couple had four children and eventually built a home. But before the home could be finished, Stella's husband died. He had led something of a clandestine life outside of their marriage and left her penniless. Stella had always valued learning and insisted that the children be educated. Her husband did not share that ideal, and so she put much of her own earnings into sending three of the four children through college. In addition to being a seamstress, she had worked at the nearby resort of Sun City for many years.

This small and tireless woman made her entire living as a seamstress for several years. At one time, when there were factories employing many people in the area, she had eight seamstresses working for her. But now the factories are closed and she is only able to employ one seamstress, part-time. She spends several hours each day stitching on one of two modern sewing machines in a spacious room with southern windows. A clothing rack holds the many colorful costumes of the village including church uniforms, aprons, and festival clothing.

Stella holds no grudge against white people, even though discrimination still seems to prevail in some sectors of post-apartheid South Africa. She recalls the kindness of her mother's white employer during some of the worst atrocities of apartheid.

"My mother had a beautiful home in Sophiatown in the 1950s and a good job cleaning for a white woman. My father had died, but we were doing fine. Some of the older children were working or living out of the home. I was home watching my three younger siblings when an awful day unfolded."

According to history, the white people of Johannesburg decided they wished to live in Sophiatown. Black people were forced to relocate to the Southwestern Township, later known as Soweto. Most of the homes of black people were bulldozed. Stella's family home was one of the last homes left standing in Sophiatown.

"Mother had been looking for another home for us, and that day she had again left to look for a house. While she was gone, the bulldozers came to take down our house. I was ten years old and my siblings were ages two, five, and seven. The men took some of the furniture out into the yard. I sat on the couch with the little ones. While they cried, we watched the big machines tumble our home into a pile of rubble."

Stella didn't know what to do, but eventually some friends saw the children and went to find their mother. Stella's mother returned and was able to get the younger children to relatives. Stella and her mother went to the home of her mother's employer.

"That kind white women took us in and hid us in her home for some time. It was illegal to do so, but she did it anyway. She had always treated us kindly. We ate from the same dishes as the white family, slept in their beds and used the same furniture. Often, black people could not even so much as take a drink from the same cup a white person used."

Stella learned from that experience that not all white people were cruel. She took every opportunity to learn as much as she could and was diligent in learning English. When her children attended school she studied their books at night and read everything that was available. She was open to learning anything and especially interested in learning about hygiene and cooking.

I attended church with Stella, not understanding any of the sermon delivered in Setswana, but basking in the warm and enthusiastic music. It seems that nearly everyone has an ear and voice for singing.

On one Sunday we attended a traditional wedding with mixed-in Western flavor. I was embarrassed to receive as much attention and rousing greetings as the bride. As I strolled amongst the nearly five hundred guests at the outdoor reception at the groom's family home, I was greeted with the familiar loud voice trill. It sent chills up my spine. I took my turn stirring the huge black pots of porridge, serving home-made beer, cutting up vegetables for a myriad of salads and inspecting the sides of beef being prepared for the barbecue grill. South Africans love to barbecue (*braie*, as it is called there, deriving from a Dutch word).

After the bride and groom arrived to sounds of a brass band and marched to the wedding feast held in a large orange tent, I partook of the meal. I astonished people later by dancing a lively jiggerbug with another wedding guest.

"Did you teach her to dance?" several guests asked Stella, as they formed a circle, clapping and laughing.

"No, she already knew how to dance." Stella replied.

I already knew how to dance, but I didn't know how much caring and generosity could be generated between our different cultures. Toward the close of my adventure in Moreuleng I asked Stella a question and the answer will always bring a smile to my lips and a tear to my eyes.

"How do you feel about having a white American guest in your home now?"

"Oh, it is like having a delicious meal," Stella said with a broad smile on her beautiful face.

Only a few short weeks later we hugged and said goodbye for the last time. I had to leave training and South Africa due

to a medical problem. I wrote a poem for my fellow Peace
Corps Volunteers, ending with these lines:

> *From South Africa I had to depart*
> *Fly back to America with a sad heart*
> *Carry on dear friends, up the steep slope*
> *Peace Corps has bound us forever in hope.*

*Starley Talbott, aka Starley Anderson, served in South Africa in
2001. Starley's stint with the Peace Corps, training group SA
VII, was shortened due to a medical problem, though her philosophy and spirit are forever connected to the ideals of the Peace Corps.
She resides in Wyoming where she is a freelance writer and recently
released her fifth book.*

LENORE WATERS

Late Evening

Sometimes the best of romance comes from the banal.

I WALK DOWN THE MIDDLE OF A WEST AFRICAN ROAD. THIS IS the road which, during daylight hours, the women of the town use to gather wood for cooking fuel and tend to their small vegetable gardens in the forest. They walk slowly, basins on their heads, babies tied to their backs with colorful bits of cloth.

This is the road on which trucks bring cacao and coffee beans to the town center.

This is the road to the Child Health Center, where mothers and teachers bring the children for vaccinations, each child screaming every time a needle goes in, no matter whose arm is stuck.

This is the road the Boy Scouts march along, practicing parade techniques. But tonight the road is quiet, very quiet.

The night is black. Of course there are no street lights, and there is no moon, which is why I can look at the sky and see so many stars. Can I recognize any constellations, I wonder. Of course, I am very near the equator, is it a southern sky?

Oh, what the hell. Does it make a difference? There are about a million stars up there; I won't be able to navigate my way through them. I wonder if the Africans, like the Greeks, found their legends in the stars.

Suddenly I become aware of the sound of a flute, an ancient shepherd's flute, perhaps.

Am I hearing things? Is it an illusion brought on by malaria pills? Am I star struck?

The music stops. The road has ended. Beyond is the forest. I turn back, back to my cinderblock "professor's house," my home for two years.

But what am I doing here, in a small African town? I have left my grown-up daughters, my job, my aged mother. Am I fulfilling a dream of the Kennedy era, do I think my being here will make a difference in anyone's life? Is it just for adventure? Or is it because I once promised an African friend I would some day come and "help his people?"

Am I here to look at the stars?

As I'm almost home, I see the elderly gentleman who is guardian of my neighbor's house. Efu looks after me, and everyone on this road. We greet each other with a "*bonne nuit.*"

A few weeks later, I find out the night music was a French neighbor playing his recorder.

Lenore Waters was born 1925 in New York City. She was an ESL teacher in Ivory Coast 1980-81. She has lived in Berkeley, California since 1976 and has been a member of the Northern California Peace Corps since 1981. She has two daughters who are very proud that their mother served in the Peace Corps.

MARTIN R. GANZGLASS

The Forty-Eight Hour Rule

The role of the policeman in an unruled land.

I AM ONE OF THE FORTUNATE FEW LAWYERS WHO JOINED THE
Peace Corps and was able to serve as both a Volunteer and
attorney.

When I arrived in Mogadishu, Somalia had been an independent nation for less than six years. The Somali Republic
consisted of two former colonies, the northern part of the
country on the Red Sea, which had been British Somaliland;
and the southern part along the Indian Ocean from Cape
Guardafui to Kismayo, which had been Italian Somaliland.
On July 1, 1960, the two became one country, with a five-
pointed white star on a field of blue as the national flag. Each
point of the star symbolized a Somali population divided by
the colonial powers in the late nineteenth century: French
Somaliland, (now the independent country of Djibouti), the
Ogaden Region (then and now part of neighboring Ethiopia),
and the Northern Frontier District of what was the British
East African colony of Kenya (and remains part of Kenya,
despite the British Colonial Administration's promise to hold a

referendum). We used to joke that if there had been another Somali population deprived of uniting with Somalia, the flag would be the same as Israel's.

Somali, at the time, was an unwritten language. All laws were printed by the Government Printing Office in English, Italian, or Arabic. The Somalis desperately needed legal translators, primarily to translate the laws from Italian into English and vice versa.

Somewhere in the process of applying for our group of Peace Corps Volunteers, the Somali government thought they had asked for lawyers qualified as legal translators. Yet we were neither told of nor trained for this job description. We did attend rudimentary Italian classes. On a scale of 1 to 10, with 10 being the highest language proficiency, we were probably slightly above 1 by the time we left for Somalia.

My market Somali was better than my Italian.

It was immediately apparent to the officials we met at the Somali Ministry of Justice and Religious Affairs, the Committee on Legal Integration, and the University, that we were not the legal translators they thought they had requested. Like many other Peace Corps Volunteers, we then had to improvise and find meaningful jobs for ourselves where we could at least contribute something.

I ended up as Legal Advisor to the Somali National Police Force, replacing a Ford Foundation lawyer whose assignment was coming to an end. (That attorney went on to become Police Commissioner of New York City. The NYPD, when he was Commissioner, was larger than the entire Somali National Police.)

The Commandant of the Police Force was General Mohamed Abshir Musa. Fresh from memories of the Kennedy Administration, I thought I was working for Ted Sorenson. The General was an intellectual, an idea man with a strong sense of nationalism, and a pragmatist. He had molded the Police Force into a national organization and inculcated a sense of national duty in his officers and men. He had overcome the divisive tribal and clan loyalties that made most other government entities ineffective.

As legal advisor, I drafted entire codes and amendments to existing laws for consideration by Parliament, prepared and revised regulations, assisted the Attorney General in a case before the Somali Supreme Court involving the unjust imprisonment of two Somali policemen, and wrote commentaries on the Criminal Procedure and Penal Codes. I even did some legal translating, with the able assistance of a police lieutenant who had gone to law school in Italy.

I also taught at the Police Academy.

Unlike in the United States, where government attorneys prosecute criminal cases, Somali police officers were the prosecutors (except for major cases, which were handled by the Attorney General's office). I taught the police officers the elements of criminal offenses and how to prove a case.

For the lower ranks, those in the field who made the arrests, I primarily taught the Criminal Procedure Code.

The Code contained a provision called "the forty-eight hour rule." Every policeman who arrested a person was required to bring the suspect before a judge within forty-eight hours of arrest. I drummed this into my students. No matter what section of the Criminal Procedure Code I was teaching on a particular day, I wrote the number "48" on the blackboard or flip chart. Before dismissing them, I would ask different policemen the significance of the number and to explain the forty-eight hour rule. I taught at the Academy every week for most of my two years in Somalia until I left in May 1968.

Somalia's brief democratic experience came to an end on October 21, 1969, when General of the Army Mohamed

Siad Barre overthrew the elected government. Peace Corps was expelled by the end of the year, allegedly because the Volunteers were American spies. Somalia entered into a dark period of dictatorship characterized by a national secret police, special military courts and arbitrary imprisonment without charges or trial.

The Siad Barre regime waged war against its own people. It fomented tribal warfare and armed one clan against another. The Army punished those thought to support any opposition, by poisoning wells and shelling and bombing cities and towns.

Two of my closest friends, the Police Commandant and another Police General were held, for several years, in solitary confinement, in underground cells in an East German-built prison. They were imprisoned because of their integrity and commitment to the democratic principles embodied in the Somali Constitution.

This particular Somali nightmare ended in 1991 when Mohamed Siad Barre, the President for Life, was overthrown and ignominiously fled the country. A new catastrophe befell the Somalis as warring factions, based on tribal and clan lines, fought each other for power. The different warlords engaged in wholesale extortion of relief agencies trying to provide food, medicine, and shelter to the hundreds of thousands of displaced civilians.

In November 1992, President Bush initiated Operation Restore Hope. This was a real international coalition. U.S. troops, along with soldiers from Australia, Botswana, France, Nigeria, Pakistan, and other nations, went to Somalia to protect the delivery of humanitarian assistance. President Clinton continued this policy of armed humanitarian intervention, although his Administration never made up its mind whether the Operation also included so-called "nation building."

In February 1993, I was contacted by someone from the State Department and asked to go to Somalia and advise the

U.S. Ambassador and the Special Representative of the U.N. Secretary General on how to rebuild the Somali judiciary and police.

I arrived in Mogadishu in April 1993 and found a city I barely recognized. After three years of unrestricted tribal warfare, Mog was totally destroyed. Buildings were pockmarked with shell and bullet holes. The stone minaret of a fourteenth-century mosque on the road to the beach had been targeted and partially destroyed. Never in the history of Somalia had Moslem religious sites been attacked by Somalis engaged in clan warfare.

The capital looked worse than many European cities that had been battlegrounds in WWII. Any metal that could be sold for scrap in India had been stripped from Mogadishu's buildings and utility poles—window and door frames, hinges, locks and door knobs, wiring, transformers—all were gone. There was a thriving open-air arms market in the center of the city. If they had the cash, Somalis could buy anything from a simple rifle to an AK-47 to a rocket-propelled grenade launcher.

There was no functioning Somali government. Two warlords, each claiming to be president and each using his own clan-based militias of heavily armed young men, controlled different sections of the city.

Prior to the arrival of troops under Operation Restore Hope, residents on both sides of the dividing line were shelled indiscriminately. The number of civilian casualties had been enormous. Thousands of refugees fled the capital and lived in refugee camps in the countryside, solely dependent on humanitarian relief for food and shelter.

Under the rules established by the military coalition, Somali police were not allowed to carry any guns except in joint operations with coalition forces. I found the police in Mogadishu investigating crimes, arresting suspects and generally carrying out their duties, armed solely with batons and whistles. This at a time when most young Somali men in the capital openly carried AK–47s.

In order to compile information for my report, I visited as many police stations in the city and around the country as I could. At one station in Mog, the policeman in charge, who was not an officer, welcomed me with a broad smile. He called me Mr. Martin, which was how I had been known during my Peace Corps service. He remembered me from the Academy. He said the police in Mogadishu had a very serious problem, and he needed my advice. I thought he was going to ask for weapons and was already prepared to tell him I had no authority to even pass that request up the military chain of command.

"Mr. Martin," he said, in an anxious voice, "we have arrested many bad people. We are holding them, but there are no judges to take them before. Under the forty-eight hour rule, do we have to let them go?"

If it hadn't been so foreign to Somali culture, I would have hugged and kissed him on the spot. After the collapse of the Somali state, and a period of anarchy, lawlessness, absolute chaos, and the indiscriminate violence and wanton murders, this decent, honest Somali policeman was concerned about the legality of holding suspects for more than forty-eight hours. I gave him my opinion that the forty-eight hour rule did not apply if there were no judges before which to bring those arrested. However, as soon as judges were appointed, I told him, the police had forty-eight hours to produce the suspects.

Unfortunately, Somalis have endured much worse since 1993. After the U.S. and the U.N. pulled out in the fall of 1993, Mogadishu descended into a spiral of senseless violence with innocent civilians dying either from being caught between warring factions, disease, or starvation. More than fifteen years later, there is still no end to the Somalis' horrific nightmare. Fighting continues today. Factions based on tribes or clans, or under the guise of Islam, kill in order to control territory and seize power. In Mogadishu, and many other areas of the country, there is no real functioning government. According to the U.N., Somalia is the worst humanitarian crisis in Africa. Yet, the decency and adherence to the law of that single Somali policeman gives me a glimmer of hope that someday, the rule of law will return to Somalia.

The former Police Commandant is alive and well in Minnesota. I testified at his asylum hearing several years ago. The other Police General lives on the West Coast and is a grandfather many times over. We usually see each other at Ramadan when he comes east to visit his daughter's family. We call each other every Sunday evening.

Although I can't go back to visit Somalia, like all other RPCVs I continue to enjoy the close and enduring friendships with Somalis I first met almost forty-five years ago. And our children have bonded with the children of our Somali friends. Perhaps together, in the not too distant future, they will be able to return to a peaceful Somalia. *Insha'llah*—God willing.

Martin Ganzglass served as Legal Advisor to the Somali National Police Force from 1966-68. He taught the Criminal Procedure and Penal Codes to police and drafted legislation. He returned to Somalia in 1993 as Special Advisor to U.S. Ambassador Robert Gossende as part of Operation Restore Hope. He has a large extended Somali family, stemming from friendships established more than forty years ago and seven Somali children consider him their "white" grandfather, a title of which he is especially proud.

DELFI MESSINGER

✦

Full Circle

Going back, to leave again.

THE PEACE CORPS TAUGHT ME HOW TO MAKE A DIFFERENCE. Although I was mainly occupied with bonobos for eleven years as a "volunteer" after leaving my Peace Corps assignment in Zaire, I also started a children's magazine there called *Bleu/Blanc*, which exists to this day.

In 2000, I traveled back to what is now known as the Democratic Republic of Congo to see what remained of my projects. On the evening of my departure from that country I had a chance to write down my thoughts and reflect on my visit.

Our truck hit a pothole, jarring my reflections. Beside me, passengers were nodding to the *slap-slap* of the windshield wipers. The sky had lightened and suddenly we broke out of the storm. As the water ran off, fog steamed up from the hot, damp pavement. On the right the sunset was russet and mauve dipping behind the Congo River.

Clever, I mused. *Work smarter, not harder.* Massala was right; a clever, roundabout way may be the most direct route to change. Then it struck me: The magazine would carry on. Amazingly, the games and puzzles, stories, cartoons, poems— the sparking of minds, the thirst for learning and literacy would be my legacy. On a shoestring, on a whim, and almost unwittingly, I had planted a smelly crop of seeds for the next generation. Those seeds were the real golden grains.

Night falls fast on the equator. Our convoy reached the outskirts of Kinshasa amid pedestrians hurrying home before nightfall. I stared at the sunset's reflected glow from the river, knowing that this would be the last time. Abruptly, the sun slid into the Congo's vast waters. The sky turned a streaky silver, and the *mamans* selling goods along the highway hurried to light their lanterns to lure the evening crowd. Traffic thickened and slowed as we passed the airport and headed into town.

I cracked a window and the clean smell of rain blew in. The palms along the side of the road lifted their lacy feather duster heads against the fading sunset colors. The throng— many still on their way home from work—were hundreds deep at the truck stops and along the dirt paths lined with wooden tables selling grilled turkey tails, soap, cigarettes, and skin-lightening creams.

God, I was homesick for this place! This vile, gorgeous, snarly, exhilarating, insane, deep, and terrible place. For two years now, I had been dreaming of this Congo and in a few days I would be leaving forever. Through tear-lashed eyes, I remembered the birds—the kingfishers that splashed in my water barrel and the nightingale that sang every evening around eight. I thought of the flocks of mousebirds that hung like long-tailed ornaments in the trees, and the grass finches that eluded our rat-trap cat. I remembered the cattle egrets overhead that gave me courage under fire.

Zaire, Zaire, I'd loved you so! And, oh, how I'd hated you. You taught me a lifetime of lessons that I would never have learned in any other way—you gave me the human side of myself. I'd been close to tears all day and maudlin thoughts floated to the surface of my mind. *No flowers*, I thought. *Why hadn't I thought to buy flowers for Tamibu?* (One of my workers who died of AIDS in the brief time that I had been visiting.)

It was dark in the car and I wiped my face clear of tears. *Don't be so harsh*, I thought. *Instead of stuff, you gave yourself and that was worth way more.* I straightened in my seat. As the clouds drifted away and the stars came out, I saw more clearly. I knew that I could leave the Congo behind, even though a part of me—the part that held the future—would always remain.

Delfi Messinger is the author of Grains of Golden Sand. *She served in Zaire from 1984-87. Her website is delfisgrainsofgoldensand-bonobos.blogspot.com.*

BETH DUFF-BROWN

✦

A Promise Kept

Going back again raises questions, retrieves expectations,
and reminds one of promises. It is never easy and, in
many places, spans tragedy and loss.

I SAT IN A BACK PEW, LIGHTLY SWAYING TO THE BAMBOO XYLO-
phones. Buttery light streamed across the white altar from the
stained-glass cross carved into the red brick church. I pre-
tended to pray, to find a private moment, to close my eyes and
reflect on what I had seen in the week since returning to this
village where I had lived a lifetime ago.

As the Catholic sermon was ending and the hymns grew
louder, I waved bye-bye to the bare-bottomed baby who had
been making faces with me and attempted to slip unnoticed
out the side door.

A vicar caught me and pulled me before the congregation,
where I had stood ten years earlier, and fifteen before that.
Weather-beaten eyes smiled in encouragement; several women
ululated and called out "Miss Elizabeth" before a stern glance
from behind me silenced them.

"I just wanted to thank you again," I said with embarrassing simplicity, as my eyes began to sting and I fumbled with
the sleeves of my white cotton blouse. "Thank you for taking

care of me when I was just a girl, for your prayers, for my child."

Before I could finish, I stood there in tears, unable to move, unable to speak, humiliated at my public display of emotion. I cried for having kept my promise to come back again. I cried for a young woman who lay dying alone, no longer able to walk to church. I cried for once again having built up false hopes with my return, for not having done more to help those tired faces now looking up at me.

They woke to church bells every dawn, ambled from the same mud huts in which I had sat twenty-five years ago, gathered to sweep the aisle, polish the pews and adjust the same curled posters of the Stations of the Cross in broken frames, tacked to the crumbling brick walls.

And I cried because the one man I had been looking for was not out there, looking back.

Truth be told, I also cried for my lost youth, the freckle-faced California girl who had arrived on their mud-hut doorsteps in 1979 as a Peace Corps Volunteer, so idealistic, brave and full of life.

This village in Central Africa was where I had come into my own. It's where I felt that first heady rush that comes from teaching a great class. It's where I overcame aching isolation and discovered the simple pleasure of just sitting alone.

Kamponde is where I prayed for rain so I could wash my long hair; where I danced around fires, learned to play a better guitar with a Peace Corps boyfriend who visited from time to time; where I walked behind mothers carrying babies to their graves.

The Democratic Republic of Congo—known then as Zaire—was where I wrote for hours by candlelight, preparing me to go on to write as a foreign correspondent from points around the globe.

I left Kamponde in 1981, the last Volunteer, pulled out as corruption overran the Institute Untu, where I taught English for two years with the conviction I was truly doing something good.

My job with The Associated Press allowed me to return to Kamponde in 1996, to renew my ties with the villagers and write about who we had all become over the years.

I had told the villagers then that if their prayers for me to have the child Chris and I had longed for were finally heard, I would somehow let them know. But I knew it was unlikely my letters—filled with photos of the blue-eyed baby girl with whom we were blessed only a year after that visit—would arrive by Congo's pitiful postal system.

Now I wanted to thank them for those prayers.

The civil war breaking out during that first return in 1996 went on to devastate the Congo. It wasn't a war over ideology or religion or tribal hatred, but about which warlord would win the battle to exploit the country's vast mineral wealth. Though far surpassing the ongoing conflict in Sudan, Congo's neighbor to the northeast, the war here has largely been ignored, as its complexity eludes easy definition. There has been no Mia Farrow or George Clooney to shine that brilliant celebrity light upon the humanitarian heartbreak of Congo.

Though it officially ended in 2002, the conflict's resulting disease and starvation has gone on to claim nearly 5.4 million lives, according to the International Rescue Committee. I had followed the statistics, wondering how many of the nameless 45,000 Congolese who still die every month from the strains of that war might be from among Kamponde's 5,000 villagers.

By the time I left for my trip in the summer of 2006, with a sense of dread, I wondered if the people of Kamponde would know they had survived the deadliest conflict since World War II.

I was traveling with Claude Kamanga Mutond, one of my former students who is today one of Congo's most well-respected and best-connected journalists. We had found each other again by accident, locking eyes in disbelief as we stood amid shouting demonstrators at an election rally we were both covering in 1995. He went on to string for the AP and several big American dailies; the Internet now allows us to keep in touch.

My interviews would be conducted in French or Tshiluba, the local Bantu dialect of central Congo, and then translated into southern-accented English by Jim Mukenge of Kananga, the provincial capital of Kasai Occidental about one hundred miles north of Kamponde.

Jim graduated from Appalachian State University in Boone, North Carolina, and then went on to be a manager at Taco Bell. "Run for the border!" is one of his favorite lines about the job he actually liked. His wife Bernadette worked down the street at a competing Wendy's.

But they missed home, gave up the American dream and returned to Kananga. She works as an administrator at the U.N. peacekeeping mission and the two of them run several small businesses. People hammer Jim about giving up life in the United States.

"Everybody has their own village and mine just happens to be here," shrugs Jim, who changed his first name when he arrived in the States, after his hero, Jimmy Carter. He speaks fluent English and French, his native Tshiluba and the Swahili of eastern Congo, which would later aid me in an interview that would leave me speechless.

I waved at children along the dirt road, some little faces frozen in fear at seeing their first white woman. My heart pounded as we crossed the rusted railroad tracks, a sign that we were near the village.

I took in the sour smell of manioc root, the smoke from brush fires set to scatter the snakes, as our jeep, lent by the U.N. peacekeeping mission in Congo, approached the church where I had spent Sunday mornings daydreaming and working out new lesson plans.

That familiar salmon sun was setting behind thatched-reed roofs, down into the green savanna where I had watched grazing gazelles from my classrooms. Barefoot women in soiled sarongs, carrying buckets of water or bundles of sweet-potato leaves on their heads, ran into the tall brush, alarmed by the grinding gears of our 4X4.

There was the dingy Peace Corps house, white with royal-blue trim, across from the church, in a compound that had once bustled with Belgian missionaries, electricity, and colorful bougainvillea.

The people of this Central African nation have been so drained by war, corruption and neglect, that I feared for the worst and hoped only for a few familiar faces. Most of all, I longed for the face of Tshinyama Mwananzoi.

Another former student in Kinshasa, the Congolese capital where I had begun my journey, told me he believed the easygoing man who had cooked for Peace Corps Volunteers for two decades had died. Though saddened, it had not surprised me. The average life span here is only fifty years, and Tshinyama would have been well past that by now.

Moments after we arrived, the village priest looked up at the darkening sky and said that the cook who had worked for the foreigners had passed. Then where was his grave, I demanded to know, with a bitterness that caught both of us by surprise.

"Life is like a circle, and you've come home," Tshinyama had said when we last met. "You haven't changed over all these years. That's because it was here that you found who you are."

Joseph was the first to emerge from the shadows cast by kerosene lanterns, barefoot and trembling in his threadbare white shirt. He clasped my hands and said: "You kept your promise."

I was stiff and weary from days of hard travel. There are only 400 miles of paved roads in a country the size of Western Europe; just one badly rutted dirt road takes you to Kamponde.

Joseph's familiar furrowed brow made me smile through my tears.

"I thank God for inspiring you to come back, Miss Elizabeth, remembering the place where you once taught our children," said Joseph, who had cleaned house for Father Paul, the old Belgian priest who, like me, was the last of his kind to live here.

Joseph and his lifelong neighbor Placide, their elderly wives and dozens of other villagers were shaking their heads, calling "Miss Elizabeth?" as they gathered at the old wooden doors of the terra cotta-roofed church, beneath the moon now rising above the mango trees.

Joseph and Placide's children had once built fires behind my house. We would often sit around together at night; I would strum my guitar, practice my Tshiluba and they would ask me questions in their broken elementary school French: How does the sun stay up in the sky? Is it true Americans have magic boxes that carry them from one floor to the next? Was your president really just a peanut farmer, like ours?

Those children were now grown—I would later learn some had already died—and I was stunned that Joseph and Placide, both in their seventies, were still alive. One in five children will not live until age five in Congo today, yet these old farmers had persevered.

But apparently not Tshinyama. Now I would put wild-flowers at his grave, share stories with his grandchildren about his magical mango pudding and his belief that God had put him on Earth—and his father before him for the Belgians—to nourish the White Man.

I could see him wiping his hands on the apron fashioned from an old flour sack, his amber eyes red-rimmed from the hot coal fire and brick oven on which he would boil his *pili-pili* pepper sauce and bake sweet banana bread.

The classrooms were ghostly quiet; a gentle breeze came off the savanna, through windows that had not seen glass in years. Cursive lessons from last year still lined the black chinked chalkboards.

I sat in one of the wooden desks, carved with sweetheart initials slashed by an arrow.

I closed my eyes and could hear the wolfish laughter of the young men, some of whom had been my own age and had terrified me at first. My rowdiest twelfth graders would make smooching sounds when I turned to the board, so I had once walked out, refusing to teach. The same class later won me back after averting their eyes when a gust of wind blew open my wraparound skirt.

The concrete-and-brick school was built and once staffed by Belgians, whose country ruled the Congo for seventy-five years, until independence in 1960. Father Paul had taught history for decades at the Institute Untu.

I never had the courage during our Sunday lunches to ask the old man with the long white beard, who still held Sunday mass, whether his lessons included King Leopold II, the Belgian monarch who amassed a personal fortune in the rubber plantations, lopping off native hands when quotas were not met.

Most of the students were now out in the fields, their backs bent as they helped teachers plant staples of peanuts, corn, manioc, and beans before the rainy season really sets in. Those teachers were on strike, demanding back pay and a long-promised wage hike.

Some of my former students are now teachers at the school. Their salary of 20,000 Congolese francs—about $45 in 2006— has not been paid in two months. The headmaster shrugged. Yes, he knew it unfair, but the burlap sacks filled with wads of government cash, typically delivered on the back of a bicycle, had yet to arrive.

Marceline Kanyi Mushimbi and Kamulombo Mutongo had been two of my favorite students. He would jump off his bench with a radiant grin, to pick the pronoun or fill in the verb. She was shy but determined to graduate with a handful of girls alongside hundreds of boys.

The two went on to marry and now, in their 40s, lament their status as unpaid teachers who must work the fields to feed their eight children.

"We are intellectuals, but our hands are all torn up from machetes, hoes and working under the sun," said Kanyi, as she showed me her calloused palms. "Even the villagers mock us: 'Look at you, the smart ones who went to school, but now you work with us in the fields.'"

Kamulombo laughed loudly and shrugged off my suggestion that perhaps fewer children would have eased their burden. "I'm laughing now, but I'd rather laugh than cry," he said. "But at least we have our eight children, which makes us proud, which makes us rich."

The next morning, after a cold bucket bath behind the rectory, Kanyi approached with a big smile and gently pushed me back into the room where I had been sleeping on a cot. She pulled a squawking chicken from beneath her orange-and-blue sarong.

I'd been telling a lie this trip, saying I was a vegetarian. As a young woman here, I tried it all: squirming grub worms, grilled python, flying termites. I no longer have the stomach.

Not wanting to offend Father Urbain Musuila, with whom we ate every night, I had brought bags of rice and beans. I used the vegetarian fib to avoid the bush meat, smoked eel, and caterpillar stew. I ate as little as possible, knowing that unless Tshinyama had prepared the food, it could lead to yet another bout with parasites.

Marie Kabuanga Mutanga's brown eyes, made larger by her hollow cheeks, pleaded with me.

Unable to speak, too weak to eat, she tugged at the rattan mat on the dirt floor of her hut. Her mother explained that her emaciated hipbones poke painfully into the hard ground.

A tin cup with plastic rosary beads and a twig of bougain-villea made a makeshift altar near her balding head.

This beautiful young woman, twenty-eight, had cooked and cleaned for the parish priest when I last visited ten years ago. She had charmed me into leaving behind some lipstick and clothes.

I had come to speak to her mother, a funny and outspo-ken prostitute with whom I used to be friendly, halfheartedly pleading with her about staying away from the students. That was back when a mysterious sexually transmitted virus now believed to have originated in Congo was spreading across the country—but had yet to be called AIDS.

"We're on our own," said Kamilongo Kamukenji, prop-ping up her daughter's head. "The village has done nothing for us. People are just more concerned about struggling for a living."

She told me her daughter was dying of a parasite. But Sister Kapinga Clementine, the dynamic Catholic nun and registered nurse who works in the village maternity clinic, later told me Marie had an incurable case of what she called the "four-letter word."

The priest for whom Marie worked has died, some say of AIDS, though no one can be sure.

Sister Clementine said malaria, pneumonia, parasites and tuberculosis, as well as lack of medicine and transportation made worse by the war, are much greater killers than AIDS these days.

There was little I could do for Marie. She brought back the pain I had often felt here, of feeling useless, of raising hopes that could not be met. I knew her eyes would haunt me forever, as do those of all the lost lives who have helped me tell my stories over the years.

I left her mother enough francs to buy a foam pad to soften her daughter's final days, and the fuzzy purple poodle Caitlin had told me to cuddle when I missed her on this trip.

The night before I left Kamponde, another pretty young woman who now cooks and cleans at the mission also asked me for some lipstick.

I had heard that some Rwandan Hutus had landed in the village. Kasaians, like most Congolese, are fiercely, sometimes violently loyal to their own ethnic groups and family lines.

As each day went by, I kept asking about the Hutus, thinking their story would help illustrate the changing face of Congo.

Everyone said there was a Hutu couple there, but no one could seem to find them. I got the impression that either the villagers were hiding them or that they did not want to be found.

On my last evening in Kamponde, I had just finished playing with a bunch of kids on the sidelines of a soccer match, when a stick-thin woman with wild hair approached me. She asked if I was the "U.N. lady," her eyes filled with fear.

When I had arrived in the U.N. emblazoned jeep, I had been wearing the U.N. press badge that helped get me past soldiers and thugs as I traveled in Congo. As soon as they heard of my arrival, Anatazi Mukaluzita and her husband had run into the bush.

They believed I was there to take them back to Rwanda to face the Tutsis, who had chased hundreds of thousands of ethnic Hutus into eastern Congo after the Rwandan genocide of 1994.

Her husband was still hiding, but she figured she had nothing left to lose.

"I told him, 'We are already dead, so I might as well just talk to her.'"

Anatazi began to cry with relief when Jim, speaking in her native Swahili, assured her all I wanted was to hear her story. She didn't want to say where she's from in Rwanda as she feared for her six children, if they were still alive.

Militants from Rwanda's Hutu ethnic minority, known as the *interahamwe*, had slaughtered half a million mostly Tutsis and moderate Hutus in the 100-day massacre of 1994. In the years that followed, some 2 million Hutus fled into Tanzania and eastern Congo as Tutsis exacted their revenge.

Anatazi, who couldn't recall what year they were forced to flee, says she and her husband were working in the fields when Tutsi militiamen attacked. They ran into the forest, Anatazi with a bullet in her left leg and a friend whose breast had been lopped off.

Alongside thousands of Hutus, they marched thousands of miles across Congo, an escape that would take them several years, until the couple collapsed in Kamponde. After the twins she was carrying were stillborn and her friend who had lost her breast died, Anatazi said she lost her drive.

"We were so tired of running. We just decided to die here and the others left us behind." She said the villagers took them in and allowed them to work their fields in exchange for food. Their situation is murky; some villagers told me quietly the Hutu couple is forced to work like slaves. But she was quick to say they were grateful for being allowed to live in peace.

Anatazi quickly hid beneath her sweater several packages of glucose biscuits and bars of soap that I have given her. When asked if they would remain in Kamponde or return to Rwanda in search of their children, she replies: "My life is in the hands of God. I have no idea."

I sheepishly watched the fat black goat being led off toward the big black cauldrons behind the church. Cooks were boiling manioc and corn flour for the hot mounds of sticky bread known as *fou-fou*. Men were coming back from the forest, balancing jugs of palm wine on sticks across their shoulders, tapped from the same trees where they get their nuts for cooking oil.

Later that evening, slowly and with great pomp, couples and their children were led into the church courtyard. Chief Jean-Baptiste Katende Kamponde—who earlier had presented me with an ancient copper cross once used as currency—and the nuns were seated near me in the best rattan chairs. The bamboo xylophones and goatskin drums warmed up the crowd.

Long wooden benches had been set in a circle. The men sat on one side, laughing and guzzling the wine and corn whiskey that would soon get them drunk. The women, as always, were off to the side. I joined them to dance, provoking cheers from the crowd and pursed smiles from the nuns.

Tshinyama's wife, Marie, stood off in the distance and raised her chin with a timid smile when I waved. His younger brother, Kabunda, argued with other men about who they had just voted for in the first multiparty elections in forty years, now President Joseph Kabila or then-rival Jean-Pierre Bemba.

They were not convinced either former rebel leader could rise above the weapons that had brought him to power and bring the country the stability they craved. Some even miss the kleptocracy of Mobutu Sese Seko, the dictator once revered and feared by those who believed his signature leopard-skin toque held the magic that kept him in power for thirty-two years.

As the night wore on, I stood before the villagers, a few hundred by now. I thanked them again for protecting me, and told them if I could, I would one day bring Caitlin to sit and share palm wine with them.

The women sashayed to the words of an impromptu song about an Elizabeth tree whose roots had grown deep in their village. The seed of that tree, "little Caitlin Kamponde," may have fallen far from this ground, they sang, but was still the beloved fruit of Kamponde.

On my first night in Kamponde, a man bicycled by moonlight for miles to catch me before bed.

I could not see him in the dark, but heard others greet him as he approached. I smiled to myself and tried not to cry as I listened to the elders asking him about his hunts, the grandchildren, the village where he now lived.

He came from the shadows; we stood grinning and shaking our heads in disbelief. We embraced awkwardly, a middle-aged American woman and an old African hunter with graying beard.

"Ahh–ahh–ahh, Miss Elizabeth, I can't believe it, you kept your promise," said Tshinyama in his sing-song voice. We asked many questions about family and other Peace Corps Volunteers, joked about who had put on or lost more weight, had the most wrinkles. He was thrilled to hear of Caitlin, looking at photos by the kerosene light.

"Maybe you can never forget me because your belly was always full?" he said in his familiar good-natured way.

Others had confused him with Father Paul's cook, who had died several years ago.

Tshinyama had cooked for the Peace Corps for a decade. When I learned in 1981 that I would be the last Volunteer in

Kamponde, I brought him up to Kananga, to the regional Peace Corps house where'd we go to get our meds and mail, and he went on to cook there for another ten years.

After the Peace Corps evacuated all its Volunteers in 1991—widespread rioting and violence had made it too dangerous—Tshinyama walked home and intended to go back to his fields. But other family members had taken over his crops. It was unclear to me whether he was ostracized or chose to leave on his own.

"You guys spoiled me and I needed to maintain a standard of living," he said with a grin. With no one to cook for and no fields to plow, he packed up his brood at age forty-five and moved to Mfuamba Kabang, some four miles southeast of Kamponde.

By now, Marie had given birth to twelve children, but had lost at least five. Someone would later tell me Tshinyama left Kamponde in fear of sorcery, believing a spell had been cast against his family, causing their babies to die.

As we had ten years ago during my first visit back, we began to plan the village feast for which he would cook.

My last morning in Kamponde, after my humiliating scene in church, we set off on foot, my pink floppy hat shading me from the sun as we headed through the green savanna toward Tshinyama's new home.

Children gathered to see the first foreigner to ever set foot in the desolate village of a few dozen square huts. It was so grim and small compared to Kamponde; once again I had to hold back more tears.

We ate with our hands, a rich meal of *fou-fou*, chicken spiced with his trademark *pili-pili* sauce, and boiled manioc leaves. Tshinyama apologized for not having the ingredients for the mango pudding so many Peace Corps Volunteers had once craved.

He showed off his homemade rifle as I took in the antelope antlers and other animal talismans used to decorate his home. Faded magazine ads of Western food on gleaming plates were tacked to the whitewashed walls of his little mud hut.

An adopted son, a young man he took in after his parents were killed, at first cried with fear that I was there to take Tshinyama away, then serenaded us with a love song for his father on a guitar he had fashioned from an Oki peanut oil can.

After lunch, and the obligatory sip of palm wine with the village chief, I told Tshinyama that it was time to go.

I gave Indian cloth to Marie, though glaucoma has clouded her eyes and I didn't know if she could see the bright paisley patterns. There were notebooks and pens for the grandkids, a red rubber ball.

Thinyama would not meet my eyes as I pushed an envelope with $150 in his hands, suggesting he buy a new bicycle and a cellular phone. I told him there was now a weak signal in Kamponde, that a few clever types were making money selling phone calls, hinting it might be a way for him to return home. It wasn't much, yet still more than the average annual income in his ravaged homeland.

We said our last goodbye before I headed back up the path. I hated leaving him in the bleak little village and pledged to try and return one last time.

We both knew it unlikely we would ever meet again.

"*Washala bimpe, tatu,*" I choked, as we grasped each other's hands, my fair freckled ones clasped between the rough dark fingers that had cooked so many meals for hundreds of Peace Corps Volunteers. It's a simple Tshiluban farewell: Stay well, father.

Tshinyama softly replied: "*Wayi bimpe, mamu*"—Go well, mother.

Beth Duff-Brown was a Peace Corps Volunteer in the Democratic Republic of Congo from 1979-81. It was there that she determined she would become a foreign correspondent and she has twice visited her village of Kamponde as a journalist to report on conditions there. She has worked for The Associated Press—most recently as the Deputy Asia Editor—for twenty years, based in Africa, Asia, and North America. She currently is a John S. Knight fellow at Stanford University.

⭐

The Utopia of the Village

We carry Mother Earth, and all she gives, within us.

IN THE YEARS THAT HAVE PASSED, I FIND MYSELF LONGING FOR the intangible—a dream that exists under the raw, rugged spaces of earth, the places where the roots of trees sleep. Under buried earth, bruised patches that both grow and decay with time. I can smell Africa in places where it doesn't exist: in dreams, in corners of the rooms in my mother's house in America, in parts of my flesh I could swear I've washed hundreds of times since I was there.

I miss the heat of Africa that I once hated. Africa is a thick, slow heat—seeping into the blood. It's a different kind of heat than anywhere else on Earth. Its heat has girth, could drown a man the way the ocean could devour him. It is a kind of unforgiving heat that will never care about people, the will of Nature that will always remain uncontrolled by human beings.

I miss the scent of Africa. I miss the developing world. I long for a place where people defecate on the sides of the street and think nothing of it—it is a way of life for them, just as using clean toilets is a way of life in Westernized cultures. I search out poverty; I am drawn to the edges of the Earth where people sleep on hay and worship the gods of the trees and thank the Divine for the food that fills their bellies each day. I long to live in silence among people who will understand something that has no words.

When I come back to my home country, I am overwhelmed. It is the place where the people all look like me and talk like me and share my language, and I am overwhelmed to be in a place where I can talk to anyone because we all speak the same language. I long to leave again, to go to a place where people don't speak my language and I have to learn to speak theirs. Or simply not speak at all.

If that place even exists on Earth.

It is called the Mute Earth and it is a silent heaven, a place where no one says anything because words cannot make sense of nonsense, and sometimes I wish to not have words although words are the things that often save me; they are my therapy.

I am a writer.

I love America because she is my Mother, my womb. Where I learned myself and grew and learned my language. And I love Africa for all the things America never could have given to me: a certain strength that comes from suffering, a strength I hope never again to live without. Africa is the raw earth, the roots of the trees struggling below the ground; Africa is Nature, and god. But they are my two children, and I love them the same, but for different reasons: America and Africa. A mother loves her children the same but in different ways. We are given the opportunity to live on Mother Earth for such a short, sacred time. We must find the significance in all things, above all within ourselves.

Heather Corinne Cumming served as a Peace Corps Volunteer from 2004-06. She returned and published her book entitled The Messages of Trees, Volumes I-IV. *In 2008 she returned to Zambia to begin the Simwatachela Sustainable Agricultural and Arts Program, which helps to promote water, food, and nutrition security and sustainability created by the people and committed to serving the needs of the people in both Zambia as well as in Sierra Leone, West Africa.*

PART TWO

WHY ARE WE HERE?

SUSANNA LEWIS

The Engine Catches

Little by little, people can make a difference.

THIRTY PEOPLE, INCLUDING FOUR TEACHERS AND TWENTY-SIX eighth- and ninth-grade girls, are crowded behind a rusty, light green, open-back Toyota truck, our bodies poised to push. "*Um! Dois! Tres!*" and we jam our bodies against the truck. We use all of our strength, but the truck only moves in almost imperceptible increments until—at last—the engine catches and we hear the whir of the motor. We chase after the truck, grab at the green metal and pull ourselves up and in.

Once everyone is in the truck, we are packed liked sardines—girls are sitting on each other, their hands are around each others' waists, and we are clinging to the sides of the truck to keep from falling out.

The wind blows at the girls' hair; their smiles are unrestrained, broad and toothy. Palm trees and mud houses blur past us as we make our way to Ilha de Mocambique.

I am the assistant coach of the Escola Secundaria de Monapo girls soccer team, and we are on our way to a game against the team from Ilha de Mocambique. Ilha is a 500-year-old town forty-five minutes from our own village, Monapo. It is a tiny place situated just off the Mozambican coast, and it served as the first Portuguese capital of Mozambique until the turn of the twentieth century. It is a hauntingly beautiful place of 300-year-old churches, navy and green waters, and women dressed in colorful *capulanas* and iridescent earrings. Ilha's gently crumbling, centuries old Portuguese buildings and sturdy Mozambican mud-and-reed houses are a fascinating juxtaposition of this country's past and present.

We can see, hear, and smell present-day Mozambique as we drive across the one-lane bridge to Ilha. It is low tide, and female figures walk on the water more than a mile into the sea, on paths worn into the sea floor by thousands of fishermen before them. They look for fish with nothing but a pail and a free hand. The air is fresh and fishy, and shirtless men ride bicycles with sacks of charcoal and cassava between their knees.

We make our way to the soccer field, which is next to the Portuguese Forteleza and the glimmering water of the Indian Ocean. The girls and I change into our uniforms inside the Forteleza and they giggle in excitement—this is their first "real" game against another team and they are nervous. The coach says a few words and I say a few more, to build their confidence and to remind them that together we are strong and that we can win this game.

We play a bigger, tougher opponent on sandy dirt, and the girls play barefoot, though I play wearing sneakers. The girls play better than they ever have before; they do what we taught them to do in our practices, and they play like mature soccer players. They pass the ball well, talk to each other on the field, and dominate the other team. During halftime, the coach and I tell them how much they have improved, and how proud we are of them. When we score the girls do cartwheels, hug, run over to me with their arms open and clasp my hands in theirs. I can't help but smile and hug them back. I have never felt so comfortable and like myself with Mozambicans before. The girls flash their big smiles and we are in the moment, we are a team.

We do the unthinkable, achieving a resounding victory, 5-0.

After the game, we push the truck to start its engine, pile into the back and make two victory laps around the island. The girls sing to taunt the other team, their voices nasal and imperfect, but somehow the disharmonies are beautiful. They sing, "*Silencio toda a gente, Monapo esta a passar!*" (Everyone be quiet, Monapo is passing!). They sing, and I sing with them. Next to me a girl blows on a whistle to accompany the singing, on my other side another girl has her head on my shoulder. Sea salts are in my nose, and the gravelly road throws us up and down against the metal of the truck. The girls' glee is palpable and my own happiness is pure. We drive back to Monapo in the fading light of the day, and when we reach our town the girls sing again, "*Silencio toda a gente, Monapo esta a passar!*"

As we pass by their different neighborhoods and girls jump off of the truck, they say to me, "Goodbye Teacher!" and give me big hugs. Even though I had been running team practices for a couple of months, and teaching these girls English for nearly a year, it was only after that game that I finally felt like I was a part of their team and a member of their community.

To me, being a Peace Corps Volunteer is working hard every day to belong, every day to learn new customs and change your perspective. You don't know that you are changing or that your community is slowly accepting you until, like those pushes that finally get the truck's engine to catch, you have an amazing, surprising moment where everything comes together. For me, the soccer game was the moment that, after months of pushing, the engine caught. After that game I finally felt confident that I was a member of my community, and knowing that I had taught my girls to be better, more confident soccer players made me feel that I had an effect on them, too.

Progress as a Volunteer is slow and often difficult to detect. Even though it may seem impossible at times, serving in the Peace Corps guarantees you one thing, that you will change and you will see change in others—even if to realize it you need a ride in a rusty old truck, a soccer ball and twenty-six wonderful girls.

Susanna Lewis served as an English teacher at the Escola Secundaria de Monapo in Mozambique. She was a part of the tenth training group in Mozambique and her service was from September 2005-07. Susanna now lives in Baltimore, Maryland and is teaching English to refugees, as well as pursuing a master's in Social Work at the University of Maryland.

KELLY J. MORRIS

Yaka

One of the best things a Peace Corps Volunteer
can do is make himself or herself unneeded.

IN JANUARY 1969, I WENT TO TOGO AS A PEACE CORPS
Volunteer to work as a community development extension
worker for community self-help construction. It was my job
to help communities and their leaders determine their needs
for classrooms, clinics, bridges and culverts on farm-to-market
roads, and other infrastructure; to prioritize their needs and
inventory their resources; and to organize self-help projects to
address their highest priority needs. The community provided
labor and local materials (sand, gravel, rocks, and water); the
local officials provided transport and skilled artisans; and Peace
Corps helped to obtain grants for the materials that were not
locally available (e.g., cement, reinforcing steel rods, wood
planks, tin roofing sheets, etc.) and organizational and technical
support, i.e. me.

I was shocked when I went to visit one of the village chiefs
with whom I was to work. It was less than ten years since
Togo had become independent. To my surprise, the chief of
Yaka welcomed me by lamenting the departure of the colonial

government and complained that the country had "Gone to hell in a handbasket" since the whites departed! We had been told that our mission was to "work ourselves out of a job." This was not what I was expecting.

I persevered, nonetheless, and worked with the chief, the neighborhood sub-chiefs, the women's group leaders, and local artisans to build several bridges and culverts on farm-to-market roads. The work went well. The people needed the bridges and worked hard to help obtain something that was in their own interest.

During the dry season, I had to go to Lomé, the capital city, to buy building materials and transport them back to our worksite about 450 kilometers inland. I rode my red CZ Czechoslovak motorcycle down to the railhead about 200 kilometers to the south. My motorcycle and I spent the rest of the voyage sitting on 100-kilogram sacks of millet in a freight car with a squad of soldiers. We bought *sodabi,* the distilled palm wine that is Africa's "White Lightning," from women who crowded the railcar at rural whistle stops and punished our innards with it for the remainder of the agonizingly slow trip.

I spent several days in Lomé buying materials, arranging to hire seven-ton trucks, loading them, and expediting them northward. My plan was to hoist my motorcycle onto the last truck and to ride back to my site on it. Fate, however, intervened in the form of a mangy street dog. As I was riding on my motorcycle down the street the night before my proposed departure, the dog rushed out from an alley, bit me on my ankle, and disappeared.

The next morning, before departing, I dutifully reported the incident to the Peace Corps Medical Office.

"Where is the dog?" the doctor asked.

"Long gone," I replied.

"Well, I have to assume that the dog was rabid and treat you accordingly," he announced.

There began a series of sixteen daily shots that he mercifully rotated in four-shot cycles between my biceps and thighs.

"I'll give you the vials of serum and the throw-away sterile needles to take with you to your post," the doctor said. "You can have the nurse at the nearest clinic inject you." I was ready to depart, only one day behind schedule.

My plan was foiled again in a most unexpected way. For several hours after my first injection, I had a reaction to the shot that left me woozy, light-headed, and unsteady on my feet.

"You aren't going anywhere," the doctor decided, "until your shots are completed."

I sent the trucks ahead and then whiled away an unplanned sixteen days in the capital city.

When I finally completed my shots and was liberated, I hopped the next train back north to my post.

The chief of Yaka was not too pleased with me when I went to check on our worksite. He berated me for my extended absence that he characterized as a vacation. Then he treated me to a long list of all the things that he and his collaborators had to do in order to keep the project going in my absence. Thanks to them, the work had continued.

"I know what you were doing," he concluded. "You were drinking beer and chasing after women. That's what you were really doing!"

Of course, he was right. Young, single, trapped, and bored in Lomé, I had spent my time, after the dizziness from each day's injection wore off, drinking beer and chasing women.

My local friends who caught up with me at the beer bar that evening found me in a deliriously good mood. I described my saga and my dressing-down by the chief, which pleased me no end.

"You white people are crazy," they said. "Why does getting chewed out by that old chief make you happy?'

"Because," I replied. "in Yaka they figured out that they
didn't need me. In this one village, at least, I worked myself
out of a job. Mission accomplished."

*Kelly J. Morris is an international development consultant and writer
who served nineteen years with the Peace Corps. Beginning in 1969,
he was a Volunteer and country staff for eleven years in Togo and
staff for two tours in Washington. He is the author of the* Bight of
Benin: Short Fiction *and the upcoming* African Democracy: A
Primer. *He is the founder and list owner of the Friends of Togo.*

ANNA RUSSO

Nous Sommes Ensemble

Perhaps "globalization" is simply recognition of a basic truth.

THE SANDY DIRT FOOTPATHS IN MY VILLAGE WOVE AN INTRICATE design in between the thatch-roofed huts. These pathways carried the community: motorcycle taxis; skittish goats hurrying to get out of the way; chickens; dogs; cattle; children on their way to school; women carrying stacks of bowls, firewood or water on their heads; people going to the fields or heading home with their harvest. I walked these paths every day, getting to know the shortcuts to the market and home, maneuvering my way around the ruts that formed during the rainy season and trying to avoid getting my bike tires stuck in the sand. Eventually, I became familiar enough with the paths that I could walk them at night without a flashlight, using the moonlight for guidance.

It was on these pathways that I first heard the phrase, *"nous sommes ensemble."* On my way to the market I crossed paths with a man coming back from that direction. We stopped, shook hands and commenced the usual greeting custom of asking a variety of questions to find out how the other person is doing. How are you, how is your health, how is work, how are your fields, how is your house and family, how are your goats and cattle, how is the heat; all the while still shaking hands. He finished by stating *nous sommes ensemble* and went on his way.

It took me awhile to register what was just said to me, *nous sommes ensemble*—we are together. What did he mean by that? Are we together in spirit, in work, in life? That was the first time we met, and I did not work with him (at least not yet). Why did he assume we were together? It was normal to stop and say hello if our paths crossed; and if I saw him again, I was sure we would repeat the multiple question greeting custom, but I was uncertain if I would end with *we are together*.

As it turns out, this was (and still is) a very common phrase in Cameroon. Heard often between passersby on the street, from guests and hosts at a party, or at the end of a long day's work; generally speaking, it means "see you later" or "see you soon." However, this simple phrase has many other meanings as well. It suggests our work together is not finished and we will meet again soon to complete it. It means you are my brother or sister, a part of my family, even if we do not share a blood relation we will always be part of the same community. It also means I am here for you; so if you need help, just ask.

A simple statement that literally means *we are together*, we are not alone. This phrase, these three little words, taught me a lot about humanity and togetherness. Despite our myriad differences as human beings, we do share certain emotions, actions, and behaviors. We are independent as individuals, but there are universals which we collectively share.

The grandmother in America who spoils her grandkids with sweet treats is no different than *la grandmère* in Cameroon who gives afternoon snacks made with peanut butter to her grandchildren. Mothers and fathers in America feel proud when their children do well in school, just as parents in Africa do. Girls in America shop for hours for the right outfit to wear to a school dance or on a date, to impress the boy they have a crush on. Girls in a small African village get dressed-up in their best clothes on market day to impress the young men who will be there.

The death of a child or loved one is no different for the subsistence farmer who makes $200 a year or for the family in a developed country that has an annual salary 200 times that amount. Despite the different circumstances, we share these experiences because we share the same world. We have this commonality of being human, which brings us closer together.

We are human—language, race, ethnicity, geographic location, and religion should not divide us. As humans, our dreams, frustrations, successes, happiness, and sorrow bond us together. This idea is probably shared by many cultures worldwide, but in Cameroon we say it out loud. *Nous sommes ensemble*. We are together.

Anna Russo served in Cameroon from 2000-2002 (Sahel Agroforestry). She moved to Rwanda in 2008 after finishing an M.A. in International Development at the University of Denver. Currently living in Kigali, she manages community development projects for a U.S. based coffee company which not only buys coffee from Rwanda but also invests in the social well-being of the farmers and their families.

J A Y N E   B I E L E C K I

✦

The Sweetest Gift

The little things do often become the sweetest.

I WENT INTO PEACE CORPS THINKING I WOULD BE HELPING THE neediest people in the world. It made me proud to think that I was sacrificing two years of my life for others. Not everyone can forgo their comfortable lifestyle or live such an uncertain life in an unknown land. I was positive I would teach the locals something, improve their lives, and begin the process of saving the world. The Peace Corps warned us about thinking too idealistically, but I knew I was different. I had known for years that I wanted to be a nurse and serve as a Peace Corps Volunteer in an African country.

This was my calling.

It was early on in my Peace Corps service, and I was in the throes of cultural shock. Some days it was all I could do to talk myself into going out in public. Today was a good day, though. I was ready to deal with the staring eyes and inescapable barrage of conversation I met with whenever I ventured into the society of Cape Verde.

My Peace Corps post was on Maio, a round, sun-baked pancake of an island in the Cape Verde Archipelago approximately 600 kilometers off the west coast of Africa. The islands are volcanic in nature, and known for their consistent weather and beaches, which came in either black or white sand. Maio, although one of the smallest islands, was outlined in beach and had the reputation for the loveliest in the entire country. Wealthy people came from all over to enjoy them. Although some money came in through domestic tourism, Maio was also the poorest and least developed of the islands.

I lived in the lower area of the village of Calheta, called the Baxona, near the beach. It consisted of two strips of brightly painted homes sharing one wall with their neighbor. This shared wall decreased the cost of construction and labor. The houses were one room, two at the most, and all made of cinder block and cement. Between the colorful homes, a cobblestone street ran from north to south and faded into the white sand beach at the south end. On the north end was the *chafaris*, a tan brick structure about eight feet tall with one small spigot. Women came once a week with their twenty-two-gallon pails to receive potable water from the *chafaris* attendant, the most powerful women in the village. On a water day, energy levels ran high. The street would be noisy and bustling with exuberant children and chattering women carrying water on their heads. Today, a non-water day, the small street was quiet and empty.

My current home was a generous donation made by a successful carpenter. It was the largest house in the entire village, with two bedrooms, a living room, a small kitchen, a bathroom, and a *quintal* with stairs to the roof. The inside was painted in yellows and blues, the floor tiled in golden brown. I also had the luxury of a built-in cement washing board and a clothesline. The roof had a large room on it for a generator and an unused tank for water.

The average Cape Verdean family on Maio lived with five to seven people in a house the size of my living room and kitchen combined.

As I left the security of my huge sky-blue house with yellow trim, I closed the white metal gate and made my way up the path to the main village. It zigged and zagged around rocks scattered throughout the tan-grey, lunar landscape. It would be a ten-minute stroll in the dead space between the two sections of the village. I enjoyed this part of the walk the most. I looked out to my left and followed the turquoise sky and the green-blue ocean until they touched at the distant horizon.

Enfameira! Enfameira! I looked up to see two young fishermen making their way to the beach. They waved excitedly and I waved back. Then three school-aged children came running toward me. They stopped abruptly before we met on the path, and then began to walk respectfully past me. They had big smiles on their faces and each greeted me as we passed. *Bom dia! Bom dia! Bom dia!* Smiling, I replied in kind.

I could hear the *funana* playing clearly on a radio and voices in animated conversation. I began my inner monologue—a pep talk of sorts. I was heading in. I cautioned myself about being over confident. I reminded myself that culture shock was an out-of-control emotional roller coaster, so low expectations were imperative to success. I knew I could anticipate a lot of talking and gawking at the strange, skinny, white creature plodding into town. Some days I dreaded this, but not today. Things were going well.

I stepped off the path and onto the cobblestone street of the central square. People smiled and greeted me while they stared wide-eyed and unabashed. A woman I didn't know stopped her sweeping of leaf-littered cobblestones to talk to me. She was my height with a muscular build. She wore a sleeveless shirt, no bra, and a knee-length black skirt with a scarf covering her hair. It was typical Cape Verdean dress for rural Maio.

I made an earnest effort to listen and understand what she said, but my concentration quickly withered. I let myself become distracted by a couple of boys playing nearby as she continued with her one-sided conversation at a rapid pace.

After a moment, one of the boys walked over to us. He stared at me, cautiously inching closer and then backing away. I imagined how brave he must feel for being so close to the pale stranger. I imagined how he would tell this story to his family and friends. Everyone would wait in suspense to hear about the strange white woman. Yes, how brave he was. I smiled at the thought.

He smiled back. Our eyes met, and we held each others' gaze for a moment. He couldn't have been more than three years old. He was skinny and naked. His big, dark brown eyes were framed in long eyelashes and a shaved head. He sucked on a piece of candy and had developed a black ring of dirt around his mouth. His nose ran with thick green snot that he wiped away with the backs of his hands. His hands were covered in streaks of black snotty mud. Slowly, he reached one of them out towards me.

He opened his hand wide. Inside, a beautiful bright gold wrapper now glimmered in the sun. I hesitated, mesmerized by its loveliness. Thinking I hadn't understood, he thrust his hand forward and nodded his head at me to take his last piece of candy. I delicately reached out to take his gift. I opened the wrapper and put the treat in my mouth. I smiled, worked to control my shaky voice, and thanked him. He smiled huge and stood next to me. We stood there together, smacking on our pieces of hard candy and enjoying it. I looked at him again, holding back my tears. "*Obrigada,*" I said once more, wanting to make sure he understood how much his generosity meant to me. Then I quickly said goodbye.

As I walked away I stumbled on the crooked cobblestones, overcome with emotion. A child with almost nothing has given me his last piece of candy. Words cannot describe how unworthy I felt to receive such a sweet gift.

My mind reeled as I tried to comprehend what had just happened. I had spent money on meaningless key chains and pens to present the locals as souvenirs of my stay. I was already living in a monstrosity of a house with indoor plumbing that no one else in the village could afford. It all seemed worthless and ridiculous compared to his generosity. I had been so sure I would leave the villagers with a better existence. I had some strange notion that sacrificing my great American life for two whole years would be the greatest thing I ever did.

And it was. Not for my original reasons, but because I was shown the true meaning of kindness and unselfishness. In the end I received the sweetest gift, and I carry it with me everywhere I go.

Jayne Bielecki worked as a water sanitation and health care volunteer in Cape Verde for two years, 1995-97. After returning to the U.S. and readjusting to life with too many toilet paper options, she earned her master's degree and took a teaching position at the University of Wisconsin-Eau Claire. She lives with her husband, two dogs, and a variety of cats on an old homestead in western Wisconsin, appropriately dubbed the Funny Farm.

MARCY L. SPAULDING

* * *

The Conference

When nothing goes right, it's hard to remain positive and energetic.

An ka musomaninw ka bolokoli dabila!
Bolokoli be tooro lase muso ka keneya ma.
(Let's stop the excision of young girls!
Excision is harmful to women's health.)
—From a poster at the Conference on Excision, Kita

JOURNAL ENTRY: MAY 16, 2001, BENDOUGOUBA: TODAY I BIKED
twenty-five kilometers to see what Malians have to say about
female circumcision (or, excision, as it is called here, also
known in the West as female genital mutilation, or FGM).
Excision is deeply ingrained in Malian cultures in most parts of
the country. There are various types, the most common being
the removal of all or part of a girl's clitoris. Some people claim
it's done for religious reasons (though Islamic teachings do not
either condemn or condone the practice), some consider it a
rite of passage for a girl coming into adulthood, some say its
purpose is to make a girl "clean" and less promiscuous, and
others just cite tradition. Sometimes the excision is performed

149

on adolescent girls, sometimes on younger girls, and sometimes on infants.

Oftentimes, excisions are performed under unsanitary conditions, and many girls may be excised at one time, using the same knife—putting them at high risk for HIV infection. Once excised, a girl can contract various infections and have difficulty in childbirth. And the excision itself can be psychologically traumatic. Practices are changing now, but the movement of Malians to educate each other about the dangers and consequences of excision is new, and the practice is still very widespread. While a few of the younger generation would like to abolish it, I've heard stories of grandmothers taking away their young granddaughters to be excised without their mothers' knowledge. There is an old fear that a girl who is not excised will never have a husband; many still believe this.

As an American, I feel shocked and horrified that such a practice could exist. For Malians, I know that the situation is much more complex. I'm always very interested to hear Malian points of view on the matter.

A doctor at PLAN International told me about the conference on excision in Kita. Of course, it was scheduled just before and during my first big health committee training session. I really wanted to go. In our Peace Corps training, we had been told about the practice, but were told not to talk about it. It's too sensitive an issue, and since the Malian Health Ministry—the organization with which I technically work—has not officially come out against it, we are not "officially" to discuss it. So I haven't talked about it at all, not until recently.

I decided it was something I would be very interested in discussing with Malians, but I would not be the one to bring it up. Until about two weeks ago, no one did bring it up. Finally, Fatima (Adama's wife) did, then my friend Lassina and some of his friends. So I had a one-on-one conversation about it with a

woman, and another with five young men. Fatima is certainly
against it, but leaves it at that. Since both she and her husband
are against it, her daughters are not excised. As for the men,
I'm not so sure about what they thought. They, too, seemed
to think it bad, but weren't too clear about why. Traditions are
hard to change, they said. I'm guessing people who are strongly
for it are less likely to bring it up, at least with me.

Due to the training session, I had almost missed the conference entirely. I returned from Kita to spend the day preparing for the health committee meeting. By nightfall, I hadn't
finished. Adama came back from the conference's first day and
I asked him about it. He told me about the pro-excision arguments of the very religious older men who were there, and
it upset me incredibly. I had to hold back tears of frustration,
which were due in part to the fact that I had missed something
important to me, merely to prepare a meeting for a health
committee that constantly has me tearing my hair out because
people so rarely seem to take it seriously.

I had even skipped out on possible vacation plans for this
committee. I could be in Senegal now, sitting on the beach.
I'm tired of making sacrifices for this committee. That's part
of what made me so angry yesterday—and why I had to go to
Kita today. I had to do what was important to *me*. So I found
a way to do it and still be responsible.

I came home right after dinner last night to finish my preparations by the light of a kerosene lamp. I got up this morning
at the crack of dawn and biked to Kita—in a skirt, blasting my
"Road Trip" mix tape on my Walkman. Aside from the difficulty of riding in a skirt, the ride felt great, and it reminded
me about passion and calling.

If you're really passionate about something, you often
cast aside common sense. Common sense, for example, tells
you that you need eight hours of sleep and that biking in

110-degree weather under a blazing sun is stupid. However, I needed to go to this conference, and I didn't care if it meant I had to stay up all night preparing for the meeting. Now I'm angry that my sense of responsibility is once again slapping me in the face. I would have very much liked to have stayed at the conference today, but instead I'm waiting here, once again, for people—*anyone*—to show up.

More and more I'm beginning to understand why so many Peace Corps Volunteers become so jaded and disillusioned. We want to *do something*. But our good intentions too often bite us in the ass. We bust our butts, and money gets *bouffed*. We want villagers to take control of their own community's health—but unless there's a tangible and immediate incentive, it's a low-priority affair. My daily life is spent just trying to *understand*, so that I can help. But people don't care about trying to understand me—oh, no, they already know all about me. I'm a rich *toubab* from a country of streets paved with gold. I talk funny, I don't understand anything, I can't do anything, and it's pretty damn funny to watch me dance. I'm considered to be extremely selfish because I don't hand out money when I walk through the village. So what good am I? What use is a *toubab* if she doesn't give things?

If the approach of the Peace Corps—"Don't hand out money, know the community, work toward sustainability"— is the only way development can work for the benefit of the people, then I am becoming more and more convinced that it's not possible. Unless people can (1) open their minds; (2) recognize which behaviors and practices benefit the community and which harm it and alter their behavior accordingly; (3) think about the future and not just the present moment; and (4) recognize in *themselves* a power and a desire to make change, then development cannot happen. People here are poor; that's a fact. But the influence of Western culture makes them feel poorer than they are, makes them want what they can't have, thus making them feel powerless and helpless.

5:20 P.M. Bintou, the president of the health committee and the most motivated person in the village, *just* arrived. When I got here at 3:00, I was feeling good, feeling energetic, and ready to work. Now I feel discouraged and foolish. If things continue like this for two years, I may have to shoot myself. I have here what I consider to be an almost ideal situation. And I have a positive attitude (though that's being crushed little by little).

I don't know how other Volunteers do it. I really don't. Well, I know some make it through only because they stop caring, or they never did care. I don't want to stop caring. So, consequently, I fear I'm going to continue to get hurt.

Thank god not every day is like this. But the roller-coaster ride I've been on for the past nine months is tiring.

Later, the same day: Well, a couple of people came. And I was clearly upset. Bintou yelled at me. Adama yelled at me. "You shouldn't have gone to that conference; you should've stayed here and prepared, called people to the meeting!" That did it. If he had any clue how important it was to me to attend that conference, or how completely destroyed I would feel had I not gone…well, I was about to burst into tears. So I got up and left to calm myself down and avoid having everyone watch me cry. And, everyone laughed.

Bintou came to me and yelled some more: "Anger is bad! Anger is bad! You have to come out here and listen to us!" I took a couple of deep breaths and went back. But I needed more than that couple of minutes to hold back the tears. I sat down, and they yelled at me for being angry. Then they picked up on the tears streaming down my face. "Wait, she's not angry; she's crying! That's bad! Crying is bad!" Not to mention, quite funny, apparently.

Adama was practically rolling on the ground, yelling and laughing. What a great way to make a person feel better. One of the joys of village life is that things that happen that are funny today are not just funny today, they're funny for days and weeks to come. I don't think crying is ever forgotten. No one took me seriously before—now it can only be worse. And the whole village will know by tonight that I cried when no one showed up to my meeting. Fabulous.

I know, of course, that the reason for my crying is much deeper. One, I needed it. In the past nine months I've cried twice. Two, I desperately need a vacation. Three, I had an emotionally disturbing morning experiencing closed minds and watching videos of little girls being cut. Four, I've been putting up with all this for nine months. Five, my emotional support system consists of people who laugh uncontrollably when I cry. Insane—you have to be insane to do this job!

May 17, 2001, Bendougouba: Yesterday's writing was very interesting—a written record of my rapid descent from energy and passion to shame and disillusionment. I felt great yesterday morning. I pursued something that was important to me, did what I needed to do even though common sense (and Adama) told me I shouldn't. At the conference Adama seemed happy that I was there. It was only before and after that he chastised me. So I was up on high—but the higher you are, the further and faster you fall. Still, I don't regret going to the conference; had I not gone, I would feel a lot worse today.

Unfortunately, I now feel less likely to have faith in the people I work with, to put my soul into something, only to be disappointed. If people don't want to take control of their community's health, I can't help them. If something is really important to me (and this job is), I put my all into it, I make sacrifices for it. And, time after time—like yesterday—I get shot down, with no one around but me to pick up the pieces.

Each time my faith is weakened, little by little. From time to time it gets restored—which is so important—but again it almost makes the falls harder.

I honestly don't know if I can continue in this way for two years. It may prove to be too much of a sacrifice, too much of myself being pushed down, taken away. I don't need to be here. I can't continue to give of myself this way with so little result. On top of difficulties with work are the difficulties of my personal life—my limited support network, my need to feel loved, my need to feel like part of a community. The kind of support I need is limited. In the village, I get some of it from Adama, Fadiala, and Bintou. But, as evidenced yesterday, that doesn't always work well, although Bintou did postpone travel plans for me last night because I was upset. Otherwise, I have Sima and Karin—my two closest teammates and two people I love dearly. When I'm alone, I have my journals and my thoughts.

As far as feeling loved—I know that I am loved here, but the manner of expression of love here is not what I'm used to. It's not explicit. At times, it's even harsh. So my loving comes from the children—the very small ones, the innocent ones who love me unconditionally, now that they've grown accustomed to my presence. Unlike adults here, I can love babies in the same way I would in the States. And they love me back the same way, too. Our love is non-verbal. It's smiles, touches, closeness, laughter. No pressure, no expectations. But again, it's limited. Granted, there is no shortage of babies, but as an adult woman I need more; I also need to feel I belong.

I feel welcomed here, but I don't feel like a *part* of the community. I feel like a novelty, appreciated in the sense that it's fun to have a *toubab* around ("What is she doing here again?"), nice to have someone to help with the work, make us look good, make us laugh. I'm very much affected by the temperament and attitude of those around me, and so I tend to derive my own mood from that. It becomes a constant battle I fight to remain positive and energetic while others are apathetic, to continue doing my best to be a member of the community and to be accepted despite the laughter. To try not to see misunderstanding on my part or in others as my own failing.

Well, I sure have done a lot of thinking in the past two days. Happy six-month anniversary of installation! It's not all bad, of course. I'm at a low point now, but I'll rebound; I always do.

Marcy L. Spaulding served as a health education volunteer in Mali from 2000-02. After returning, she published her journals in a memoir entitled, Dancing Trees and Crocodile Dreams: My Life in a West African Village, *the book from which "The Conference" is excerpted. Marcy misses her friends in Mali and once in a while craves a big bowl of rice and tiga dege na, a dish which she has woefully been unable to recreate at home. She also misses taking baths under an open sky. Marcy currently lives (and loves!) in San Francisco, California.*

MARSA LAIRD

*

Girls' School

Though the hopes of earlier times have often been dashed,
the belief in the power to change can remain.

I PRESENTED MYSELF TO THE HEADMISTRESS TWO DAYS LATE.

My heart was hammering and my legs felt weak as I stammered out an apology. I had been felled by food poisoning, I explained, and this was my first day out of bed.

She said nothing.

I tried a touch of humor, remarking that I had hoped for a quick death, but that it seemed I was destined to hang around a little longer. Her lips compressed into what was clear evidence of a dour Scottish disposition. She ordered me to return in two hours to teach my first class.

The school she presided over was the first in Somalia to educate young ladies beyond the ABCs, and I and a fellow Volunteer were to be the first teachers of the new upper grades. During our training, one of the lecturers had commented that when we taught boys, we taught boys; but when we taught girls, we taught an entire generation. So I walked back to my house and tried to keep up my courage, this goal in mind.

When I returned two hours later, I was terrified.

The girls, ages twelve to sixteen, were already assembled in their classroom. At a nod from the headmistress, they stood at attention and recited in a sing-song voice, "Go-od mor-ning, Miss Marsa." Then she was gone, and I was alone with the girls, rows of them.

They looked beautiful in their white-cotton school dresses, concealed under long wraps of colorful fabric pulled over their heads whenever they left the school. This was less a matter of religion at that time: the prevailing attitude was that girls and women were the property of the men in their families. The wraps had the added advantage of hiding the girls' liveliness and curiosity from outsiders.

That was why I was here, to liberate them! This was going to be my mission, to help the girls take their rightful place in society.

While I was formulating these lofty thoughts of youthful, untested idealism, I realized that if I didn't gesture to my students, they would stand all day.

The large, sparsely furnished classroom opened to the outside along the entire length of one side of the cinder-block building. Besides the students' desks, it contained a long table and a blackboard on legs. That was it. Glancing around, conscious of the expectant looks on the girls' faces, I saw an open closet. The shelves were piled high with ruled copy-books and boxes of pencils. Nothing else. But I was a Peace Corps Volunteer. Our motto, like the Boy Scouts—or was it the Coast Guard?—should be *"semper paratus."* I would ad lib. I could do that.

I was already thinking ahead, planning to inspire them with the story of Madame Curie, who had won two Nobel Prizes in science. (Maybe an edited version of Eve Curie's biography of her mother was available in a series of English readers for African students I had seen elsewhere.)

I asked my pupils about their ambitions. After some hesitation it turned out, remarkably, that they all wanted to be doctors and own color TVs. I told them I would bring a tape recorder the next day—which, in 1962, was about the size of a small suitcase—to interview them and let them hear how they sounded.

They were transfixed, although I wasn't sure if they knew what a tape recorder was.

Everything seemed to be going really well when I became aware that they were looking down at a point near my feet. Some of them were even holding their hands up to their mouths trying to suppress titters. As I looked down, to my horror, I saw a huge, fat worm with a segmented body and many pairs of legs slowly crawling along the cement floor towards my sandaled feet!

It turned out to be a millipede. I had never seen one of these creatures before and didn't know that they were only ugly, not dangerous, so I yelled in fright, banging my head against the blackboard as I ran from its path. My students were completely delighted, shrieking and clapping their hands with pleasure.

I looked at my watch and saw with relief that it was time to dismiss them; the girls appeared disappointed that there was no more entertainment on the program. As they shuffled out, I reflected with more than a little trepidation that this was only my first day as a Peace Corps teacher.

My students looked beautiful as they paraded across the square with just a touch of self-consciousness. A crowd had gathered to watch the different contingents march past to honor the first president of the new Somali Republic, Aden Abdullah Osman. That image remained vivid twenty-five years later as a group of Returned Peace Corps Volunteers walked across Memorial Bridge to Arlington, Virginia, waving handmade blue-and-white Somali flags and singing the Somali anthem "Somalo Wanachsen" (Somalia is Great). My students would be middle-aged with their own families now, Madame Curie forgotten.

The millipede fiasco on my first day at the Girls' School in Hargeisa brought my students and me together. They developed a protective feeling toward their ignorant American Peace Corps teacher. They giggled over private matters when they were supposed to be studying, but I still think they were trying to please me. What the girls liked most were games and dancing. Especially dancing. They also liked to sing.

One girl followed me around whenever she had the chance, offering to do things for me: "Can I, can I, Miss Marsa?" She had a narrow face, large eyes and a curved forehead, a facial feature distinctive to many Somalis, adding to their unusual good looks. I had a crush on one of my teachers, too, when I was about her age.

I would come over to their dormitory after supper from my house nearby to say goodnight. My maid-in-waiting would always take my hands when I stopped by her bedside and murmur "You are my dream," in the exaggerated flowery way Somalis often used when expressing themselves. They have a gift for oral poetry.

One day, this touching ritual came to an end. The school discovered that the girl had tuberculosis, and she was sent home. Later I learned that she had died. This taught me not to get too close to any of my other students, although I liked most of them and encouraged their extracurricular chatter with me as a means of practicing their English.

Their favorite method of practice was using my tape recorder. They were fascinated by the mechanics of it and loved to hear themselves while I attempted to correct their pronunciation.

At the end of the school year, a Volunteer organized an English poetry recitation contest and I entered one of my students. She had worked very hard recording her English, spending hours with me after class. I picked Wordsworth's "Daffodils" for her to learn because it was available and I liked it. To hear her intone "A host of golden daffodils," with her hands clasped to her heart alternately brought tears to my eyes and suppressed laughter to my lips. She won the contest!

The girls liked fairy tales, listening raptly to stories of abducted children, orphans, cruel stepmothers, wicked witches, handsome princes, and enchanted animals. Afterward, I would have them draw their favorite parts and write captions. They often chose sad episodes. Their drawings were childish; they weren't used to figurative art, and in the past had only painted interlaced designs of flowers and birds. One example I saved shows a mother with her hands up to her face and a boy half her size with hair like palm fronds who floated in the air. The caption reads "o. don't tak my child."

The lesson my girls found particularly distasteful was English grammar. I didn't blame them. We used booklets printed by a British company that specialized in teaching English to African students. Many of the exercises consisted of paragraphs with blanks in which they had to write the proper tense of the verb indicated. The chief obstacle to this was that the Brits couldn't get it into their heads that East Africa was not a suburb of London. The girls didn't know about Liverpool Station or afternoon tea. So I used to substitute examples that were familiar, such as Mrs. Hasanabi's Dry Goods Shop, or "a herd of sheep."

It's forty-five years now since I taught in Hargeisa. Some of my students are probably dead. Hopes for the Somali Republic have all but vanished. Today the place where my school stood is part of a breakaway region of the original Somali Republic called Somaliland. It's not recognized by the United States, but it's doing well in comparison with Somalia, which is largely devastated. A while ago I received a letter and a few photos from a fellow-Somali RPCV who is involved with a fundraising project to support a maternity hospital in Somaliland, the first of its kind there. At the hospital babies are delivered and women are trained to become nurses, midwives and first-aid workers. And two young women are studying to become doctors. They appear in one of the photos in traditional Somali dress, their eyes staring intently at the camera.

Looking at their smiling faces, I remember again the words of our Peace Corps lecturer all those years ago who said that when you teach a boy, you teach a boy, but when you teach a girl you teach a generation. Perhaps Marie Curie's accomplishments may not have been entirely forgotten after all.

Being a Peace Corps teacher in Somalia from 1962–63 changed Marsa Laird's life. She got a graduate degree in ancient art, which gave her the chance to do some excavating in Iraq before the bad days shot down her career. So, she taught art to college students in New York City for twenty years. And, as it turned out, the time spent teaching English to girls and boys in Somalia, whose own language wasn't even written then, was good experience for dealing with kids who resisted art at all costs.

STEPHANIE BANE

✦

Testimony

Disease, so distant, brings all of us home, all of us together.

I BARELY KNEW HELENE BEFORE HER SON DIED. SHE FLUTTERED around the edge of the family, slavishly devoted to her older cousin Yvette.

Yvette ran a health clinic. We sat together in the shade of a mango tree one hot afternoon, talking about health issues in the community. Unasked, Helene brought us a tray of hot sweet tea. She served Yvette with her head bowed. The tea was sticky with sugar. In Chad, the sweeter the tea, the greater the sign of affection and respect.

"Why don't you sit down with us?" Yvette offered.

"No, thank you."

Helene turned to me, a very serious expression on her face.

"Yvette saved my life. I love her like my mother."

The remark was unexpected; I thought I'd misunderstood. Before I could ask the obvious, Helene walked away. I looked to Yvette.

"I got her out of a terrible situation in the city," she said vaguely. It was the only explanation she would offer.

Yvette was the first wife of Thomas, the village chief. Thomas had four wives, three in our household and one in a neighboring town. He took care of them all financially, and all of their children. But Yvette was the wife of his heart. He considered her his partner in the development of the community. He would do anything for her. So when she asked that her adult cousin Helene and her toddler be allowed to come live with them, it was done. Never mind the expense of supporting them, or the shame Helene clearly carried with her. He even paid for her to go back to school.

Helene was humble and shy. At school, though she sat near the front, she never spoke. In the crush of ninety students, it was weeks before I even realized she was in my class. Then I would see her, watching me with wide, clear eyes, taking everything in.

When she occasionally found courage to make conversation with me at home, her French was beautiful, much better than my own. But that was rare; she would send her son David to see me in the afternoons, an emissary between us. He would totter back and forth while Helene labored over the evening meal and I wrote anxious letters to my mother, who had recently been diagnosed with breast cancer.

Yvette was out of town, or it would never have happened. Helene would have told her David was sick, and she would have done something about it. I didn't see it myself, even though I spent time with him. He would bring me a mango or some other treat that Helene asked him to deliver. He wasn't afraid of my white skin. He leaned against me if he was tired. I gave him a taste of whatever I was eating and listened to him chatter if he had something to say. I never understood a single word. He was only three, and he spoke to me in N'Gambaye. I answered him in English or French. Mostly we just smiled at each other, easy companions.

The morning of the day he died, I saw Helene holding him. He was dehydrating rapidly. He looked shrunken, like an infant. She had mixed some honey with water, hoping he would drink more.

As the day wore on, the older women in the village heard what was happening, and gradually came into the yard. They sat around Helene, not saying much, just keeping her company. I didn't understand. I was getting ready to attend a school play with one of my students when I heard Helene start to wail. I ran out of my hut and saw her holding David close, crying out.

Terrified, I stayed where I was. The old women sat quietly, letting Helene cry until she was spent. Minutes passed. Another old woman entered the concession. She must have been waiting outside—for the commotion then the calm—before she entered. She was the woman who prepares the dead for burial.

Helene started screaming when she saw her. She screamed over and over and clutched David to her chest. She wouldn't let her take him. The old woman, loving and awful, pried David from her arms.

As swift and cruel as it was, letting Helene linger over David would have been worse. It was not long after two o'clock and the temperature was high. It was easily over 110, probably over 115. He'd been dying for hours, and the smell of it was already on him.

I retreated into my hut. I sat at my desk on my wooden folding chair, staring at the wall. The heat was unbearable, but I had nowhere else to go.

It was quiet outside. I could hear the low voices of the old women as they cared for Helene. I listened to the murmur and slosh as they bathed her in buckets of cool water. She sobbed quietly, and cried out once or twice.

Eventually, I heard more noise and shuffle. I went to the door and saw that the women had placed several mats together in the shade of a nearby mango tree. They led Helene, who was faltering and could barely walk, to the center. They'd dressed her in someone else's clothing; the outfit she'd worn every day I'd known her was gone. She sat upright with their assistance; when they let her go, she slumped to the ground. They began to seat themselves around her. More women came into the yard and joined the group on the mat.

I turned back inside, panicked. I didn't know the rules. I didn't know what was expected. The person I could have asked was prostrate with grief outside my door. Most of my friends in Chad were men; I wasn't part of the rituals of women. I wasn't sure if I was welcome. Sweat dripped down the backs of my legs, and I prayed intensely that whatever I did next would be the right thing. I decided to join the women on the mat.

The few yards I had to walk from the doorway to the mango tree were long. Everyone but Helene turned to look at me; she lay motionless, eyes shut. I'd never met most of these women—they weren't educated, didn't speak French, and had no reason to socialize with the white schoolteacher. I braced myself for a negative, suspicious reaction. The women shifted slightly to make room for me as I took off my sandals and sat down. They turned their attention back to Helene.

We sat together for an hour or more.

Helene was in shock, still and silent. The women wept on her behalf; most were mothers, most had lost children. I cried with them; the sorrow of it was terrible.

At dusk, a man came to let us know that preparations were complete for the funeral. We stood up and made our way slowly to the graveyard. Thomas joined us, together with the men from the village. He nodded in greeting, but did not speak. He was pale, and his face was grooved with pain.

The men sat on rough wooden benches in the open air. We sat in front of them, still clustered around Helene on a mat. The service and the singing in N'Gambaye were brief. David's little body was swaddled in the familiar cloth of his mother's skirt. The grainy light of the evening passed; when it was over, we walked home in the dark. It had only been five hours from the moment he died until we put him in the ground.

Two or three days later, Thomas summoned me to speak with him. We sat together outside of his office. He still wore the devastated expression I'd seen on his face at the funeral.

"Did she tell you how sick he was?"

"No. She didn't. I didn't know until the afternoon that he died."

"Me neither," he said. We sat in silence for a long time looking at the dirt, our feet, our hands.

"I have a truck," he finally said. The hospital in Moundou was only an hour away.

"I have money," he said.

"I do, too."

"I don't know why she didn't ask us for help." He shook his head. He looked up; our eyes met. Neither of us would say it out loud, for fear the truth would come alive and find its way to Helene. To know it right now would break her. It was only dysentery. David didn't have to die. We were too rich for that.

The week after the funeral, one of the older women in the village asked me for money. They were all chipping in to buy Helene a new outfit, to replace what David was buried in. I knew they were struggling to come up with enough, and I could easily have paid for the all the cloth and tailoring myself. But they wanted to give her something. So I gave enough for the cloth, and left the cost of tailoring to them.

Helene missed school for the next two weeks. The heat was still brutal, and she was listless and barely functional. She lay motionless on a mat during the afternoon hours. She lost weight, her skin looked yellow.

She showed almost no emotion until Yvette returned. When Yvette walked into the yard, Helene leapt to her feet. She let out a miserable, ululating cry and ran to her. Yvette let out the same cry and opened her arms. The rest of us clustered around. Someone pulled together several mats under one of the mangos, enough for the whole family. Yvette sat in the center, with Helene at her feet.

Thomas joined us and gave a speech to welcome Yvette back home. He talked about what had happened in her absence. He told us he was shocked that death could come to the family, that he had believed his wealth would protect them. I cried, and so did Thomas' second and third wives. We had all been grieving silently, along with Helene, and it was good to share it again.

Yvette told us about her trip. She had been summoned to the capital by the wife of President Idriss Déby. She waited at the presidential palace for weeks but was never received. She bitterly regretted that she'd been gone, and for nothing, when David got sick.

The household resumed a normal rhythm, though Helene decided to drop out of school. She had missed too much to catch up, and she was exhausted. Yvette fussed over her, urging her to participate in the life of the family. Slowly she started to engage, preparing meals again and helping the older children with their homework.

For me, life in the family and the village got sweeter. The women relaxed around me. Wherever I went, I was more welcomed than before.

The heat finally broke; the first rain of the year swept through the village. It happened one night at dinnertime, and it was a torrential downpour. I usually shared a meal under the stars with Yvette, but the rain forced us into our huts.

I heard a knock at the door; it was Helene. She had a tray of food.

"I asked Yvette if I could eat with you tonight," she said. She was nervous.

"Come in," I said. "This'll be fun!" I hoped I sounded enthusiastic; doing this was hard for her.

I cleared off my desk to make room for the food. We ate together in the lantern light. The rain hammered on the roof. It was so loud we had to raise our voices; for the most part we sat in silence. It was cozy.

After we finished eating she gestured toward the letter I'd shifted onto the floor when she came in. "Who are you writing?"

"My mother," I said.

"Do you miss her?"

"Yes, terribly. It wasn't so bad when I first got here, but now she's been diagnosed with breast cancer. I'm worried about her all the time."

"Breast cancer!"

Helene was shocked. Breast cancer is something Chadians don't talk about. But I wasn't going treat it like a shameful disease. I was very direct.

"Yes. She had a mastectomy. Her entire right breast was removed."

Helene was silent. The expression of shock was gone, and she didn't look judgmental. In fact she looked happy. Excited.

"I want to show you something," she said.

Instantly she lifted her shirt up to her neck. I tried not to look surprised.

"I had breast cancer," she said.

There was a long raised scar above her right breast. She touched it.

"I had a tumor, and a surgeon in N'Djamena removed it. I'm cured now."

We both looked at the scar for a minute.

"How scary," I said. She nodded. Breast cancer doesn't often get treated in Chad. There's too much stigma, and there just aren't the medical facilities.

"Did you have to have any treatment after surgery?" I asked. "My mom is going through chemotherapy because her cancer might spread."

Helene looked at me blankly. She shook her head. "I'm cured."

I regretted asking. There was no chemotherapy in Chad, whether she needed it or not.

She was still holding her shirt up, reluctant to cover her scar now that it was out in the open.

"I've got this scar, but it's nothing to complain about. I should have died."

That was the situation Yvette had saved her from. Helene didn't share the details, but I could guess. Her husband might have refused to let her seek medical care. Perhaps he shunned her because of the disease. He clearly didn't want her any-more, even after the operation, or she wouldn't be here with us. She wasn't likely to remarry, and now her baby was gone.

Slowly she pulled her shirt back down over her breasts.

"Do you want some tea?" I asked.

"I would love some."

We talked about other, easier things as I made tea over a Bunsen burner near the doorway. I put all the sugar I had into the pot.

Stephanie Bane was in Chad from 1993-95. She currently works as an Account Planner in an ad agency, and is getting an MFA in creative writing from Pacific University in Oregon.

DOROTHEA HERTZBERG

African Woman

What we learn, when we watch what others endure.

YOU CAME IN LATE TONIGHT TO THE HOSPITAL; IN A SHARP AND rusted metal chair you sat. You looked straight ahead into the dim flashlight.

Behind you two men stood.

They have accompanied you and steal your voice.

They will have a man-to-man talk with the doctor about how *you* feel and the pain that *you* bear.

You will look at the floor and listen as your baby screams for you from behind the metal door. The doctor will overprescribe you medicine for the pain in your breast. The men will go and buy it.

Your baby's urgent cries intensify and a woman brings her to your bosom.

You hold your breath in fear, wondering which breast your malnourished child will suckle. His cries turn to a whimper as he clasps onto your nipple. Oblivious to your pain, his little fingernails and teeth grip your swollen and agonized breast.

You wince and bear down on your lip as the baby sighs and takes in its heavenly sips. The pain is unbearable, you begin to pant, every muscle straining and tense. The two men have returned with satchels of medicine, as they behold your struggle...and now it is their eyes that turn to the floor.

In this moment they relent and recognize that it is you who feeds Africa.

Me, I sit in horror and awe. This kind of strength is unknown to me. An acceptance to nourish and bear the suffering of a nation—without pride, without choice, and without apparent anger—you succeed in raising Africa.

A gold bracelet bound tight around your wrist, symbolizing that you are but an object to be given to a man. Two gunshots go off into the night, and you become an arranged wife and mother for life. Your chances to dream fading with the sound of the explosion.

With hidden knees and humbled curtseys you carry a heavy burden. Each day as the sun streaks the sky you will cultivate the land until all of its children have feasted.

Will I ever know this kind of courage?

Prior to joining the Peace Corps as an APCD for Health in 2008, Dorothea (Dee) Hertzberg served as a Peace Corps Volunteer (1999-2001) and as a Health Technical Trainer for Peace Corps Pre-Service Training (2002 and 2003), both in Burkina Faso. Dee has consulted for several international agencies including: The Carter Center, Intrahealth International, the United Nations Development Fund for Women, JHU-CCP and JHPIEGO. Dee holds a Master's of Arts in International Development and a Bachelor of Arts in Social Thought and Political Economy.

EDMUND BLAIR BOLLES

*
*   *

My Rice Crop

*Getting more than we gave has been the experience
of most Peace Cops Volunteers.*

I said, "Have a shoe," and handed the headmaster's wife a potato from the school garden.

Exchanges like that happened when I pushed the edge of my Swahili skills.

I excuse myself: there is a similarity between the word for shoe, *kiatu*, and the one for potato, *kiazi*, but strangers in a strange land tend to be ridiculous, never more so than when they try to adopt some of the local ways.

There was the time I took my sixth and seventh graders out to transplant rice from the nursery to the farmland. In theory, this project was an important demonstration of a better way to grow rice, the village's staple crop. Transplanting was a proven way to increase yield per acre: I knew that because it said so on the sheet of mimeographed paper that the Peace Corps had given me; I was in no position to doubt it: I didn't know what rice in a nursery looked like.

Flashback to the first night of Peace Corps training. One of the women in the group dropped her voice and asked, "Do any of you know about farming?"

173

The cat had popped from the bag. We were all typical Volunteers, fresh out of school, bright-eyed and citified, knowing nothing about farming. Yet somehow we had been selected to teach agriculture to the primary-school children of subsistence farmers.

We did bring enthusiasm to our task, running to find and grab a hoe when there were not enough to go around. We didn't want to miss the chance to work under the summer sun. And when it came time for one of us to volunteer to castrate a lamb, I stepped forward.

Truth be told I had no idea what I was doing. I knew zilch about farming and zilch about Africa. That means I knew zilch squared about African farming. During training, we consoled ourselves with the witticism, "Farming can't be that tough, or so many people wouldn't be doing it." It turned out to be not so easy.

No, wait! There was something easy—radishes. I popped radish seeds into the soil and in no time at all, even without much rain, I had a row of salad vegetables. Forty-five days from planting to harvest with no maintenance. Now that's easy. It was also pointless. The people didn't eat radishes and didn't like radishes. And I couldn't eat a fifty-yard-long row of radishes by myself.

Eggs were easy, too. Almost every villager had a few chickens free-ranging, scratching a living from the ground and providing the occasional egg as a bonus for its "owner." Rooster-doodle-do echoed around the teachers' houses every dawn. I had some hens of my own. The Peace Corps had provided me with the leghorn and two New Hampshire reds I kept cooped up behind my house. They were twice the size of the village birds. One of the local roosters eventually discovered their presence and used to hang around outside my chicken wire making eyes at them.

Between my three birds, I got two eggs a day. There was always a white one from the leghorn and a brown one from the reds. Every so often the reds outdid themselves, and I had a three-egg omelet for breakfast. My students were thunderstruck by the fertility of the birds and the size of the eggs. Their own birds did not deliver eggs with any kind of regularity, and the eggs they did manage were small, not quite robin's-egg sized.

The villagers could see that eggs flowed onto my table like honey and were properly impressed. Even so, they were not ready to follow my example because, while my eggs came easily, they were not free. The only reason my birds stayed fat and fertile was that I fed them every day. I made a feeder (probably half of the practical things I have ever made in my life were made during my Peace Corps years) and bought large bags of feed at a store a hundred miles away. Who could afford that? By American standards, the eggs were very inexpensive; by the lights of a Tanzanian villager they were prohibitive.

The kind of farming the villagers did was hard work. Preparing the ground was just plain backbreaking labor, and then harvesting was even more painful. "Stoop labor" we call a lot of that harvest work. I found I could do it for no more than five minutes without keeling over. Picking tomatoes while bending over a plant is not as immediately exhausting as using a hoe to build a ridge for planting, but the blood rushing to the head made me dizzy. The students were more determined than I and lasted longer, but they didn't find it much easier.

One of the lessons I learned in the Peace Corps is that hard work is hard work, no matter who you are. You'd think I would have known that before going to Africa, and in a way I did, but there is knowing and then knowing. First-hand knowing is best and before the Peace Corps, I knew very little at first hand.

Like rice. I had eaten plenty of rice before going to Africa and was pleased to find it was my village staple. Maize or millet was a more common staple in East Africa, but my village was on a flood plain at the base of a highland massif, perfect for growing rice during the floods of the long rains. *Mpunga* was the Swahili word for rice, and it was a big word in Kidodi village. Naturally, as the new agriculture teacher, the first the school had had in years, I was determined to have a good rice crop. The parents complained that they sent their kids to school so they would *not* have to farm. Yet there I was.

The school did have plenty of land available for planting out behind the school building, and it probably once had a fine garden, but nature had reclaimed it. In Africa, nature does not fool around: I couldn't see very deep into the field, which was overgrown with elephant grass. At least, I guess that's what it was. Anyway, an elephant could have hidden in it, so tall were the blades.

Using hoes and machetes we cleared a place for a nursery where we could start growing our rice. My Peace Corps sheet on rice said to plant it in a nursery and then transplant it. The local method was to plant it straight in the field, so our project would demonstrate a superior yield from a superior method the villagers could adopt.

When it was time to transplant the rice from the nursery, I led my kids out to the field. The nursery had come along fine, although it seemed to have a lot of fresh grass growing alongside the rice. I told the students the plan. Carefully remove the individual rice plants from the soil and carry them over to the larger field for replanting. Sure, said the kids, and began carefully removing the grass.

Nope, nope, I said. They stopped and looked at me.

Take the rice shoots, I said, and plant them over there.

At once they began again to take the grass. We went through the routine one more time before the penny dropped in my slow-moving brain. The grass was the rice. What I thought was rice were weeds. So, O.K., they know what rice looks like and I don't.

After a certain amount of bending and getting dizzy, we moved the rice from the nursery to the field, just in time to take advantage of the great rains. More water came down from the highland slopes, bringing fertile soil with it and sitting on the ground. All the villagers were looking forward to harvesting a year's worth of eating, and seeds for the next year's planting besides.

When the rains stopped and the water began to recede, the people of my village began an action not mentioned on the mimeo sheets. They built makeshift platforms that rose above the rice and sent their children out to sit on them. When birds came into the fields, the kids on the platforms would sling stones at them to chase the winged grazers away. I did not discuss it with the head teacher, but probably he would have been agreeable to setting up a similar system at the school. I wasn't agreeable. The students had come to learn, not to miss class while they acted as living scarecrows. We would lose some of the rice that way, but that was the price.

It turns out, however, that birds are not partial grazers. By the time the water was down and others were in their fields harvesting rice, our rice was gone. Did the transplanting system lead to better yield per acre? Only the birds knew for sure, and they kept mum.

One day a year later I noticed that I could see clear across the whole school grounds. The school's field of tall grass had been cleared, worked, and planted. And not with rice nor with radishes. We now grew things schoolchildren could grow and people would eat, foods like okra and eggplant; tomatoes, too, despite the agony of the stooped harvest. I wasn't any less prone to dizziness, but I couldn't let the kids work while I voiced enthusiasm.

They called me teacher, but I did an awful lot of learning.

Edmund Blair Bolles served in Tanzania from 1966-68. He is the author of over a dozen books, including A Second Way of Knowing *and* Einstein Defiant: Genius versus Genius in the Quantum Revolution.

DONALD HOLM

* *
*

Gentle Winds of Change

*Tilting at windmills…or trying to build them where they have no
business being: perhaps that's the joy of Peace Corps.*

As if out of a fairy tale, on one side of Makele, Tigray, in
northern Ethiopia, on a rise, stood the castle of Ras (or prince)
Mengesha, descendant of centuries of Tigray's monarchy. His
lovely wife, Princess Aida, was a granddaughter of Emperor
Haile Selassie.

Since the dawn of civilization, Makele had been a caravan-
trading center, especially for salt. Perched at 8,000 feet in the
Abysinnian Highlands, to the east an escarpment plunged
below sea level to the Danakil Desert in the Great Rift Valley.
There, nomads cut salt into blocks from evaporated lakes.
Camel caravans toted their precious cargo on ancient paths that
snaked up the escarpment.

Not everyone lived happily ever after, however. In the era
of Solomon and Sheba, whose legendary kingdom was located
there, Tigray was a granary, producing an abundance of the
millet-like grain called *teff*, the main ingredient of Ethiopian
flatbread, *injera*. After millennia of cultivation in a gradually
drying climate, yields steadily declined. Precious little topsoil

179

remained. Farmers steered their oxen-pulled plows around rocks littering the fields. The specter of famine loomed.

My task was to teach English as a second language to seventh and eighth graders in the town's lone school. I was honored that one of my students was the son of Ras Mengesha and Princess Aida, who may normally have sent him away to a boarding school for his education, but had elected to keep him at home now that the Peace Corps had arrived.

My students taught me practical things about their world, as I taught them about mine. They showed me local points of interest, like the market. Trading in salt was the center-piece. At the teeming camel section, my students gave me tips on how to select a good one. Strangely enough, one of the most important ways to recognize a camel's mettle, I learned, involved the animal's ability to stick its long tongue way out, halfway to its knees, with saliva drooling to the ground as the camel went into a stupor. "Oh, sir, *gobez, gobez* (the Amharic word for *strong, awesome*)," they would shout.

We were always looking for ways to enrich our contribution. One PCV developed expertise in building latrines, which he succeeded in erecting at various points around town.

Another Volunteer, Dick, and I stumbled across an abandoned windmill kit in a field behind the school, in wooden crates with weeds canopied around them, displaying fading logos of the clasped hands of the U.S. Agency for International Development. To cynical PCVs, this was typical of USAID. Our school had two General Electric stoves collecting dust in our faculty room, with ovens used as filing cabinets. Just the thing if you were looking to track down a "hot item." The problem: our school had no electricity. At a Peace Corps conference in Addis Ababa, I asked a USAID rep attending how it was possible they would send us electric stoves. His nonchalant response: "We had new stuff coming in, so we had to move it out."

But was the windmill kit, like the electric stoves, really a white elephant? Strangely enough, it seemed to Dick and me that a windmill might actually make sense. With the persistently encroaching desertification, ladies had to fetch water for their households from muddy pools in a river trickling miles from town. They lugged the essential liquid on swayed backs in earthen jugs that weighed as much as the water they carried, an agonizing task. As I slept at night, I dreamt of these ladies smiling as water gushed from an imaginary windmill in the center of town.

We picked a central spot that the local government said we could use. It was like an erector set on Christmas morning, trying to figure out which part went where. Our efforts drew amusement from people on their way to the market. What were these zany Americans trying to do? Construct a launch pad for a moon rocket?

Over many Saturdays, we put together the first tier, then the second. Complexities sprang up. How on earth were we going to drill the well under the windmill? Just as intimidating, how in the world were we going to be able to lift its heavy motor to the apex? We blindly worked on, with the spirit and enthusiasm typical of early Volunteers, that we could change the world by force of will alone.

We needed a miracle. Then, one quiet afternoon, a small plane dropped down at the airstrip, a pasture on the edge of town where goats grazed. The American Ambassador had breezed in from Addis Ababa on a field trip. He was staying at the castle hotel at the other end of town, a bookend to the castle of Ras Mengesha and Princess Aida, constructed for the occasional VIPs and to encourage fledgling tourism.

The Ambassador invited all eight Volunteers in Makele for drinks at the castle that evening, following his call on Ras Mengesha and Princess Aida.

I put on my ratty, rust-colored sports coat and my green polka-dot tie that didn't match. As we arrived, we over-heard the Ambassador speaking to one of the staff working at the hotel, who was presenting a bottle of *tej* honey mead, Ethiopia's national drink, as a gift to the Ambassador from the Ras and Princess. The servant asked the Ambassador what he would like him to do with the *tej*, and the Ambassador growled, "Dump it down the toilet, I've given enough of my intestines to this country." We looked at each other and shud-dered, knowing this insult would be reported back to the Ras and the Princess. It was not an auspicious start to the evening.

The Ambassador went around and asked each of us what we were doing in Makele as Volunteers. When most of us responded that we were secondary school teachers, he impa-tiently raised his voice and tiredly blurted out, "But what are you *really* doing to help these people?" This sparked pangs of guilt. We harbored such high expectations when we had ide-alistically answered President Kennedy's call to do our part in bringing the developing world out of poverty.

Dick and I volunteered that, well, we were working on weekends to build a windmill. The Ambassador's mood changed. "Why that's ideal," he beamed. Given the increas-ingly arid climate, and the steady strong winds coming up from the escarpment, we sensed that he was thinking big, chasing windmills in his mind spreading across the horizon like oil derricks.

In the weeks that followed, Dick and I felt even more inspired to complete the windmill, constructing a third tier.

One Saturday afternoon as we were lunching at the town's only restaurant, a great commotion occurred. A helicopter swooped down into the market, scattering camels and donkeys and people in every direction. Most of the people in the mar-ket had undoubtedly never even heard of a helicopter, much less seen one. For them, it was as if a spaceship had docked. Dick and I took swigs from our warm beers, and wondered what this could possibly be about.

Two well-built men in U.S. Army fatigues stormed into the restaurant asking where they could find Perry and Holm (Dick and me). The lead man, with blond crew-cut hair and sporting colonel eagles on his lapels, snapped to us long-haired, unkempt PCVs, with obvious irritation, that they were Army engineers sent by the Ambassador from the small Army base in Asmara to team with us to finish the windmill. Their helicopter was capable of lifting the windmill's gearbox into place. But first, they wanted to check out the overall feasibility of the project.

We took them to the site. The Army engineers went back to their helicopter and returned with sounding gear and augers. They launched into tests. Whenever we tried to assist, they barked that we were getting in their way, so Dick and I returned to the restaurant and sipped some more on our warm beers.

A couple of hours passed. The two Army engineers, by now sunburnt with sweat dripping down their faces, paraded into the restaurant again. The colonel snarled that that there was no aquifer below. The site we had chosen would produce not more than "a cup a day." The two stomped out of the restaurant; their helicopter thrashed up a repeat whirlwind of dust and commotion as they departed in their "spaceship."

And the windmill? Dick and I thought about tearing it down, but our final days crept up on us so quickly, we never got around to doing it. For all I know, it stands today as a metaphorical monument to the spirit of the Peace Corps in its early days, a testament to tireless effort and goodwill, tempered by the sobering acknowledgement that development remains a worthwhile goal, but one which cannot be achieved nearly as easily or as quickly as early Volunteers may have imagined.

With it comes the resignation, call it wisdom if you like, that the impact of the Peace Corps has not been in spectacular, strong gusts of wind, in showy projects like windmills, but rather in day-to-day tasks like teaching school in remote locales, acts of kindness that are good in themselves, fostering gentle, yet steady, zephyrs of change that enhance the image of America, and through us, increase America's understanding of perspectives of the developing world. That is what we have *really* been doing.

Donald Holm, PCV in Ethiopia from 1965-67, is a semi-retired Foreign Service officer whose career has taken him to South America, Southeast Asia, Western Europe, the Eastern Caribbean, and back to Africa. He currently lives on a ridge, often buffeted by Chinook winds, looking out on snow-capped mountains above Boulder, Colorado. Come to think of it, with the emerging energy crisis, what an ideal spot for a...?

JENNIFER L. GIACOMINI

✦

La Supermarché

Can seeing what something can be make people want it to be?

AFTER LIVING IN VILLAGE FOR JUST OVER A YEAR, I TOOK MY mama, Elise, to dinner at a German-owned restaurant. Elise had wanted to travel to Kara for a while, but had to put it off. Each time she prepared for her departure, something came up in the village prompting her to stay. Last time, her husband simply refused to let her go. I think he didn't want to endure his thirteen-year-old daughter's cooking during Elise's absence.

Finally, I had an idea: I would take Elise to her brother's house and out to dinner. I would pay for everything. Just as I knew he would, Papa agreed.

So, one Friday morning, we biked to Guèrin-Kouka and eased into comfortable seats in the second row of the taxi. Elise had her eye on me, a form of sisterly protection. She watched me navigate the system with the familiar taxi drivers who tried to make sure I was comfortable.

We arrived in Kara a few hours later and much dustier. The driver took the back way, allowing us to enter Kara near Elise's brother's house. Only Elise's youngest brother Jean, a student, greeted us. He spent his off-seasons in Katchamba and was just a few years younger than I. I invited him to go with us.

We sauntered to the restaurant, dodging cars, bikes, children, and livestock on the road. La Supermarché, a German-owned restaurant and grocery store, provided desired treats from America and Europe. I often browsed the grocery, longing for the luscious cheeses, meats, candies, and cookies. They were way too pricy for my meager Volunteer salary; I bought a cheap candy and went on my way. The adjacent restaurant, however, was my favorite. I could purchase a hamburger and fries, along with a beer or two. It provided a welcome change from my regular village meals of *pâte*, or polenta, with pepper sauce.

I had spent many hours in this open-air restaurant, dining and watching CNN or BBC on the large-screen TVs mounted to posts supporting the straw roof. The restaurant opened into a garden filled with colorful flowers, a beautifully manicured lawn, and a children's play set. It was a welcome piece of home and momentary escape from Togolese life.

Elise shyly informed me that she had never before been in a real restaurant. She had traveled but, like most, had eaten street food at outdoor food courts. This didn't really surprise me; the cost of one meal at a restaurant could feed her family for a week. I was, however, surprised when Jean told me that he too had never eaten at a restaurant. He had been a student in Kara for four years, and I often saw students at restaurants, mostly drinking beers but occasionally dining. I couldn't believe he was never one. *Il n'y a pas d'argent*— there's no money.

We opened the menus; their faces fell, shocked by the steep prices. Elise wanted to ask questions, but the only one she mustered was if the restaurant had everything on the menu. I explained that you get to order anything you want and someone else cooks it and serves it.

However, oftentimes I would order an item at a Togolese restaurant and only then would the server inform me that they didn't have it that day. I would order another with the same result. This often occurred several times before finding something they did have available.

I persuaded Elise and Jean to order cheeseburgers and fries. I mentioned other places one might encounter them, like a barbeque or a picnic. I then launched into a tirade on the fast food nation America is quickly becoming. They didn't quite understand, so I gave up.

We ordered, and I got up to use the restroom and wash my hands and face from the dusty taxi ride. I warned Elise and Jean that, despite the African custom, the servers do not bring a bowl of water for washing. If they wanted clean hands, they should go to the restroom. Neither of them seemed to care.

When I returned, Elise leaned over and whispered, *"Ma sœur, je dois pisser."* My sister, I have to piss. She asked if she could go on the lawn. I was so glad she asked; I promptly told her no, she had to use the restroom. While this may seem crass to some, I knew the mannerisms and customs of the Togolese and knew it was common to find an outside corner and urinate.

So we proceeded to the bathroom. It was hysterical! Elise had never even seen a toilet, much less used one. I had to pantomime the entire process of entering a stall, shutting the door, using the toilet and flushing it. I only made it about halfway through this act before she burst out laughing. You mean I have to pee in there? Sure, said I, this is the only place we go *chez-nous*. Every residence has at least one.

So, Elise decided to have a go at the foreign device. It took her several minutes; I do believe she was nervous about using it correctly. Meanwhile, I contemplated a world that allows such a massive difference in septic technology. They dig holes, squat in the forest, and use sticks or corncobs for toilet paper. Not all facets of Togolese life are on par with the Western world.

I snapped back when I heard Elise flush. She practically fell out of the stall. I showed her the sink, soap dispenser, and paper towels. She was unsure of the hand-washing process and kept muttering, *"Les Américains-la,"* those Americans. She couldn't believe that clean water came from the faucet all the time. She didn't have to walk a few kilometers, collect it, and then walk back with the heavy basin balanced on her head. It was so easy and clean. She stood there and watched the water just run for a full minute.

Finally we returned to the table and Elise ordered her brother to go wash. I think she wanted Jean to have an eye-opening experience like hers. He took me with him to explain, but he wasn't as much fun. He had seen and used both a toilet and sink before.

We returned to the table to find Elise looking at our meals, no idea what to do. I explained garnishes and showed them how to pick up a cheeseburger with both hands and take a bite. Yum. Elise was horrified. Eat with BOTH hands? To use the left for anything but wiping was probably the biggest taboo in Togolese culture. I had to explain toilet paper and soap and that it doesn't matter because we consider ourselves, and both hands, clean.

I told her to cut the burger in half and just eat it with her right hand. She happily munched away and really enjoyed it. Her brother also cut his burger in half, but began eating it with a fork. He ate it one ingredient at a time, forking the bread, then the cheese, then the meat, etc. I tried to explain to him the culinary delights of the melding of all these into one bite. Unsuccessful, I tried a different approach. I explained that to eat this dish with a fork would be like eating *pâte* with a fork. No one does it. He didn't care.

Following our trip, Elise and I had several conversations about technological advances and women's rights. I was left with deep frustration because she understood suffrage and technological improvements, but she never wanted to do anything about them. *C'est la vie en Afrique.* Life in Africa revolved around that fatalistic attitude, stunting development and making it difficult to accomplish much. The villagers in Katchamba thought that it would be great to have latrines, running water and electricity, but would not work to accomplish these goals.

Instant gratification worked perfectly. Why save money when we may not be here tomorrow to use it? Death was such a huge part of life that it became their reason for not looking into the future. Let the women spend hours upon hours collecting potable water and send the children off into the woods to defecate. Why save money for the future when they must feed their families now?

We had several village meetings to discuss building latrines or an accessible well in Katchamba. People wanted them; they just wanted someone else to buy and build them. I refused to do it myself without help from the village in planning, saving money, and implementing the project. The chief and other elders told me to continue my work with the health clinic and not worry about building something the village won't work to maintain.

I believe the women knew the benefits potable water and less waste could offer the village. And that it would make life less exhausting. But every argument ended with the men saying no. The women continued arguing, but their husbands just walked away. One day, maybe, these women will learn to stand up for what they believe and follow their sisters from fifty years ago in women's suffrage. Maybe, just maybe...

Jennifer L. Giacomini served in Togo from 1999-2001, after gradu-ation from Hamilton College. She is now the Executive Director at Grand County Rural Health Network in Colorado.

✳

Mokhotlong

You can't learn a culture without attempting its language.

THERE IS A GIRL OUTSIDE MY RED WOODEN DOOR.

Her world is there. She does the family's washing and cooking in her patched skirt and bare ebony feet, two meters from my front step. She plays games there, sings hymns there. And she communicates with the neighbors from there through the tremendous trumpeting power of her tiny lungs.

Her name is Sebueng, and while my Sesotho is not at all fluent, I think her name would translate to "in the place of the one talking." Basotho children are named after the circumstances of their births; perhaps her mother was busy in conversation when her baby took her first breath, or perhaps someone was talking with her to try and distract her from birthing pains.

At any rate, the Sesotho language is grammatically simpler than English. The *se-* prefix generally indicates that the noun is a person (although not always) and the—*ng* suffix denotes "in the place of." It is when the Basotho throw idioms about cows and entrails at me that my language skills falter. But, as they say here, *"Seqanqane se seng le se seng sea iqomela"*: Every toad jumps for itself.

Welcome to Lesotho.

Its claim to fame is that it has the highest low point of any country on Earth, and thus it proudly calls itself "The Kingdom in the Sky," or, more commonly, "The Mountain Kingdom." And it is believable: as I looked this morning at the tips of the mountains of my humble village (elevation approximately 3,200 meters) surrounded by billowy clouds looking as if their rocky heads had punctured the cap of the world, it truly felt like I was in the sky. In fact, just a hop, skip, and really long hike away is the mountain Thabana-Ntlenyana, the highest point in Southern Africa.

I live in the village of Thoteng, an offshoot of Ha Senkoase in the district of Mokhotlong. *Mokhotlong,* if you remember that suffix, translates to "in the place of the Mokhotlo." The Mokhotlo is a *very* strange-looking bird, a bald ibis in the books. I have heard it referred to as "that Dr. Seuss bird." With its shimmery blue-black feathers and tremendously long, thin, curved-yet-somewhat-pointy reddish beak and white head, I think the good doctor would have approved. Out of all ten districts in Lesotho, ours is (supposedly) the birds' only home.

I saw three Mekhotlo on the day I moved in, and they continue to be an ominous yet oddly comforting presence. They somehow herald change, earmark already memorable occasions, and remind me that life, full of weird little creatures like them and me, should never be taken too seriously.

While one might think my spelling of *Mekhotlo* a typographical error, it was spelled so on purpose. Nouns in Sesotho belong to one of about six different classes based on prefixes, and the formation of plurals and pronouns, ubiquitous in ways unimagined by native English-speakers, dictated by the appropriate noun class.

These noun classes present problems for new Lesotho PCVs who just want to know the word for *this*. Had our infinitely patient trainers begun to explain the intricacies of noun classes in week one or two, saying that the word *this* could be *ena, tsena, mona,* or a number of other words, depending on its referent, our brains might well have exploded, so we had to grit our teeth and accept the response, "Oh, don't mind, we'll get to that later."

With *this*, we began our long journey to fully understand the definition of the word *mamello*—"patience."

I thought I was patient in America. I had become a good listener. I did not yell when web pages took longer than thirty seconds to load or when I was stuck in traffic. I meditated occasionally. I even steadily trudged along through diet and exercise until, over the course of a year or so, I had lost sixty pounds.

But I had never waited for a taxi (in the form of a Toyota minibus, which holds fifteen passengers) for over four hours to fill so that I could go home. I had never tried to teach before, much less English (which must be the *hardest* subject to teach due to unexplainable, illogical idiosyncrasies), in dirt-floor rooms packed with seventy-plus teenagers who spoke a language that I didn't know. I had never lived without electricity or running water, and believe me, that takes patience.

And walking suddenly became a problem. At my slowest natural stride, I soon realized I outpaced everyone else in the vicinity. "Why are you running?" they ask as I amble slowly up a hill. "You are always in a hurry!"

Above all, I had never before had to lose myself—let go of my ingrained habits and assumptions—in order to be able to even start to understand folks from a different culture.

Meetings, for instance, take place *ka nako ea Basotho,* "at the time of the Basotho," or, as we Volunteers like to say, on

Basotho Time. Things start when people are there—meetings, taxis, funerals—and once I let go of preconceived notions I wasn't even aware I had, I realized that this method of living is actually relatively free of stress. You'll get there when you get there, and chances are that we'll wait up for you. It's no Motel 6, but it'll do.

One serious problem I had with the Sesotho language is its lack of vocabulary revolving around the word *love*. To say, "I love you," one says *kea o rata*. However, to say, "I like tea," one says *ke rata tee*.

What does this mean? Does this mean the intensity of your love for tea rivals your love for me? Or does this mean your love for me is so commonplace that it equals your love for your morning cup of tea?

The Basotho have a term for white people, *makhooa* (singular is *lekhooa*, part of the "le/ma" class), but they also use it as a derogatory term for people who believe they are better than everyone else, people who act superior.

I don't like it, and I don't tolerate it when used in reference to my friends or me.

I had never been personally exposed to racism in America. At least, not to the extent that I have seen it in South Africa. But all I have seen here, in Lesotho and just across the border, makes me extremely sensitive to judging people based on their color. And to point me out as different—as a *lekhooa*—that puts me on my guard. We are all, underneath the multicolored clothes of culture, human.

We all celebrate. We all dance and sing. We all cook and eat, even if the ingredients differ slightly. We all ask questions. We all have seen strange birds, but I swear the strangest live here. And we all suffer loss, each accepting and facing grief in his own way, in his own time—perhaps even in Basotho Time.

One can even see similarity in the languages. When I told a coworker that my cat was pregnant, he said, "*E jele yeast!*" "It ate yeast," only a baby step away from "she has a bun in the oven." And that same man, when he accidentally hurt my hand, took it and kissed my palm, a manifestation of "kiss and make it better."

"*Eseng lekhooa; ke 'M'e Thandiwe Kao,*" I say. "*Na, ke ngoana oa Moshoeshoe. Ke motho joalo ka oena.*" ("Not *lekhooa*; I am Madam Thandiwe Kao. Me, I am a child of Moshoeshoe—the founder and first king of Lesotho. I am a person, just like you.")

I even live with you, here behind my red wooden door. I work with you, for you and for your children. I have given up my own family and friends to be a part of your lives for this short time, to be a part of a new family. I am a mother of over 200 children whose faces light up when I walk onto campus. Their pain—your pain—is my pain. And my hope is that one day, you will not see me for my skin, but for the laughter I have shared, the knowledge I have imparted, the hard work I have done, and the tears I have shed in this beautiful place: the place of the Mokhotlo—my home.

After graduating summa cum laude from Appalachian State University in 2005 (B.A. English), Allison Scott Matlack served in Lesotho as an education volunteer (English teacher) from 2005-07. She got married in October 2008 to a fellow ed volunteer (see, Peace Corps romance does work out!) and they are busy readjusting to "the real world." The complete version this story is excerpted from what sealed her acceptance to the Sewanee School of Letters, an M.F.A. creative writing program. She keeps her eyes open for a bald ibis or two. Rea le hopotse, Lesotho!

SANDRA ECHOLS SHARPE

Changing School

*Collisions of culture and necessity are not necessarily
limited to those from far away.*

IN JANUARY OF 1965, I BOUGHT ALL OF THE NECESSITIES TO FILL
my Mbeya, Tanzania school compound: reading materials,
science equipment, paraffin (kerosene), some clothes, a book
locker, and my certification from NYU-Syracuse that assured
my qualification to teach as a Peace Corps Volunteer. But
when you are in Mbeya, should you do what the Mbeyans do?
Meca, the Land Rover driver, loaded my paraphernalia, drove
through the town, turned onto the Chunya road, and headed
uphill toward a church mission compound six miles from the
center of Mbeya.

Ah! Wonderment...a stream-washed cloth, sun-dried...
draped around a linearly plaited hill...a multiplicity of potato
plants all growing in magnificent brown-green rows.... Mud
houses, maize fields, people carrying fruit and vegetable baskets, local buses, and fields of pyrethrum flowers traverse the
Rift Valley road. In less than thirty minutes, Meca's unbridled
Rover turns left wildly onto a narrow clay strip, jerkily pot-
holing its way down a gradual incline. As it crosses an eroding

one-lane wooden bridge, we roll past the dispensary and come to a full halt in front of a row of teachers' houses.

The view on the left is of a white stucco building, that dispensary. It has a faded rouge porch with an open door. It looks vacant and hollowed out like an old gourd. Medicines have long since evaporated with the cool, misty, morning rains of the season. In front, five slab-mud, cement-covered homes are nested in a valley of rolling hills, picturesque and soothing to a tiring traveler. A morning rain plays a mighty drum roll on the corrugated roofs, welcoming me to the compound. Stately eucalyptus trees hurl down, from scented branches, rolls of raindrops.

At eight o'clock, Meca unloads all of my worldly possessions in my home, wishes me well and leaves.

One hundred steps from the teachers' quarters are the classrooms. The elongated mud-brick building features windowless windows and doorless doors. The dark entrances empty their content of sky-blue A-line dresses, white shirts, and khaki pants. The teachers inspect them and beckon to me to join them. The students stand at attention. As I walk toward the school compound, a huge round field appears. In the dry season, it will host sports events, community ceremonies, and school events. On the far side of the field are the gardens and storage buildings, which house dried beans, rice, and other foodstuffs. I am introduced and asked to take my place with the teachers. Now we wait for the new headmaster.

Smiling, an older teacher, a traditional man, watches the road as a new headmaster comes to replace him.

Striding in to the rhythmic music of his *irimba* (thumb piano), Mr. Mpacama arrives at the Ngoba Upper Primary School to begin his duties as headmaster. The Board of Missionaries placed him here to upgrade the school. Because he is a strict, punctual man, they expect him to be a great disciplinarian.

With the changing of the guard, indulgences disappear. If I want coffee or tea, I must bring it in my thermos every morning. I must also supply my own biscuits (cookies). Early, around 6:30, the pounding feet of children run to the middle of the school compound to receive assignments. The headmaster tells group one, "Sickle the high grassy areas around the school only, and then sort the cuttings into a compost heap." He says to another group of older students, "Begin kitchen duty." They clang large pots and pans as lunch is prepared. The cutting and simmering of large quantities of vegetables, boiling of rice and tea and the slicing of papaya or seasonal fruits are daily routines. The sweeping of the compound, and mopping the storage areas, and liming the latrines are a necessity for maintaining sanitary conditions. The headmaster even initiates the inclusion of a sewing class. It is scheduled at the end of every day, therefore lengthening the average amount of time students spend in school.

Mr. Mpacama checks each group's work, then signals for the students to return to the front of the school and line up. He blows the whistle and says, "Tusagewa, begin the exercises! Let them run one mile around the school compound!"

"Yes, headmaster!"

While most students run and chant, a small group remains to whisk away footprints from the drying schoolyard.

Promptly at 8:00, I ascend the concrete steps to the headmaster's office. The smooth, mud-finished interior wall and the recently scrubbed concrete floor lend a muddy creek-water smell to the khaki pants and white shirt he is wearing. The headmaster says, "Welcome again to my office. Please sit down. Let me see your lesson plans for the week! I'm happy to see you are including the sewing lessons after school as part of your teaching load! The bolt of fabric, newspaper for making dress patterns and the needles and threads will be in the storage cabinet by 4:00 P.M. for you to use."

"Thanks," I say. "May I also use the microscopes tomorrow for the unit on one-cell organisms, and may I show pictures during geography class of the flora and fauna of the Indian Ocean coastline, around Dar-es-Salaam?"

"Yes," he replies.

I continue, "Sarah and I share photos and borrow reading materials from other Peace Corps Volunteers' book lockers. We pool information when we can illuminate the ecology of the coast. Our students are now seeing the natural beauty of the area."

The headmaster replies, "Please feel free to exhibit resource materials in your classroom." I leave his office and head toward the teacher's workroom.

My feet keep walking, but my mind is a whirling cloud, drifting into history. Zanzibar: I will have to teach about the diaspora! I will have to teach about Mombassa.

Rain comes! RAIN. RAIN. RAIN. Foamy gray water, gallons of it make the compound, in an instant, look like thick mud soup, with our small teachers' cottages stewing around in the middle.

The cold rain subsides. The one village car and the cottages shake off the vision, fill up and look like sanctuary. Now the chanting of the math students and the lecturing voices of the other teachers become louder as rainwater trickles into the compound.

The headmaster leaves his office and walks to his car. He says, "I am going downtown to pick up more cans of oil, sacks of rice, and medicine. You give first aid to many of the students with your own ointment and band-aids. Thank you!" The headmaster continues, "If I don't see you any more today,

I will see you tomorrow *mwalimu* [teacher]. Enjoy your *chakula* at noon!"

I return to the teachers' workroom until the history period begins. The day passes slowly. At the end of forty minutes, geography class begins. Then I teach English; we review for a test. Pressure is on! Students must pass the eighth-standard exit exams before they go to high school.

It is not long now before we see a 1956 Austin-Healy burping along the one-lane dirt road toward the school with Mr. Mpacama and perhaps two students in it. We could not see them clearly because the car windows are taped with newspaper. The shifting gears and ill-repaired clutch seem to enhance the old-fashioned scolding they receive. When the car stops, the badgering continues.

"It amazes me that none of your teachers could see you run away from school, in the middle of the day, over the bridge, up the hill to meet the bus! Why do you do this?" says Mr. Mpacama angrily. "Just to buy fish! I saw you wave your hands, and stop the bus. Then you boarded it, unpacked the fish, and placed them on the steps, stacking your purchases on the bus steps! You have no discipline! You should be studying! You caused the bus to be much later than usual getting to Mbeya town! This is a bold act! Meet me tomorrow after school, and I will give you your punishment!"

Apologetically, the students look at him and say, "We have a Friday ritual; we purchase fish for our families!" After school, Mr. Mpacama calls a meeting at his home briefing us about the incident. Hunger grips us; we nearly taste his boiling curry meat and *ugali* dish cooking on the stove.

He informs us that the school suffers from a lack of discipline. There are too many broken bricks that need to be re-made. The compound suffers from a lack of paint; just like many of the students, it suffers, needing revitalization. The fiery head master says, "It is sad that our school is behind Itope, Iringa, and Mpala, and other well-known schools in the district!" He continues, "Yesterday, during school hours, two of our model students left the compound to buy fish from a local bus driver. The punishment I will give requires the efforts of the entire seventh and eighth standards since others probably have been guilty of the same misdemeanor. Beginning tomorrow afternoon, students will make bricks to replenish the exhausted supply."

There are hisses and cheers among the faculty. One teacher cautions him, "But, Mwalimu, the tradition of our school will be ruined if students make bricks for a punishment." Nevertheless, the headmaster insists and teachers are dismissed.

Next day, after school is over, the seventh and eighth standard students meet in the compound.

As work begins, the old teacher, who is a traditional man, watches again. He pulls off his shirt and jumps into a pit. The arduous task of making bricks continues as he and the students dig three huge pits in the ground. Mounds of cut grasses are thrown into these holes and chopped up into small particles. Then the water bearers bring large cans of river water and dump it into the pits. Students jump in and press the wet clay with particles of grasses into a smooth consistency with their feet. Still others line up and scoop out the wet clay mixture and pour it into wooden brick molds, rectangular wooden frames. Each holds enough mud to form one brick. The old man and the students finally dump the first solidifying brick on the ground to dry, followed by the second and third ones. Unfortunately, I must oversee the brickmaking project. I feel like a camel herder.

At the end of the atonement week, two enormous pyramids of sun-dried bricks are piled up in a vacant space near the road. The old teacher is no longer watching or sitting by the side of the road. The bricks are fired using huge eucalyptus trees. They turn hard and indestructible.

The rain descends gently upon the cooling pyramids, but it does not abate the old teacher's anger. He walks five miles to visit the district officer whose office is in the government *boma* (center). The old teacher explains the punishment to the district officer. Mr. Mpacama is summoned.

The district officer says, "Headmaster Mpacama, how could you inflict such a horrible punishment on your students? You know they walk barefooted seven to ten miles a day, over mountains and through valleys of maize to get to school each day. Surely, you could have punished only the two guilty students and allowed the others to go home to help with the afternoon chores! Surely, you could have waited until spring to make the bricks."

Mr. Mpacama says, "Sir, look at the progress here. We have planted gardens. Now we sell vegetables to customers at the market and have cash to pay for many of the school's expenses. Also our soccer team is excelling and more of our students are passing the standard eight exams this year!"

How could Mpacama possibly have achieved all of this having been the headmaster at for only short time? "Enough!" the district officer replies. "Since traditionally the making of bricks is a labor of love and not of atonement, I dismiss you from the school."

Mr. Mpacama was sent—loudly protesting—to pick tea on a plantation in Tukuru, in the southern district of Tanzania. According to the old teacher, who is a traditional man, certain rituals of work must be maintained in order to give stability to a community. These rituals outweigh any notion of progress the headmaster could conjure up. To the old teacher, the headmaster is like an empty can, for the Swahili proverb even says, "An empty *debe* can [for carrying kerosene] makes the most noise!"

Sandra Echols Sharpe served as a teacher in Tanzania from 1965-67. She now resides in Greensboro, North Carolina.

ALAN BARSTOW

*

The Season of *Omagongo*

*Sometimes the things we see and believe might better
be seen and believed a little differently.*

TATE SHIKONGO TELLS TIMO TO FETCH THE WHIP: "*ETA ONGO-
dhi*," he says in Oshindonga. He adds in English, "Bring it
here. I want it."

Timo returns with the three-foot water hose. His nine-
year-old frame, all beanpole arms and legs, walks easily. He
hands Tate the hose with his right hand, his left hand cupping
his right elbow, and keeps his eyes lowered in the way the
Owambo people of northern Namibia show respect to their
elders. Then Timo tries to jump away, but Tate's calloused
hand grabs his wrist. He holds the hose above Timo and says
in Oshindonga, "You left the cattle to wander into the fields."

"Yes," Timo says, his eyes shut tight above his bullish
cheekbones. Tate whips him twice and Timo cries out and
tries to break free.

"Because you were playing soccer," Tate says. The thick
muscles of his arms—arms that I've seen plow fields, fix
engines, fire AK-47s—stand out as he whips Timo again and
again.

"The cattle ate the *mahangu*," Tate shouts. "The cattle destroyed the crop."

Tate Shikongo's eldest son, Petrus, is sitting next to me with the twenty-five-liter *omagongo* gourd between his feet. He removes his thin-rimmed glasses, wipes them on the collar of his business shirt, and laughs a thirty-years-ago-Tate-whipped-me-for-letting-cattle-into-the-field laugh. Tate Angula, the headman of Okatope village and Tate Shikongo's older brother, sleeps peacefully next to us, barefoot in the sand.

I've seen Timo whipped before—the first time, two weeks after I'd moved into Tate Shikongo's homestead during training in late 2002; I couldn't sleep until I heard the midnight rain on the aluminum roof of my room. I signed up for Peace Corps to teach English as a foreign language just out of college; I wanted to work in development, travel to little-known places, learn a new language and culture; I believed Peace Corps to be the best face of the U.S. government.

A year after 9/11, as Bush made plans to invade Iraq, I arrived in Namibia confident that what Volunteers did here— teach in schools, coordinate AIDS awareness activities, find the common ground between Namibians and Americans—was a better way to spread goodwill and curb terrorism than invading countries. But, during the times that Tate Shikongo whipped one of his grandchildren, I've turned away, thinking no matter how much Oshindonga I speak, how accustomed to the traditional food and drink I become, or how accepted and welcome my work here is, *These are not my people. I am different.*

Tate Shikongo can seem the antithesis of a lot of what I stand for. He disciplines with corporal punishment, has a conservative interpretation of the Bible, and fought as a guerrilla and terrorist. Yet, I'm drawn to him and I respect him. He fought as a guerrilla fighter for his country's independence from the racist apartheid regime of South Africa. At seventy, he still works as a mechanic to make enough to care for the AIDS orphans he welcomes into his home. He cries at any mention of his dead wife. I refer to him as *tate* (pronounced *tah-tay*), which means *father*, not just because he's my elder, but because he's like a father to me.

Tate lets Timo's wrist go after the beating. The boy falls back, his skinny chest rushing for air. Tate flicks the hose against his own leg and hands it to Timo, who replaces it in the house and returns with a used tongue depressor and a Black Cat Peanut Butter jar filled with tar-like ointment. Tate takes the jar and rubs the ointment on the ringworm rashes on Timo's legs and arms, reminding him to stay out of the stagnant pools of water as he herds cattle. There are no welts or marks from the hose—nothing save his labored breathing shows that he was beaten at all.

Timo joins his cousins in their hut for sleep. Tate and Petrus talk about the fields, the crops, the rain. Tate Angula snores evenly. Only my ear still hears Timo's cries and the smack of the hose. I know Timo should be punished for neglecting his chores, but I don't think a whipping will teach him. I force this to the back of my mind, reminding myself that I've seen children face far worse than corporal punishment, like being hungry, orphans, or HIV-positive.

Tate Shikongo says to me, "Alona, you are too much quiet."

I am Alona, but Alona is not me. I told Tate Shikongo my name was "Alan" the first time I met him and I traced it in the sand. Tate said, "Good name. Bible name."

"My name isn't in the Bible," I said.

With the authority of a man whose father was one of the first Owambo ministers, ordained by Rhenish missionaries, Tate said, "Alon brother for Moses. Moses no speak word of God. Alon carry message. You are Alon. You spreading message."

I had been in Namibia for less than a week and didn't know there is no "R" sound in Oshindonga—"L" and "R" are interchangeable, so Alan becomes Aaron becomes Alon. Nor did I know that Owambos believe personal qualities can be attributed to people through names and, thus, what this name said about me. I was eager to be accepted, to feel a part of the family, and I hoarded whatever endearments I received, including the affectionate "a" they tagged onto the end of *Alon.*

Now, when he says my Namibian name and I think the of the significance of it, feeling impotent to prevent Timo's beating and somehow culpable because I witnessed it, I think to myself, *My name is not Aaron. I have no message.*

Petrus takes the dipper from the *omagongo* gourd between his feet and fills a wooden cup with the lime-green beer. He offers it to me and I drink it, tasting limeade and tonic.

He asks, "What do you know about the season of *omagongo,* Alona?"

"Not much," I say.

Petrus says March is the season of *omagongo.* The small, green *marula* fruit is picked, peeled, pressed by a cow horn, and left to ferment in gourds, with fruit flies hovering like steam. "It's a good and bad time," he says. Good because it is a time of rest between the planting and cultivating of the crop and the harvest, when the stalks of millet stand like warriors, spears in the air, and the Owambo watch the rain turn their dusty, semi-arid land into a crop-bearing land, when the sun is shrouded by rain clouds and the rain falls like a mother's touch, nurturing the land after nine months of drought. It's a bad time because everyone is drunk for weeks. So drunk, Petrus says, tribal law bans carrying a *panga*—a machete— because people often get into arguments during this time. He nods at Tate Angula, the village's headman, who represents the tribal king, and says it's all so ludicrous the tribal courts will not hear any disputes in this season.

Petrus refills the wooden cup with *omagongo* and hands it to me, saying, "When you marry at Tate's house, Alona, I will give two cows." He laughs. "But my brother, you are always too quiet."

"You longing your home," Tate Shikongo says.

"No," I say, taking another drink of *omagongo*.

"Tell us what you're thinking," Petrus says.

Not wanting to talk about the whipping, I ask, "Who will be the next president of Namibia?"

Petrus coughs and says, "Pohamba."

"Why?"

"He's the most popular because he's the Minister of Land Reform. The people want land."

I ask about land reform.

Petrus coughs again and says that during the apartheid regime of South Africa's colonial control of Namibia, the blacks were forced to live on small homelands that were surrounded by fences, known as red lines, and the rest of the land was given to white farmers. Since Namibia's independence in 1990, the government has struggled with how the land can be bought from the white farmers and distributed to the people. "The whites set unfair prices. Say this cup of *omagongo* is worth five dollars, but the whites ask one hundred dollars for it. The government can't pay the price. There's hundreds of thousands of hectares of farmable land outside the red lines, and the people who own them live in Germany."

"Some in America," Tate Shikongo says. His eyes are big and wet in the light, as they are when he's talking about his time in exile or his dead wife. He's shirtless and sitting on the end of a rusted gas cylinder. A misplaced bone crowns each of his shoulders. The one on the left is the legacy of his time as a prisoner of war; the one on the right, he told me, grew to match it. When I had asked him about it, Tate Shikongo said, "Your government sends teachers, but they should send doctors."

Petrus takes a long drink and says that even after independence in Namibia, the red lines still inhibit his people's growth because they cannot afford to purchase land outside of the homelands.

He takes my cup and gestures to the broadness of the night around him. "You see, with the good comes the bad."

I take a long drink of *omagongo*, sweet and rank, and although I've been drinking it all day, in this, the season of *omagongo*, I'm not drunk.

The *omagongo*. The dry, empty air. The chorus of bell frogs. The clink of wooden cups. Tate says, "Twelve o'clock. Time for sleep." Petrus and I keep drinking. "I'm tired," Tate whispers. No one moves.

"Tell me, Petrus," I say without making eye contact. "Why am I here? What do you want me to do here?"

He puts his cup down and covers its base with sand so it won't spill. "To do," he says. He puts his hands together and looks at me. "Americans must always have something to do."

Petrus spreads his arms and I follow the broad movements of his hands beyond the bubbles of light in the trees to where the homestead ends in darkness. There's no moon. Although I've lived in Namibia for a year and a half, the southern sky is still foreign to me: the upside-down Big Dipper, Orion rotated 90 degrees, the kite-like Southern Cross, scores of other constellations I don't know. The southern sky holds shapes and patterns that I'm only beginning to recognize.

Petrus says, "You've come here to teach, Alona, but you're learning more than you're teaching. When you return home, spread your message. Teach your people."

"Twelve o'clock," Tate cries. "Time for sleeping."

Petrus wakes Tate Angula, who stands up slowly, pats me on the back, and says, "Alona, you marry. I give the cow." He laughs. "*Kala po nawa. Stay well.*"

"*Inda po nawa,*" I say. "Go well."

He follows Petrus out of the homestead, and I hear Petrus' truck start. I watch the headlights in the tops of the marula trees until they're absorbed by the darkness. Tate takes the *omagongo* gourd and goes inside.

I move the oil barrel in front of the opening in the homestead fence so the goats and cattle won't wander in during the night. Walking back, I pass Tate's window, fixed open. My young, white face is reflected in the glass. *My name is not Aaron,* I think.

Inside the house, Tate switches off the electricity and I feel my way through the darkness, past the framed picture of his wife, his diploma from the German university he attended as a refugee, and the mortar shells—relics of Namibia's war for independence—that hold little souvenir Namibian flags. My hand brushes against the hose Tate whipped Timo with, the same hose that will be used in the morning to draw water from the tap. I pinch the hose in my hand, feel the veins in the rubber. *With the good comes the bad,* Petrus had said.

I undress in the room I slept in as a trainee, crawl under the mosquito net, and lie on top of the blankets. I wonder what Timo was thinking before he fell asleep after the beating, if he cried in the hut amongst his brothers, if he learned to never leave the cattle untended. I look at the corrugated tin roof above me.

Their voices surface in the silence of the room: *war, your father and your mother, God bless America, Alona, Alona, Alona.* I'm a Volunteer and my country is at war. I know Petrus is right, I'm learning much more than I ever thought I would.

As he always does, Tate calls through the house, *"Alona, ka lale po nawa."*

"Yes, Tate, sleep well, also."

Alan Barstow taught English as a foreign language in Namibia from 2002-04. A writer and teacher, Barstow has published several pieces about and inspired by his experiences as a PCV. The full version of "The Season of Omagongo," *of which this is an excerpt, appeared in* American Literary Review. *He is forever grateful to the Peace Corps for opening up a new world to him, and for the families and friends he met in Namibia that opened their homes, lives, and hearts.*

ERIC STONE

* *

Tapping

*Being away, with the patience that can bring and the
examples one comes across, can teach us for our return.*

I AM IN A SUBWAY CAR IN MANHATTAN AT 8:30 IN THE MORNING
on a Monday. People squeeze themselves into a narrow box-
car like cattle, pressing and pushing. Eyes are cast downward.
Nobody speaks. With furtive glares they eye one another,
but do not speak. Tension, annoyance, determination. There
is a single-mindedness and focus which I find striking. This
focus makes me feel lost. Newspapers begin to quickly unfold,
headphones are turned to the highest volume, eyes are closed,
hands grasp the bar tightly, with tension. A man bumps me and
apologizes twice. They all look ambitious. A young teenager
girl steps on an older man's foot. She immediately apologizes
and moves backward.

Before Africa I, too, was an ambitious busy American. I
thought myself and my existence quite important. I had so
much to prove and do and become. So I traveled to Africa
in a flurry of excitement, deluded in a maze of self-centered
ambition. I departed a real New Yorker with a real New York
attitude.

Thankfully, I was not foolish enough to think I could make much of a difference. But one dark night I found myself staring out a window into the endless black landmass of rural Kenya, its darkness going as far as the moon hidden behind hills, and ambition oozed away. Instead a need to nurture, a desire to be there in the life of a child, became the only thing that mattered.

I am in a doctor's office waiting room on the Upper West Side of Manhattan. I am alone. On the radio plays a light FM song that makes me want to cry in horror. These types of songs make me feel cheap and manipulated like a tool. Overly produced instrumentals, tampered vocals, swelling strings to make one feel gushy and nostalgic. The secretary, a large-framed, attractive African-American woman, clicks her long pink fingernails on the desk without looking up.

"Sign these papers and make sure to give your insurance number." I fumble through my wallet, flipping small plastic cards. The insurance card is missing. I start becoming anxious. "I cannot find the card," I say. She still is not looking up and now seems annoyed. She makes a gesture with her eyebrows and purses her lips together sarcastically. "If you don't have the card you'll have to pay the full fee. If you can't pay the full fee, you can't be seen." She did not make eye contact and appeared disgusted.

"How much is the visit."

She snaps back, "Four hundred dollars."

"I found it," I say, feeling the card in my side pocket.

A white older male with a large protruding stomach walks out of an office in the back. He walks toward me, is serious, direct.

"I am Doctor Devins. Come back. Where is the pain?"

"Since October I began feeling..."

"I said where is the pain, not when did it start."

"I feel a pressure like I want to have a bowel movement. It sometimes feels sore. Then I found blood."

"Lie down." He is firm, appears harried, humorless, mildly irritated. He behaves as though he is being put out, bothered, doing somebody a favor he wishes not to do.

"You waited a long time to see somebody," he states, sounding accusatory.

"I am not normally in a rush to have totally strange people stick objects up my ass," I say. His attitude provokes me. And it was also the truth. "I mean would you like to be in this position?"

He chuckles sarcastically. "Oh, I do this all the time," he says.

"Yes, but I don't," I say.

"O.K. You're really really tense. You need to relax." I am curled up on a cold steel table with my pants down as he prods me.

"You must be joking," I say. "If there is a time to be tense this is the time," I say. I tried to make awkward conversation. "I like this building a lot," I say.

"Good, you can buy it," he says.

Although he tells me what he is going to do before he does it, he is cold in his affect and manner. "I will put a tube in and pump some air. I will gently put in a small scope, which you will not feel. It is one centimeter in length and has a small camera on it. The good news is it will not hurt, but will feel uncomfortable."

The examination is done relatively quickly but without any further conversation. At one point, he walks out of the room and I feel ridiculous, vulnerable, and confused; flattened out in such a strange position like a slab of beef on a butcher's block.

At the end of the day, we are really just bodies of water and blood. In moments like this it becomes clear and obvious. He comes back in with jelly. "This will be cold, and this may hurt because this will be my finger this time which is fatter than the other instruments."

"I am thrilled," I say.

The examination is now over. "Put your pants back on."

"I feel like a cheap whore," I say, trying to be funny, trying to soothe both him and myself. He did not laugh. He laughed at nothing. I struggle to pull the pants up quickly.

"I am worried," I say. He is nonreactive.

"We're going to check things out with another doctor." This makes me worry even more. "I found a small growth, either a tumor or a polyp. Could be anything."

Theses are the scenes one dreads in life: You on a table sitting in front of a doctor. The doctor looks at you and directly, with little emotion, says words like "tumor" and then refers you to a specialist. You see the patient, or yourself, deflate like a balloon. "What are the chances it could be cancer?" I ask. The second line of dialogue and dread.

He does not look concerned; his voice doesn't become soothing or softer; he does not lean into me or touch my hand like I would naturally do for somebody else in such a position. There is not a single thing he says or does that is assuring, convincing ,or comforting. He seems unmoved and unaware that I am nervous, scared and confused. He speaks to me like a child, scolding and accusatory. "You really waited too long. Really unwise. You really did yourself a disservice. You'll have to have a surgical procedure, a colonoscopy, and have a biopsy. Then we will know more."

I left the examination flustered, perplexed, and terrified. I was angry at the insensitivity of the secretary, the doctor, the cold and clinical inhuman feeling of the overall experience. He told me nothing. He made me feel bad. I knew that night I would go home to a Manhattan hovel with nobody to talk to, home with my thoughts, a tight New York existence, pressured and detached. No girl holding a plastic pitcher above my hands, no empty bowl beneath them. No warm water to gently caress my palms. No mother setting plates in front of me. No cramped, lightless house to sit in for hours with neighbors and mamas and children. No shaky fence to climb. No flickering lantern light to guide me. No moon to hope to see.

Seven large African mamas are sitting on old wooden benches. These ladies are enormous, sturdy and steely, as tough as tanks. In a sweltering room, they fan themselves and their offspring diligently with close attention. Their breasts hang out freely as babies suck heartily. Sick African children. Toddlers curled up against the gargantuan, assuring frames of their mothers. The babies and children look sullen, exhausted, defeated. The air is stiff and miserably uncomfortable. The sun blasts through a small window heating the room into a fiery furnace. Sweat pours off all our faces; women wipe their cheeks with pretty white cloths. They dab the heads of their babies. A door creaks open but nobody is behind it. A mama slowly stands, enters the door. Two toddlers follow her. I have a fever and am coughing. I hunch forward. The women notice.

In Luo, one says, "You have a touch of malaria. You must see doctor first. You are sicker than us. You are a sickly white man. Your body cannot take what we can take. Please, you must see doctor before us all."

The other women shake their heads and hum, yes. Children's eyes never stop staring at me. Children's eyes fixated, obsessed, fascinated. Sick children's eyes, so lovely and so wide. "Yes, the *mzungu* has a touch of malaria. Please see doctor first." They seem to have a consultation then come to a mutual consensus. I am defensive and silly. "I have a flu! I am not stricken with malaria. You Africans, you say everything is a touch of malaria. You cannot have a touch of malaria. You either have malaria or you don't. You don't have a touch of it! Can you be a touch pregnant? Imagine? Imagine being a touch pregnant?"

They laugh and are highly embarrassed. In Africa the word pregnant is never uttered. A woman could be bursting with twins in her ninth month and will not admit she is pregnant. The word shall never form and fall from her lips. The babies could be hanging out in labor and she will not utter the word.

I like teasing them. "Imagine being a touch pregnant." They are howling now, cackling and embarrassed. Sick mamas carrying sick babies, having walked for ten or twenty miles from the fields and villages, seeking medical treatment from a town Indian woman with colorful medicines in glass jars— they are laughing. "*Mzungu* you are stricken with malaria. You must see doctor first. We are stronger than you." One emerges, walks toward me and puts her hand on my head. She begins humming, then moaning loudly. The other woman follows her, chanting, humming, then moaning.

Suddenly they are singing beautifully and melodiously. I am chilled with goosebumps. The children's eyes, wide as saucers, never flinch away from me. They are as still as statues. Waving their large arms to the heavens, they are now praying to God to heal my sick and stricken malaria-infected self. The tiny door creaks open again. The singing comes to an abrupt halt. "Go. Get the malaria treated. Your touch of malaria." They scream laughing.

Behind a small desk held up with skinny legs sits an Indian woman of about fifty. She has large, black-framed glasses perched at the end of her nose. Her hair is poofed out, with slim, neatly trimmed sideburns that look painted on. She has gold rings on her fingers. Streaks of white shoot through certain parts of her hair, embellishing her already striking and refined bone structure, an extra flair of dramatic exoticism. Her long nails are manicured into perfect triangles and painted a bright purple. Her eyes are wide and green and almond-shaped like a doe's. They are glistening and seem too large for her delicate features.

"I want you to know I make my own medicine," she said. "You see those?" She points to dozens of glass jars lined in neat rows on shelves. "I made all those myself. Aren't they beautiful? How colorful they are, right? I imagine you might want to take one or two home because they are just so beautiful, can't you tell?" She is smiling like she just told a joke. The jars look more like sweet candied syrups for children than medicines. I wanted to drink a whole one myself.

"They look so sweet," I say.

"Now tell me," she says softly, making direct eye contact. "How are you feeling?"

I tell her I am vomiting, feverish, exhausted, aching. She writes these things down on a little pad, like a waitress taking an order. She shakes her head "yes" silently. "Very typical. This is Africa you know? Everybody feels this way." She laughs. "I am joking. You must laugh in life in the midst of our struggle or you will be crying day and night, no?" She is smiling, waiting for my reaction, listening. "Tell me about yourself? How are you feeling in Africa? You come from so far away. This is a different life, hee?"

"It is difficult."

She shakes her head in agreement. "You see those taps over there?" she asks, pointing to a small porcelain sink and a spigot. "Water has not come out of those taps since 1969. It is a decoration piece. The sink is used for storage. And you see that light switch behind you? Hasn't turned on since the Emergency in India probably before you were born, 1975 or so."

"I was born in 1975," I said, proudly, but not sure why.

"Imagine. Life is fascinating and so complex and mysterious, is it not?"

I agree.

"You will be checked for malaria, and for other things through a blood test. Don't worry. But in order to assess your condition I must know about your soul. Who is this man sitting here? Where did he come from? Why is he in Africa? How has this place affected him? Have you given any of this much thought?"

Before I could answer she said, "I have seen many whites. I have been sitting behind this desk talking to sick and dying people for over thirty-five years. Imagine that? Imagine that in thirty-five years behind this desk I have never gotten bored one time? Interesting and fascinating, hee? Life is so mysterious like that, do you not agree? I see in your body, in your face, you are not dying. In three, four days you will be O.K. Although you will have a blood test, I am sure you are fine. I am able to see things, things almost instantly now. I now see things other people do not see. It is a sad and blessed gift I have received. Imagine I see so much suffering daily and nightly. I cannot tell you how many I have treated for no pay. In thirty-five years I have only been paid about half of what most owe me. They are so poor here, as you know and as I know. I just accept it. I accept that they cannot pay. I love to help people. I really love it so much, and I never get bored."

She told me about a white man who stayed in Africa for several years blowing bubbles. Another one developed a fever of 103° for three years, but had nothing wrong with him. Another slept for weeks after consuming too many potatoes.

"You are Indian," I say, as though she does not know it. "I love Indian food." The very idea of tasty spicy Indian food seems intoxicating and extremely appealing in a country devoid of such delicacies. The contrast between the mouth-watering complexities of Indian cuisine with the tasteless Kenyan staple diet of dry, heavy, plain food is striking. Kenyan cuisine that merely fills the stomach, food that convinces a person he or she is full and satisfied, survival food, food that sits in your stomach like an ancient brick.

"I am so happy to hear it that you love Indian food. You are multicultural, hee?" She laughs. "A most fascinating word, hee? 'Multicultural,'" she says again. "Isn't that a beautiful word? It means the soul is not alone, the soul mixes with many, many cultures being shared and experienced." She shook her head, seeming pleasantly surprised and astonished by this concept and by her own description.

"A wonderful word. And Indian food is wonderful," I say. "I love *motto paneer.*"

"I make a wonderful *paneer.* I will make it for you one day," she tells me.

When would she make it for me? A doctor, a foreign Indian woman who knew me for all of three minutes, offering to serve me her home-cooked *paneer.* The idea of it, the gesture of it, the notion of it, was almost more appealing than the actual act of it.

"Now tell me your life story," she says.

"From 1975?" I ask.

"As I examine your body, you talk. How are you feeling in Africa? You must miss your mother so much. And I can assure you that people get maladies and sickness when they are sad and alone."

"Sometimes they mock me," I say. "The teenagers mostly. They make fun of me. They modulate their voices trying to sound very nasal. They think whites talk like this. They make fun of me." I tell her this like a schoolboy on the playground tattle-telling to a principal or teacher. I am surprised by the sound of wound in my voice. When verbalized, this sounds absurd, even embarrassing, and I am immediately ashamed for having told her. Wounded, stabbed in the very heart, by shoeless hungry African teenagers, hurt by young women who will become middle-aged women who will become old women, always without rights, without options; women dominated by men, men in poverty. I am wounded by their silly mocking, mocking which is not mocking at all.

The doctor chuckles, leans forward and takes both of my hands into her hands. I feel the rings on all her fingers, and the softness of her skin. She pats and squeezes my hands firmly, then holds them for long minutes. I did not expect this gesture, how I longed for this gesture without knowing until this moment. "They mean no harm," she says. "That I am certain of. One cannot be certain of so many things in this life, but this I am certain of. It is merely ignorance. It is fear. It is fascination. It is a powerful desire to make you feel seen and appreciated. In fact, believe this or not, it is a great honor. They are giving you the time of day. In Africa this is the biggest compliment—seeing somebody, really seeing them. If they knew you were wounded they would be devastated, they may even cry. An African has many faults, many just like everybody. But an African would almost never deliberately hurt the soul of another, honestly. They are reaching out to you. You have much, so very much, to offer them. Open your soul to these ignorant and vulnerable young people."

I struggle to contain wells of tears in my eyes, tears I know she can see.

"Children can be cruel, but these children are not cruel. They are deprived and depraved. They know so little of the world. You have given them hope. The white man stirs up so many emotions in people here. There is so much history. But the teenagers. They are in awe, they honor you."

"I understand now," I say, and mean it.

She pulls my shirt up. "An enviably flat stomach," she says patting it. "Breathe deeply."

"Where do you get your water" I ask. "You have no water in your taps."

"The women bring it. I pay them something small. They enjoy working for something small rather than handouts. Handouts are what ruined this country."

"You must be frustrated to have a sink in front of you that hasn't worked in decades," I say.

"One accepts things. You see it as corruption. It is all corruption. You can see the young people walking around here. They get a few shillings, and they are trying to save for a radio, a television. But yet they live in a grass house. They build their homes out of cow dung and yet they have a television inside it? What is this sense? It is the thinking of corruption. Our politicians have billions and mostly everybody in this country is dirt poor, dying of diseases from hundreds of years ago? Does it make one ounce of sense that people here are dying of typhoid? Imagine! Typhoid. This is a disease from the Middle Ages you know. This is life in corruption. Breathe deeply. I am now going to feel your neck and look down your throat."

"You never get bitter here?" I ask. "You see the corruption and you are making no money. You are trained in India right?" She nods yes. "In India you could make quite the salary correct?" I ask.

"Let me tell you. In India with my degree I could be living like a princess. I moved to Africa forty years ago with my husband, a Kenyan born in Homabay, a Luo. We came here to Kisumu, to his family. Then I went briefly to train in the U.K. I did my residency in a hospital in the U.K. But I was in agony, let me tell you, between just us. Total despair and despondence. People in the U.K., they act so arrogant and so serious. It was so cold there on every level, let me tell you. Standing far apart from one another. Nobody seeing anybody. So I came back to Africa. I make pennies a day you know. But in the evening, at the end of the day, and the end of this lifetime what will I say? Will I say goodbye to my gold and my pennies? At the end we only remember the good we did. It is the good we did that matters, the people we helped. We are not alone in this universe. We are part of everybody else. The tapestry is here." She points to her face and to my heart.

"I get bitter," I say. "I get so angry at all the injustice. I wish I could be like you."

"You have to accept. And you have to enjoy. Enjoy everything. You have a choice. You can enjoy. Please enjoy. Be happy. Learn to be happy." She is pressing gently on my neck, looking into my ears, rubbing my arms, smiling. "In you I see something. You are really a good old old soul."

"Thank you."

"You have a malady of some kind. A small, small malady. But you will be fine. You must drink lots of boiled water, lots. Rest and sleep. This malady may be a virus. But I am in the mindset that it is more of a soul malady. Your soul may be shifting a bit. This is common. But if you stay in Africa you will mend that soul and then it will shift again. That is life. You have to work with that shifting."

How does one respond to this? This was like a scene in a fairy tale, the wise Indian sage giving advice from the beyond to an ignorant, lost and searching young person set adrift in a foreign land. And yet it felt real, solid, comforting and healing. As I emerged from the table I felt a touch of relief, I breathed a little deeper, life seemed lighter and more hopeful. I thanked her kindly and asked how much I owed her.

"You pay what you can pay. I do not wish to strip a Volunteer of all funds and assets. You are suffering enough.

As I say, I have what I need to enjoy everything. You enjoy everything too."

As my hand grasps the doorknob I stop still and stare at her. I want to take the entirety of her in: her delicate face with eyes too wide for refined features, the dramatic flair of white shooting through her hair like a lightning bolt, the shiny gold rings on her fingers, the rows and rows of colorful medicines in glass jars, her stifling hot little room, the wooden desk she has sat behind for thirty-five years listening to the agonies and sufferings of the sick, the forgotten, the despondent.

"Oh, can I buy you a slab of *paneer*?" she asks. "I know how much you like it."

"I am fine," I say. "I am finer than I have ever been."

I wonder how many people had left this small room feeling better, healed slightly, or even completely, without swallowing even one pill. I wonder how many people died in this office, or died before reaching this office, or died after leaving this office—dying from so many easily curable diseases. I wonder how many people actually did pay her. I am convinced she did it all for free, never charging a soul. She lived off her husband's earnings, earnings she found more than sufficient. She has treated thousands in thirty-five years. She never charged a single one.

"I feel a lot better," I say. She smiles like she expected me to say this. She knows the rarity of grace has bestowed itself unto me. She raises her hand, wiggles her fingers, the rings making sounds like bells.

"Believe me when I say you can enjoy everything," she says. "Nothing is too good to be true. Just laugh more. See people and really see them. See it all. See the tapestry."

I experienced the failures of nations on the faces of Kenyan people. I realized what oppression and human greed and the thirst for power does to continents, to countries; how it obliterates self-worth, self-esteem, self-determination. I realized what white dominance is, and how it massacred and stymied a once proud and dignified continent of kingdoms and tribes. I realized the true meaning of corruption, how is sceps into every element of ordinary human life, how performing a simple errand can land you in jail or beaten or raped. I realized that life is complex, that culture is everything, that people are fundamentally selfish, that people are fundamentally good. But what I realized most of all was that humans, when stripped to the raw, need only their feelings and relationships to exist. When money and power and possibility is unknown or stripped away, people are left with their feelings and relationships. I learned how communities in Africa thrive in times of need, and how they accept and love the outsider once they feel non-threatened. I learned that Africans are the most forgiving people I've ever met. I learned that communication can surpass any language barrier, that cultural divisions can be broken down, that honesty and humility can reach beyond borders, beyond race and poverty.

The concerns I have now are no longer the concerns I once had. The people I once knew are no longer the people I knew. The county I knew is now a foreign country. And yet as I run by the Hudson River, I see the shimmering lights of the Statue of Liberty shining, illuminating the water. I think of the immigrants who witnessed that torch for the first time, those who risked their lives on ships to enter this country seeking a better life. I think of the many people all over the world who still dream to come to this country in spite of any hatred or resentment they may have for America. I think of the many Ugandans, Sudanese, Kenyans, Somalians, and Ethiopians I encountered throughout Africa—in the post offices, fields, bodegas, on street corners; the smiling running children who will never leave their village—and feel tremendous appreciation to live in a country devoid of daily bribes and diseases easily treated. I feel profound sadness that the world is so imbalanced.

Days stressing in New York City. Disconnecting from people attempting to connect. Meetings with acquaintances in restaurants that feel more like appointments. We meet, we part, we enter our small boxes.

After graduation from New York University, Eric Stone taught ESL/ ESOL in China, Brazil and throughout New York City. He then joined the Peace Corps, launching and managing an HIV/AIDS, malaria and TB care and support center in Western Kenya from 2004-06. He went on to earn a master's degree in Social Work & International Affairs from Columbia University, and is now a social worker with the Department of Veteran Affairs.

PAUL P. POMETTO II

The Drums of Democracy

"They" may try to stop it, but the drumming lives on.

MANY PEOPLE IMAGINE THE SOUNDS OF AFRICA TO BE THE ROAR of a lion, the laugh of hyenas, or the calls of exotic birds. This may still be the case if you are camping on the ledge of Ngorongoro Crater in Tanzania or staying in a guesthouse in one of Namibia's or South Africa's national parks. In Ouédo, where I was living for two years as a Peace Corps Volunteer, the most acute sounds of "my Africa" were the drums. Every night, there were the sounds of the drums.

Prior to assignments to our villages in 1974, the Peace Corps had flown us to Cotonou, the economic capital of Dahomey, and trained us for three months in the culture of the nation, French (the national language), some Fon (the language in the region of my future assignment), and basic agricultural methods (grain storage being my project). We learned within our first weeks the importance of using only the right hand for eating and greeting, the practice of tasting all liquids before offering them to our guests, and other basic courtesies. We also learned fairly early about animism and the importance of the voodoo culture in everyday life to Dahomeans. This included the sacredness of pythons and a similar respect for baobab trees, wherein people believed some of their ancestors resided. During one of our first receptions, which was at the home of the Peace Corps Director, the staff consulted a witch doctor to ensure that it would not rain on the event. Daily rains were part of this particular season. Indeed, it did not rain in the yard where the reception was held.

Ouédo was located on a dirt road perhaps eight miles from Abomey-Calavi, which was the closest town with a post office. Back in 1974, Volunteers depended on *la poste* for receipt of mail and monthly allowances. Each of us had been issued a small motorbike—a *mobylette*—that facilitated trips to the post office and our job sites. Cotonou was about ten miles south of Abomey-Calavi. The official capital of Dahomey—Porto Novo—was further east, toward the Nigerian border. I also used the *mobylette* to visit the farms where I was promoting and assisting the construction of small, cement grain silos. At the end of each day, I liked to either take a walk or a ride on the bike to visit different homesteads. Dahomeans were most hospitable and seemed always to enjoy my visits. Over time, they returned visits to my tin-roof bungalow. This is how I learned about the Fon people and some of the practices of their voodoo beliefs. I would learn later that millions of people practice this religion all over the globe, including in the United States.

On one of my rides down an unknown path, I spotted a *revenant* (meaning "ghost," in the French language) in the distance and it was coming my way! I had learned about these ancestors coming back from the other world, but had never "met" one up close. It appeared like a small haystack floating or dancing up this narrow dirt alley with high grass and trees on either side. Even though I understood a human was inside this costume, it startled me as I struggled to turn around the bike in the narrow walkway to race the other direction.

A visit to the Temple of Pythons in Ouidah was particularly impressive to our group of Peace Corps Volunteers. The temple was simple—round and made out of clay—but it contained dozens, perhaps hundreds, of pythons. We were coached on how to approach these symbols of deity, and at the appropriate moment, to touch or pick up one of the snakes. We had already been instructed never to disturb a python that was crossing our path or the road. In a car, we nearly always came to a halt to permit a python to cross the road. Unfortunately, there were times at night on paved roads when we didn't have enough time to stop, though some of these snakes were strong enough to survive such bumps in the road.

One day in 1975, my assistant ran into my hut to inform me that the nation had changed its flag. He was concerned because I had just paid for a tailor-made flag of Dahomey for my own collection. Nonplussed, I simply asked the tailor to make me another flag, using the new design. About a week later, he mentioned to me that a few more changes had occurred. Dahomey was now the People's Republic of Benin, there had been a revolution, and Marxism-Leninism was the new philosophy of President Mathieu Kerekou. I also learned that it was against the law to make the new flag. One had to purchase flags that had recently been made in North Korea. More importantly to Ouédo, the president had banned voodoo practices and the playing of the drums!!

The silencing of the drums changed the entire environment of my village. Ouédo had no televisions or theaters; it had no electricity or running water. I was content to spend some of my free time reading by the light of a kerosene lantern, but I missed the music of the drums. There were exceptions, however, including one for July 3, 1976—my twenty-fifth birthday. I had talked with Dahomean (now, Beninois) friends and neighbors about having a great celebration, in part, because they had invited me to so many family ceremonies. Fortunately, one of my friends was the brother of President Kerekou's driver, and I was given permission to have the party. There was food and drinks for all who visited from Ouédo and other villages. Stilt dancers excited the gathering and the drums played wildly.

Though the earlier spread of both Christianity and Islam had banned voodoo practices to no avail, Kerekou made a brave attempt to end this practice; however, by the 1990s, he had dropped the Marxist-Leninist policies, the "People's" in the nation's name, and the ban on voodoo practices. When, in 1991, Kerekou stepped aside to permit the victorious Nicephore Soglo to become president, many around the world took notice. Benin had become the first African nation wherein a democratically-elected president followed a dictator without bloodshed. By the time Kerekou won the free and fair elections of 1996 and 2001, the nation was celebrating an annual Voodoo Day! Kerekou retired from office in 2006 upon the election of the current president, Boni Yayi.

The drums have continued to beat as a democratic and peaceful society evolves in this area of West Africa. In fact, the call of those drums reached 1600 Pennsylvania Avenue, N.W., Washington, D.C., otherwise known as the White House. That President and Mrs. Bush visited Benin in March 2008 was a testament to that nation's growth, to U.S. and international support for Benin's evolving institutions, and to the recognition of a culture that even includes animism as the national religion. Peace Corps celebrated its fortieth year in Benin in 2008.

Paul P. Pometto II is Deputy Chief of Mission at the U.S. Embassy in Djibouti. His long career in the Foreign Service is the consequence of two years of service as a Peace Corps Volunteer in Benin, where he served from 1974-76 in the grain storage program. Paul is a native and resident of Washington, D.C.

PART THREE

GETTING THROUGH THE DAYS

RYAN N. SMITH

Boys & Girls

A snapshot of African life in the twenty-first century.

RIGHT NOW IT'S 106 DEGREES, AND I'M IN MY HOUSE WHERE IT'S only in the 90s, writing and listening to the radio. My host-brother, Ibrima, is at the neighbor's compound, drinking tea, talking to his friends, and listening to 50 Cent. My host-mother, Jarkong, is outside pounding rice, preparing for lunch. She started at noon and won't be finished until 2:30, when the men return from the mosque. Fatou, the eldest daughter, sits next to Jarkong, tediously removing rocks and bugs from the rice. Her daughter, Niima, has her head under her shirt, breastfeeding.

After lunch, the brothers will return to 50 Cent and other pleasantries. The women will scrub the bowls and pots; this time, Niima will be strapped to Fatou's back with a long piece of fabric, knotted just above her pregnant stomach. Fatou and her husband have four children, all girls. For Fatou, each attempt at a boy means more rice with bugs that need to be removed, more time with a baby strapped to her back.

Between meals you can usually find about half of the women washing the family's clothes by hand. The other half are tending their vegetable gardens, a twenty- or thirty-minute walk from the compound.

As the babies finally fall asleep, two of my host-brothers watch an early '90s episode of *The Bold and the Beautiful* on a tiny black-and-white television hooked up to a car battery. The women iron clothes or sort vegetables to be taken to the market tomorrow. Ibrima is still over at the neighbor's, where he is working on his eleventh cup of tea for the day, and where he'll likely be until midnight or later. He'll be the last one to get to bed tonight. Tomorrow, before sunrise, Fatou will be the first to wake, will strap Niima on her back and start walking to the garden. Her vegetables aren't going to water themselves.

Born and raised in Central Illinois, Ryan N. Smith served in The Gambia from 2007–09 as an Agro-Forestry Extension Volunteer. He served with his wife, Leslie Coleman, and they enjoyed baking dessert breads in their solar oven and sneaking into coastal resort pools. Ryan has a B.A. in Environmental Policy from Illinois Wesleyan University.

BOB HIXSON JULYAN

I'd Wanted to Go to Africa, But the Peace Corps Sent Me to Sierra Leone

Youth, snakes, fantasies, age, and a country's later tragedy...

WHEN I ARRIVED AS A PEACE CORPS VOLUNTEER IN THE SIERRA Leonean village of Yonibana in August 1965, Sierra Leone, the Peace Corps, and I were age mates. We all were young, untried, unformed, with the eager optimism of youth, fledglings for whom the future was open and auspicious. In 1961 Sierra Leone had achieved its independence from Britain, the Peace Corps had been created by President Kennedy, and I had left high school to enter college. Now just four years later, we all found ourselves together, ninety miles upcountry from the nation's capital, Freetown, in a village whose name, Yonibana, means "big ant" in the local Temne language. I was to teach English in the village's new secondary school.

A Peace Corps vehicle dropped me off at what was to be my home for two years, a well-built cement house, painted yellow, with six empty rooms, a porch and, behind, an outhouse-shower and a small building with a kitchen and room for a houseboy or, in my case, five schoolboys. Like the rest of the village, the house had no electricity or running water.

I was the first and only PCV assigned to Yonibana; an agricultural missionary who'd worked in the village the previous three years was on sabbatical, and aside from two locally born Lebanese traders, I was the only non-African for thirty miles.

Just what I wanted.

For this was Africa! The Dark Continent. Land of mystery and adventure. True, the secondary bush around Yonibana wasn't exactly the great game plains of East Africa, nor were the people of Yonibana—khaki shorts and trousers, gaudy cotton shirts bearing portraits of Kwame Nkrumah and President Kennedy, and cheap plastic sandals—exactly the tall Masai warriors with red robes, ostrich-plume headdresses, and *assegai* spears I remembered from *National Geographic*. Sierra Leone, despite its name meaning "Lion Mountain" in Portuguese, didn't even have lions, nor any of the continent's other iconic animals. I made a bad joke about this contrast: I'd wanted to go to Africa, but the Peace Corps sent me to Sierra Leone.

No matter. I was young, and even Sierra Leone and Yonibana allowed me to indulge my explorer fantasies, which even then I knew were only that.

At the Christian Missionary Society bookstore in Freetown I bought a leather-bound journal and, in true explorer fashion, began recording my adventures and observations:

October 5, 1965: I went into the bush today with two other teachers and some students to cut sticks. After we finished, and as we were walking back, we talked of snakes. The most dangerous snake in Sierra Leone, they said, is a small, brown snake, about eight inches long. It is called anlofot *and "the king of snakes," for though small it will kill all others. It appears when the rains come; it has a nasty temper and doesn't hesitate to attack. The snake charmers and snake jugglers will handle all varieties of snakes, even poisonous ones, but they will not touch this small, brown snake.*

Tales such as these helped me to believe I was indeed living in the land of danger and adventure. And, perhaps morbidly, I turned to snakes to confirm this. After all, in the absence of lions, leopards, and rhinos, snakes were the most dangerous animals around.

Soon after hearing about the "king of snakes," I was sitting on my porch when villagers spotted and killed one of these snakes that had been crossing the dirt street toward my house. Another time, while walking alone in the bush I came across a grass hut inside which a man had something suspended by string over a fire. Thinking he was smoking meat, I asked him what kind. He just looked at me strangely; then I saw that the "meat" was the head of an enormous rhinoceros-horned viper. The man was preparing magic, not a meal.

I took long hikes through a nearby forest preserve and always saw something unexpected.

May 1, 1966: In the trees overhead there was a large number of bee-eaters. A bird more gracefully designed I can't imagine—slender curved bill, long forked tail—and quick and nimble in flight as well. As I sat there watching the bee-eaters, a movement in the bush beneath caught the corner of my eye. It was a green snake, at least four feet long, and it was moving in and out and along and around the vines. My first thought was that it might be a green mamba, and indeed I later confirmed it to be so. It glided quickly from branch to branch, its blue tongue flickering in and out. I watched it for some time with the glasses, and when it slid out of sight, I rose to look closer, but it had vanished. After seeing the snake, I no longer felt at ease sitting beneath the tree.

I was almost desperate to find in Sierra Leone and Yonibana what I expected from Africa. I took photos of grass-thatched huts, even if all the other houses in the village had metal roofs. I took a two-day backpack trip into a remote area and, with a native guide, climbed the 1,945-meter Bintimani, the highest point in West Africa west of Cameroon. I studied Arabic with a Muslim teacher from Senegal, drinking tea with him by candle-light, and I sat with a local Lebanese trader and drank sweet local coffee. At night, I listened to the beating of drums from the nearby forest where the Poro and Bundu secret societies met.

November 20, 1965: There is a Bundu bush about fifty yards from my house. Now that the dry season has come and the harvest is in, people have time to work with their secret societies. Last night the Bundu Society was performing initiation rites, so there was drumming and singing and clapping of hands all night long, wild merrymaking.

Despite the local people not being Masai, I fell in love with them, especially with their humor. I liked and enjoyed my students at the secondary school and, while I knew I wasn't exactly Albert Schweitzer, I nonetheless felt I was fulfilling the Peace Corps mission of fostering international understand-ing. At night, by the light of an oil lantern, I sat with African schoolboys and teachers on my porch, and together we laughed and told stories and kidded one another, while on the porch of the house across the street tiny children sang native songs.

November 29, 1965: This evening, some schoolboys came by the house and asked me to point out some constellations; they needed to see some for a science class assignment. One question led to another, and soon a student asked me about thunder. I told him what science says it is; they, having listened to my version, began telling me theirs. Here in Africa, fear takes many forms, and there are few accidents: every mischance results from some spirit, witch, devil, or even someone having special power. Here in Yonibana there was a woman who was able to cry the thunder. If a thief were about the town, she would swear the thunder and swear as well to the people that soon the thief would be found out. Sure enough, within a week a mighty crack of thunder would be heard, even if the sky was completely clear of clouds, and the thief would be struck dead, even if he was in a house.

The Africa of Yonibana was good, at least most of the time. Outside the village, Africa wasn't so good. I made journeys at least once a month to the capital city for supplies and to connect with other PCVs. They tended to live together in compounds. Instead of schoolboys, they were waited upon by houseboys, servants. The youths they taught were often arrogant and cheeky. The city was noisy, crowded, and filthy. Theft was a pervasive problem. My fellow PCVs certainly weren't having any of the African adventures I was having, though we did share adventures as we traveled around Sierra Leone together: climbing the Bintimani, visiting the remote beach at Shenge where rusting cannons lay on the beach, and traveling to the diamond area of Kono, where a local diamond trader allowed us to hold uncut diamonds acquired illegally. We drank palm wine and fiery *omole*.

As our two-year assignments wore on and exoticism waned, we began feasting upon tales of just how delightfully dysfunctional Sierra Leone was. Every expatriate had a favorite WAWA (West Africa Wins Again) story.

March 5, 1967: I was anxious to go to Magburaka because Yonibana is boredom's native home. Also I was looking forward to listening to Kent's running diatribe against Sierra Leone. He keeps sane here because 1) he drinks, and 2) he openly ridicules this country he can't stand.

Sierra Leone went from being ersatz *National Geographic* to something out of Gilbert and Sullivan. The Freetown newspaper story of the body found missing most of its internal organs had the police quoted as saying, "We have not ruled out foul play." The prime minister, the Sierra Leoneans called Toadface. A country as awkward and inexperienced as any adolescent, stumbling and bumbling. Even the military coup was comic opera. Who could take seriously soldiers who rode around in lorries painted with mottoes such as: Help us O God, Black Zorro Again, and Shanghai Joe?

The second school year ended, and I and my fellow PCVs departed. After I'd loaded my belongings into the local missionary's truck and we were driving away from Yonibana, I looked back at my home of two years and the school boys with whom I'd shared it—and I wept.

That was forty years ago. The country no longer is comic opera but dark tragedy. Coups devolved into civil war and then into anarchy. Bands of teenage brigands, ragged but heavily armed, roamed the countryside pillaging, raping, murdering, and—their special signature brand of savagery—severing victims' arms and legs with machetes. Most foreigners departed, including the Peace Corps; the government collapsed. While the civil war and anarchy finally have ended and foreigners are beginning to return, Sierra Leone, despite significant natural resources, has remained the nadir of global economies; the 2007 United Nation's Human Development Index of nations ranked Sierra Leone at the bottom.

The Sierra Leone I experienced, the Sierra Leone that disappointed me for not being Africa, was indeed Africa, the *real*

Africa, of ordinary people facing disease and inadequate health care, pervasive corruption, food shortages, and lack of opportunities. What most Americans see—the animals, the photogenic tribesmen, even the exotic snakes—are just an Africanized version of Buffalo Bill's Wild West Show.

I identified the "king of snakes" through a field guide as a night adder, *Genus Causus*: "Although this snake is poisonous, its venom is not very potent and causes mainly pain and swelling. There are no recorded deaths caused by this snake." Death is caused by diseases and people.

With all that has happened to Sierra Leone in the forty years since we were young together, I wonder: was it all just a fantasy? If my snake adventures were just youthful fancies, what of my hopes of making a difference? Were they, too, just fantasies? Perhaps.

Yet without fantasies—and the idealism and optimism they engender—I and countless other young Americans would not have left home for places like Yonibana—and we needed to go there, if only to encounter the real Africa. And there are still young Africans who need to stop by these Americans' verandas in the evening and together tell stories and kid each other and talk about the world not only as it is but also as we wish it to be.

Bob Hixson Julyan has taken a different course than the country in which he served from 1965-67. Unlike Sierra Leone, he changed his name, from Hixson to Julyan, and he gave up his independence when he married his wife, Mary, and began a family. He is the author of several books about history, geography, and outdoor recreation. He and Mary now live in New Mexico, far removed from equatorial Africa, where dangerous snakes have rattles on their tails.

JED BRODY

Breakfast

*What is it they say about a good breakfast being
the most important meal of the day?*

MY ALARM GOES OFF AT SIX, BUT ROOSTERS ARE ALREADY crowing. They've been crowing for three hours; I've learned to sleep through it. I open the metal-slat windows. Twenty minutes ago, someone at the mosque ascended to call the faithful to prayer; this, I haven't learned to sleep through.

Blinking sweat from my eyes, I glance at the thermometer: 33 degrees Celsius. I try not to think about what this means in Fahrenheit. I delay getting dressed, packing my bag with lesson plans and a bright yellow meter stick. I place my stubs of colored chalk in my shirt pocket before putting it on just for that extra second of relative coolness.

Outside, motorcycle exhaust and crinkled brown stalks contribute to the fragrance of the morning.

I ride my bicycle two blocks, to have breakfast outside the school. I pass the old man I pass every morning. He's riding a bike that might be older than he is; he's wearing the kind of cap Oliver Twist wore. He shifts his weight from side to side as he pedals, the folds of his robe flowing like tall grasses. I wonder where he's going. Again I don't ask.

I smell mango peels drying when I reach the women selling food. I'm early; one woman hasn't finished setting up. Her small son, no more than eight, is carrying a long wooden bench on his head. He's having a little trouble with balance. He looks like a seesaw that got up and walked away.

I hear forks scraping metal plates. I lean my bike against the fence and walk around the chickens pecking at fallen rice; some are sprayed hot pink so their owners can identify them. Several students are standing together and eating. "Do like me!" they say, extending their plates in a symbolic offer to share what they have. "*Merci! Bon appetit!*" I reply.

I approach the beans and rice table. Eight or nine students jostle, waving their empty plates in the face of the woman who serves them. Her head is ornamented with a gauze-like black-and-orange scarf and glittering balls of sweat. Her outfit, yellow and brick-red, depicts baby chicks and eggs. "*Bonjour,* Yovo," she says affectionately." "Yovo" means "foreigner." "*Bonjour,* Mama," I answer.

Shoving aside protesting students, she selects a plate for me. She reaches for the mountain of cooked rice rising out of a metal basin. As her metal scoop scrapes away a plateful, steam gushes. She ladles on some chickpea-like beans, the beans that I'm going to eat forever in the afterlife, if I'm good and kind. Finally, she dips her spoon into the sauce, past the red oily superficial layer on which green hot peppers float, through murky regions dense with mashed tomatoes, until at last she reaches the source of flavor.

When I finish, I lower my plate into a sudsy bucket; a young girl scrubs it immediately. As I hurry toward the classroom, I prepare for the lesson I'm about to give.

Jed Brody was a Peace Corps Volunteer in Benin from 1996-98. He teaches physics at Emory University. He has not had a driver's license since 1995.

KATHLEEN MOORE

✴

Daily Life

It's in the small things that we learn the most.

IN JANUARY 1965, THE PEACE CORPS SENT ME TO EMDEBER, AN isolated village in the highlands of Ethiopia. The people there are called *sabat bet Guragi,* the seven houses of Guragi. Just living there from moment to moment took a concentrated effort. Drinking a glass of water, for example, was not something I did hastily or without thinking. I held the glass under the tiny spigot of the water filter while it slowly filled with liquid, the color ranging from pale orange to deep red depending on how long it had been since the filter was new.

While the sediment in the water settled, I looked out the back door at the hills in the distance, wondering how to teach the passive voice, say, to my ninth-grade English class. Finally, I sipped the water slowly so as not to stir up the little pile on the bottom of the glass. When I got close to it, I poured the remaining drops on a struggling carrot plant.

Everything was connected: the garden, the students, the river, and drinking a glass of water. I became accustomed to

the complex routines of living in that grass house and found I
did not want a life that would require less of me.

I awoke in the morning to the crowing of a rooster held
captive in my outhouse so the hyenas wouldn't get him, but
I didn't move from my flea-infested mattress until I heard
the rhythmic *thud, thud, thud* of coffee beans pounded in a
wooden mortar, a soft, comforting sound, a morning sound.
It meant that Demaketch, my landlord's daughter, would soon
bring me good, strong coffee.

She tried to sneak in with the coffee and slip out like a
shadow. I wondered what she thought of me. She knew me
more intimately than anyone; she washed my clothes in the
river, pounding them on the rocks and drying them in the bright
sun to make them clean again after the red dust of Emdeber had
crept in and even dyed my skin red. She cooked lentil stew for
me Monday through Friday; I never ate it all because I knew
she would eat what was left when she came to wash the dishes.

On Saturdays, she cleaned my house and put a new coat of
cow dung and water on the floor. I wouldn't come home until
the smell was gone, so she had lots of time to look through
my books, stare at photos tacked on the wall, examine my
wardrobe and marvel at my kitchen utensils, even slip a little
sugar into her pocket. It was Demaketch who brought me the
eucalyptus branch to put in the sugar when I found ants in it.
Next day, they were gone.

I often got to school after the students had said the Lord's
Prayer, just in time to hear the last refrains of the national
anthem, "Ethiopia, Hoy!" It reminded me of my school
days when we prayed every morning and said the Pledge of
Allegiance, "one nation, under God," putting patriotism right
up there with godliness.

First through seventh-grade classes were in rooms made
from thin eucalyptus trees with a half-hearted attempt to fill
in the cracks with mud. Forty to fifty students squeezed into

each. The only light came from a small square cut in the wall that passed as a window and from the doorway. There was no door. There were no desks, just benches, worn so smooth that the students' skinny bottoms slid off. Most of them didn't have paper or books or pencils. I talked and they repeated. I wrote a few words on our tiny blackboard, passed out scraps of paper and stubs of pencils, and they got on their knees behind the benches, put the paper on the bench and copied my words. I cried after each class for the first week.

Then I got over it.

Watching a child play with a homemade toy car—a piece of wood to which he had loosely nailed four bottle caps as wheels that rattled like those on the Land Rovers that occasionally came to Emdeber—it dawned on me that there were no wheels in Emdeber other than those that came attached to vehicles and then left with them again. There were no carts, no wagons, no pulleys, no bicycles. Nothing rolled. There were only feet and backs and hips. Women and children and donkeys carried everything from babies to stacks of firewood to clay jars heavy with water.

The Guragi way of life had not changed over the centuries. In larger cities there were hospitals and high schools, post offices and telephones, electricity and foreigners; influences that, like thin cracks in an antique Chinese vase, doomed it to break apart from the pressure of change. Emdeber had no cracks except for us, the Peace Corps Volunteers. Emdeber's language, food, customs, beliefs, and social structure were yet untouched, and we were privileged to live in that secluded time capsule for two years.

How is it possible to live in a place so different from what you have known that you might as well be on the moon? The truth is that place doesn't matter. The truth is that language doesn't matter. The truth is that running water and electricity don't matter.

If I had had running water, I would not have known Ato Tesfaye, the man with a donkey who brought me two metal cans full of spring water each week. I would not have known when his baby daughter died. I would not have walked behind his family to the cemetery, would not have shared the grief of a mother who had had four babies, buried two, and was no older than I.

If I had had refrigeration and could have bought dead chickens, then my boys would not have had to put the rooster from Friday's market in my outhouse to keep it from being eaten by hyenas. Then I would not have been aware of the hyenas nor understood their part in the grand scheme of things. I do not like hyenas. They are ugly and make horrible sounds. But there are predators in this world, and I needed to learn how to live with them and not be captured and eaten by them. I needed to know, too, that there is safety and protection from these creatures and, when it is offered to me, I can accept it and share it.

There was room inside my *saar-bet* house for all of us, teachers and students, Americans and Ethiopians, even a little kitten and puppy that surely would have been a hyena's dinner. While those ugly animals laughed outside in the darkness, pretending their hunger was funny, we inside had light and laughter and love. The hyenas gave me that truth.

If we had had a paved road out of Emdeber, we surely would have used it most weekends to visit larger cities where other Peace Corps Volunteers lived. We wouldn't have spent all our time in Emdeber and the nearby villages peopled with Guragis. We could only go as far as we could walk, but we found as much mystery and surprise just miles from our doorway as others did who traveled greater distances. We visited the wealthiest man in *sabat-bet Guragi* who we had seen ride through town on his mule with his entourage of men and boys walking barefoot beside and behind him, carrying spears and swishing the flies from his face with their *chiras*. We were amazed at his huge *saar-bet*, the beautiful hand-carved furniture, and his handwritten books of genealogy tracing his ancestors back to Adam and Eve through generations of Old Testament kings and prophets.

We visited the sacred tree, the center of animist worship, an ancient, pre-Christian religion that no one admitted to but many still believed in at least a little bit. The tree was so old and so huge and so beautiful that it must have been home to spirits older than time and unrestricted by theology. We celebrated with a Muslim sheik, so wealthy he owned a generator and could produce electricity for his village whenever he wanted to. Thousands of Muslim families came from all over Ethiopia to honor him, bringing with them camels that looked as out of place there as they would have at home. We saw the camels slaughtered; their long, bloody necks and heads left lying on a grassy slope while men butchered and women cooked the meat. We ate the camel stew as the honored guests of the sheik, sitting under his pavilion with his wives and trusted friends. If we had had the wheel, I would have missed so much. A place like Emdeber puts everything in perspective. You come away knowing what matters and what doesn't.

After serving in the Peace Corps in Ethiopia from 1965–67, Kathleen Moore worked for the Public Health Department in Detroit's "ghetto" until the riots broke out in 1967; then went to Wisconsin to work in a Job Corps Center where the boys had been told by a judge to "go to jail or go to Job Corps." Then to Minneapolis for the War on Poverty, the Model City program, and finally the county welfare department. She is retired and plans to return to Ethiopia to teach English again—bringing it full circle to end up where she started out.

LINDA CHEN SEE

Watoto of Tanzania

Out of the mouths of babes…or understanding the
sources of joy in the realities of poverty.

WATOTO MEANS CHILDREN IN KISWAHILI. THEY ARE POTE POTE
(everywhere). Like the breeze and the sun and the sky, *watoto*
were a part of our every waking hour. They are the heart of
Africa.

Watoto taught us our first Kiswahili word. When our plane
landed in Dar es Salaam, we were herded into open-backed
Land Rovers. Jostled along in the sauna heat along the coast,
we rode through streams of people. Women, covered in bright
cloths of all colors and designs, humpbacked with babies tied
onto their backs, clasped smaller hands beside them.

Children pointed, yelling, "*Mzungu!*" "*Mzungu,*" we learned,
means European. We were rightfully "*Merekani,*" Americans,
yet we would remain "*mzungu.*" I can still clearly hear a child's
voice yelling, "*mzungu*" as if I were in Africa today.

We stayed at a Salvation Army lodging. In the tall palm
trees around our cabins, large brown bats hung upside down
in bunches, chattering and screeching when one or another
accidentally bumped a neighbor. I had a small band of children

who followed me. They knew no English, so I would point to an object and state its English name. They responded with the Kiswahili equivalent. *Popo* is bat, *jua* is sun, *ua* both fence and flower. *Mtoto* is one child, and *watoto* are children. I was taken heart and soul with their openly friendly ways, and their quick, eager smiles and laughter.

After a brief stay in Dar es Salaam, we were transported to a coastal mission village named Bagamoya. Its translation is "lay down my heart," given because of its involvement with the slave trade. Countless Africans saw their homeland for the very last time there.

We stayed at a Teachers' College for Kiswahili language training. Another group of Volunteers had already passed through.

The local village children were delighted with this second wave of *mzungu*. The former Volunteers had started a project to ship shoes to Bagamoya. We saw many *watoto* in shoes, some laughably oversized, but protecting small feet from the parasitic worms known as chiggers. Chiggers can only be removed by being cut out.

One of the first children they had helped was a boy of ten years named Joseph. He had an infectious smile as wide as his face. We saw Joseph every day. With us, he seemed to find his place in the world, being both liked and accepted.

A year later, when I visited Bagamoya on my own, I found a bit taller Joseph, still wandering the Teachers College. He yelled my name and ran to where I sat, placing his head on my lap and hugging my legs tightly, bringing tears to my eyes as I hugged him back. I couldn't help thinking that we had abandoned him.

Joseph had a sister named Paulina. She was also part of our *watoto* followers. There was also petite, naturally beautiful Kaboko, and Faki, a boy the others had warned us was a thief.

I have a picture of Faki taken on the steps outside our dorm. While most of the children smiled, Faki scowled, eyes narrowed, hands outstretched, palms up with an expression that said, "Give me the camera." One day, Faki came running up to our group to return a teacher's forgotten wrist watch, a very expensive black market item.

The unspoiled beach and crystal turquoise ocean of Bagamoya were irresistible. The first time we went into the water, the *watoto* walked out with us, holding our hands. Only when we ventured out to where they couldn't stand did their wide-eyed terror as they clung to us tell us they didn't know how to swim. Living this close to the ocean, yet they had never learned to swim. We never met any parents, never saw families enjoying the beach or the ocean. Adults were preoccupied with surviving.

We were assigned to our posts. Mine was Ngudu, a village about forty kilometers south of Mwanza, a city on Lake Victoria.

Another PCV, Debbie, had arrived one month before me, and was living in a guesthouse. Our German-built home was being painted and repaired. She had been checking on its progress, and was accustomed to hearing, "*labda kesho*" (maybe tomorrow). It was a phrase we would hear often.

One early morning I walked into town to buy some matches. I had checked one *duka* (shop), and was told, "*hamna*" (we have none). Standing outside, I heard shouting nearby and then saw a bare-chested man wearing a long off-white cloth wrapped around his waist down to his feet. He started yelling in some tribal language. His anger frightened me. I was new in town, still just "*mzungu*," and saw no familiar faces, just averted eyes. I started walking quickly toward another *duka*, followed by his yelling. I ducked inside the doorway and hurried in among those gathered, waiting for my eyes to adjust to the dark interior. Suddenly, a child started screaming loudly. I turned around expecting to see my crazed follower. The screaming child had run behind the counter and was being held by an adult. Our eyes locked, hers in terror, mine in shock. I was the source of her fear.

A lot of children there had either never seen a *mzungu*, except for a missionary doctor giving painful injections.

We left our German home about six months later, at the government's request, for a smaller one in a village called Ngudulugulu. We settled into our routines and, again, *watoto* became the central part of my life.

There was a footpath between our house and our outhouse, and many little bare feet passed by, to school or town. The *watoto* always greeted us, some mumbling shyly, others curtsying respectfully. Beyond was a pit where we threw our paper trash followed by *watoto*, happily searching for anything salvageable. Every evening, we watched small boys returning home with herds of cattle, sheep and goats in clouds of dust.

I worked in fisheries and Deb in forestry. The government breeding ponds for our tilapia were located in a southern village called Malya. I made many trips to and from Malya, mostly to collect fingerlings to stock other ponds. We each had a *piki piki* (motorcycle) for transportation, and I could carry about one hundred fingerlings in a can previously used for cooking oil. On my return, some of our *watoto* would greet me. They would appear just as I rounded the curve at the bottom of a hill outside the main path to our home. I would hear chanting of "Maisha" and see the *watoto* waving to the beat of the chant. Maisha was the name of the monkey I had adopted, and who was very popular. The *watoto* would run beside me, still chanting, close enough to touch me, until they finally wore out near the top of the hill.

One of my fish farmers was a man named Shripolonge of Ngudulugulu. He was tall, soft spoken, and always wore clean yet tattered long-sleeved shirts, shorts, and a tan sun hat. Like most of my fish farmers, he simply called me "Mama." These farmers were highly motivated men and often approached me to dig or improve a fish pond. Shripolonge had built a pond years ago, fringed with banana trees and sugar cane. One day I stopped to talk to him, but couldn't find him around his pond. So I walked across the path to his mud hut with thatched roof. Tanzanians didn't knock, but yelled, "*Hodi*," "Is anyone home?" Hearing no response, I *hodi*ed my way to the back. As I approached the other side of the hut, I spotted a baby sitting in the shade along the outside wall. When she saw me I noticed her surprise, and prepared myself to hear a terrified cry. I spoke softly, "Oh, please don't cry. I'm leaving." She studied me and then smiled so shy and sweet, I laughed. I sat down and talked in Kiswahili until I remembered she probably only knew Kisukuma, so I talked in English. She sat, calm and patient, smiling her understanding as I told her about my day.

We bonded. Finally, a sibling showed up, a small child herself, and adeptly lifted the baby to a protruding hip. I waved my goodbye and the baby smiled. I later learned that the baby, Lugwa, was the youngest of the family, less than one year old. I would see some of her first steps and hear some of her first words. I brought her homemade dresses at a village *duka*; cans of juice and beans for her family when I could find them; and tomatoes, potatoes and onions from our open-air market. I prayed that some of the food trickled down to Lugwa. In time, she raised up her arms when I approached, and I picked her up and sat her on my lap. I used to talk to her and sing her songs; when I hugged her close I smelled the earth and smoke.

I used to think about adopting Lugwa and taking her back with me to the States, especially after her mother died unexpectedly. From necessity, her father remarried quickly. But she was loved by her family and the villagers. She had an industrious father who provided fruits and vegetables grown without chemicals and home-raised fish and rabbits. She had days of sun, warmth, and too blue skies. She witnessed complete rainbows spanning an endless plain, and dancing to the beat of drums, and singing within the village. There were clear cool nights lit only by millions of stars and a large moon, and so still you could hear the silence.

I remember tops of heads outside high glassless windows, some comically bobbing up and down trying to get a look at the *mzungu*. They followed me and were awed by my *piki piki*. They watched as I turned the key and the monster roared to life. They screamed and backed away, but remained transfixed. I would look at their little shocked faces, and playfully pat the seat behind me, saying, "*Twende!*" (Let's go.)

Screams, heads fervently shaking no, *watoto* backing away.

I often heard *watoto* singing as they walked together in small groups, or in huts or at schools. The sweetest song I ever heard, though, was at a village accessed only by footpaths. I was helping a woman make a clay stove inside her hut. As we were mixing the sand, clay, and water with our hands, we heard singing outside. I asked the woman "*Vipi?*" (What is that?) and she responded "*Sijui*" (I don't know). I told her I'd be right back and walked behind the hut to where three small girls in ragged dresses stood lined up all alone beside a footpath. They had short reddish hair, and distended bellies, signs of malnutrition. Yet, they were singing in beautiful harmony: to no one. It was joy, pure and simple, and extraordinary for something so ordinary. I listened until the clay on my hands started to dry and itch. I walked back inside the hut as the girls sang on.

Of course, there was a dark side. There was disease, malnutrition, death, and tears. But I remember the light. I remember the countless *watoto* who had time to be kind to me—a stranger in their world and time, who always had willing hands to push my stalled *piki piki*, drag a net through a pond, or walk Maisha. I lived in a world stripped of greed, envy, jealousy or power. There's a lot of happiness to be found in a world rich in spirit yet poor in material wealth.

The *watoto* especially taught me much—to live in the present, smile and laugh often, to be kind and learn from those different from yourself, and if ever the joy within you overflows, just sing.

Linda Chen See (Hain) was a PCV in Tanzania from 1981-83. Her experience brought her much joy and showed her the connection we have to each other. She is currently writing a realistic fictional book with many memories of that time.

KAREN HLYNSKY

Begging Turned on Its Head

*Begging, perception, giving, and reality: coming to
terms with our own preconceptions.*

"A BEG, *DU YA, FI, FI SEN*!"

"I beg you, please, give me five cents."

Wearing blue shorts and white shirt school uniforms, four
boys followed me toward the market. Even without uniforms,
the Bic pens the boys carried showed that they were pupils.
Barefoot, they wore their feet like shoes, their hard, calloused
soles spreading beyond the bottoms of their feet from years of
walking without shoes.

"*Fi, fi sen, du ya, fi, fi sen.*"

Laughing at the chance for a few cents, they were innocent
of the fact that their bellies would swell from malnutrition
during the coming lean weeks. They thrust out their hands to
me, giggling as they braved talking to a white woman teacher.

With no other excuse to talk to me, begging was a way to
connect.

I turned to them as usual and laughed back, "You give me
five cents!"

"What?" they said, "A beg du ya!"

Extending my right hand to them and pointing with my left, first to them and then to myself to make sure they got the pronouns right, I repeated, "YOU give ME five cents!" Enjoying the joke, the silliness of MY begging THEM for money, they ran off still giggling, kicking the dust up.

In a country that neither understood nor tolerated solitude, a person alone drew others like a vacuum. But what of the beggar who sat alone on in the shadows of Koidu's post office steps? Why were there no children at his feet giving him silent company?

There was no obvious reason that he should be a beggar— no leprous hands or feet, no blindness, no withered append-age. Yet every Saturday, he was ready for those of us who'd just come from the bank with money for stamps or airmail letters.

Because he had no obvious reason to be begging, I saw him as an intrusion—someone to ignore, circumvent, shake off. But as I tried to scurry past him undetected, he'd cry out with his sandpaper voice, "Money, ma! Money, ma!"—the "ma" getting coarser and broader each time. "MAAAH, MONNEEEYYY!" Perhaps, if he caught hold of my unwill-ing eye, I'd give him a twenty-cent piece to quiet him until next week.

I would see the old beggar after traveling from my small town to the district capital—a hub of commercial activity. In the wet season, the clay roads were eroded and slippery; in the dry season, corrugated and dusty. Either way, the twelve-mile ride usually took an hour, usually with seven other people crammed into the backseat of a possibly brakeless Toyota. After one such trip to the city, my nerves already jogged raw and my patience worn thin, the poor beggar appeared and began his mantra. In one of those precious moments of long overdue honesty, I looked him square in the face, gritted my teeth and shouted at him, "Not today, pa! NOTHING TODAY! Next week maybe! Maybe next week!"

Before I could rush by him, in his most polite voice he thanked me. I finally got it. For all those weeks he had not been begging for money at all, but for recognition—recognition of his presence there, his appeals, his mere humanity, and the fact perhaps that his greatest wrong was simply that he had become old and that his children, if he did have children, were not caring for him in his old age.

We began to be respectful of each other. When I saw him I greeted him kindly with the "Pa" that he deserved, giving him money when I had it and an apology when I didn't. He, in turn, always thanked me.

Meanwhile, around the corner, the lepers enjoyed socializing together in front of the supermarket where expatriates and a few well-off Africans bought imported food to remind them of their ties to somewhere else: two-ounce cans of tuna from Portugal, lentils from Lebanon, butter and bottled herbs from England, processed cheeses from Switzerland that came in bite-size, individually wrapped wedges. There were special treats that could only be bought from the coolers in the larger stores of the cities—ice cream sandwiches and Cadbury chocolate bars that melted as soon as they left the air-conditioning of the store.

And there were shrimp chips imported from Japan. In the box, they were quarter-sized translucent pastel wafers, but drop them into hot oil and they crackled and swelled up into the airy crispness of cheese curls. We bought them, not out of fondness for cheese curls, but because, in the utter stillness of the evenings in our villages, watching shrimp chips cook was entertainment. We bought them because they were decadent. To buy them was to claim that we were not part of the poverty outside the store.

The lepers, consequently, had chosen a good place to pass the day. Three or four of them would sit in a row on mats outside the doors of the supermarket as we shoppers with shrimp chips in our baskets and chocolate bars melting in our hands dropped coins into their fingerless palms. They didn't pay us much attention. Unlike the beggar on the post office steps they seemed happy, cheerful even, as they talked quietly amongst themselves. They had a good view, from where they sat, of people coming and going into town, of the Lebanese markets, of the Moslems praying in front of the mosque.

I suspected they even knew who'd made a strike at the diamond fields, if they didn't employ miners themselves. One of them, it turned out, owned most of the taxis in town. It made sense really—not that that particular leper owned taxis—but that if a man did own taxis that he couldn't drive, and if he happened to be a leper, what better place was there to pass the time?

Karen Hlynsky, who served in Sierra Leone from 1974-75, has been a program and curriculum developer for high school teachers and students with a special interest in teaching young people about environmentally sustainable development.

PATRICIA OWEN

*
*   *

Time

Understanding the music of the spheres is lost in a land of clocks,
regained only with patience, and easily lost again.

THE HEAT WAS DISSIPATING AS I DREW WATER FROM A WELL FOR
my evening bath in Saare Kutayel, a village in Senegal. Sherife,
a little boy about ten years old, stood next to me, chatting away
about the cows he had been herding and helping me haul up
heavy buckets.

Suddenly he grew quiet, softly touched my arm, and said
with wonder, "Look." He pointed up in the western sky,
over the heads of a small knot of villagers peering in the same
direction. Between the thin layers of parting clouds was the
smallest curve of silvery light cradled in the vast darkness. This
new moon signaled that Ramadan, a month of holy fasting for
Muslims, would begin in the morning.

Living in Africa for over a year by that time, I'd already
developed a whole new respect for the sun, moon, and cycles
of time. More than once I'd awoken in the middle of the night
to what I thought was a shining flashlight, only to groggily
discover that it was the full moon. Having made its trek over
the top of the big mango tree, it was now blasting into my

mosquito net. And I'd long since learned to time my arrivals back to the village before dark on moonless nights.

I once got a late start from a faraway village. I rode my bike miles in blackness over a bumpy trail, with pounding heart, reassuring myself that the sinister clumps of trees around me were familiar patterns leading me home. Just the week before that, under a full moon, everything had been lit up like a fairyland. I had no idea that a chunk of cold rock over 200,000 miles away could make that much difference.

In the African language that I learned, Pulaar, the word *"lewru"* means "moon." I was stunned one day when a native speaker told me that he was going to visit his relatives *"si lewru mayii,"* when the moon dies. I had to give this long thought before I understood that he meant "the end of this month." The word *lewru* works perfectly for both because, naturally enough, the phases of the moon define the month. When the moon has passed through its waxing and waning, of course, the month is over.

In conversing with African friends about future plans, they referred to *"lewru tubako,"* *tubako* meaning white person. If I said a training event was going to be happening "next month" for example, they would clarify, *"Lewru tubako?"* which means, "the month (or moon) of the white person." Though meant kindly, and for clarification, the question would inevitably make me cringe. It was like having to admit, "It's true, we are arrogant enough to cast aside the whole natural order of things, the innate rhythm of the universe, and rely on an artificial, arbitrary system for keeping track of the passage of time."

Solar time presented a similar disparity. There were no clocks, and having a watch was mostly just a status symbol. For written communication about time, pictures worked best. Often, I'd sit with people who just returned from the clinic with their paper bags of medicine, and I'd make little drawings, indicating when they should take each pill. If the directions said three times a day, I'd draw a picture of the sun rising, the sun centered high in the sky, and the sun setting. Verbal communication about time required a different vocabulary. Among old people, all times hinged on the five daily prayer times. Since we were close to the equator (latitude 14 degrees north), the sun was in about the same place throughout the day all year around. This meant that the correspondence between the position of the sun and the time of day was always about the same. Even if people in my village didn't personally practice the Muslim tradition of daily prayer, this rhythm of the day was clearly ingrained. Once I said to Aawdy, an older man, that I'd be by his hut *"bimmbi law"* (early morning) to go with him to look at his fields. This resulted in a discussion, as to whether that meant *subaka* (6:30 A.M.) exactly, or just sometime before mid-morning.

Arm waving also worked well to convey time of day. My villagers taught me that, instead of struggling for the words or concept of a particular time, I could say "I'll see you tomorrow when the sun is here" and throw my arm up.

My neighbor Mariama loved learning anything new, so we often had discussions about time. During slow afternoons she'd say, "Let's do the calendar." I'd retrieve the little boldly colored calendar that an American friend had given me for a Christmas present. As we sat shoulder to shoulder on a woven mat, she would look at each page, clarify the name of the *"lewru tabako"* and count each date in that month, her finger running over the numbers in each row.

Mariama was fascinated about how Westerners tell time and liked to compare the time on her watch with mine. I knew we had made progress in cultural exchange one day when we were discussing a meeting I had the next day in another village. "I'll be leaving when the sun is about here," I said, pointing over the cornfields and toward the river. "Oh," she said, barely looking at my earnestly positioned arm, "about ten in the morning?"

When I left Africa, I spent a few weeks in France, a dip into luxury. One day I was sitting in soft chair in a big house on Cezanne Avenue in Aix-en-Provence, reading a book and drinking tea. A wave of anxiety pulsed through me. I put my book down and wracked my brain; I had no deadlines, no appointments, nothing forgotten. And then I realized. I didn't know where the sun was. Or, what phase of the moon we were in, or which constellations marched across the sky. I got up and looked out the window to get my bearings and realized that this was no doubt the first of many recalibrations my body and spirit would be making as I returned to the Western world.

Patricia Owen dutifully went to work every day as an executive for a non-profit organization for twenty-five years and then gave it all up to go to Senegal to be a sustainable agricultural extension agent with the Peace Corps from 2003-05. She now lives as an artist and peace activist.

LAWRENCE GROBEL

* * *

Learning to Play the
Game of Life

*Many lessons are learned in foreign lands—including the one
Dorothy Gale learns in* The Wizard of Oz: *We needn't
ask questions of strangers, for the answers lie within.*

WHEN THE PEACE CORPS SENT ME A LETTER OF ACCEPTANCE AND
told me my country assignment was Ghana, I was disappointed.
I had indicated I wanted to serve in Africa, not South America.

Then I realized that Ghana was not Guyana; disappointment turned to joy.

I knew nothing about Ghana other than the fact that it
was sandwiched between Togo and the Ivory Coast in West
Africa and not between Suriname and Venezuela. But it was
1968: the year the Vietnam War was in full rage, the year
Martin Luther King, Jr. and Bobby Kennedy were assassi-
nated, the year Mayor Richard Daley let loose the Chicago
police on anti-war protestors outside the Democratic National
Convention.

It was a good year to join the Peace Corps.

When I got off the plane, along with the thirty other
Volunteers that summer—the first group to be trained in
country—I found out just how different Ghana was. I saw
men walking around in wool suits when it must have been

100 degrees. Women balancing huge, carefully stacked trays of produce—papayas, oranges, plantains—on their heads while they carried babies on their backs. All the officials in their varied uniforms were black. White faces stuck out in a crowd, children stared and called us *obruni*. Mosquitoes descended upon us as if we were pure sugar. Local traders and prostitutes saw us as fresh meat.

We had come from the land of plenty, and it was expected of us that we'd share what we had with those who didn't because they would do the same if positions were reversed. They even had an appropriate saying, one often seen on the local *tro-tro*'s: "All Die Be One Die." They had sayings for almost anything, painted on walls, on mammy wagons, on the sides of lorries, at eating and drinking establishments known as chop bars: "Skin Pain," "Time is Money," "Book No Lie," "And So What," "Poor No More," "Why Worry Drinking Bar," "Loose Your Belt Chop Bar," "Don't Mind Your Wife Chop Bar," "Life Is a Game Store."

We had arrived in a third-world country and were about to enter their game store with their rules. We were shuffled off to a training college in Winneba to learn them.

It was once the Kwame Nkrumah Ideological Institute, where Chinese and Russian envoys came to instill their ideologies on those who ran the country, until Nkrumah was toppled and the communists kicked out. Now it was America's turn, and we were her ambassadors: a group of carefully selected college graduates about to be placed in secondary schools and field positions throughout the country, to help undo whatever muck was done before, and to show by example why democracy had it over group-think. At least that's what Washington presumed.

In fact, we were a bunch of draft-dodging, dope-smoking, well-intentioned idealists who preferred the Beatles and Bob

Dylan to Timothy Leary and Eldridge Cleaver. We were coming with open minds and hearts, looking for adventure and new experiences. If we could pass on knowledge, that would be great; but many of us were unsure what knowledge we had to pass on, and were far more aware that, in the give-and-take, we'd be taking more than giving. After all, we were the strangers in this strange land and we had a lot to learn.

We didn't get much chance to explore Winneba initially because the training was vigorous. There was language (Twi) in the mornings, group interactions in the afternoons, and sleep in small dormitory rooms at night. A psychologist observed our behavior and veteran Volunteers told us what we could expect. A nurse patted our bites with calamine lotion and warned us to take our anti-malarial pills, boil our water, and stay away from rabid dogs. If we ever got bitten we'd have to undergo a series of painful injections in our stomachs unless we brought the animal to be tested. If we were in some distant village, we'd have to kill the dog, cut off its head, and put it on ice until we were able to get to Accra.

The annual Deer Hunting Festival brought the entire town into the streets. It rivaled anything I've seen in Pamplona during the running of the bulls, the Palio di Siena, or Mardi Gras in New Orleans. We found ourselves dancing in the streets with fat Ghanaian women who laughed at us and put white powder on our faces.

Beer was plentiful and came in bottles much larger than the Coors and Buds we were used to. It was strong and cheap and, after a few rounds, you could get very friendly with those more interested in what you had in your wallet than in handshakes or pats on the back. I remember sitting with another Volunteer and a trader who was trying to sell him a Rolex watch for forty cedis, which was the equivalent of forty dollars. The Volunteer wasn't interested, but I was and got him down to fifteen and two beers. When the thing stopped working an hour later, I opened it up and saw an aluminum band holding cheap parts in place. We were in the Peace Corps, but we were on our own. This was the price of admission.

"Have you been warned not to come into town on Wednesdays after dark?" an English doctor asked at a local bar.

"Yeah, something about a giant evil spirit who roams the streets."

"It's true, you know," the doctor said. "I've seen it."

This spirit, in the form of a seven-foot man, left his beach cove to visit his wife on Wednesdays. Everyone knew who the wife was, but no one claimed to have seen the spirit-husband. If he saw you looking at him, you would be frozen in position for the rest of the night. It sounded like a tale to keep people off the streets one night a week. But this doctor said he had been attending a patient on the forbidden night and, when he went to his car after midnight to return to Accra, he locked eyes with the spirit. His car went dead and the doctor sat glued to his seat, hands on the wheel, until the morning. "Then the damn car started and I was on my way." He had our attention; though even with the beer, we hadn't been in Ghana long enough to take him seriously.

It was impossible to get used to the bugs, but you did learn to ignore them. It was harder to ignore the children when they peeped through the holes in the tin bath house, stifling giggles as I tried to bathe with my large bucket of cold and small can of boiled water. It took a few attempts to get the hang of it, wetting my body down, soaping up, then mixing the waters and pouring it over me to get clean. Washing my hair was the real challenge, the kerosene lamp providing the only light.

On special occasions, I did my best to be clean. An invitation to dinner at the home of the town's only doctor was such an event. Dr. Ampofo was a university trained medical doctor, as well as a renowned sculptor whose works were exhibited in galleries around the world. He had studied in the U.S. and England and was head of the Tettah-Quarshie Hospital. He participated in a program with the Smithsonian Institute where he would send them interesting local flora rich in medicinal value to be studied. The doctor told us that he often used the services of the surrounding fetish priestesses to help him cure patients that didn't respond to Western medicine. He never told his patients, he said, because once they journeyed to the hospital, they were putting behind their beliefs in juju and ancient practices.

"You should go to Larteh," he suggested over wine. "That's the home of Nana Oparibia, the fetish priestess whom Kwame Nkrumah used to consult before he made any decisions. She's a very powerful woman, and she trains many others in the art of healing and prediction." As Larteh was only a few towns north of Mampong, and since I had the draft still very much on my mind, I thought it might make for an enlightening excursion into what truly was the Africa of my imagination.

The hills leading to Larteh were steep, and markers along the way had become part of the legend of the town. A large red anthill shaped like a pregnant woman was really not an anthill at all, a man sitting next to me on the lorry told me. It was the remains of a stubborn pregnant woman who was told by a fetish priestess not to walk into Larteh with sandals on her feet. She didn't listen. As one of the chief reasons women came to the shrine at Larteh had to do with conception, this story made perfect sense: the priestess's feet were never to touch the ground, thus, out of respect, one must approach the fetish compound barefooted.

The place was not a tourist attraction, but one of business. Women who went into "possession" throughout Ghana and found themselves speaking in tongues were often sent to

Larteh to become trained in the fetish arts. On the white walls leading to the compound were large wasp nests, which were symbols of good luck. The wasps, which lived in pairs, were lean, long, black, and scary. In one corner I saw a broken toy doll placed against a large black cauldron, where barren women made their offerings. Off to the side were the bones and skulls of animals that had been sacrificed. Inside the cave-like rooms were various carved stools painted white, symbolizing the deified spirits of ancestors. In the open square of the compound were a dozen women all wearing white cloths, their bodies covered in white clay, their hair plaited and coated with a red powder. Opposite them was Nana Oparibia, the head honcho, sitting on an elaborately carved stool, her sandaled feet resting on a white goat skin. Her advisors sat on simpler stools on each side of her. There was no mistaking the woman's imposing presence, and when she saw me, I knew I had to lower myself before her.

"Get on your knees," one of the trainees who could speak English whispered to me. "Make your offering."

I did as she instructed and crawled before the high priestess with the bottle of gin I had been told to bring. She took it from me, twisted off the cap, and poured three drops on the ground before pouring some into a clay cup and handing it to me. I assumed this was her way of insuring the gin wasn't poisoned, and I swallowed it in one gulp. The Nana said something and her advisors laughed. She poured more gin into the cup and handed it to me again. I drank it, there was more laughter, and she did it a third time. The gin was strong, and I didn't like it. If she insisted I drink the damn bottle I was going to get sick, so I waved my hands trying to say it was enough, but she pushed the cup at me and I drank. Later I found out that I was supposed to drink the first offering in three sips, but as I had done it in one she was only following tradition by having me down three large gulps.

My head swimming I started to ask her if she could answer a question, but Nana Oparibia didn't speak English and the woman next to her, who did, said I must stand and greet the twelve women in training. I went around shaking hands with each of them. The fourth woman I touched took my hand in both of hers, locked eyes with mine, and started to shake. I tried to withdraw my hand but she held it tight and words that sounded like "*Antay Antay Antay*" came out of her mouth. She let me go when her body seemed to lose control, and she began jumping around like a soul possessed, which she was. The other chalked women began clapping their hands and singing as she hopped around, her arms waving as if she was a bird in flight. Then a second woman got the spirit and joined her, their heads bobbing up and down like lizards, their cloths unraveling as they danced. Their exposed breasts showed their ages: one was long and wrinkled; the other small and firm. They whirled and shouted for fifteen minutes as the others encouraged them. When the spirits left they collapsed to the ground, were covered with their cloths, and left alone until they recovered.

I didn't know what I had done to set them off, but it indicated to Nana Oparibia that I was troubled and through her advisor she asked me why I had come. I tried to explain how my country was fighting a bad war in a foreign place and that they were taking young men like me against their will and forcing them to fight. I didn't want to have anything to do with this war, I said, but I wasn't sure if I could escape it. That was why I was in Ghana, and why I was coming to see her. Could she see into my future? Or, if she couldn't, could she spray me with some magic potion to protect me?

It was a mouthful for the woman to translate and the priestess answered with her own mouthful, which was translated back to me this way: "Your eyes are light, your skin is pale, you don't believe the way we do, so how can you come to me for help? If you don't want to fight, don't. And thanks for the gin."

I had only been playing in the Life is a Game Store for a few months, but I was getting the hang of it. In Ghana, I would learn during the three years I served, part of the game was learning to live your life understanding boundaries and knowing which lines could be crossed and which must be avoided at all costs. All Die Be One Die, it's true. But there was plenty of time to learn that one.

Lawrence Grobel taught at the Ghana Institute of Journalism from 1968-71. He created and directed the Masters in Professional Writing Program for Antioch College West in 1977 and currently teaches in the English department at UCLA. He is a contributing editor for Playboy *and has written ten books. He recently completed a novel and a memoir (*You Show Me Yours*). This essay is an excerpt from that memoir. His website is www.lawrencegrobel.com.*

JOY MARBURGER

A First Real Job

*Memories of a time before the civil war, before the conflicts that
nearly destroyed a country that is now trying to rebuild.*

I DECIDED TO JOIN THE PEACE CORPS IN 1969, DURING MY MAS-
ter's program at Bowling Green State University. My decision was based on several factors: disillusion with the Vietnam
policy, a need to explore the world, and dissatisfaction with my
program. A question in the Peace Corps application asked in
which country I wanted to work—my response was India or
somewhere in Africa. I had no clue that Africa was so diverse
in geography, cultures, and nations.

I ended up in Sierra Leone, or "Salone" in Creole, where
I would be a secondary school teacher. The name dates back
to 1462, when a Portuguese explorer sailed down the coast
of West Africa. There seems some dispute whether it was the
shape or climatic conditions that influenced Pedro da Cintra
to come up with "Sierra Lyoa," meaning Lion Mountains,
since the coastal regions looked like "lion's teeth." Sixteenth-
century English sailors called it Sierra Leoa which evolved into
Sierra Leone. The British, who took over the country from
the Portuguese, officially adopted the name in 1787. British

philanthropists founded the "Province of Freedom," which later became Freetown, a British crown colony and the principal base for the suppression of the slave trade. The local name for Freetown before the Europeans came was Romarong, meaning the place of the wailers. This name came from the sounds of the constant weeping and screaming of victims of storms and cross-current disasters at the mouth of the Sierra Leone River.

A military coup was occurring when we landed at Lungi Airport in Freetown. There were about fifty of us, and we were herded into the receiving room by AK-47-toting soldiers. We were eventually cleared to begin our six-week training; living with families to undergo "cultural adjustment" and learning the Creole language. The training experience was memorable: the very hot food with staple ingredients of rice, cassava, and palm oil; the custom of eating the food with your hands; the different attitude about what is "personal property"; and the total submersion in inquiry-based teaching methods.

My assignment was to teach biology and general science at a girl's secondary school in Moyamba, the provincial capital of the Southern Province. The school was operated by a Catholic order of nuns, the Sisters of St. Joseph. I lived in a modest cement-block house equipped with electricity and running water. I had three housemates, also teachers at the school; two were also PCVs and another was a Canadian Volunteer. Since the Canadian and one of the PCVs had been there for a year already, they had hired a "steward" named Brima who took care of all the household tasks. Brima had a great sense of humor, as did the other three Volunteers.

After dinner in the evening, we would tell stories, including Brima. Local neighbors would drop in unannounced, and the stories would continue. We had a local "band" in the neighborhood, which would play traditional Salone songs at least once a month with hand-made instruments.

Teaching science to Sierra Leonean girls ranging from twelve to twenty-one years was a challenge. The educational system was based on the British. Instead of grade levels 7-12, there were forms 1-5. The whole point of students going on to high school after elementary school was to pass the Ordinary Level exams to get into a college or technical school. These girls were a select, small minority of the general female population. They were attending school through government scholarships or family savings. Some came from wealthy families in Freetown. Many came from the rural areas around Moyamba; their family income amounted to about $360 a year. The school fees were around $30 a year, so this was a substantial sacrifice. Many did not finish high school, either because of family responsibilities, or because they were married off.

In Moyamba, I became known as the "rescuer of animals in captivity." Local people who had captured wild animals to make pets of them (or eat them) would bring them to me. I would pay them a leone or two (one or two dollars), and after observing the animals for a while, I would release them back to the forest, where no one would see me doing this. I had, at one time or another, a bush baby, a mongoose, a python, and an African falcon.

The students and I also had encounters with dangerous animals coming onto the school grounds: one day a tsetse fly (that causes sleeping sickness) came into the classroom through an open window, and all the students ran from the room. One student killed the fly, and I insisted on inspecting it so I could identify a tsetse fly. We also had a green mamba come into our library. That snake was quickly removed by the groundskeeper.

My most memorable experience with poisonous snakes occurred when I was preparing lesson plans in our dining room. All the other Volunteers were in town. Brima had finished cleaning up. I happened to look up from the paper-work just as a snake slithered under the front door, and then went under my bedroom door. Brima killed the six-foot spit-ting cobra with a broom!

I try to keep abreast of what has happened to Sierra Leone since I left in 1972. Civil war conflicts ravaged the country from the late 1980s until 2002. Much has changed there since I was a Volunteer; there are now websites and other electronic information about how the country is rebuilding itself. I often wonder what happened to my students, and whether they and their families survived the conflicts.

Joy Marburger, who served in Sierra Leone from 1969–72, is the research coordinator for the Great Lakes Research and Education Center, National Park Service, Indiana Dunes National Lakeshore, Indiana. She received a M.S. degree in biology from Bowling Green State University, Ohio and a Ph.D. at the University of Maryland in Agronomy. She is currently a member of a friends group working to return the Peace Corps to Sierra Leone.

SERA ARCARO

* *

It's Condom Day!

The comedy of crossing cultures crops up when least we expect it.

YOU JOINED PEACE CORPS TO CHANGE THE WORLD IN SOME small way. This idea, conceived by the idealist in America, came to fruition in Namibia, in the form of teaching English. You would change the world, or the lives of many people anyway, because learners who were highly proficient in English would have a better chance of qualifying for the university, would enable them to obtain better jobs, and would improve their standard of living.

It seemed to make sense at the time.

A year and a half later, your naïveté is gone; you have realized that the world changes, regardless. All you can do is nudge a few people in the right direction, presuming you know which way that is. Given the high rate of HIV infection (20-30 percent of the population has the virus), you have come to terms with the sobering realization that all the English in the world won't help if your learners die prematurely from AIDS.

You want to nudge them towards life.

This is why you find yourself, one day, standing in front of a class of thirty-six twelfth graders who are giggling nervously because you, their beloved English teacher and newly-minted "Life Skills teacher," has just announced, rather gleefully, that "It's condom day!" You triumphantly produce two wooden penises and a boxful of condoms. "Now, I know that, of course, none of you are having sex now"—a brief spasm of confusion: they look guilty. *Does she really think we're not having sex?*—"but you probably will sometime in the future. Now, how many of you plan to have fourteen children?" The girls all shake their heads adamantly, clucking at the very idea; several boys raise their hands—obviously imagining all the fun they could have producing fourteen offspring. You continue, "How many of you plan on dying from AIDS?" They are duly sobered; no one raises a hand. "O.K. then. That's why you must use a condom every time you have sex."

You start with a game. The learners form four groups and each is given nine sheets of paper, each with one of the steps to using a condom correctly. Their task is to put them in order. The first group to finish will win sweets.

You've never seen learners so engaged, bent over the papers, "This one is second to last..." "No, you must check the expiration date first..." "Which one comes next?" A group says they're finished. You check the order. You find it a bit disconcerting to see that they've put "tie the condom" before "have sex and ejaculate." After a few more false victories, one group finally manages to put the steps in the correct order. Knowing that the kids will listen more to each other than to you, you have one of the more articulate learners explain the steps.

It turns out that the condom should be tied after having sex and removing the condom. Go figure.

Next, you ask for a volunteer to demonstrate how to put on and remove a condom, using one of the wooden penises. Sakeus jumps up. He may have failed four out of his six subjects last term, but this is his area of expertise; he will teach and the others will learn. Without any self-consciousness, he selects a green-colored condom and proceeds to accurately demonstrate how the prophylactic should be used. The class is attentive, only chiding him when he comes to the "have sex" part.

"How? Tell us how!" They feign ignorance.

You feign interest in something outside the window so they won't see you laughing and you won't see whatever gestures Sakeus might be making with the wooden penis.

After Sakeus' condom demonstration, it's time for a femidom (female condom) demonstration. You hold up an empty, two-liter plastic Fanta bottle and announce, just for the fun of it, "This is my vagina." (English class and Fanta will never be quite the same for anyone again.) Luckily for you, Kristina volunteers to demonstrate how to use the femidom on the Fanta container.

The class *oohs* and *ahs* over the femidom's larger size and its two rings, and is especially enthralled by the *fthoink* sound when the femidom is removed from the bottle.

You encourage them to ask questions, answering them with only minor tinges of embarrassment. Finally, the learners ask the ultimate question, "Can we have condoms?" Of course. Although you don't want to admit to yourself that they are really having sex, the façade is shattered when the learners maul the box of free condoms and ask if you have any Cool Ryder or Sense brand condoms, because they "like those ones better."

Later, Ndapewa is upset with you. "Miss! What are you doing with those condoms? You are encouraging people to have sex! They should abstain until they are married!"

"Yes, I know," you say, pausing to think of where to begin. This is always the debate. "But they are having sex anyway. I am just encouraging them to do it safely." It is no use citing research that there is no correlation between condom distribution and increased sexual activity, but that there is a correlation between condom use and decreased STDs. Instead, you demonstrate reality on a nearby learner. "Gabriel, don't have sex. Wait until you're married."

"Yes, miss," he says, while reaching for more condoms.

"See? I can encourage abstinence, but he will do what he wants. He's going to have sex, so it's better that he protects himself." Ndapewa sighs in resignation. You feel the same way. You get to do this with eight more classes.

Most of the classes proceed about the same as the first, except one time the English teacher next door, Mr. Nuushona, enters the class to make an announcement. He is oblivious to the situation and doesn't seem to notice anything unusual, such as your desk being covered in condoms. A learner, in some twist of cruelty, invites him to "stay and hear the lesson, because it's very interesting." Mr. Nuushona is a compliant guy, so he says, "Yeah, sure."

You find yourself suddenly embarrassed. You, who had been brazenly swinging wooden penises around while discussing the pros and cons of femidoms and condoms, have been brought to a complete standstill. Then, slowly, you begin to laugh, because it's the only way to unfreeze, and the class also begins to laugh, but everybody is trying to hide it. Finally, Mr. Nuushona gets his bearings and realizes that something is amiss. He glances at your condom-covered desk, at the femidom packet in your hand, at the Fanta-vagina, and suddenly it all clicks. He does not want to be here! This is not the safe confines of an English class! It has morphed into a perilous Life

Skills class. He was tricked! He darts out the door before you can give any explanation.

But you must stay, and somehow you continue.

Sera Arcaro served in Namibia from 2002–04 and currently teaches English to high school students in Raleigh, North Carolina. She still keeps in touch with her Namibian students through Facebook; many have successfully completed college and some have gone on to study in places such as Russia, Sweden, and Germany.

B R Y A N T   W I E N E K E

* ⋆ *

The Civilized Way

New ideas, even in teaching, never work quite as expected.

ONE OF THE BIGGEST PROBLEMS I FACED IN TEACHING A PRACTI-
cal skills course at Kolo Agricultural School in Niger was
finding opportunities for the students to perform activities
themselves rather than watching their instructor. There was no
problem with the plowing; the school owned plenty of farmland to sacrifice to student inexperience. Nor was there any
problem with teaching them how to de-parasite the animals
because the school owned twenty oxen and one bull, and some
degree of inexactitude in that process would probably not kill
any of them.

It was different with the castrations. It was rare that a local
villager brought in a bull at the right time for me to demonstrate the process step-by-step with the students gathered
around to listen and learn. It was even rarer that we would
have more than one bull so I could castrate one and have the
students do the second.

This difficulty is what caused me to accept an offer from
Boureima, the school herder. He had grown accustomed to

me, and I had boundless respect for his ability with the herd. When he told me that the people in his village had bulls they needed castrated and he wanted me to do it, I jumped at the chance. It would give my students an opportunity to have firsthand experience in using the *pince burdizzo*, the huge pinchers that Peace Corps had provided to achieve the desired result without piercing the skin, thereby greatly reducing the risk of infection. I was also pleased by Boureima's offer because this may have been the first time that the Fulani herders in his village would allow their bulls to be castrated using anything but the traditional method, which consisted of pounding the scrotal sac to smithereens with sticks.

The idea of taking my 7 A.M. class to Boureima's village seemed a good one. By the time the twelve students arrived at the corral that Thursday morning, Boureima had already let the school herd out to pasture, and I had prepared the necessary equipment. We left immediately: the class was scheduled to last only two hours, and the students had another right after. Since Boureima had told me his village was only a short distance down the road, I figured that it would take fifteen or twenty minutes to get there. We would then have more than an hour to perform the procedures before heading back. Two hours seemed plenty of time.

Boureima led us. Although he was an older man, slightly stooped with leathery skin and wizened features, he walked faster than any other human being I have known. Much faster. In his loose-fitting robe and sandals, he moved down the dirt road as if on skates. While I had known Boureima and worked with him on a daily basis for six months, I had never seen him on the open road.

The students and I struggled to keep up. I reminded myself that Boureima walked to work every day and had told me that he lived nearby, so it couldn't be that much further. But he just kept walking. Several students began to fall behind and, while I yelled at them to keep up, I understood why they were falling behind. This man was a machine!

We walked for forty-five minutes without slowing and were miles away from Kolo Ag School. It was 7:50 A.M. when Boureima asked the students and me to wait under a tree while he went over and spoke with the village elders.

I sighed. There was nothing to do but wait under the tree. Boureima walked the hundred yards to his village, which was a grouping of ten or twelve low-lying nomadic tents with cattle milling about. Cattle are an essential element of life for the Fulani, and managing them effectively is one of their great skills. As with the Tuareg, the Fulani had been accustomed for years to living in the desert, never stopping for any length of time, avoiding cities and towns. But times had changed with the drought, and they had settled here, twenty-five miles from Niamey, for months, perhaps years, waiting for the rains to resume and their nomadic life to become possible again.

I tried to appreciate this unique glimpse into a mysterious and fascinating culture. From under the tree, we could see children playing with the oxen, skinny four-year-old kids jumping up onto 800-pound animals. The parents stood by, laughing enjoying the game, evidently impervious to any danger. When I was able to overcome my fear for the children's safety, I could not help laughing as well.

At the same time, I could not help feeling impatient. It was already 8:15 A.M., and Boureima had still not finished talking to the village elders.

Finally, he walked back to where we were waiting and invited us to join him. He explained in rapid-paced Zarma, that one of the students interpreted, that it was necessary for us to talk with the elders and allow them to get to know us before we discussed business. This was customary. Through the student interpreter, I reminded Boureima that we did not have much time. He nodded, but I knew that getting Boureima to follow a schedule was about as likely as getting those bulls to castrate themselves.

It took ten minutes of conversation with the elders in broken Zarma before Boureima brought up the idea, as if he had just thought of it, of our using the Western-style equipment we had brought to castrate bulls from their herd. Everyone nodded and agreed that this was a good idea. The men dispersed and began to shoo the children away. Boureima helped his fellow villagers; I had never seen a bull taken to the ground so effortlessly and quickly. When he was down, no matter how much the Fulani protested that I was not to participate, I insisted upon being the one who tied the bull's legs together. After all, I would be the one kneeling behind him, and I wanted to be sure that the rope was secure and tight.

I castrated the first bull myself, explaining each step to the students as I performed it. They paid very close attention and helped by holding the ropes taut. When we had finished and the bull was released, the students seemed quite impressed. So did the Fulani, who seemed suddenly to realize that a procedure—which had always taken them an hour, caused great pain to the bull, and created the risk of serious infection—had just been done in ten minutes with very little pain to the bull and virtually no risk of infection. They applauded and began looking for another animal to castrate.

They brought forward a second bull. While I watched and assisted, I let the students do everything this time, including the closing of the *pince burdizzo*. They did a very good job.

The Fulani were so excited by the expediency of this procedure that they began to round up every young bull in the herd. Soon, they had a line of twenty bulls waiting their turn. A few of them were too young, but for the most part, it would have been both impolite and inhumane not to have done them. If we had not castrated those bulls with the *pince burdizzo* that day, they almost certainly would have faced the "stick method." Nine o'clock, then ten o'clock passed while we were castrating one bull after another; I refused to leave before we were finished.

By the time we had castrated all the bulls of age, every member of the class had handled the *pince burdizzo* for at least one bull, and most of them had done two. It was an extraordinary day. When we finished, the village elders brought out a gourd of milk and offered it to us as a token of appreciation. It was, of course, unpasteurized milk in a land where tuberculosis was far too common, but it would have been an insult not to accept. They offered the gourd to me first as the leader of our group. I took it and drank, then passed it on to my students.

We got back at 12:30. The students had missed their 9:00, 10:00, and 11:00 classes and part of lunch. When we arrived, I was informed that the Director wanted to see Boureima and me.

Monsieur le Directeur was not an agronomist. He knew little about the agricultural techniques being taught at Kolo or about the fieldwork I was teaching. He walked around the school dressed in a leisure suit, expensive leather sandals, and a multi-colored ascot. He also carried a cane. We PCVs called him "F. Scott Director."

It was obvious that he was furious as Boureima and I entered his office. His face was contorted, and he could not keep his seat. I had seen him angry before; he seemed to consider it one of his duties to yell at the school's African employees regularly, but I do not think I had seen him *this* angry.

He knew where we had been, but he aimed his abuse at Boureima, not me.

"How could you keep the students out this long?" he screamed in French. "How could you take them so far away? You made them miss their other classes. Why didn't you tell us what you were planning to do?"

Boureima sat still with his head bowed and said nothing. There was nothing for him to say. It had been my decision.

"Monsieur," I interrupted. "I'm the one who took the students to Boureima's village. It's my class, not his. It isn't Boureima's fault we were late."

He refused to listen. "You are new, he is not," he said, looking at Boureima. "He should have known better."

He continued to yell at the herder, then told us both to get back to work. When we were outside, I apologized to Boureima for getting him in trouble, but he only smiled. He did not take it personally and seemed less disturbed than I was at the Director's outburst.

"I will see you tomorrow," he said with a glint in his eye. "Maybe we will stay at the corral."

Bryant Wieneke, a volunteer in Niger from 1974-76, has produced a series of peace-oriented suspense novels available through www. peacerosepublishing.com, the website for his own publishing company. He works at UC Santa Barbara and lives in Goleta, California.

JAY DAVIDSON

Who Controls the Doo-Doo?

*Confidence about one's body can be severely tried where sanitation
is not quite all that might be expected!*

DURING OUR PRE-SERVICE TRAINING (PST), AFTER SEVERAL
weeks of staying with our host families, we gathered for
a few days at the town's broken-down excuse for a lycée,
where our daytimes were filled with the routine of medical,
cross-cultural, and technical sessions. The highlight was when
everyone assembled for a Town Meeting, also known as the
"no-talent show."

By the end of PST, the offerings at the Town Meetings
were getting increasingly vulgar, with more and more skits,
songs, and poems devoted to diarrhea and other illnesses. My
favorite entry in that vein—and the only one I can remember,
now that I am writing this almost five years after the fact—was
the one in which a fellow trainee shouted out the question,
"Who controls the doo-doo?" He taught us to reply in unison,
"You do! You do!"

If only it were that easy to exercise mind over (fecal) matter!

One of our language facilitators got married twelve days
before our swearing-in, an excellent way for us to witness a

non-American wedding reception: we never saw the bride or a ceremony of any type. All we did was sit around in a stifling, enclosed courtyard. Then, just in time to stave off our hunger, we were served some of the goat and rice that constituted the celebratory repast.

I was careful to go for the rice and vegetables, avoiding the bits of goat. One fellow trainee had pointedly observed the eating habits of the town's free-range goats, exclaiming, "No wonder we're all getting sick! We're eating the goats, and the goats are eating *garbage!*"

In any event, on the night of the wedding reception, just after going to bed, I experienced gastric distress. I had been invited to sleep on the roof of the home of Stacy, a first-year PCV who lived just across the street from my host family. Sleeping on the roof meant taking advantage of any available breeze, making it just a little more bearable in the hot-as-Hades town of Kaédi, where nighttime temperatures were always higher than 90 degrees Fahrenheit.

I had asked our training director if I could sleep there, citing the fact that my host family not only didn't have an accessible roof, but had a television blaring in their courtyard until the wee hours of the morning. Half the neighborhood assembled to watch it—and me, the *toubab* with the strange habits.

At about 4:30 in the morning I awoke with my urgent need and headed downstairs to the bathroom. I tried to psych myself into believing that I was in charge, mumbling to myself, *Who controls the doo-doo? You do! You do!*

Well, I was *trying* to control it!

I got downstairs, reached the front door of the house and gave it a yank, only to find that it had been padlocked. It was too dark for me to be able to read the combination, thereby releasing the door, allowing me to enter the house. I was *not* able to control the doo-doo. The liquid poured forth, into my running shorts, down the back of my legs, and all over the step in front of the door.

I had visited the house a few times before, and I knew that Stacy got her water for doing laundry from an outside spigot. But I did not know *where* that freaking spigot was. At various points during the next few hours, when I was feeling well enough to try to find it, I groped around in the dark to see if I could find the water supply, but I never did find it. All I could do was wait there in the yard, squatting against a tree, until somebody sleeping on the roof awoke, descended into the front yard, and could tell me the location of the water so that I could clean up.

By sunrise, the little critters that were causing the havoc in my body were fully in control. I was weak, queasy, and depressed. One of the first-year Volunteers asked if he should arrange for a Peace Corps car to come and take me to the infirmary on the campus where we were training.

Wow! They can do that? was my answer. Yes, they could, and yes, they did! The nurse gave me medication, I had to drink a liter of water with disgusting oral rehydration salts, and I stayed all day and that night in the infirmary. I napped much of the day and slept nine and a half hours that night—all in glorious air-conditioned comfort!

There was a tremendous storm that night, necessitating that everyone move from their usual outdoor sleeping places to the hot indoors. The following day, just about everyone was talking about the awful night that they had. But I had finally had a good night sleep, which totally transformed my attitude. Whereas the day before I was feeling that I would not be able to survive until swearing in, now I was thinking, *Only ten more days? Is that all? Bring 'em on!*

Jay Davidson was a teacher for thirty-four years in San Francisco. When he retired in 2003, he joined the Peace Corps and served as a Curriculum Development Specialist in the Islamic Republic of Mauritania, West Africa, from 2003-05. He can be reached via his website, www.jaydavidson.com.

BINA DUGAN

The Ride Home

Almost anyone who has traveled the way Africans do will recognize at least a part of this experience.

THE INSIDE OF THE GREEN-AND-WHITE B&C BUS FEELS HOT AND humid, and has since we left Magunje and began traveling on the dusty, red clay and gravel road. I angrily wonder if the sun, recognizing our displeasure with the roads, has given us a more unbearable problem on which to refocus our exasperation. The suffocating conditions intensify with the growing number of people and bags crammed into every crevice of the bus; even the aisles fill, making passage difficult. Human sardines, we slowly soak in our own brine of perspiration.

Sitting on the right side—the sunny side, the three-seater side—I feel sweat forming into large beads on my face, neck and chest, and rolling lazily, following the contours of my skin. Occasionally I mistake the movement for that of a fly and brush it away.

When the road offers few potholes (a rare occurrence), the bus increases speed, creating a breeze and brief respite from the heat. An added bonus is the fleeting disappearance of the smell—a sharply pungent mix of sweat brought on by heat and hard work, *Chibuku*, tobacco, wood-smoke, greasy hair-cream, roasted *mealie-cobs*, babies, and recently washed clothes never purged of these odors.

"*Hasina matickets*," barks the conductor, searching for passengers who, somehow, have boarded unnoticed and haven't yet bought tickets. How he thinks this could happen mystifies me, as no one (including me) travels without at least two large bags, one full of clothes and another of food. Some adventurous people add children, a radio, and household goods like buckets, washing basins, pots and pans. Women especially carry a large burden, with a baby tightly wrapped onto her back, a toddler or young child passed over bags obstructing the aisle, and a bag of unground *mealies* in a plastic woven bag tied closed with twine balanced expertly on her head. Alighting from the bus, additional luggage may be lowered to her from the top carriage, carefully but quickly, by a muscled loader. With incredible agility, he climbs on top with the bus still moving, using the railing, the door hinges, and the door itself as leverage.

"Zvipane, Zvipane. *Uyai, uyai*," the conductor calls, announcing the next stop and encouraging all people departing here to inform him of any goods they need removed from the top carriage, so the loader can retrieve them quickly.

A growth point, Zvipane has been identified by the government as centrally located and deserving of development, and this status means the town has a restaurant. The existence of a restaurant means that we will stop here for twenty minutes for the crew to eat lunch—a large plate of *sadza* (the polenta-like staple food) with a few pieces of grizzled goat meat and an oily spoonful of green vegetables—so no passengers heed the conductor's suggestion to depart quickly. While the crew relaxes in the restaurant, the passengers eat at the bottle store—dry loaves of bread, crisps (potato chips), cold minerals (soft drinks)—or buy outside from the female vendors—guavas, mangoes, wet-but-not-frozen freezits (popsicles), and sweet reeds (a thin cousin of sugar cane). Scrawny dogs with pronounced ribs slink through the groups of people, heads and tails held down, wary of the kicks of cruel men.

Some, exhausted by the ride and the sweltering heat, return to the bus, hoping to enjoy an empty seat for a few minutes. Teeth or nails in the corners of windows conveniently open Cokes, the slow bending of the aluminum cap producing a hissing that signals the upcoming quenching of parched throats.

The driver announces our departure by noisily turning over the engine and giving a few short blasts of the horn while the loader urgently yells "*Handei*" and bangs his fist on the hot metal door. Soon after departure, the conductor announces the first stop: "Chiroti Pa Chikoro," (the stop at Chiroti Secondary School). No one responds, so we continue.

Beginning our descent to the Sanyati River, a collective anticipation builds and all conversation ceases. The steep road contains deep gullies created by quick-flowing rainwater making the descent slow and treacherous. The absence of homesteads and fields—and the abundance of the lush, green "bush" taking over the road—underscores our anxiety: Why does no one live here? What dangers lurk? What wild animals roam?

When we finally reach the bridge, all heads face out, peering through the grimy windows at the river. Everyone wants to inspect the water level; neighbors speak freely about the effect the rain and river have on their own homesteads. The river, now full and rushing quickly west toward Lake Kariba (sixty kilometers away), resembles iced coffee—the result of heavy rainfall stealing the rich topsoil of unfortunate farmers upstream.

The river signals my arrival at home. After nearly eight hours on this "chicken bus" (aptly named because of the crowding and occasional presence of chickens), only thirty kilometers of the worst roads remain, so bumpy that not holding your tongue behind clenched teeth will likely result in biting it off. Black-and-blue striped tsetse fly traps come into view and Peter Store, where the tsetse fly-control barricade is situated, looms ahead.

Betraying the importance of his job, the Animal Control Officer approaches the bus—large, black net ready to capture unwanted flies—with his blue overalls uniform tied by the arms around his waist revealing a hair-speckled chest and a belly stretched to the limit by beer. Before checking for tsetse flies, he buys two loaves of freshly baked bread from the driver (our only daily source of bread and the *Zimbabwe Sun*). After slowly inspecting the exterior of the bus, he half-heartedly lifts the barricade and, with a salute, sends the bus on its way.

Traveling up the hill with the horn blasting continuously, we pass schoolchildren trudging home. Munoda's store and the DDF (District Development Fund) radio antennae appear. "Musampakaruma, Musampa," calls the loader as he again climbs to the roof. I'm home.

Bina Dugan, English Teacher/Library Developer, Zimbabwe 1995-97, continues to teach English and improve the communication skills of non-native speakers in her role as a freelance ESL tutor/coach/editor, and as an Adjunct Professor in the American Language Program (Speech) Department at Bergen Community College in New Jersey. She no longer takes the bus, save for the occasional fifteen-minute (air-conditioned) trip into Manhattan.

STEPHANIE GOTTLIEB

The Little Things

Bringing oneself into a foreign place sometimes
brings the foreign place closer.

THE SUN PEEKS THROUGH MY STRAW HANGAR. THE THWACK OF an axe from across my courtyard and the neighing of donkeys signal another day has begun. In Burkina Faso, the last thing I need is an alarm clock. As if set to a timer—even though usually NOTHING runs on time—my village comes to life as the sun peeks over the horizon. The people—and animals—start their day whether I am ready for them to or not. There is no snooze button.

I jump out of bed, thankful for the morning coolness flowing over me, knowing that, in three hours, the sun will beat down and I will have to take refuge from its rays. The mornings have always been my favorite, not only for the gracious breeze and cool air, but for the sounds and sights of my village coming to life.

My mornings are all the same. I lace up my shoes, take a gulp of water, and set off. I pass several of my neighbors, all of whom have been up for hours already, preparing breakfast and lunch, washing the children, cleaning the house, and preparing to set off to the fields—it is the rainy season, and everyone has a field to tend to. As I run, I wave hello and pass my morning greetings to my neighbors—"*Aw ni Sogoma,*" I shout as I jog by—"Good morning" in my village's local language of Joula. We rush through the greeting ritual.

At this point the odd looks have subsided, and most people just know me as the crazy American girl that "*faires le sport.*" Running is never done unless one is trying to get away from something, or in playing soccer...and most certainly not done that often by a girl.

I continue on my path through the mango groves teeming with ripe fruit. Their scent fills the air, and I have to resist ripping one off a tree and eating it right there.

I don't know if I will ever be able to buy fruits from a supermarket again.

I wave to the villagers and children who are already in the grove, picking mangos for sale in the market. I pass as the children make their way to school in the morning, carrying their little rice-sack backpacks as they bound along. I dodge the various cattle, goats, and pigs along my route. Passing the river, I can see the dark outlines of the hippos as they float lazily amongst the marsh grasses, and I continue on into the rice fields. The view is spectacular, and a far cry from nine months ago when I was staring at the New York skyline from my office window. Oh, how much my life has changed in such a short time.

As amazing as all of this is, it is the end of my run that I look forward to the most. As I crest the hill out of the mango grove, the familiar cry pierces the air. There is Brahim, my two-year old neighbor.

"Madame! Madame!" he cries as he sees me come over the hill. He darts towards me from his courtyard, his little legs carrying him as fast as he can go. His eyes are lit up, and there is a smile on his face that could light the world. Normally we shake hands, high five, and I pat him on the head...but today is different. As he runs up I put my hands out and up he jumps giving me the biggest bear hug that he can muster. He has been so shy up to this point, and his affection surprises me. Most children—having never seen a white person—howl at the sight of a *"fantasme"* (ghost), but not Brahim.

"Bonjour," he says, the only word of French he knows. He props on my hip and I jog him back to his mother. He pops down to the ground, gives me a hug and then runs back to his house.

I wave goodbye and finish up my run, just a little more energized than the moment before. Happy...content...his hug is one of the highlights of my day...and something to look forward to every time I crest that hill to make my way home.

Stephanie Gottlieb, who spent two years in Burkina Faso (2006-08), currently works as the Communications Director for a non-profit that serves the African Immigrant community, African Services Committee.

BRUCE KAHN

* * *

There Will Be Mud

*Getting from one place to another has always proven one
of the centers of the Peace Corps experience.*

LOOKING BACK FORTY YEARS, I FIND THE MOST VIVID MEMORIES
of our Peace Corps service in Malawi to be the times Pam and
I spent traveling. Hitching rides from our town in the middle
of the country to Blantyre, nearly sixty kilometers away; taking the day bus to visit other Volunteers; and sitting in the
crowded night compost bus that carried the overnight mail
("cum post"), wedged in amongst the chickens and a variety
of small and pungent livestock. And yes, the few times that we
hitchhiked—me with a broken arm and Pam seven or eight
months' pregnant—to visit the Peace Corps doctor.

The ride from Ntcheu to Blanytre was dicey, kilometer
after kilometer of bumpy dirt road (or wet road, depending
on the season). Mix in one Volunteer with a broken arm and
another within a mere month or two of giving birth—you get
the idea. Such were the joys and travails of getting around in
Malawi.

Being young and optimistic kept us going. Eager to find
respite from our first term of secondary school teaching, we

decided to venture out to two neighboring countries for a little rest and recreation. We'd meet up with another young married couple in Blantyre and set out on our first train ride. Our plans were ambitious. We were going to ride the train into Mozambique (still a Portuguese colony), spend a few days at the seaside resort of Estoril, aka Rhodesia-by-the-Sea. From there we'd hitchhike to Salisbury, Rhodesia (soon to be off-limits to Americans), and take the train back to Blantyre—all before school resumed in January.

Forty years ago, Blantyre was a bustling, cosmopolitan city serving as the de facto capital of the country. Nearby Zomba was the official capital then, but Blantyre was the hub of Malawi's trade and finance. It had a number of good restaurants, two British-style bookshops, a supermarket, several better than average hotels, a lively old market with delectable street foods, and a drive-in theater. It even boasted a bohemian café with a rumbling, snorting cappuccino machine. I still remember the heady combination of coffee and spicy samosas—a unique blend of Europe and Asia in Africa

We stocked up on food to get us through our twenty-six-hour trip. Bread, cheese, nuts, cold drinks, and whatever fruit we could safely eat without having to wash them thoroughly, bananas always the safest choice. From Blantyre we made our way by bus to the nearby town of Limbe, which would be our starting-off point. Limbe, in sharp contrast to bustling Blantyre, was a sleepy little place.

Besides a smattering of government offices and schools, Limbe was home to Malawi Railways. The railway system, a relic of the British colonial era, was sturdy, somewhat slow, but usually reliable.

That day, it proved to be anything but reliable. While waiting, we heard disappointing news: trains were having trouble crossing the Malawi/Mozambique border. Now that the rainy season had begun, the dirt was turning to mud. The low-lying southern district bore the biggest brunt of the rains. "When will the train to Portuguese arrive?" I asked a conductor in my best Chichewa. "Soon, *bambo*," he said. "Soon."

Soon turned out to be six hours later. Meanwhile, we waited among our fellow passengers. The Malawians took the long wait in stride. The men squatted near the platform, smoking and chattering to pass the time. The women and children gathered in small groups, laughing and enjoying each other's company, the children often glancing our way, not sure what to make of us. In time, the train chugged into view.

Settling into second-class seats, we were eager to set off on our journey.

The train ride to the border was unremarkable. The train stopped occasionally. As it did so, local vendors lined the platforms, selling their wares; children stood waving or holding their hands out in hopes of getting a few pennies from the *azungu*, these strange white people staring back at them; and women crowded around, many to bid farewell to husbands or brothers bound for the mines in South Africa.

In the heat of December, the farther south we traveled, the more exotic the vegetation became. Malawi has no jungles to speak of: the wildlife is mostly limited to the northern part of the country. Yet the low altitude and the verdant, tropical setting made it seem as if we had landed in an Edgar Rice Burroughs novel. At the time, everything we were doing seemed like an adventure, but we were content to read, play cards, and nap while the rickety train rolled towards the border.

As we approached the border, things literally came to a halt. By this time the train had moved from the lush countryside to something resembling a muddy, overgrown swamp. Any minute, we thought, the train would start moving again and we'd be on our way. As time passed and the heat became more oppressive, we saw our fellow passengers getting off the train, smoking their cigarettes, and talking to one another. Something was going on, but we didn't know what it was.

In time, the conductor appeared. *"Moni, bambo,"* he greeted each of the men politely. And *"Moni, mai,"* he greeted the women. A bridge just across the border, he told us in British-inflected English with bits of Chichewa mixed in, had washed out. The train couldn't go any further that night. We could sleep on the train, and the next morning another train would come up to meet us on the other side. We would need to leave the train in the morning, taking our *katundu* with us, walking across the bridge, and getting on the other train. No problem.

We asked the conductor about getting sheets and mosquito nets. And, oh yes, about food, as well. Sorry, he said, no sheets, no mosquito nets, and no food. The four of us looked at each other and settled in for a long night of stifling heat, high humidity, no food, flies, and what seemed like every mosquito in Southern Africa.

Throughout the night, we could hear babies crying, men walking through the train trying to get some relief from the heat, women talking just loud enough to hear, but too fast for us to understand. Did any of us get to sleep? Probably not. Were we sore, unhappy, hungry, and mosquito-bitten? No doubt. At the time it seemed that we would never survive, but we did, and have laughed about it many times since.

As I think back on it, this was just one night of discomfort for us. For many in Southern Malawi, the presence of flies and mosquitoes was a daily fact of life. Flies carried diseases that caused blindness, and mosquitoes, of course, malaria. (This was many years before HIV and AIDS decimated this country of extraordinary beauty and its equally beautiful people.)

The next morning, we carried our bags across the bridge and slogged through the mud, stopping only to swat flies and squish mosquitoes, for a good thirty minutes to reach the train that was waiting for us. We were anxious to move on. The train did just that after a while and then stopped again at the first town in Mozambique. Its name escapes me now, but we were there long enough to wash up as best we could, eat at a charming little Portuguese restaurant, walk around the town, and prepare for the rest of our trip.

When we finally arrived at our destination, we had spent fifty-two hours on the train. I was never so happy to see a clean bed and a bathroom with a shower. The mosquito bites finally disappeared, and we spent a few days relaxing in the sun. We felt alive and happy, and we were determined to enjoy the somewhat decadent lifestyle of the Rhodesian elite, even if only for a short time. These four young Peace Corps Volunteers had made it through the first leg of this trip.

The rest of that vacation was not quite so eventful. We hitchhiked to Salisbury, the four of us in two cars that were traveling together. The Rhodesians who picked us up took us to their home, gave us dinner, and took us to a hotel. With only weeks to go before the U.S. closed its consulate in Salisbury, we had little time for sightseeing. We were fortunate enough to visit one of the most beautiful sights in Africa, the awesome Victroria Falls, as well the ruins of Zimbabwe.

Except for those spectacular sights, Rhodesia proved to be an oppressive place. After living in an independent black African country, albeit one with a one-party dictatorship, the vileness of apartheid seemed all too real.

We opted to fly back to Blantyre on Air Rhodesia, wary of another train ride. When we returned to Malawi, Pam and I to Ntcheu, and our friends to Mulanje, it was like going back home.

Our students and fellow teachers wanted to know all about our trip. People in town greeted us with smiles, and the shop-keeper at the town store welcomed our return when we rode our bikes there to buy cold drinks.

And what of hitching rides to Blanytre, one of us with a broken arm and the other seven or eight months' pregnant? My broken arm is another story for another time, but suffice it to say that our daughter Barbara was born about nine months after our train trip.

After his stint as a PCV in Malawi from 1969-71, Bruce Kahn went on to teach ESL in Malawi, American Samoa, Iran, and at Georgia Tech. He has been a technical editor at IBM in Atlanta since 1984. When not editing technical documents, Kahn is an avid crossword puzzler. He has attended the American Crossword Puzzle Tournament since 1997 and has played the on-air puzzle with Will Shortz and Lianne Hansen on NPR's Morning Edition Sunday.

SHAUNA STEADMAN

*

The Hammam in Rabat

Getting down to basics in Morocco.

RABAT WAS ONLY A FEW DAYS OLD TO ME. I WAS WORKING UP
the courage to leave the security of the training-site hotel and
venture out alone into the streets of *djellaba*-clad men and
veiled women in Morocco's capital. I needed to call my children and grandchildren to let them know that I had arrived
safely in the country that was to be my home base for the next
twenty-seven months.

There was no phone at the house of my host family. There
were, however, strange beds, loud prayer calls five times a day,
several pastel-colored chickens, and lots of foods that I had
never eaten before. The chicks were le Eid gifts. The food,
it seemed, was for startling my palate. I was roommates with
Jackie, a fellow PCVer from Puerto Rico who spoke French
well. She was my language savior.

Around the corner, Kumi was in the same fix as I, an older
Volunteer with minimal language skills. Our host families were
related somehow, so we often spent time together. The second
week in country, our "hosties" decided we needed to visit the

305

hammam, since there was no way to adequately bathe in the
houses.

It was an 80-degree day in late September, in Africa. We
left our houses wrapped in American street clothes, Moroccan
djellaba, veils, heavy coats, scarves, and we carried towels on
our arms. We were told that we would catch cold after the
bath if not well prepared. We carried baby-scaled plastic stools,
plastic buckets, soaps, shampoos made out of some kind of tree
sap, scrubbers and extra underwear. And trepidation.

A traditional Arabic hammam is a communal building with
a dressing hall and three rooms. There are no dressing stalls.
The rooms get progressively hotter as you slip and slide further
into the abyss. Around the perimeter of each room there is an
iron pipe with spigots that dispense cold water every two feet.
The pipe is about twenty-four inches from the floor, so you
have to sit. The hot water is poured from another spigot into
the bucket that you bring with you.

You eliminate any unnecessary items in the dressing room,
arriving at the first room naked. Genders are given opposing
days for bathing, except for boys under the age of seven or so,
who come with their mothers.

It didn't take Kumi and me long to understand that this
was going to be an adventure. Kumi is Korean: olive skin,
brown eyes, and black hair. I am Scandinavian: ice white skin,
blue eyes, and red hair everywhere. I definitely felt the brown
eyes of every Arabic African upon me. There are not many
Scandinavians in Morocco.

Turns out that there weren't enough stools or buckets to
go around for our group of four adults and several children.
Kumi and I would have to sit directly on the cement floor. I
envisioned all sorts of exotic infections in the making.

I ended up in the dunce seat, manning the filling of the
bucket position near the one "hot" spigot. The room was

packed and the buckets were coming at me like Lucy on the chocolate conveyor belt. Oooooh good.

I remembered gym class showers during junior high with little fondness. This, too, was turning out to be the mother of embarrassment. Our host families and their relatives were getting quite a kick out of this situation. Kumi was just trying to get herself washed up so we could get OUT of there. AND the buckets kept coming.

I have sailed a bit and I understand water dynamics a little, so I invented a game. I could use the hydroplane of the soaked floor to "sail" the filled, rounded-bottom buckets to the prospective bather, thus eliminating the line of inquiring eyes standing over me. I began a sort of ice curling technique that quickly caught on.

Kumi and I soon found that our new friends had forgotten that we were strangers and were enjoying the game. In fact, our ranks had swollen, drawing from the population in the other rooms. Soon, the laughter was dispelling any myths about "them" and "us."

I was able to get washed up and "spa-ed" back together. In the process, I learned some culture, broke some taboos, and lightened up a tense situation. Our bodies were steaming when we left the hammam, and our hearts were full. Still, I never visited the hammams much after that. I learned how to take sponge baths at home until I got an apartment at my site in Essaouira. My first month there, I made a shower out of plastic tubing and a plastic tablecloth material that rose in splendor over the outlet of my Turkish toilet.

Shauna Steadman served as a Peace Corps Volunteer in Morocco from 2003-05.

PAUL NEGLEY, JR.

Straight Razors in Heaven

*New experiences can also be small experiences—
but that makes them no less satisfying.*

LOUIS ARMSTRONG SAYS IN A SONG THAT, WHEN HE DIES, HE wants to be buried in straight lace shoes and a Stetson hat, with a twenty dollar gold piece in his watch chain. He did not ask to be shaved. What the Great Satchmo knew, and I just learned, is that there are straight razors in heaven. So put on your best clothes, get all pretty, and get shaved by the blessed.

I got a haircut yesterday, in what would be an old-fashioned barber shop back in the United States. Here, it is the only way to get one's hair cut. The place has the feel of an all-guys sports bar with long black leather sofas and cigarettes.

A big jolly fellow with crooked eyes greeted me. He was polite and gave me an excellent haircut. He even compli-mented me on my hair, saying that no one in Morocco could know how to cut it except him. I believe him, too. This was the first good haircut I've gotten in Morocco! He said, "No trimmers, scissors only, is the way to make it look nice."

I felt a little pampered and admired. As he perfected a side slant to give me a fresh look, he asked, "Would you like a shave?" He noticed that I had a four-day beard and was weathered from the six-hour bus trip to Agadir.

I am open to new experiences, but a man who can only see out of part of one eye, who looks at me sideways to see me straight?

Having four inches of the sharpest knife known to man held next to my neck by him caused only a brief hesitation.

He lathered me up with a brush and the thickest shaving cream I have ever felt. I felt like a car soaped up and pushed through an automatic wash. That brush tickled and hurt, then teased me and lied to me. When he was done with the lather, I didn't think it could get any better; I had relived every relationship I had had in the last ten years.

Then he pulled the razor out. An old grandfather of a beauty, it had an ivory-colored handle. I thought "Please God, be gentle." I was nervous; it was my first time.

Though I like to flirt with danger, this was no philanderer. I was marrying this guy, trusting him with my life with that blade to my face.

With the first touch, I flinched deep in my heart, but my face was as still as butter. The second slice, and I entered into a garden of no fear. "I can control my fear, use it, manipulate it, make it disappear." The third took me out of my trance; I knew that I could not master my fear as he could not master my cleft chin. It had taken me nearly five years to learn intricate art of "clefting."

He nailed it with perfect form.

He turned down for the neck. A slip of the wrist and life's end comes. The headline in the *Post*: "Moroccan Barber Terrorist Murders American Peace Worker." Then, like the initial warm relief of urinating in your pants, I achieved total nirvana. I was enlightened.

He finished and the guilt set in. I really did feel like the boy who peed his pants. "What do I do now?" I begged in my thoughts. "Do I promise to come back?" The barber smiled, "Like new" he said to the daunting image in the mirror. I *was* new.

My God, I was beautiful, shaved. I leaned into the mirror, amazed, breathless. I reminded myself of the monkey who sees his image and doesn't recognize it. Only I was attacking the mirror in narcissism, not fear, staring in utter disbelief that I could be so attractive.

After a few minutes, maybe hours, the blessed barber took notice and asked, "Would you like some cologne?" My mind raced: "Yes, of course, I want cologne. Spray me down because I am going out tonight, pretty face."

He sprays it on his hands and, bam, a fiery slap on the face. My eyes watering, the image in the mirror blurs then melts away and a crying little boy remains. When I sober up from the aftershave, the barber is holding my hand. He gently lifts me from the chair and sets me on the sofa. I am a baby in his mother's arms. I am confused, bewildered, but all trusting.

"Stay for some tea," my mother says, and I snooze and drool in my newborn warmth.

A baby doesn't anticipate that every experience will be new and amazing, it just is. A twenty-five year old getting a haircut doesn't expect to be reborn.

If you have never been shaved with a straight razor, I am a jealous riot of envy for that first experience to come. So, when I die bury me in straight lace shoes, a Stetson, a twenty dollar gold piece for my watch chain, but don't you shave me. That last shave will come from an old grandfather straight razor in heaven.

Paul Negley Jr., a PCV in Morocco from 2004 to 2006, pursued two master's in International Affairs and Natural Resources Sustainable Development at American University and UN University for Peace (Costa Rica). Presently, he works in Pech Valley, Afghanistan with USAID.

JANET GRACE RIEHL

* *
*

Big Butts Are Beautiful!

Our styles, and the way we view ourselves, can change dramatically when we learn to see with the eyes of another culture.

Naledi was my name in Botswana. When I arrived, I had asked my language teachers for a Setswana name. They said, all right, but it's not something casual to give a name. It's not something we can do on the spot or even overnight. They told me, "We'll keep our eyes on you, and think about it for awhile, and then let you know what your name is."

Every week I'd ask how my name was coming. They'd say, "Wait a little longer."

One week they came in and said, "We've got your name. It's Naledi."

I asked, "What does that mean?"

"It means 'Star,'" they said, "and that's how we feel about you." Which was a good thing. But Naledi is not an exotic name in Botswana. It's not any more unusual than Susan or Mary would be in the United States. The good thing about my name being Naledi was that there are so many beautiful songs heralding and celebrating the stars, *naledi*. As I walked around the village, children sang these songs to me. Being serenaded wakes a body up. In Africa, you don't have to be standing on a balcony, either.

Now, I'm going to teach you one of these songs. It's a call and response song—the most common pattern in Africa. It means, "Star, star...star of the morning. Wake-up!"

Naledi.

Naledi. [Echo]

Naledi.

Naledi. [Echo]

Naledi ya mosong.

Tsogong.

Not only did I get a new name in Botswana, but I changed the way I felt about my body. You see, I come from a long line of women with big buttocks. You all know what it means to have big buttocks in the United States, where we grow up thinking you have to have a big bosom to be beautiful. Makes it kind of hard on us gals that are bigger South of the border than North.

But, fortunately, in my early twenties, I struck the body-image sweepstakes and got my measurements imported to Africa—first to Botswana and later to Ghana. In these countries, a woman's large buttocks are lavishly and openly admired.

I'll never forget the day in Botswana when this first happened to me. I walked through the village minister's compound, and he launched into a litany of praise about my big buttocks in Setswana that set my ears on fire:

Minister: *Nalediway!*

Myself: *Ke nna, Rra. [That's me, Sir.]*

Minister: *Nalediway! Maraho waharho wa atona mahomasway.* *[Your buttocks are amazingly big.]*

Myself: *Maraho wame, Rra? Ow!*

[My buttocks? Oh, goodness, gracious.]

Minister: *Eeee, Mma. Maraho waharho wamouncle taaaaata!*
[Yes, Ma'm. Your buttocks are incredibly beautiful.]
Myself: *Keitumetsi, Rra. [Thank you, sir.]*

"It's true, Naledi," said his more understated wife as she awarded some love pats to my rear end. "Your buttocks are traditionally built—just like a Motswana woman! *O Motswana tota!*"

I cast a look around behind me with an increased appreciation of what I'd been carting around back there all my life. The feeling grew that I had something good going on behind me. It was the secret side of me that I couldn't fully appreciate because I could only see my buttocks in stillness reflected in a mirror, not in motion, as those around me did.

This feeling of secret wealth was reinforced when I bicycled fifteen miles over deep sand tracks between the village to the capital city. I'm not talking blacktop, here. I'm not talking gravel. I'm not even talking dirt. I'm talking sand. My bike was a balloon-tired bike with no gearshifts on it. Has anyone ever ridden a bike like that recently? I'm talking about the bikes with the fat, fat tires. I stood up to pump, of course, in order to cut through the track. With every downward stroke, the tires sunk down into the sand something like four inches.

Villagers working out on their lands stopped to lean on their hoes to view my buttock muscles straining against the fabric of my long, traditional skirt. Then, all along my bicycle route, as if by prearrangement, whole farming families waved and greeted me with the same chant of appreciation the minister and his wife had showered on my previously unnoticed buttocks:

Nalediway!
Maraho waharho wa atona mahomasway.
Maraho waharho wamouncle taaaaata!

That is how I came to know that big butts are beautiful, and that mine is just as beautiful as any others.

Some of you have big butts like me and some of you, well, we'd have to send out a search party to find your butt, it's so small. But, no matter what size your butt is, we can be happy we have this precious treasure. We can all feel like stars, right here in this heaven on earth. Ladies, *Bo-Ma*, show your gents what you've got. Strut your stuff just a bit. Remember, your butt is beautiful, especially if it's a big one.

Janet Grace Riehl served in Botswana from 1972-73 where she taught English as a second language. She is an award-winning author, speaker, and creativity coach. Her down-home family love story beyond death is Sightlines: A Poet's Diary. *Her poems, stories, and essays are published in national literary magazines and in three anthologies. Janet currently struts her stuff in St. Louis, Missouri where she shakes it up with class.*

BOB WALKER

Monsieur Robert Loves Rats

Little slips can have odd consequences!

IT PROMISED TO BE A LONG MOTORCYCLE RIDE TO THE VILLAGE where I would be working that day. It was barely dawn when I finished my breakfast, but the rhythmic, earthen *thump* of a woman pounding cassava flour, punctuated by an occasional rooster call from the village on the hill above our house, signaled that others were also beginning their morning. I broke the still of the dawn, kicking over my motorcycle's engine and accelerating past our bamboo gate into the fog.

Before coming to Zaire, I never knew how cold it got in the mornings of dry season. The chill air rushing past as I negotiated the rutted, red-clay roads made my hands stiff and uncomfortable. My wife and I occupied a double post, each working with our own fish farmers, but we had worked out a strategy where, every few months, we switched to see how our partner's work was progressing. It was a beneficial way to critique and lend perspective to each other. Today, I would be visiting some of my wife's farmers at the far end of our post, so I had made an early start on what promised to be a tiring day.

Relieved to arrive after a physical, forty-minute ride, I turned off the main road and was greeted by a cacophony of children. Having heard my motorcycle from a long way off, they had assembled in typical large numbers. They scrambled to keep up, running perilously close alongside, laughing with excitement as I attempted to maintain control in the deep, soft sand of the village's central thoroughfare. Finally stopping at one of our farmer's houses, I stepped off with a wall of smiling kids' faces tightly crowded around me. Adults pressed through the throng to greet me while a wizened village elder swatted at children with a short stick, attempting to clear space for me to move.

"*Niama!*" the thin old man scolded, referring to the children as insects. He clucked through his teeth in disgust, ineffectually swinging his stick as the kids laughed and playfully dodged. When the other adults joined the effort to disperse them, they gradually moved away to a respectful distance. A circle of local neighbors, the village elder, and fish farmers replaced the children; all had out-stretched hands ready to shake. Many gripped their right forearm with their left hand in emphasis of earnestness and respect intended by their greeting.

Shaking hands, I took care not to miss one, and to pay attention to the elder, acknowledging the respect owed him. Subsequently, a chair was produced and a glass of water, and I was encouraged to sit and drink. After an appropriate pause, I said, "We have much work to do at the ponds, and if the farmers will assemble, we should go immediately into the forest to visit their work." I knew that there would be plenty of time in the village spent eating, drinking and socializing; I didn't wish to lose the cool morning hours.

Hiking down from the village into the forested valley, we arrived pond-side. I began to review the list of daily tasks so important to successfully raising an abundance of large fish in the six months from stocking to harvest. Feeding the fish, cutting the grass, adding compost, keeping the overflow pipes clear—a farmer's diligence to routine completion of these and other tasks was the key to a rewarding harvest. There is no better teacher than good example, so I worked along side the farmers. Grabbing a narrow bamboo pole lying near the bank, I inserted it into one of the overflow pipes at the top of the dike. Overflow pipes allowed rainfall accumulation to harmlessly exit the pond, maintaining an appropriate level. A blocked pipe would allow floodwater to pass over the top of the dike, eroding it and potentially blowing out the pond.

Immediately there was a cry of "*MPUKU!*" as farmers scrambled, machetes in hand, eager to dispatch the family of rats that emerged from the pipe. A young nephew was ordered into the forest to collect large leaves, and the freshly killed rodents were bound in neat, green little packages for easy transport back to the village.

That was when I made the *faux pas* I would regret for the rest of my service.

Thinking of my cat and how much she would appreciate a nice rat-meal, I thought to ask if I could take some home. "Could I have those to take home for my..." I started to ask.

Well, the truth was that I wasn't thinking, because otherwise I would have realized that this prized catch was valued protein destined make a welcomed meal for the farmer's family. And here I was, stupidly asking to take some home to my cat! Thankfully, I realize my mistake mid–sentence. But how would I explain that I had changed my mind?

It turned out that I wouldn't have a chance to explain. The farmers seized onto the idea that I must absolutely love rats. "Oh, Monsieur Robert loves rats! We are going to bring these up to the village and eat them together because you love them so much!"

There was no escaping what had now become a social obligation, so I made the best show I could of graciously enjoying my rat-meal.

As I was saying goodbye to return to my house that afternoon, a tight, leaf-green rat-package was pressed into my hand to "take home to my wife to enjoy." Every time in the months to come that I visited this village, I knew in advance that I would be served a proper rat-meal. After all, everyone knew how much, "Monsieur Robert loves rats."

Bob Walker and his wife Tina served as Peace Corps fisheries agents in Zaire from 1987–89. Living and working in a remote village, they spent the first two amazing years of their marriage without telephone, electricity or running water, but lacking nothing of importance. Today they are raising two kids in the Washington D.C. area.

DANIEL FRANKLIN

Imani

The friends we make and lose comfort us and teach us—
and allow us to learn even the saddest lessons.

MY EARLY DAYS IN BASMA WERE NOT EASY. BASMA, A TRADI-
tional village of subsistence farmers located in northern
Burkina Faso, is not located on any maps. Directions invariably
include instructions to "turn off the dirt road." Life in Basma
is barely changed from centuries ago; people live their whole
lives without ever seeing a traffic light or having a cold drink
on a hot day.

Upon my arrival in September of 2001, I was proud of the
progress I'd made in French during training, only to find that,
outside of a handful of people who'd attended elementary
school in a neighboring village, nobody could even say *bonjour*.

Villagers comforted me after the events of September 11th
(news of which reached Basma on September 14th) by assuring me that it could not have happened: 110-story buildings
simply do not exist.

I had expected the first weeks to be difficult. But when
weeks turned to months and things didn't improve, I began to
lose faith—in my program, in my village, and most of all, in

myself. Though my Mooré (the local language) was improving, progress was slow. I sensed that my village was nearly as frustrated with me as I was. I was adding nothing to the village, and didn't feel that I was getting anything from it other than nonstop diarrhea.

Why had I volunteered for this?

Just as I was on the verge of giving up, I found Imani.

When I found her, just weeks after her birth, Imani had been separated from her mother. I almost didn't see her: a tiny, abandoned puppy shivering next to a baobab tree despite the powerful mid-day sun. I could sense her fear, confusion, and utter sense of aloneness. I understood it exactly.

I had long ago given up pretensions of saving the world, but at least I could save one helpless animal. I had my mission.

Imani is the Swahili word for faith. I chose it not only because I thought it was a beautiful name, but also because it was one the villagers could pronounce. I had already lived in the isolation of my village for over three months, but it was Imani's presence in my hut that finally created the home for which I'd longed. Before Imani, long days spent struggling to communicate and trying to find my place in the village were followed by endless nights of loneliness and tedium. I read several novels a week in an attempt to escape my reality, and passed hours staring at pictures of family and friends, melancholy in my heart. All of that changed with Imani.

Imani helped me in more ways than I could have imagined possible: she kept me company; she helped me learn Mooré words such as *nemdo* (meat) and *n deemda* (to play); she showed me parts of my village that I hadn't even known existed until our walks took us there. Most importantly, nurturing her transformation from a hungry, abandoned puppy to a full-grown, healthy dog inspired my own efforts to survive and flourish in the village. As I focused on helping her gain strength, I forgot much of my own despondency and concentrated instead on what I needed to do for her. The frustration of living on boiled flour and leaf sauce was rendered irrelevant when faced with the task of making dog biscuits from those same ingredients. For the first time since my arrival in Basma, I had faith in myself. I had *imani*.

My work in the village improved dramatically as my rediscovered optimism provided a fresh outlook on my experiences. Different languages don't preclude communication; they only make it more challenging. Criticism for poor language skills is evidence that someone wants to talk, and maybe they're even offering to be a tutor. I became less hung up on my frustrations and failures, and more cognizant of my successes. I began to develop friendships with co-workers at the health clinic as well as with the villagers around me. A little *imani* changed my life in Basma.

A year into my service, the experience had completely turned around. I was integrated into my village. I had friends, and even an adoptive family. Though fluency in Mooré still eluded me, I had achieved a strong proficiency. There were still plenty of difficulties and challenges, but even on my worst days, knowing that Imani was at home waiting for me always brought a smile to my face.

One weekend in November 2002, I went to the capital to e-mail my parents. I came home several days later, and sensed immediately that something was amiss. Imani was gone. I searched all around my hut, and all around the village, but she was nowhere to be found. I was crushed, but consoled myself with the knowledge that dogs often run away. Perhaps she felt that I had abandoned her. Perhaps she had run off somewhere and gotten lost. I could not shake the fear, however, that I had done something to make her leave. I asked around, and sensed a strangeness in people's responses, but assumed it was because nobody quite knew how to deal with such a distraught American.

Then my adoptive brother told me. I thought at first that maybe I hadn't understood what he'd said: "*Bamb da rime fo baaga,*" he repeated, "They ate your dog."

My stomach heaved; I was overcome with vertigo. I was crushed, unable to respond. I felt that I had bridged so many cultural divides, but this was one I did not want to cross. Had Imani run away, I likely would have deluded myself into believing that she was alive and well, just waiting for the right time to come back after some carousing in neighboring villages. Had she died, I could at least view it as part of the life cycle. But knowing that she had been killed by my villagers for a night's supper was harder to deal with. I lost all faith in those around me when I lost Imani.

I'm not sure if there is a "normal" mourning period for an eaten dog. It took me several weeks before I could look at anyone without wondering if they had partaken. I found myself reverting back to my pre-Imani routine: I spent most of my time in my hut, passed hours each day reading, and cut myself off from human contact.

After a time of this self-imposed seclusion, however, I forced myself to come to terms with my loss. Imani had meant so much—she had opened up the village to me, and she had helped restore my faith in myself. But she was gone, and no amount of self-pity or grief would bring her back. More importantly, I still had a job to do, and I was not about to quit. Serving out my time in misery would be to no one's benefit—least of all my own.

So, I got myself back to the place I'd been when Imani was in my life. I attacked my work with vigor, and achieved some of the greatest successes of my Peace Corps service. Though I thought often of Imani, all that she had shown me did not leave with her. My friends and family in the village were still the same wonderful people they had always been, regardless of whether or not Imani was by my side.

Much as I learned during my years in Burkina, there are some cultural differences that I will never appreciate. However, I did come to a realization that is still with me to this day: Imani showed me strength that I did not know I had. Losing her did not take that strength away from me. To this day, *imani* is within. I have faith in myself.

Daniel J. Franklin served in Burkina Faso from 2001–04. He is currently an attorney in New York City.

PART FOUR

CLOSE ENCOUNTERS

FLOYD SANDFORD

* * *

Hail, Sinner! I Go to Church

Sometimes, it seems as though giving just isn't enough.

ON NOVEMBER 8, 1964, I ATTENDED CHURCH FOR THE FIRST time since arriving in Ibadan. I was invited by relatives of one of my biology students to be one of several special participants in a Sunday service at The Blessed Church of Christ (Ijo Ibukun Ti Kristi) in the Oke-Ado area of the city. The day was lovely, and passersby returned the few Yoruba phrases of greeting I knew with their own greetings and smiles as I sauntered along Liberty Stadium Road in full Nigerian dress from Adeyoola Chambers to the church, a forty-five minute walk. It was the church's big event of the year, a festive harvest celebration. Seven special guests from Ibadan had been invited to participate—Mr. Amusan, a general trader; Mr. Adekoya, an accountant; Mr. Shogbesan, an insurance broker; Mr. Ayoola, a solicitor; Chief Ogunlesi, the Director of Broadway Printers; Mr. Olomo, a politician from the Ibadan Ministry of Finance; and me, tutor at IBHS.

The program for the occasion was detailed in a small, nineteen-page booklet with a pink cover. It consisted of songs

327

and spoken passages. At the beginning of the service, to the accompaniment of joyous singing and hand-clapping, as befits a harvest celebration, all seven of us marched in single file—I at the end of the procession—and took our designated seats on a raised dais facing the congregation. The church was packed, about two hundred people. I was the only Caucasian in the room and had worn a brand new traditional Nigerian outfit made especially for the occasion.

One of my students, Musa, had introduced me to an honest, hard-working tailor in the city. He had made me a beautiful traditional Yoruba man's outfit. It consisted of a flowing outer garment, a *sapara* (*agbada*), worn over a matching shirt (*orbuba*) and trousers (*sokoto*). All were made of cloth with alternating narrow blue and white stripes. The *sokoto*, tightened with a drawstring, closely resembled pajama bottoms. On my head, I wore an attractive tan-and-beige-patterned felt *fila*.

The service was long, lasting about two hours. As the morning festivities wore on, the church approached sauna-like conditions. Midway in the service, each special guest was recognized in turn. All seven of us were listed in the program, each with a full page devoted to us, including a special song in our honor. The six Nigerian honorees had songs in Yoruba. I was listed last, and my song was in English: "The harvest is passing, the summer will end." My song began with the phrase "Hark sinner while God from on high doth entreat thee," a curious coincidence, as I was certain none of the program planners knew I was an agnostic and infrequent churchgoer.

Growing up in Smithtown, on Long Island, New York, my main reason for faithfully attending the First Presbyterian Church on Main Street each Sunday was because I enjoyed singing in the choir under the direction of choirmaster Don Gardner. Mr. Gardner wrote several pieces of religious music including "Man Does Not Live By Bread Alone," which the choir often sang at Sunday services, but was best known for the song "All I Want For Christmas Is My Two Front Teeth," a ditty he dashed off one evening, while enjoying the company of his incisor-less granddaughter.

I had absolutely no idea what to expect during the church service. I had come only because it seemed unfriendly to turn down the original invitation. All I had been told was that it was a harvest celebration, that the congregation would be honored by my attendance, and that I was expected to bring a donation. No one had bothered to mention that it was a highly publicized special church occasion, or that the other honorees included important local officials, successful businessmen, and well-off politicians.

I had a ten-pound note in my trouser pocket, at that time equivalent to about $24. I had given some thought to my donation. I wanted to be generous and let the congregation know how much I appreciated the honor of being asked to participate. But I didn't want to embarrass the other participants and project myself as a fat cat, filthy rich American; $24 amounted to nearly a week's worth of my modest Peace Corps subsistence allowance.

As I sat on stage with the other honorees, I began to wish I had brought a few one- and five-pound notes in the event that I decided to reduce the amount of my donation during the service. Looking out over the congregation, I began to have concerns and reservations. Would they interpret my ten-pound donation as excessive, perhaps even offensive? Was I about to project a blatant and unnecessary show of wealthy American arrogance? Too late now, I'm here, and all I have with me is the single ten-pound note.

After nearly an hour spent reciting religious passages and singing eight anthems, many of them with multiple stanzas and long solo parts, the special part of the ceremony began.

The choir and full church congregation stood up and began to sing "*Omo Arowosola ti nro bi ojo....*" Mr. Amusan, the general trader, proudly arose from his seat, and began dancing. Aha, so dancing is part of the ritual. Well, I can handle that, I thought.

He danced slowly and gracefully, keeping rhythm with the music's beat, to a box located off to the side of the stage. I hadn't been aware of the box until then. Arriving at the box he reached into his pocket, deposited something inside, then shuffled back to his seat, keeping beat with the music all the way. As he was returning to his seat, an elegantly dressed Nigerian woman standing by the collection box, who had been singing some of the solo vocal parts throughout the service, reached into the box and held up the offering for all the congregation to see. "Twenty pounds," she announced. The congregation responded with cheers and shouts of approval. Mr. Amusan smiled, faced the audience, graciously received their praise, then took his seat. Good grief, I thought.

Then it was the turn of Mr. Adekoya, the accountant. A soloist began singing the first verse of his specially selected song "*F'Olunun wa o Olorun Ibukun iba Re to to, K'a to korin o ajuba Emi Mimo....*" Several portly older women from the congregation left their seats and moved into the center aisle of the church, singing and shaking, as Mr. Adekoya danced across the floor to the money box. In slow, subdued fashion he glided gracefully across the stage. Nearing the box he picked up the tempo, showing off some special dancing skills. Then, finishing with a flourish involving several twirls of his body, he stuck his hand in the box. "Twenty pounds," the box keeper announced, holding up and waving about a crisp twenty-pound note for all to see. More cheers from the congregation.

The insurance broker and the solicitor were even more generous. Sitting on stage watching their performances, facing the multitude, I was feeling sick to my stomach and increasingly uncomfortable. Rivers of perspiration poured from my arm-pits. My hands were clammy. I sensed the blood draining from my face, my clothes becoming damp and clinging.

Then Chief Ogunlesi took to the floor in his elegant traditional dress. Exhibiting fancy footwork, he danced across the stage and really upped the ante. "Fifty pounds," the woman announced to the congregation, which responded enthusiastically with joyous shouting and clapping. I sat motionless and stone-faced. The seat of my *sokoto* was sopping wet. When I shifted slightly I could feel the back of my *sapara* plastered with perspiration to the back of my chair. What had I gotten myself into? Could this be really happening? Or was it all a bad dream, related somehow to last evening's meal of highly seasoned curry?

Then it was Mr. Olomo's turn. Looking at his elegant apparel, a beautiful white *sapara* with elaborate embroidery and gold braid, I had a gut feeling that he was going to surpass everyone, duly impressing all assembled with his generosity. I was not disappointed. Rising almost triumphantly from his seat, he immediately pulled from his pocket a crisp new one hundred-pound note, which he held up and waved above his head as he began to dance across the stage. The consummate politician, he obviously intended to make the most of his opportunity to play to a full house.

His dance was lengthy and over-the-top. There were elaborate embellishments: body twirls, arm and leg extensions, and knee bends with crouching that brought his body close to the floor. As he danced, he kept waving the hand holding the note. Pleased with the size of his donation, he put on a terrific show. The congregation went wild.

At the end of his performance I felt about as big as a microbe, or one of the suspended dust motes visible in the beams of light streaming into the church through the stained glass windows. Had the floor opened up and swallowed me from view, I would have been thankful. Good Lord, had someone deliberately arranged the program honorees in the order of presumed wealth and anticipated size of gift giving? Nearly every participant preceding me had made a contribution an order of magnitude greater than the one previous. Did these folks think I was a Rockefeller? Didn't they know I was a helplessly middle class American, subsisting on a Peace Corps living allowance of less than $5/day?

I yearned to be delivered from my impending embarrassment. Let this agony be over quickly. Why hadn't someone told me about the nature of the harvest celebration, the gift-giving obligation of the honorees, the magnitude of gifts commonly given? Why had they placed me last on the list of potential donors? I was about to be humiliated in front of two hundred people. The women's chorus began to sing "Hark sinner while God from on high doth entreat thee...."

Everyone was on their feet, smiling, swaying, and hand clapping. Mr. Olomu and the others all turned their heads in my direction. It all seemed like a bad dream. I slowly rose up from my chair, all eyes on me, and started to move with the music, the seat of my *sokoto* and my *orbuba* darkened by perspiration.

"And warning with accents of mercy doth blend...."

My clothes were plastered to my body. Had I just stepped from a sauna, I couldn't imagine looking any more bedraggled. The rim of my *fila* was wet. Sweat coursed down my face, as I sensed myself anemically and inelegantly shuffling towards the insidious box and the fated announcement. I didn't want my dance to be anti-climatic following the politician's energetic performance, but I had no enthusiasm, no joie de vivre, as I sensed myself creeping along like an amoeba with an iron deficiency. I felt like an Arthur Murray reject, that my life force had left me.

"Give ear to His voice lest in judgment he meet thee...."

I imagined what everyone was thinking, sitting on the edges of their seats. "What's he going to do to top Mr. Olomo?" I could imagine all the pent up energy ready to be vented in cheers and shouts at the announcement. "Two hundred pounds from the American tutor!" My song seemed to go on forever. The previous participants had measured their dancing so that their arrival at the box and the return trip to their seats coincided with the length of their song. Had they practiced beforehand? The trip to and from the collection box couldn't be more than thirty feet, but I felt like I was moving in slow motion. Oh, God, let their be some sudden event to distract the congregation. A sudden storm, perhaps. A massive thunderbolt. Let their be a miracle. A total solar eclipse, that blackens the church. Let this ghastly day be over.

"The harvest is passing, the summer will end."

I turned and looked out at the congregation. The atmosphere inside the church was fever pitch, everyone standing, hands clapping and bodies swaying, all primed for the climax of festivities, the reservoir release of all the accumulated pent up energy, the shouts of joy and jubilation. I reached the accursed box at a point about midway in the song, deposited the soggy crumpled ten-pound note that I had clutched in my clammy hand for what had seemed like an eternity, and began the long dance back to my seat. Agony, misery. I wanted to run back to the seat, to have my moment of ignominy end quickly. But what then? I would be sitting in my chair facing the congregation while the choir was still on the third verse, with the final verse yet to come. Better I keep moving, even if it seemed like I was maneuvering through thick molasses.

Soon after I dropped the sweat-dampened wadded note in the collection box, and was nearing the security of my seat, I heard the woman announce "Ten pounds." The silence in the church was oppressive...soon followed by what agonizingly sounded like a few audible gasps...then feeble polite applause. Mercifully, the service concluded soon after.

I stayed briefly at the reception following, watching members of the congregation besiege Mr. Olomo, gushing over the magnitude of his Christian charity. He looked really pleased with himself. After the obligatory polite niceties, I slowly moved toward the door, nodding to people as I passed, and beat a hasty retreat. That was my first and last appearance at the Blessed Church of Christ. They say that religion comforts. Not so for me that day.

Floyd Sandford is the author of African Odyssey: the adventurous journeys of a Peace Corps Volunteer in Africa, *from which this is an excerpt. He was a Peace Corps Volunteer in Nigeria from 1964–66.*

CAROL BEDDO

✦
✦ ✦

A Visit From H.I.M.

Our relations to power can become quite real,
especially when there is love involved.

LEANING IN THE SHADE OF THE METAL WAREHOUSE BUILDING, I'M one of about ninety villagers who have come to the dirt airstrip to welcome Emperor Haile Selassie to Bahar Dar. We stand still and silent at the sight of the distant plane, an exotic silver insect aloft in Africa's enormous blue bowl of a sky.

As the plane touches down, women demonstrate enthusiasm with their loud falsetto trill. Men call and humph in deep voices and some clap their hands or rhythmically stamp their doulas, sturdy wooden walking sticks, on the ground, creating a deep syncopated layer of organized sound beneath the women's continuous, high trill.

Not only am I the only non-Ethiopian in this crowd, I am the tallest, the palest, the only blonde; and I'm the only person who's not a peasant.

Not one of my fellow teachers is here. The bank president and vice-president are not here. Perhaps the airport director is inside this warehouse that serves as the airport building, but he is not to be seen.

Showing up to greet the emperor is left to the common people.

Two men in khaki roll out a narrow red carpet in the general direction of where the plane will come to rest. The crowd is dressed in their usual traditional best—white, homespun cotton dresses for the women, their heads and shoulders covered with white shawls. The men wear long tunics over jodhpurs, both of white cotton twill, white gauzy shawls draped over their shoulders. I'm wearing an ordinary brown cotton dress my mother made and, while everyone else is barefoot, I'm wearing locally made leather sandals with upturned toes that protect my feet from our stony paths.

So now I will finally see H.I.M. in person, in my village. I am here in Ethiopia only because he requested Peace Corps Volunteers. He wanted fast growth of education in the provinces and, to achieve that, he wanted young, healthy Americans who would be willing to live in distant villages until Ethiopian graduates from the teacher training college could replace us.

The Emperor and I have a connection, a reason he could actually know of me. But will he know me if he sees me?

Guy told me that Haile Selassie knew who I was the night we realized our relationship was changing. Our feelings for each other were intense, even though liking each other was all I ever intended. Guy lives and works in Addis Ababa, a professional person, and I'm in the northern highlands. I did not expect a satisfying relationship.

"There's something that I need to tell you," Guy said that night in Addis as we were saying a long farewell in the lobby bar at the Itegue Mennon Hotel. I was due to fly back to Bahar Dar early the next morning. "It shouldn't make a difference for us, but it is better that I tell you."

"Hmm, that sounds interesting, but difficult," I said.

"It is both."

"O.K. Go ahead. Tell me."

"Well, you know how in our country all marriages are arranged?"

"Yeah. Sort of."

"I know this will sound odd to you, but I must tell you. I hope you will accept what I say. It does not change anything about us. It's just one more thing I need to work out in my life."

"O.K."

"I have been, how should I say? Promised? I am supposed to marry someone." Guy's soulful brown eyes, so typical of the handsome Amhara people, white half moons below the chocolate brown irises, always made me feel warm inside. I continued looking straight into those mournful eyes, calmly listening, waiting. "This is one of the things the Emperor speaks to me about."

I knew he spoke with the Emperor; I'd been in his Addis Ababa office when he received calls. I had assumed they spoke about Guy's marketing activities at the tourist organization, and they probably did, too, since it was the Emperor who had placed him there. But they spoke in Amharic, and quickly. There was no way I could understand a word.

Engaged? I was stunned. And His Imperial Majesty was involved?

"Who is it you're supposed to marry?" An easy, bland question.

"The Emperor and my family betrothed one of his girls, Hirut, to me when we were children."

"Do you love her?"

Guy laughed long and loud, but his eyes did not look cheerful. "Love is not the point, my darling Carol. We're betrothed by our families. That's all. We were betrothed for reasons not having to do with love."

"And now?"

He laughed again. I was not finding anything funny. I gave him a straight, serious look that he understood to mean he ought to get on with answering my question. "Hirut is living in the north, in Lallibela, and she is in love with an American." Guy looked at me in a peculiar way, as if I should see the irony. And while I might, I couldn't stop to enjoy it. "She lives in a more primitive place than you. No running water. No electricity. No industry. I feel sorry for her there. The American is an architect restoring stone churches. Wonderful, don't you think?"

"I guess."

"Wonderful: Hirut and I are promised to each other and we both are in love with Americans." Guy slapped his knees. I couldn't laugh; this was the first time he'd said that he loved me. "My dear Carol, this does not affect us. I don't want it to. But I wanted you to know—not to hear from someone else."

"An arranged marriage," I said.

"Yes."

"But without a wedding date."

"That's right. With our families' acceptance, we've been putting it off for many years. That was easy when I was abroad studying, but now—we don't know how much longer we can do this."

"Is this the family problem your father asks you to fix?"

"Only a little part of the problem," he said. "But, yes, it is one of the things he speaks to me about."

"Can't the Emperor just make you do what he wants?" I couldn't believe I was having this conversation. "I mean, he's the king, right? Don't kings just get to have things the way they want?"

"The Emperor is not like that. He's very kind. And patient. Also, he's very curious about you."

"About me?" I said, surprise quickly turning to a small panic. Couldn't Peace Corps find out about this? Wouldn't they send me home, pronto? "Oh, shit!" We were told in training that we were to be very discreet. As fresh Volunteers, we translated this to mean we could do anything we wanted, as long Peace Corps staff did not hear about it. And now the Emperor himself knows about me. More importantly, he knows about Guy and me.

Today H.I.M. is coming. Queen Elizabeth and Prince Phillip are soon to make a state visit, and H.I.M. will bring them here to Bahar Dar to show off his rural outpost at the source of the Blue Nile. He has an experimental farm on that hillside. H.I.M. is proud of his agricultural successes.

So now I'm standing at the airstrip, to show my respect just as everyone else here intends. In some crazy way it seems to me that if H.I.M. really knows who I am, if he does know I'm stationed in Bahar Dar, he would be insulted if I didn't appear? So why am I getting nervous and having second thoughts? Because I'm an obstruction to the Emperor's plans? But I didn't intend to become an obstruction. I don't want to feel as vulnerable as I do at this moment. But I won't avoid this.

The Emperor's plane touches down, and the mighty roar of the propellers drowns out the women and men who've kept up their falsetto trilling and rhythmic thumping. Two men in khaki uniforms roll out the stainless steel stairway. A third man runs to deliver another strip of red carpeting, and they begin unrolling it from the top of the staircase, creating a continuous red walkway down the stairs to the carpet on the ground, which leads into the metal warehouse building, a decidedly inelegant entry to Bahar Dar.

The plane door opens; a hush descends. We wait, breathless. Everyone else must have already known what to expect, because they begin laughing even before I see the little dog, a tiny, brown, fluffy lap dog at the top of the red-carpeted stairs, the smallest dog I've seen since I arrived in Africa. He stands at attention, perched on skinny legs on the stairs' top landing. As if receiving an "at ease" order, he descends the stairs, hopping on all fours onto each stair one at a time. He reaches the bottom of the stairs, turns back to look up at the open door, then sits and obediently waits.

All at once the women begin trilling again, keeping at it until H.I.M. appears. He stands at attention in his military uniform, his billed cap, and a cape with a tall, embroidered collar encircling his neck. Once again we fall into silence as we gaze up at H.I.M., and H.I.M. gazes out at us.

As the Emperor takes his first step, everyone around me bends at the waist into a deep bow, and I know they can no longer see H.I.M. Suddenly I have an odd thought: I'm American and we don't bow down to monarchs. Or do we?

Still uncertain, I remain upright while H.I.M. descends. As soon as his foot touches ground, everyone around me is no longer merely bowing, they are dropping to the ground on all fours, hands outstretched in front of their heads. H.I.M. and I are the only two standing, and I'm a half-foot taller. Never have I felt so conspicuous.

H.I.M. picks up his dog and tucks him under his left elbow. The dog's tiny face peers out from the edge of the cape. H.I.M. begins a slow, straight-shouldered, regal walk on the red carpet, head held high, just as in every photo and newsreel. But seeing him in person, I'm struck by how small he is, a perfectly formed, slim, handsome little man. He and his dog are in perfect proportion. Does he know that? Was that his plan?

H.I.M. walks, chin up, eyes straight ahead, cradling his dog, a walking stick in the right hand. He never looks to either side. I'm hoping there's a chance I might be less noticeable here in the shade, against the wall at the back of the prostrated crowd.

Suddenly he turns his head sideways, in my direction. Oh, my Lord, those melancholy brown eyes of the Amhara people look into mine. Without thinking, I lower my head and break our gaze. I didn't know until just now, but clearly I've absorbed some cultural etiquette; I should not make direct eye contact with someone from a higher station. It just came naturally to bow my head this way, and I'm glad. It feels right.

I raise my head, and he's still looking me over. He seems to invite eye contact, and I'm astonished by a brief, discreet look of acknowledgment, as well as a hint of a royal nod. I know I will remember those eyes forever, eyes filled with intelligence, sorrowful patience, and compassion. A deep, bountiful compassion in which I'm certain I am included.

Carol Beddo, a PCV in Ethiopia from 1964-65, returned to her Peace Corps station in 2003. Visiting Bahar Dar nearly forty years later flooded her with memories, and she began to wonder: Who was that young woman? Carol is coming to understand how the experience provided the foundation for the rest of her life as a community activist and as a consultant in public policy, political campaigns and elections. Life with her husband of forty-plus years is rich with family, and she's grateful that her three grandchildren desire a lot of her time.

ROBERT E. GRIBBIN

Moon Rocket

What is the meaning behind the landing on the moon?

I SEE IT IN MY MIND'S EYE—FROM MY HOUSE IN SONGHOR—
wind-blown tufts of light-green sugar cane surging like a
great sea on Kenya's Kanu Plains, washing gently against the
thousand-foot heights of the Nandi Escarpment. Thirty miles
distant, Lake Victoria Nyanza is glimmering in the late afternoon sun. The image is clear, but complicated by other images,
faces, smells, sounds—by the sheer exuberance of memories
that so indelibly marked this time in my life.

As a Peace Corps Volunteer in Central Nyanza, I was charged
with supervising the construction of a rural water system designed
to pipe potable water to 1,200 farms on three government-spon-
sored Settlement Sugar Schemes. I worked with a group of eight
men whom I trained in the skilled work of the project. When
resting, we kibitzed and talked. They had many questions.

Maurice always began. With a twinkle in his eye, he probed
the differences he reckoned inherent between whites and
blacks. He questioned me incessantly about why I had come
to Kenya. I'm not sure he ever really understood my response.

Presuming that I knew the answer, maybe I couldn't articulate it well. Altruism was beyond Maurice's comprehension; a thirst for adventure seemed to be a satisfactory motive.

Another exchange went like this:

"Robert," Maurice asked, "Is it true that Mzungus (Europeans) eat frogs?"

I pondered. "Yes. Some Mzungus eat frogs, but only the legs. When fried up they taste a bit like chicken."

Maurice looked skeptical. "Really," he frowned. "Frogs." He concluded, "Mzungus are very weird."

I responded, "You know, Europeans think that eating termites is strange."

Maurice absorbed this information, then shot back a surprised query. "Why?" he asked, "termites are good."

A telling exchange occurred in July 1969. Americans had just landed on the moon. The guys were interested in this news—more so than I had expected.

"So, Robert, is it true that Americans have landed on the moon?"

"Yes," I responded pointing to the wisp of a moon still visible in the morning sky. "They are up there now."

This engendered discussion of rocket ships and airplanes, which demonstrated these rural men's lack of appreciation for the science and the technological accomplishment of the moon trip. Francis, who was more cynical than his colleagues, observed, "If Americans can build airplanes, then certainly they can build a rocket." He was puzzled, however, that it had taken so long to get to the moon. "After all," he noted pointing again to the moon, "You can see it right there!" This again raised the question as to whether the landing had really happened.

Ligolo, older, taller and stronger with his front teeth knocked out in the traditional Luo style, and who rarely participated in these exchanges, cleared his throat. The men craned anxiously in his direction when he asked, "So Robert," he paused, "What color is God?"

I was stunned. I had no context for the question. Yet it obviously lay at the heart of their concern. James, the most worldly of the crew, who sported sunglasses and who had shed his family name Oyier in favor of Bondi, in honor of Agent 007, came to my aid.

"Robert," he explained, "we Luo people believe that God takes several forms and that he lives, at times, on the moon. The issue goes to the nature of God: if he is good, he is black like Africans. However, if he is evil, he is red. Ligolo's question is fair. If Americans have gone to the moon, they must have seen God. So, what color is he?"

It was a good question. From further discussion, I learned more about Luo beliefs, but had no answer. We agreed to look together. I brought back international editions of *Time* and *Newsweek* from Kisumu the next week, and we scrutinized the stories and pictures for help, but—of course—found none.

I realized afterwards that this had been one of those moments when each of my friends took one more step into the modern world and away from tribal traditions. The trappings of old beliefs diminished in the new reality.

Before too long the issue of God on the moon faded away. Soon Luo owned and operated trucks and buses, and, perhaps subconsciously reflecting this religious heritage, started bearing names like *Moon Rocket* and *Apollo 12*.

In the years since, I have reflected often and with sadness on how man's crowning technological achievement of the twentieth century unintentionally undermined beliefs that had sustained Luo people for generations.

Robert E. Gribben was a PCV in Kenya from 1968-70, building rural water systems at Muhuroni and Hoey's Bridge. Subsequently, he joined the Foreign Service and went back to Africa off and on for another forty years. He visited his projects several times over the years and found them up and running and well staffed by the men he had trained.

THOR HANSON

✦

Bury My Shorts at Chamborro Gorge

Sometimes our encounters are a little closer than we might find comfortable, though a little less immediately dangerous!

> *"Just listen to this stomach of mine…. The way it sounds, you'd think I had a hyena inside me."*
> —Humphrey Bogart, *The African Queen*

WHEN PEACE CORPS VOLUNTEERS MEET, THEIR CONVERSATIONS follow a pattern as predictable as the phases of the moon.

During my time in Uganda, we would gather in the capital city every few months for some kind of workshop, training, or just to visit and take a break from village life. After the usual greetings and a few stories from the bush, talk invariably turned to the two topics on everyone's mind—food, and its eventual results. Or, more crudely: what's going in and how it's coming out? We all dreamt aloud about supermarkets, pizza delivery and food courts, while at the same time lamenting the sorry condition of our bowels. With roundworms, giardia, amoebas, and other intestinal challenges as common in the Ugandan diet as bananas or beans, digestive discussions could prove quite lengthy.

In my work, I spent most days in the forests of Bwindi Impenetrable National Park, where I was habituating mountain gorillas for the park's fledgling ecotourism project. Sharing lunch (and parasites) from a common bowl with the trackers made me a frequent visitor to the Peace Corps nurse; I had bragging rights to more de-wormings than any other PCV in the country.

I had learned the simple, vital rule of gastric survival in Africa: never trust a fart. Unlike passing gas in the temperate zone, where foul smell is your primary risk, tropical flatulence carries with it a host of embarrassing possibilities. The schoolyard adage "silent, but deadly" becomes more menacing: "silent, but...sorry."

Many parts of the world suffer from the unfortunate combination of abundant diarrhea and a distinct lack of toilets. In Uganda, every one of us lost a latrine race at one time or another, and sharing these stories became a sort of contact-group ritual at any Peace Corps event. One Volunteer found himself with his pants around his ankles, searching for shrubbery on a busy Kampala street corner. The gate guard from a nearby embassy finally took pity on him, offering soap, bath water, and a clean pair of pants.

Another friend learned to survive long taxi rides by lining his shorts with newspaper, a technique I could have used on a certain day in Queen Elizabeth National Park.

Queen Elizabeth, or "QE," encompasses nearly two thousand square kilometers of savanna and lowland forest on the floor of the Great Rift Valley. It borders Virunga National Park in Congo (Zaire), making one of the largest contiguous protected areas in all of Africa. As part of the training for our park ranger-guides at Bwindi, I had arranged an exchange program with QE's Chamborra Gorge, a narrow, forested chasm that snakes through the grasslands from the edge of the rift escarpment to the shores of Kazinga Channel. A fellow Volunteer, Cathy, had spent the past two years habituating Chamborro's resident chimpanzee population for tourism. The Bwindi rangers and I would spend several days there, seeing Cathy's project, learning about savanna ecology and chimpanzees, and touring the local community to see how other villages dealt with life on the edge of a national park.

"The millet here is sour," concluded Bwindi guide Enos Komunda shortly after our arrival. He and the others seemed to enjoy the trip, but missed Bwindi immediately and sent radio messages back to the park every day. Although we had traveled less than sixty miles, it was a major outing and the farthest any of them had ever been from home.

I rose early one morning to accompany a group of tourists into the gorge. Cathy had asked me to help evaluate her newest guide, Milton, and I looked forward to spending an hour with chimpanzees, comparing the experience to gorilla viewing.

Heavy sunlight shone red through the dry season haze as we prepared to set off. The morning temperature already approached Bwindi's on a hot day, but cool breezes rose up from the gorge, bringing the promise of forest and shade. Cathy's "Fig Tree" Camp sat on a wide grassy plateau, over-looking the park's dry plains and the gorge itself, a steep-sided chasm carved by the rushing Chamborra River. The savanna stretched away across the level floor of the Rift Valley, stopped in the west by the sheer face of the Rwenzori Mountains, book-ended by the shimmering waters of Lakes Edward and George. Through it all, the gorge cut an incongruous ribbon of green, a winding, rainforest microcosm trapped in a sea of dusty plains and arid acacia.

We drove along a rutted game track that followed the rim of the gorge, passing groups of shaggy grey waterbuck and a small herd of Uganda kob, the graceful, long-horned antelope pictured on Uganda's national seal. They stopped grazing to watch us, tails flicking, coppery coats a pale reflection of the iron-rich soil. After a slow mile, we found the trackers waiting in the shade of a thorn tree. They had left camp at dawn to hike along the edge of the forest, listening for the unmistakable whoops and ascending shrieks of Chamborra's thirty resident chimps.

Unlike gorillas, who leave a clear trail through the undergrowth, chimpanzees can travel long distances without ever touching the ground. They spend more than half their time in trees, and are best located by following their vocalizations. While a troop may contain dozens of individual apes, they live in constantly shifting social structures of sub-groups and families. Calling out in the morning hours allows scattered individuals and feeding parties to maintain contact over a wide area, announcing dangers or the discovery of a particularly delicious fruit tree. The trackers concentrated on pinpointing the noise, then raced towards the chimps along the gorge's intricate network of forest paths and game trails.

I introduced myself to the tourists, a pair of middle-aged couples from the States, then turned things over to Milton. He reviewed the rules and regulations of tracking. His briefing sounded polished, very similar to the one we used in Bwindi. After a few questions, we began our descent into the gorge. One of the tourists dropped back to chat with me.

"We couldn't get gorilla permits," he explained, referring to the increasingly popular tracking program at Bwindi. "All sold out. If we're going to see any apes at all on this trip, then today's the day."

I assured him that the chances were better than eighty percent. Although the chimps were highly mobile, and less predictable than gorillas, the gorge confines their movements, and they rarely eluded Cathy's trackers.

The trail sloped sharply downward. Soon we were at eye level with the forest canopy, a wall of green dominated by the crowns of towering figs and ironwood. Black and white colobus monkeys lolled like strange pied fruit in the treetops, basking in the morning sun. We passed directly beneath them; they peered down unconcerned, like wizened shamans with their white-bearded faces and long-fringed coats. Considered one of the least-evolved primates, colobus monkeys lack opposing thumbs and have chambered, ruminant-like stomachs. They digest vegetation with the efficiency of cattle, and live in tiny home ranges, surrounded by a feast of rainforest leafage. Chamborra supported one of the densest populations in Africa, with dozens of family troops scattered across the canopy. Every morning they greeted the sunrise with their gravelly calls, like a chorus of huge, baritone tree frogs.

My stomach gave a disturbing lurch as the trackers led us towards the river, but dyspepsia had become a way of life and I dismissed it. We walked along a hippo trail, worn smooth and deep where the great beasts climbed out of the river each night to graze. The forest felt refreshingly cool; stray beams of sunlight filtered down though the canopy-like veins of gold in a shady underworld. Crossing the stream on a wide log, Milton stopped and motioned towards the treetops on the opposite shore. A dark shape melted away into the green, followed by an ear-shattering cry. We ran, trying to catch up with the chimp as it brachiated high above us. Finally, it came to rest on a broad limb, squatting with its back against the trunk, chewing absently on a handful of leaves.

We had stopped running, but my stomach was still very much in motion, rumbling ominously, with occasional twinges of pain. I tried to attribute the feeling to excitement, but my thoughts crept back to the greasy roadside tea house where Enos and I had shared a plate of eggs. In spite of the shade, I began to sweat.

Two more chimps appeared on the branch above us, a sub-adult and an old male with thin, wispy hair, and age-marks spotting his broad, dark face. They joined the first and all three began grooming one another, lined up along the branch like stone carvings in the eaves of a great cathedral.

The tourists snapped photographs, and the man I'd spoken with gave me a smile and a double "thumbs up." But I watched the apes with an increasing sense of urgency; my stomach continued to roil. Finally, I drifted to the back of the group and motioned for Milton.

"Very good briefing today," I began with a smile, "but you didn't mention what to do if a tourist needs to make a "long call" while they're in the gorge. What is your policy on that one?"

He looked puzzled. "I don't know. It's never happened."

"Ah," I whispered. "Well, in Bwindi, we always tell people they should borrow a *panga* (machete), dig a hole, and bury their waste so it can't infect the animals."

"It's never happened," he repeated sternly. "But I guess we would do the same."

"Good, good. Remember to say that next time." I patted him on the shoulder and looked at my watch while he returned to the tourists. Twenty minutes to go. Then the long hike up to the van and the drive back to camp.

I lasted for another quarter of an hour, pacing unobtrusively at the back of the group, before an audible percolating sound and a sudden cold sweat told me it was now or never.

"Milton," I whispered, tight-lipped. He was staring intently up at the chimps and didn't hear me. "Milton!" He looked back, startled, and several of the tourists turned around. I smiled, trying to look casual. "Give me your *panga*," I mumbled, "Your *panga*. Now!"

I took the blade, nodded to the trackers, and sprint-shuffled down the trail like a Japanese dancer in a tight kimono. Ten yards, twenty…too late. My body let loose and I felt a sudden, overwhelming relief accompanied by warm dampness in all the wrong places. The smell was indescribable.

Just out of sight of the tourists, I dove into the underbrush and ripped off my pants, scrabbling around for dry leaves to clean up the mess. I was frantic. The group would be coming this way any minute and here was the Peace Corps Volunteer: naked from the waist down, burying his underwear in a shallow grave. After brief consideration, I buried my socks too.

Thankfully, Milton overshot his hour with the chimps by five minutes, and the tourists were still packing their cameras when I sauntered back to the group. I handed Milton his *panga*, then quickly took my place at the rear, as far downwind as possible.

The talkative man lagged behind again, questioning me about life in the Peace Corps.

"I've thought about volunteering after I retire," he said eagerly. "But I had no idea the Peace Corps did this kind of thing. How marvelous!"

I nodded and smiled, trying to stay out of olfactory range. Finally we reached the top of the gorge, and everyone piled into the jeep, a small, crowded vehicle that had been sweltering in the African sun.

I lingered on the trail, pretending to look at a bird and hoping they'd leave me behind.

"Mr. Tour!" Milton called.

"I'll just walk, Milton," I said confidently. "See you at camp."

"No, no," he explained. "There are lions. You can't walk here alone."

"O.K., then." I shrugged and climbed into the back seat, squeezing between the trackers, and the friendly man who was considering the Peace Corps. The door slid shut with a loud thunk. There was a moment of horrified silence as my presence became unmistakably known in the stifling interior of the car. Everyone lunged to unroll their windows and the driver took off, bouncing away over the rough track, trying desperately to make a little wind.

No one spoke on the ride back to camp, and I could feel the man next to me trying to edge away on the narrow seat. From the look on his face, I think I cost the Peace Corps a likely recruit.

Dr. Thor Hanson, who served in Uganda from 1993-95, is a conservation biologist and author based in the Pacific Northwest. He spent his Peace Corps years habituating wild mountain gorillas in Uganda, an experience he described in his first book, The Impenetrable Forest. *Since then, Hanson's research and conservation activities have taken him around the globe. His second book,* Feathers: the Evolution of a Natural Miracle, *is due from Basic Books in 2011.*

NANCY BILLER

✦

Near Death in Africa

*Systems and expectations, especially in the wake of
colonialism, can alter even the best of intentions.*

I HAVE RETREATED TO THE FAR CORNER OF A HIGH SCHOOL
classroom. My eyes are closed; I try to transport myself to a
place where I can see how absurd it was for me to choose
to come to Africa to meet my death before the age of
twenty-three.

There had been earlier threats. Lying under a mosquito net
during training weeks at the Lycée Féminin in N'djamena,
Chad, after suffering from weeks of dysentery, I heard the
French nurse say "*oh la la*" when she took my pulse; I was sure
I was going to die. The day I accidentally bit into a chicken
bone and a piece of my front tooth chipped off: I was saddened
to think that all the orthodontic work I'd suffered through
eight years earlier would hardly have been worth the effort.
My teeth and other body parts would be destroyed bit by bit,
a consequence of having requested Chad for my Peace Corps
experience. At my posting in Bongor, a French doctor finally
found Shigella in a stool sample, easily cured with antibiotics.
I maintained intestinal health by consuming yogurt on a daily

basis, making it from powdered milk and a bit of starter purchased across the Logone River in upscale (French butter and yogurt available) Maroua, Cameroon. The yogurt idea came from advice I'd found in Adelle Davis's *Let's Eat Right to Keep Fit*, one of the few books I'd packed when leaving New York.

The fear I felt in the Terminale classroom with screen- and glass-free windows was different. I was suffering from something other than a microorganism attack or nutritional deficiency.

I was an English teacher for students in their last year of high school. These students had spent many years without teachers who, in France, would have prepared them by that point for the baccalaureate exam that provides those who pass with advantages in seeking employment or a university education.

My students were bright, but they did not have enough training to pass. I did not have enough skill to make up for the years when the English teacher had not shown up or had left in the middle of a term.

Toward the end of the Terminale year, teachers administered the "*bac blanc*" in their respective subject areas. The grade earned would be considered in the overall term grade. The *bac blanc* was something like the PSAT—a practice exam giving students an idea of how they would fare on the real *bac* (administered in the capital) and to help them concentrate on areas of weakness. Those areas were deep and plentiful for my students. Nevertheless, I administered the exam and imposed rules. I explained that any time a student spoke to another during the exam I would deduct ten points. I believed that I was doing the right thing, creating test conditions close to what they would experience in N'djamena later in the year. A number of students challenged me by speaking repeatedly; this would be reflected in their grades.

After the *bac blanc*, school was closed for days while the teachers graded exams.

One of those days when school was closed, after I had completed my grading, I ran into some fellow teachers at a badminton game hosted by the Chadian/Russian physician couple in town. The teachers were from the Soviet Union and they taught Russian. The year was 1978. Having grown up at a time when US school children were taught that the Soviets might invade at any time and when the apartment building where I grew up had prominent fallout shelters, I was amazed when I first arrived at this high school to find myself in real-life contact with Soviets.

By the time we were correcting the *bac blanc*, the amazement had dissipated. The teachers asked me how my students had done on the exam. I trusted them as colleagues and reported that, sadly, the results were very poor. In contrast, apparently, Russian scores were strong.

I believe that those Russian teachers then informed my students that they would receive poor grades in English, setting the stage for what happened when we returned to school after the break.

The day I handed out graded exams, my bright, strapping students were ready. They rose up, insisting that I give them higher grades. They surrounded me, arms in the air, fists clenched, demanding justice. I backed into the corner and closed my eyes.

I expected to be crushed. Other teachers and students passed by and saw what was happening. Some kind soul called for the help of the *censeur*, (the individual in charge of discipline). It seemed like hours before he arrived and, along with the *chef de classe* (class leader) cleared a path for me to pass between angry students.

My Peace Corps experience taught me that I did not have the talent to be a good teacher. But it also gave me my first glimpses of the beauty and grandeur of Africa, the dignity of its people, and the enormity of their challenges. I now have two sons, both enrolled in an academically competitive public high school. Their teachers are sometimes less experienced than parents would like, and are absent almost as much as the students would wish but, thanks to my experience in Chad, I know how incredibly fortunate my children are. As I tell those boys I love so deeply, and anyone else who happens to ask, my Peace Corps experience, despite what seemed near-death experiences thirty years ago, was just about the best and most important of my life, second only to motherhood and all the challenges it presents in the technology-laden, materialistic society in which we live today.

Nancy Biller served as a high school English teacher in Chad (in Bongor and Sarh), from 1977–79. Her commitment there ended abruptly when civil war broke out half way through her second year. All Volunteers were evacuated to Yaounde, the capital of Cameroon. As the Administrative Director for Global Health Programs at the University of Pennsylvania's School of Medicine, she has the privilege of advising many young and idealistic medical students who are interested in volunteering in low-resource areas of the world.

JACQUELYN Z. BROOKS

Boeuf Madagaskara

The food we eat…put before us perhaps more graphically than might be expected!

I LIVED ON THE SOUTHERNMOST TIP OF "THE RED ISLAND"— Madagascar—where I taught English to the Malagasy. Fort Dauphin was a dusty, run-down little town with no repairs to the roads since the French left in the 1950s. In spite of their poverty, the Malagasy were happy, loved parties and entertaining the *vazah*, their word for stranger.

I seldom left the harbor town of Fort Dauphin. One evening, on his way to the local hotel, a PCV named Greg walked onto my verandah, which was overhung with lovely wild orchids and jasmine much like an old southern plantation. Smelling the French jasmine, Greg said he understood why I never went traveling, but he wanted to invite me to his village just outside Ambovombe in western Madagascar.

I had once been there to a teachers' meeting. It had been market day for the Malagasy cowboys who herded the huge hump-backed zebu, raising so much dust we had to duck into a local bar. The whole time I was in the bar sipping a Malagasy Three Horse Beer, I watched the frenzied cowboys with their whips and guns as if transported to a Western movie. I wasn't eager to visit that part of the country again.

I told Greg that, much as I'd like to go to the celebration for the opening of the school he'd built, I had no transportation. He knew I was trying to get out of it.

"Don't worry, cutie," he said. His face was streaked with dirt and sweat, his shirt caked with red earth from biking over unspeakable roads. "This is not a date. I need a lovely *vazah* in the front row to make my school opening official. The principal from Fort Dauphin lycee and two of his English teachers are going in his truck. I told him you might ride along."

The morning of the celebration, we set off as the sun rose. I wore a clean dress because Malagasy women never wear slacks or jeans. We bounced and swerved over broken rutted roads for over three hours. The two teachers next to me were dressed beautifully in white dresses with printed *lambas* tied around their waists, but they smelled very bad from lack of deodorant and toothpaste. I had grown used to their acrid smell; what is more I had grown to love these teachers for their courage in schools that had no books, paper or even screens on the windows. They were paid the equivalent of ten dollars a week and most lived in shabby rented rooms, going home to their families on weekends. Lanto and Nuorina sang as we bounced along, songs about cows, cyclones, moonlight, and untrustworthy lovers.

Greg's school was a beautiful two-room building made of adobe from the red clay nearby. Three big plane trees planted years ago by the French shaded the schoolyard. All of the villagers in their best *lambas* and brimless hand-woven hats were milling about, setting a few cracked wooden chairs in a row facing the new school. Lanto and Nuorina insisted I must sit in the center, flanked on one side by the lycee principal and the village chief and, on the other, by the oldest man in the village and the representative from the Ministry of Education. Greg, too, had a seat in the front.

"I think you'll like lunch," Greg said with a twinkle. "They have a special feast planned in your honor."

Greg was teasing. The man from the Ministry would be the highest-ranking official. I didn't mention that in my pocket I carried three tomatoes and two shallots in case there was only steamed manioc root for lunch.

After overlong speeches by the man from the Ministry and the village chief, two men appeared from behind the school dragging an unwilling zebu, called *omby* in Malagasy, directly in front of my chair. The oldest man in the village rose and broke off a flowering branch from a shrub. He waved it over the *omby's* back, speaking softly to the animal, patting his back, then stroking him with the branch. Distracted, the *omby* did not see one of the strong young men who grabbed it by the back legs and flipped it over on the ground. Simultaneously, the second young man straddled the *omby's* neck, pulling back its head. In one swift motion the man slashed its throat. The animal convulsed as a fountain of blood poured out. I sat still as a stone in my chair, willing myself not to faint. Several men stepped forward to open up the *omby's* side, peel back its skin and begin cutting off the steaming meat from its exposed ribs.

The principal whispered that the rib meat was the most tender; one of the young men came rushing toward me with his hands full of it. He thrust the dripping still-warm meat into my hands. I accepted with as much poise as I could muster. I rose and bowed to the crowd who applauded and chanted something about the "gracious *vazah*," me. I hoped to find someone or some place I could get rid of the meat, but Nourina and Lanto linked arms with me and led me to the cooking fires.

The village women, crouched on their haunches in front of the open fires, smiled in greeting. They skewered my raw, bleeding meat. Someone passed a rag to wipe my hands. I was shaking all over, whether from rage at Greg or shock at seeing an *omby* killed and gutted, I wasn't sure. I remembered the tomatoes and shallots in my pockets. The women removed the skewers from the fire with their bare hands and calmly slid my vegetables onto the sticks.

The man from the Ministry wanted to take a photo of Greg and me in my blood-stained dress. Greg put his arm around me, but I gave him a sharp jab, my privilege as "guest of honor." Not to give Greg the satisfaction of seeing me cry, I walked over to the cooking fires.

I was given a large tin basin full with rice atop which sat my zebu-meat and veggies en brochette. Nourina and Lanto shared my meat with their own basins of rice. The zebu had been cooked to perfection: blackened to a crisp on the outside, the inside not raw but succulent and juicy, delicately flavored by the shallots and tomatoes. No barbecue sauce, no seasonings of any kind were added.

I asked what the old man had said when he whispered to the *omby* in its last minutes. Nourina translated in her best English, "The old one said, 'We are grateful that you came to the celebration; we are sorry to have to take your life. You are a noble animal. And thanks a lot for the nice lunch.'"

Dr. Jacquelyn Z. Brooks served as a Teachers' Supervisor in the Peace Corps in Madagascar from 1997–99. She has retired from teaching and is writing a novel. She lives overlooking the harbor in Gloucester, Massachusetts, where she claims to be a recluse except when entertaining her very large family.

KARA GARBE

✳
✳ ✳

The Baobab Tree

*Appreciating beauty in a time of sorrow is a
legacy of much Peace Corps service.*

I DIDN'T PLAN ON BEING DRUNK AT THE FUNERAL. IN FACT, I
hadn't planned on being at a funeral at all, nor had I planned
on being drunk. We were on a long ride and, as always, I was
nervously eyeing the water level in my Nalgene bottle. Further
contributing to my dehydration by downing a few bowls of
dolo, the local brew, was the last thing on my wish list, but
Michel wasn't one to refuse the free alcohol that people always
offered his white friend.

Michel was my friend, interpreter, drinking buddy and
spokesperson. Everyone in Bomborokuy knew to look for
me at his house if I wasn't at my own, and shy villagers wanting to approach me with questions about America or requests
for money went through him. He had recently also become
my travel partner and watchful bodyguard when we were in
foreign territory. I needed his help more then usual in the
small villages outside Bomborokuy, since almost no one spoke
French. Although Michel had been forced to quit school in
fourth grade because his parents couldn't afford the tuition, he

spoke French more fluently than I did, even though he had probably gone months without speaking it before I'd arrived in the village.

Two weeks earlier, on a bicycle trip through the bush, we had been invited by a woman in some small, unnamed village to stop and have a drink, and I'd promised to return to take her picture. People were always asking me to take their picture, to give them money, to marry them or adopt their children so that we all could have a better life in America. I refused almost all those requests, but for some reason I said yes, and Michel held me to my promise.

We took photos like eager relatives at a family reunion: the woman with her baby beside the door of her hut, me holding her baby, her beside her husband, Michel and her beside the moped, me laughingly trying to grind millet on a large flat rock with something resembling a rolling pin.

A group of children crowded into the background of each photo to stare at me with wide eyes, faces so shocked that they registered no emotion. Michel told me he doubted they had ever seen a white person before.

Then we ran into Celestin—who seemed to know Michel, but I couldn't figure out how—and the drinking began.

Celestin led us to a cabaret so familiar it could have been in Bomborokuy. Like all village *cabarets*, it was a family's courtyard that had been turned into a temporary bar to sell the *dolo* the family matriarch had spent three days brewing. Wooden benches ringed the treeless courtyard. Three mud buildings leaned into one wall, their rusted metal doors hanging open limply in the sun. The matriarch squatted on a stool beside a huge clay pot, large enough for me to bathe in and poured *dolo* into bowls cut from dried calabash gourds. She glanced up as we walked in, meeting my eyes for a moment before returning to the pocket of coins she folded into the corner of her *pagne*.

Almost as soon as Celestin led us to an empty bench, a steady stream of villagers—emboldened by a few bowls of *dolo*—approached us to shake my hand and start conversations that went far beyond my basic grasp of Bwamu. Michel fielded the visitors. He grinned, laughed, gestured. The villagers nodded at me and at him, smiled, waved their hands and raised them up toward God, praising the one who had brought an American into their midst. I'd heard this story before; villagers in Bomborokuy had told me it was God's doing that I was there, as though teaching middle-school English was going to alleviate the poverty, the heat, the high rates of infant mortality, the threat of malaria and AIDS, the dwindling supply of water as the dry season wore on. I told my students that education could give them the ability to provide answers to these problems. Some days I actually dared to believe it would.

I bought a liter of *dolo* for about thirty cents and the three of us shared it. Celestin seemed to understand French, but preferred to communicate with me via Michel. He asked about American food, about my role as an English teacher in Bomborokuy, about whether I would ever marry a Burkinabe. I gave my standard response: only if he did all the cooking and cleaning. (That always shut up the men.) I laughed as Michel interpreted. Smiling, Celestin lifted the half-empty liter from the ground to refill our calabashes.

As Celestin put down the empty bottle, a hunched-over old woman approached Michel, barefoot, a faded red dress clinging to her thin shoulders. She asked him a question.

"*Ameriki,*" Michel said. I recognized this as the Bwamu version of the French word *Amérique*, America.

They exchanged a few more sentences, and I recognized variations of "America" and "the United States" in Michel's responses. He began laughing.

"What is it?" I asked without looking up, consumed by my attempt to balance my bowl of *dolo* in a soft depression of dirt. The calabash bowl became increasingly difficult to balance the longer you sat in a cabaret.

"She doesn't know what America is," Michel said, slapping one hand against his faded jeans and breaking into a laugh. "She's never heard of your country."

After we left the cabaret, Celestin took us to the funeral. Perhaps he thought the unprecedented visit of an American woman was a fitting tribute to the deceased, or maybe it was simply poor form to visit a village on the day of a funeral without paying respects. Celestin led us into the courtyard where we sat down quietly on a long wooden bench under the hot sun.

Women and men grieved separately, the women in the cool shade of buildings, the men on benches and mats in the courtyard. But I stayed close to Michel and took a seat with the men, breaking the gender roles as no Burkinabe woman could ever do. This funeral would go on for days, a marathon grief session involving family and friends sitting quietly at the home of the deceased. Relatives came from other villages to sit, nap, eat, sleep, and quietly shake hands with others who came to sit, nap, eat and sleep. To remind the bereaved that no one is ever, ever alone.

We sat in silence, staring at our hands, at the cleared patch of dirt beneath our feet. The solemnity of the moment calmed the giddy, *dolo*-induced laughter that had been shaking me free just minutes prior. Finally Celestin indicated with a nod that it was time to leave. We again shook fifteen or so hands and walked out of the courtyard. I focused carefully on putting one foot in front of the other in a dignified, un-wobbly manner.

Celestin led us back to the courtyard where the woman paused in her clothes washing to greet us like we were old friends, shaking our hands to welcome us back, grinning and chattering with Michel. When he told her we were heading back to Bomborokuy, she grasped my hands in a thick handshake, stared into my eyes and spoke a few long sentences in Bwamu. Michel interpreted.

"She says, you should find a good husband and have many many babies, God willing."

I grinned. "*Bari-a*," I said. *Thank you.*

Celestin rolled our moped out from the shade of the house and led us out of the courtyard and toward the path that would lead us back to Bomborokuy. He shook our hands and thanked us for visiting. Michel climbed onto the moped first, steadying it for me as I gracelessly slung one leg over the vinyl seat and slid into place behind him. He kicked the moped into gear, and we waved once more as we started down the path.

I kept my hands on Michel's waist to steady myself as he steered the moped around rocks and patches of sand.

"How do you know Celestin?" I yelled toward Michel's ear, struggling to make my voice heard over the moped's engine. He half turned back toward me.

"I don't." The visible half of his mouth turned up in a grin. "I met him today, just like you."

It shouldn't have been a surprise, but the friendliness of the Burkinabe was always sneaking up on me. I laughed into Michel's green nylon shirt and turned back for one last glimpse of the village, its mud houses quickly fading into the landscape. The people we were leaving were most likely judging the entire Western world based on my drunken behavior in the two-hour period I had spent in their village. I was sober enough to be relieved that the pressure was now off—it was just me and Michel, him in his green soccer jersey and faded black jeans, me in a *pagne* and t-shirt, my legs pressed against the backs of his thighs, my hands pressed coolly on his waist, trying not to be too aware of his body.

I looked around the fields as we rode, trying to imagine the tall stalks of corn and millet that would fill the space in a few months. The dry period had sucked each wisp of vegetation back to the ground, scattered bushes and trees were the only green spots on the brown landscape. The naked soil revealed clearly formed rows of mounded earth where millet had once grown, tall and sustaining. I stared at the land, my eyes mesmerized by the quick passage of ground closest to us, the slow constant presence of the horizon in the background.

We rode in silence, the wind whipping pieces of my hair out of its ponytail. I fingered loose strands away from my mouth and eyes and leaned into Michel's back. To my left, a single baobab tree stood perfectly framed in an empty field. The baobab was one of the most majestic and stunning trees I had ever seen, its thick trunk swollen with water to survive the dry season, its wiry gnarled branches scratching toward the sky. As I stared at the baobab, my hazy mind registered it as the most beautiful tree I had ever seen. Beautiful. And simultaneously, the thought came unbidden: *All beauty passes. And this, too, shall pass.*

I was filled with awe. It wasn't sorrow, not even knowing I would outstrip the beauty of the Baobab, that we would continue down this path until the tree was far from sight, that one day even Bomborokuy would be just a memory, that my life itself was as constrained by time as this moment was. But the ancient baobab seemed to reach beyond that, seemed to suggest a vast certainty in its steady, eternal reach for the sky. African and Arabic legends explained the baobab's unusual anatomy by saying the tree had been planted upside down, its branches like roots, twisted and splintered and seeking. I leaned forward to Michel's ear, bringing my entire body into contact with his.

"La vie est belle," I said. *"C'est pas vrai?"*

He turned his head toward me without hesitation. *"C'est vrai.* It's true. Life is beautiful."

Kara Garbe is currently working on her MFA in creative writing and completing a memoir about her time in the Peace Corps in Burkina Faso (2001–04). You can read more of her writing on her blog: karagarbe.blogspot.com.

LEITA KALDI DAVIS

The Sports Bar

Easing the Cold War—just a little—in Senegal.

THE SPORTS BAR, A WATERFRONT DIVE, RECALLED DAKAR'S long history as a port where rapacious Europeans and opportunistic Africans had made deals for centuries, most notably in slaves. Not surprisingly, there was still a lively flesh trade going on inside.

Tables surrounded an outdoor dance floor with a raised "observation deck" on one side. Behind the mobbed bar, toilets turned into smelly bogs and urinals with shoulder-high partitions doubled as sex stalls where a prostitute could be rented for a few francs a minute. The prostitutes were gorgeous women of hues from lemon tea to black coffee, in skin-tight jeans and straining halter tops, skirts slit to the waist, camisoles, black mesh stockings suspended from lacy garters.

The girls swayed around the dance floor luring drunken sailors—Arabs, Pakistanis, Africans, Europeans—to bump and grind. Or else they sat giggling on the sailors' turgid laps.

The girls were usually adolescents from Senegal, Guinea-Bissau, Ghana, and Mali. The few Liberians made a hit with

the English-speaking clients. They were fleeing Charles
Taylor's grisly "diamond war"; they might have heard a door
slam when he was elected President that year. Some of the
hookers made a lot of money and returned to their villages
with the honor money brings to people hungry enough to
overlook its source. Others languished in drug-induced stu-
pors until they were suddenly too old to hook and ended up
on the human trash heaps that littered Dakar's streets.

The Sports Bar featured a floor show of violence, starring a sailor who would slap up a prostitute or girls fighting
with each other over a trick, or pimps straightening out their
gazelles. The "vampire ladies," cocaine dealers from Morocco,
sometimes swooped into the bar, faces powdered white, wearing Cleopatra wigs, black dresses, and stilettos. They would
circulate among the crowd, dropping packets here and there
and collecting money from the prostitutes. They did not
hesitate to treat a defaulter to a broken bottle in the face or
a spiked heel to the head. The sailors, instead of interfering,
would applaud and laugh, while some magnanimous spectator
might buy a drink for a girl pulled up off the floor. Meantime,
the music never missed a beat. A DJ kept the reggae and rap,
the sambas and AfroPop churning.

I watched from the observation deck, drinking beer with
a group of PCVs. Someone pointed out a young white man
who was dancing wildly, flying, stringy hair so wet with sweat
it splashed dancers near him. He gyrated around on huge flat
feet until the music slowed; he twirled to a stop like a spinning
top. To my astonishment, he focused his blue eyes on me,
shuffled over to the deck and asked me to dance. Why would
this bizarre man ask me, a white-haired, aging woman, to
dance? Well, O.K., I had to admit I was looking pretty good
in my "bar blouse"—a bright patchwork sleeveless number—
and purple pants. My hair was fluffed and I supposed I had the

allure of an older woman who might happen to be rich. I'd
never been rich, but in Senegal, I was getting used to seeing
dollar signs instead of stars in men's eyes.

The fact was I'd been longing to dance since I walked
into the place. I rose and walked toward the dance floor. The
Volunteers whooped, "You go, girl!"

"I may be old," I yelled back, "but I'm not dead yet."

We flailed around to the wails of Youssou N'Dour, the
man's wet hair occasionally spraying my face. Baba Maal followed N'Dour, and we pounded our way through another
number. When we finally wound down, the man thanked me
for the dance and led me back to the deck. Gasping for breath,
my heart thumped so violently I thought everyone could hear
it. My arthritic knee threatened to buckle. I tried to smile, my
mouth trembling, and sat down as my undaunted dance partner scraped a chair up next to me. Sweat soaked his limp nylon
shirt. He was about thirty years old, with narrow shoulders and
a flabby chest, a round face, marble-blue eyes and a cupid's-
bow mouth. He pointed a stubby finger to his chest and yelled
above the din, "I am Sergei. Sailor from Odessa. My ship in
port." He swept his finger at the Volunteers around us. "You.
You are American? Wot you do here? You missionary?"

I shouted into his damp ear that we were Peace Corps
Volunteers. He'd never heard of it. "We do development
work."

"A-h-h-h," he yelled. "Bot you waste your time here." His
arm swept toward the dance floor. "Dese people...I luf dem...
but you can not *develop* dem!" He swiveled his eyes toward my
friends. "I vould like to meet zeez American. But dey afraid of
me. I am Russian."

His words, like a gauntlet flung to the ground, sent me to
my feet. "Guys!" I announced, "This is Sergei. He's a Russian
sailor and he thinks you're afraid of him."

The Americans looked up, wiped beer foam from their mouths, laughed and yelled, "NOT!... I don't think so..." and one by one shook Sergei's hand. He beamed as they gathered around him, asked him about his ship, about Odessa. He asked them about their lives in the States, whether they had left spouses or children to work in this bewildering Peace Corps; if they really believed in peace; if they were rich. We ordered more beer, and went on to talk about the old Cold War and even African development.

The dance had worn me out and I soon waved to everyone and hobbled out on shaky legs to find a taxi. A bottle smashed somewhere behind me, heads bobbed up and down in the urinals but there, in a far corner of the Sports Bar, international diplomacy was blossoming like an orchid in the jungle.

Leita Kaldi Davis worked for the United Nations and UNESCO, for Tufts' Fletcher School of Law and Diplomacy and Harvard University. She worked with Roma (Gypsies) for fifteen years, became a Peace Corps Volunteer in Senegal (1993-96) at the age of 55, then went to work for the Albert Schweitzer Hospital in Haiti for five years. She retired in Florida in 2002. She has written a memoir of Senegal, Roller Skating in the Desert, *and is working on a memoir of Haiti.*

PAULA ZOROMSKI

One Last Party

Getting there can often be quite the task—and can
prove more important than the "there" there.

ALL I WANTED TO DO WAS GO TO THE PARTY. I WAS MORE DETER-
mined to attend the Fulani fête than an American teen was to
drive into the woods for his first beer party.

Hot sand and thorns had hardened my feet. The wind knotted my hair around its barrette and the sun browned my skin. I
longed for a hot shower; even for a cold one. Water was scarce.

My African friends told me I had become ugly. My skin was
too dark, my body too thin. A steady diet of millet and milk,
long walks searching for grazing camels, and living in the Sahel
had trimmed my body fat.

I never could understand how events were scheduled. It
had something to do with the moon, tribal chiefs, and hungry
cows. I told Gado and Mariama, husband and wife, that I had
enjoyed the previous party. I reminded them of the day we
had watched old men in straw hats race their camels across the
desert. I told them how captivated I was by the young men
with their yellow painted faces dancing, singing, and flirting
with girls.

Gado told me that it would be very far away from our place. I did not know what he meant. I didn't know if it was far or he simply didn't want to go.

After a week of hints, Mariama told me that she wanted to attend the festival. Gado would not refuse his wife. The next night, then, he told me to prepare my things. We needed to leave early in the morning.

Mariama and I were ready before the sun rose. I tightly rolled my sleeping bag and mat, setting the bedding on my camera bag. I wiped my face with cold water and put on my favorite black shirt, one embroidered with bright, multi-colored polka dots around the neck and sleeves. I tied a piece of black fabric around my waist, African skirt style.

The temperature was quickly rising, and Gado was moving slowly. We couldn't make the trip without his navigation. Finally, as the sun began to cook our part of the desert, he was ready. It was 10:00. The hottest part of the day had begun.

Hassane asked if he could ride with me. This made me happy because he was a good camel driver. I had never learned how to prevent my camel, Mai Chin Abinci (One Who Eats), from tasting every leaf and blade of grass within his reach.

We rode for a long time. The sun was beating down on us. My entire body was covered with black fabric: only my eyes weren't covered. I couldn't bear to have even my eyes exposed. The sun and wind hurt, sucking moisture out of me. I couldn't hold my body upright. I leaned against Hassane and the camel. I spotted a bush with a tiny shadow. I craved shade and begged Hassane to drop me off by the bush. I told him that he could pick me up tomorrow.

Hassane assured me that we were almost halfway there. We were almost at the market where we would eat, drink tea, and rest. Hassane wasn't lying. Soon, we were in a small market town filled with traders.

Gado told us that we could get down and have some tea. I could not respond. My camel thudded its belly down in the sand. I couldn't unclench my thighs. Hassane climbed off the camel and pulled my left arm and leg. My legs were stuck in a grip on my camel's sides. I pushed on the hump with my hand, and rolled off my camel's back onto the hot sand. I couldn't get up. I curled up under my black fabric. Mariama vomited from the heat. Gado brewed a healing tea and made us drink. We rested in the shade and ate meat. When the sun went down, Gado walked us both around the market. Then, he convinced us to get back on our camels and ride to the party.

We rode in silence.

Once we had arrived, Gado set up our camp and brewed tea. He added sugar and herbs to give us strength. After tea, Mariama met relatives, Hassane and Gado joined the camel racers, and I walked around by myself.

I was too tired to take a photograph, but I was happy to see the boys dance.

Paula Zoromski served in the Peace Corps teaching math in the Central African Republic and Niger. She got the travel bug at a young age and went to summer school in Mexico, traveled the Sahara desert on camelback with nomads, hiked the hills of Honduras, and danced in the streets with pink hair at Carnival in Trinidad. Paula, a world traveler, photographer, and writer, passed away in 2009 at the age of 41 from breast cancer.

TOM GALLAGHER

* *
*

The Peace Corps in a War Zone

*From the beginning, Peace Corps Volunteers
dealt with much more than peace.*

MY FIRST HINT OF ERITREAN REVOLUTION CAME WHILE I WAS
still in Peace Corps training at Georgetown University in
Washington. A small newspaper article appeared on a bul-
letin board telling of a bomb that had gone off somewhere in
Eritrea. A couple of months later, in Agordot, the Education
Officer for western Eritrea, Sheik Hamid Mohammed el-Hadi,
took us on a tour of the town. In front of the government
office, he pointed to a small circle of stones which marked the
spot where the bomb had exploded.

Hamid was the most dignified man I have ever met. His
six-foot-tall frame, always covered in a perfectly ironed *jalabia*,
seemed more to flow than to walk. While most of the towns-
people wore their turbans in the loosely wrapped Sudanese
style, Hamid wore his in the neater Middle Eastern/Indian
style. The turban/wimple framed a serene, honest, handsome
face. If his skin were 1 percent lighter he could have passed for
a Hindu mystic. Although he was still not forty, he had already

earned the title "Sheik," which means an old man, or, as in Hamid's case, a wise man.

His education was spotty, consisting of grammar school and a year or two at a teacher training college. He had taught himself by reading and spending as much time as he could in the company of the wiser teachers at the mosque. A few years before we met, the American Consulate General in Asmara had awarded him an exchange-visitor grant to spend thirty days on an educational tour of the U.S. He loved every minute of it and was tickled to death when he heard that the Peace Corps would be sending Americans to Agordot.

As Hamid came to trust us, he became our source of fascinating information about the war that was taking form all around us. A staunch man of peace, he was also sensitive to the legitimate grievances of the Muslim population. He would not actively join the revolution, but he enjoyed every story of their guerrilla strikes in the hinterland.

Eritreans, Hamid said, had never been happy with the Allies' decision to give Eritrea to Haile Selassie's Ethiopia. Disposing of the Axis' only colonies in Africa—Libya, Italian Somaliland and Eritrea—was not a priority issue for the West in the late 1940s. Haile Selassie, who had considerable international popularity, wanted access to the sea for landlocked Ethiopia. Why not let him have it?

As Hamid explained it to me, the Eritreans of the 1950s saw themselves as more worldly than the Ethiopians. Their location on the sea had given them access to the outside world for centuries, while the Ethiopians, isolated as they were in their mountain kingdoms, had less contact with new ideas and inventions. The Eritrean experience with sixty years of Italian colonialism had left them with skills in mechanics, business and other aspects of modern economy that were unknown in Ethiopia. Eritrean Muslims were uncomfortable with a government that had a state religion that wasn't theirs. Tigrinya speakers in both Tigre Province of Ethiopia and in Eritrea regarded Haile Selassie and his Amhara kinsmen as upstart usurpers of a throne that rightfully belonged in Tigre. Nonetheless, Eritrean Christians saw an affinity with the Amhara, with whom they shared a religion and a language group, if not the particular dialect. Many Eritreans made a genuine effort to make the new arrangement work.

One day as I was teaching a seventh-grade history class, we heard a muffled blast off in the distance. I didn't pay it any heed until later in the day when people told me that a bomb had gone off at the Senior District Officer's office. The bombers left a calling card in the form of an announcement over Radio Khartoum that this bomb had been set off by a group called the Eritrean Liberation Front. It was the first time that Hamid Idris and his friends had given their movement a name.

Only once in my first year in Agordot did the war come a bit too close. I had just turned the light out when an explosion went off just outside my bedroom window, just a few feet from my head, but with a wall in between me and the event. I heard a man screaming in pain and others running to his assistance. There was no door on that side of our house, and by the time Paul and I got some clothes on and got out to the street, the whole thing was over and he was being carried off to the veterinarian.

Our house was just across the street from the police station. Rebels had set a crude land mine in front of the station in the dark hoping to hit one of the officers. They succeeded, but this time the victim was a Muslim officer who was known for his fair treatment of people.

As I look back over my life from the perspective of sixty, I realize that that moment was the closest I have ever come to actual combat despite having been intensely, but peripherally, involved in nine or ten armed conflicts. It seems, my reaction should have been more profound. It wasn't. I just went to sleep, and don't remember thinking or talking about it much at all.

I spent the summer of 1963 in Asmara. By then, the Eritrean Liberation Front had staged several hit-and-run operations on targets in the highlands near the capital city, making the point that they were not just a small movement in the western lowlands. They had also begun to demonstrate some of the military panache for which they would later become noted.

I was sensitive to the non-political nature of the Peace Corps and did not want to embarrass the institution by taking sides. At the same time I wanted the people I lived and worked with to understand that I understood their predicament. It was a narrow tightrope to walk. Nonetheless, the fact that we did not preach did not mean that we did not present a point of view reflecting our American bias in favor of democracy.

As Eritrea and Ethiopia slipped ever closer to total war, the government's efforts to stifle opposition grew. One day, I was teaching a sixth grade class in English. As usual, the only background noise was the sound of goats and camels being paraded down the street alongside the school, and the murmuring from the market. Suddenly there was a deafening and increasing roar that seemed to come from nowhere. Earthquake, I thought, although I had yet to experience an earthquake. As the roar turned into a shriek, the school went berserk. Kids were jumping out of windows to run...where? Animals panicked and so did everyone in the market. They all ran about senselessly, except for my class, which followed the teacher who hit the floor. The noise came from three F-85 fighter-bombers that flew directly over the school at a height of about ninety feet. They were supposed to frighten us from rebelling.

When it was over, my students and I arose from our igno-
minious positions, the kids all laughing. I knew that I was the
subject of the humor, but I wasn't sure why. I asked what was
so funny, but, at first, got no reply except for more giggles.
Finally Mohammed Ali Elmi, a Somali boy who was the
brightest in the class, closed his eyes, stood rigidly at attention
as if expecting the worst, and said: "But sir, we have never
seen a white man become whiter before." The Ethiopian Air
Force had had its desired effect on me.

The F-85s, by the way, were donated by the people and
government of the United States of America. As Americans,
we were in a difficult spot in Eritrea. It was an American
Secretary of State, after all, who had made the decision to
give Eritrea to Ethiopia. Part of that deal was a promise from
Haile Selassie that he would allow the U.S. to maintain a then-
important communications base at Asmara. In return, the U.S.
touted His Imperial Majesty as a serious defense against communism. To keep Russia at bay, we gave him every manner
of military hardware that he asked for—and he was greedy.

Unfortunately, rather than discourage communism, our
support for the feudal lord encouraged all those who hated
him to look at communism as an alternative to the U.S.-
backed regime. The Eritrean revolutionaries, along with those
from Tigre, the Somali tribes, Amhara dissidents and others
who opposed the Emperor, became communists and Maoists
in the 1960s, 1970s and 1980s, mainly because they saw the
U.S. as the enemy. We were constantly bombarded with questions from students as to how a democracy could go to such
lengths to support a king.

The hardest one to answer was the student who asked me
why the Ethiopian soldier wearing the donated American uniform and carrying a donated American M-1 rifle had killed his
grandfather the night before. What could I say?

Through the years of struggle, I heard various rumors about the town of Agordot itself, most of which were catastrophic: in 1975, I heard that Ethiopian bombing of Eritrea had been so severe that there were "not two stones connected to one another west of Keren." Fortunately, that wasn't true. Paul Koprowski and I took a sentimental journey back to Agordot in 1997 when Eritrea was enjoying a post-independence boom. Almost every structure we remembered was still there, although the town is much larger now. Where once there were only 12 students in the eighth grade there is now a secondary school with 1,100 pupils. A paved road, lined with Russian-built tanks destroyed during the war, passes through and beyond Agordot as far as Barentu.

Tom Gallagher was the second Returned Peace Corps Volunteer (Ethiopia, 1962-64) to enter the U.S. Foreign Service. Ten years later, he resigned in disgust over the Vietnam War and the Nixon foreign policy. He became a social worker; and for ten years directed the largest public outpatient mental health clinic in the U.S. in San Francisco. On a volunteer basis, he also served as Director of the Counseling Program at the Gay Community Services Center of Los Angeles, which was the largest gay-oriented mental health program anywhere. In 1994 he returned to the Foreign Service where, among other assignments, he served as the State Department's Country Director for Eritrea, Sudan and the Democratic Republic of the Congo.

SUZANNE MEAGHER OWEN

✦
✦ ✦

Holding the Candle

Things we hide are, elsewhere, open and celebrated.

MY ROOMMATE JUDY AND I COULDN'T SEEM TO KEEP OUR TUNIS apartment clean or deal with hanging laundry out on rooftop lines. However, we had generous enough Peace Corps allowances to afford the luxury of hiring a woman to come to our aid one morning a week. We found her in the classified ads and tried to be as sophisticated as possible interviewing her, a new role for both of us.

Aicha won our hearts with her broad smile, gold teeth, discrete tattoos, and flowing *sefsari*, which she folded and left on a chair while working. After two workdays, she asked if she could come more frequently without charging more. We said we'd definitely pay her more, but she protested and said she was much happier being with us (and the other maids she met hanging laundry and sun-drying peppers and tomatoes on the baking hot, blindingly bright rooftop) than at home.

She had gradually filled us in on her life: two little kids and a tyrannical, underemployed husband.

After teaching our TEFL classes at Institut Bourguiba, Judy and I walked back to our apartment, picking up enough provisions at various shops along the way to make lunch for Aicha and ourselves. She was very tolerant of our cooking gaffes and always appreciated every bite. We felt good about giving her a balanced meal. Simple as it was, it was probably her main sustenance on workdays. Aicha taught us domestic Arabic, and she learned more French and some English from our animated exchanges.

After a year and a half, Aicha gave birth to a third child, a son. She hadn't counted on having more children whom she couldn't afford and didn't seem to understand how it had happened. We gave her some linguistically challenged explanations. All three of us laughed loud and long. While she was still nursing, we escorted her to the birth control clinic, which was, I think, a Peace Corps project set up by the group which preceded us.

One day, as she was leaving the apartment, she turned more serious than I had seen her previously and asked me to assist at the circumcision of her infant son. Flattered by her request, I enthusiastically agreed to do so. Judy did not seem the least bit envious!

The next time Aicha came, I asked her what my role would be; she found a candle and handed it to me. When the appointed day arrived, I wound my way through the souks to the humble house she had led me to on a practice run. After she made her request, I'd asked a few male friends if they remembered their own circumcisions. Without exception, each shuddered, unable to imagine why I'd want to witness one.

Aicha was counting on me, so there I was, hoping that my hand would be steady enough, and that my squeamishness wouldn't make me faint!

Half a block from her house on a narrow cobblestone street, I heard lots of people in a festive mood speaking rapid-fire Arabic at her open, traditional blue door. She emerged to greet me and kissed me on both cheeks, looking beautiful with lots of kohl, freshly hennaed hair, lipstick, bracelets, and a colorful silk *safsari*. She led me into a small, low room, lit only by one high window and packed with her family and friends. All the furniture except one table had been removed. Aicha introduced me to her husband and her mother. She asked me to stand beside the table, handed me a candle, lit it, then disappeared to fetch her infant son, Radjeb.

Her husband and the "circumcisionist" appeared from the shadows next to me, then Aicha and little Radjeb, whom she laid on a cushion on the table. As the knife was lifted, suddenly, three trumpets blared loudly at the back of the room, causing me to jump in shock. No doubt some candle wax dripped to the floor as I reacted to the deafening, frenetic notes, but I was riveted by the task of casting the only light on the delicate operation.

The blade flashed; Radjeb shrieked in shock. The tiny foreskin fell from him. He continued wailing in his mother's comforting arms as the trumpets continued, conversations started, and the women ululated.

Over my third cup of potent sweet mint tea during the gathering afterwards, I learned that the relative darkness was meant to calm the baby boy, and the trumpets to distract him. I was proud to have brought light to this meaningful moment.

Suzanne Meagher Owen was a Peace Corps Volunteer in Tunisia from 1964-66.

ENID S. ABRAHAMI

*
* ★ *
*

A Morning

This stark tale of female circumcision cries. Just cries.

7:30 AS THE SUN RISES, A GROUP OF MOTHERS, GRANDMOTHERS and girls between the ages of one and five congregate in the compound next to mine. Each child has been meticulously washed and ritually draped in cloth of exquisite colors and intricate patterns.

8:00 The sky is crystal blue. One by one the women walk in single file *en brousse* to the neighboring village of Taibatou. There are nine girls all in all. One is my niece, Bintou, five years old and the oldest of the group. The others range in age from one to four years. Wrapped in different colored *pagnas*, each girl is carried by her mother, Bintou by her grandmother, my village "mother." I stay toward the back of the line.

8:30 We reach a small compound made up of four huts. Three children squat around a fire eating breakfast. Another two chase each other around. They are laughing. We are ushered into one of the middle huts—dark and musty. The back door is slightly ajar—a strong stream of light blares through. The voices of women can be heard coming from the backyard.

And then it begins. With a most piercing scream. So full of pain and anguish. All in the voice of a two-year-old child. Hidden behind the door. One can only imagine what is happening. My stomach turns.

8:42 A girl is carried out from the back through the hut to the front. She is wrapped in a gray sheet. It drips with blood. A drop falls on my shoe. Her face in shock. And she trembles.

8:43 Another one is carried to the back.

8:45 The horrid screams begin again.

8:48 She is carried out. Naked and profusely bleeding. Her young vagina resembles a piece of red meat.

8:49 Another one is carried to the back.

8:52 And the screams begin again.

8:57 And she is carried out. Naked and profusely bleeding. Her young vagina resembles a piece of red meat. Raw and mutilated. She moans.

9:10 I decide to go and see what takes place out back. With my own eyes. To witness and record. I am as ready as I ever will be.

9:12 Maybe not.

9:12 I step out back. A small rectangular yard, fenced and bare. There are seven women milling about. I can't look at faces. So I look on the ground. Blood is splattered. A rusty dull knife lies near a small can of water. A strange putrid smell surveys the air and enters my nostrils. I need to sit down. Beyond the confines of this space, Africa greets me. Neighboring huts. Trees of all sorts. Dry lush brush. A crisp horizon line. So very beautiful. And so in opposition to everything happening within the borders of the crinton fence.

9:13 A girl is dragged to where we stand. It is Bintou. She locks eyes with me, for only a second. Tears roll down her cheeks. She makes no sound. Already she looks in shock. I can turn around at any moment. Grab Bintou and leave. Put it all behind me. But I don't. I won't. I need to be a witness. The question is for whom and why?

9:14 The moment has come for Bintou to be cut. Seven women move quickly and without hesitation. Bintou, legs forced open, arms outstretched, lies on her back in between the legs of another. Face up. Open to the sky above. She is strapped. Held down. She can't move an inch. One just needs to look at her face. It tells all. The entire story.

The woman in charge takes the knife. Forces Bintou's legs wider. Gets a hold on a clitoris probably too small to really grasp. The thought of grabbing Bintou and escaping floods through my mind. But I am frozen. And then it begins. Knife in right hand, she begins. Like cutting a steak. Back and forth. Back and forth. Not a clean sweep. Not quick and momentary. My head spins and nausea takes hold of me. I am determined to stay, however.

9:15 Back and forth. Back and forth. Just a piece of red raw meat. I sit on a stone.

9:17 Bintou is placed almost in front of me. Still naked. Trembling. Bleeding. I try to comfort her with my eyes. And try to erase any sign of disgust and horror from my visage.

9:24 More red meat sliced. More shrill screams. More. More More. Will it never end?

9:26 My eyes, for refuge, wander out to the Africa laying beyond, stretching across. It is unchanged. Just as it was before. Except the body surveying the landscape has forever changed. Never to be the same. Silence invades me.

9:30 There are now two sitting directly in front of me. Bintou and Khudaijaa. The oldest two. The traumatized two. Hopefully the last two.

9:33 Nope. It's not over yet.

9:35 I can't anymore. I stand up and make my way out to the front courtyard. Five trembling girls, shell-shocked and wide-eyed, sit in a circle around an open fire. I look from one to another. A disturbing thought enters my mind. If one or two of these girls should die would the door for challenge be opened? From this group of nine, who would they be?

9:40 I turn off my senses. I feel like sour milk. Curdled and ugly.

9:42 Women talk to me. Ask me the most trivial of questions. Are any words coming out of my mouth? I can't tell.

9:50 It's over. Time to leave. Head back home. Girls are picked up. And carried. And strapped to the back. The walk begins. The march commences. And the singing starts. With a head reeling I focus on the basic task of walking. Of putting one foot in front of the other. Everything around me fades just a little. Becomes a background drop. White noise. Static.

10:15 We arrive back in our village of Missirah Tabadian. To the same compound where just a few hours earlier everything seemed so different. All nine girls are laid down side by side, each with a colorful ribbon tied around her head. Marking her as excised. The village comes to see them. Like in a museum.

10:25 I return to my hut. Exhausted. Tainted. My mind is a blank and at the same time flooding.

10:30 I think I just may throw up.

Enid Abrahami lived and worked as a Peace Corps Volunteer in Missira Tabadian, a small village located in South-East Senegal, West Africa from 1998-2000. Upon completing her Peace Corps Service, Enid decided to become a nurse with the hope of returning some day to the developing world to provide sustainable health care and education to underserved areas. She is a proud single mom of a remarkably curious two-and-a-half year-old boy, Mika, and a gentle fox-like dog she rescued from the streets of New York. This story is one that is featured in her memoir, Rain Washes Over Me Under the Moon.

GENEVIEVE MURAKAMI

A Brother in Need

Persistence is perhaps the most important
attribute of a Peace Corps Volunteer.

AS A RURAL HEALTH VOLUNTEER IN A VERY SMALL VILLAGE OF Fulani farmers and herders, I spent one day per week working at a health center in a neighboring town. Although I was not a health care professional and could not provide medication, the people of my village thought I was some kind of healer and often brought their sick to me before making the trek to the health center, hoping for a quick fix, free of charge. I treated minor cuts and gave advice when I could, but most of the time I had no idea what was wrong and ended up referring them to the nurse.

Roughly two months into my service, Diallo, a man who lived in my compound, became extremely ill, and my village family asked me to see him. I looked at his feverish puffy face and his swollen joints and the way he winced when I touched his elbow. With a weak voice, he told me all his joints hurt. I guessed he had an infection and it appeared very serious, so I suggested we go to the health center right away. My family knew I meant business; nobody goes anywhere during the midday heat in the hottest inhabited place on Earth.

It took us an hour to transport Diallo the two miles by *charrette* (a donkey-drawn carriage). His friend Kamara held him in his arms to break the stress of the jolting ride on the rough, red dirt road. Kamara's soulful eyes peered out from the turquoise fabric that encircled his head and face, looking down worriedly at his friend.

This was but one of many acts of tenderness I would witness among these people. I too was worried and, as the sun beat down on us, I prayed we would make it to the center before the nurse closed it for lunch.

But we were late, and I was forced to interrupt the nurse's much-needed afternoon nap. I felt I was pressing my luck since the nurse and I were relatively new in our working relationship; we had not yet formed much of a bond. We both spoke French, but that was about all we had in common. His living quarters were attached to the health center, so people came to him day and night for treatment. There was no such thing as an appointment, so the poor man never got much of a break. Standing in his doorway, squinting at us as his eyes adjusted to the bright sun, he seemed annoyed at my request, but he groggily agreed to see "my village brother."

A nurse in Senegal can make medical diagnoses and prescribe medication much like a doctor, even though he receives far less training. During a consultation there is almost no communication between the nurse and the patient: the patient tells the nurse the complaint, the nurse does some examining, writes a prescription, and tells the patient how to take the medicine—but does not usually tell them the medicine's name or explain how it works. Most of the rural people are illiterate, keeping them even more in the dark. This is why it came as no surprise to me when the nurse did a little pressing on Diallo's joints and sent him away with a prescription.

The nurse abruptly told me he was going back to sleep and walked off. I offered to wait until the pharmacy reopened after lunch to pick up the prescription, while Diallo was taken back to the village to rest. After I bought the medication, I read the insert to find out exactly what kind of drug it was. I expected an antibiotic, but it was a muscle relaxer! My heart fell; intuitively I knew this medication would not help him.

I wondered: Should I just give Diallo the medication, or should I go back to the nurse and try to get the prescription changed? This would involve second-guessing a professional who I had to work with for the next two years. I had no credibility; I was not a health professional. And I had annoyed him by interrupting his nap.

Diallo could only afford to pay half the price of the prescription, and I covered the other half, which was the equivalent of a few dollars. Drugs were fairly cheap, but money was hard to come by. I felt like we were just throwing it away on this medication.

Finally, I went back to the nurse's house, but he did not respond to my knocks. Due to a lack of electricity, I had to get back to the village before the sun went down, and I could not go back empty handed. I pedaled through the African bush, the cool breeze against my face, which normally made me happy, but which did nothing for the sick feeling I felt inside.

My only choice was to give Diallo the pills. My skills in the village language were not yet strong, and I didn't know how to tell him what I really thought. Besides, I didn't have a back-up plan. In the villagers' eyes, any medication is better than no medication and I figured they would have more trust in the nurse's decision than in my opinion. Having taken this kind of drug myself in the past, I knew that at least it would make him feel good. Still, it felt wrong; I did not believe it would cure him.

With sweat running down my back and tears on my cheeks, I watched him take the pills. It wasn't in my job description to cure him, but I had gotten myself into this mess, and I felt a responsibility to do my best for him. I stayed up half the night scouring my health books by candlelight, but found nothing.

The next day, although Diallo seemed more peaceful, his condition was worse. His face was getting puffier and his skin, once golden brown, had developed a gray tint. The joints in his arms and legs were getting larger and more painful. My village brother had rigged a sling made out of brightly colored African fabric, because Diallo couldn't tolerate the pain of his arms hanging at his sides. He could barely walk, but managed to shuffle over to my hut and ask if he could hang out with me. He said my hut was cooler and he wanted some of my "special water" (I filtered it). But it was all I had to offer. I looked at him sitting on my bed, sicker than anyone I had ever seen in my life. I ached to protect him.

Hoping that he felt better than he looked, I asked him, "*A samori sedha*?" (Have you healed a little?)

"No," he replied, and the sinking feeling in my stomach increased. His swelling made me think of circulation problems, and I had a feeling it was not going to get better.

I had a bad feeling. This man was my age—twenty-six— and, as far as I was concerned, this was not his time to go. I was not about to chalk this one up to Allah's will. Up to this point nobody had died in my village, and I really wanted to keep it that way. Besides, Diallo and I had lived about twenty feet away from each other for the past two months. He had grown on me. This sweet, soft-spoken man was my friend, and I had never lost a friend before.

Feeling helpless, I told him I thought he needed to see the nurse again. He then told s me that he had decided he had an "African illness" and it needed to be treated the "African way." This meant using traditional medicine. He told me he was going to see a traditional healer the following day. Since we were on "African time," I knew it would probably be a few days, and I felt it might be too late by then. This African culture uses traditional healers as much, or more often, than Western medicine. Since I was fairly new to the culture, hearing him say this was unexpected, but I shouldn't have been surprised. This is a man who wore a charm around his neck with a mirror embedded in it to ward off bad spirits.

What I was up against here? How far should I push Western medicine on him? All I had managed to do so far was stress out his body getting him to and from the health center. Should I let it go and let him deal with the illness the African way? I knew little about their traditional medicine; how was I to know if it wouldn't be the better solution?

This was one of many instances when Africa would humble me.

Later that night, I kept picturing Diallo shuffling around with his arms out in front of him like a zombie. I could not bear it. How could I just lie there looking up at the stars while my friend was probably dying? And, really, what did I have better to do? I was new here and did not have much work yet. My "job" for the first six months was to learn the language and gain the trust of the people, integrating myself into this extremely different culture.

I decided I couldn't let this one go and picked up one of my books again. To my great surprise and by the grace of God, I came across a drawing of an African man who looked to be in the same physical condition as Diallo. He had the swollen face and the swollen painful joints. It was like someone had drawn a picture of Diallo himself and slipped it into my book. How had I missed this page before? The image was labeled *Rheumatic fever,* which happens when strep throat is left untreated and the bacteria progresses to the heart valves. Penicillin, an antibiotic, was listed as the medication to treat it.

At breakfast the next morning, I asked Diallo if he had had a sore throat recently and he said yes. Things were starting to make some sense. It dawned on me why we get tested for strep in the U.S. whenever we have sore throats, and why it needs to be treated. I told Diallo I thought I might know what was wrong, but I needed to consult with the nurse first. I asked Diallo if he wanted me to do this; I did not want him to think I was totally disregarding his plans for treating his condition the African way. He said yes, and away I rode on my bike.

Feeling a little more confident now that I had a reference, I showed my book to the nurse. The book was *La, Ou Il n'y a pas de Docteur,* the West African version of *Where There is No Doctor.* The nurse told me he used to have the same book, and I think this gave me some credibility. I showed him the picture and I told him I thought this is what "my brother" must have. I told him that the medication he prescribed was not helping, and that Diallo was, in fact, getting worse. I knew I was risking seeming disrespectful, but a life was at stake. Fortunately, the nurse did not get angry or defensive. He said he originally thought Diallo had an articulation problem of the joints, but he agreed with me that Rheumatic fever was most likely what was really going on. Since it probably would have killed Diallo to be transported to the health center again, I went out on another limb and asked the nurse if he would be kind enough to ride his motorcycle out to my village and give Diallo a shot of long-acting penicillin. He agreed to do it, and Diallo got his injection that evening.

The next day Diallo started to look better; within a few days the swelling and pain were almost gone. He received an additional shot, per the book's protocol, a week later and after that, besides some residual weakness, he seemed back to his old self.

Diallo thanked me, but it did not appear to be that big of a deal to him or anyone else. The villagers went about their business as if nothing really happened, though I felt I had witnessed a miracle. I didn't think anyone, even Diallo, realized he could have died. But I was wrong.

Although he felt better, Diallo was still too weak to continue working in the fields under the hot sun. He was a guest of my village family and was earning his keep by working in their fields. He decided to go back to his native country, Guinea, to be with his family.

Before I knew about his plans for leaving, he stepped into my hut one morning and asked me if he could have a picture of me. Irritated, because he was the umpteenth villager to ask me for a photo, I asked him why he wanted one. He told me he wanted to show his mother a picture of the girl who saved his life.

That was how he really thanked me.

Genevieve (Wittenberg) Murakami was a Health Volunteer in the village of Allah Bougou, in the Tambacounda region of Senegal, West Africa from 1999-2001. She is currently a Registered Nurse who cares for newborns and new mothers in the postpartum unit of a local hospital.

STEPHANIE OPPENHEIMER-STREB

✦

A Tree Grows in Niamey

American connections, a brother's death,
bring a Senegal volunteer to Niger.

THIS IS A STORY OF FATE, CHANCE, AND REMEMBRANCE. IT SPEAKS of the power of relationships, no matter how brief. And in the end, it is not entirely mine.

My own Peace Corps experience in Senegal years ago made me eager to return to West Africa. The desert and cultures of Niger had fascinated me for years, and I embraced the opportunity for a six-month stay. As the departure date approached, I found myself in a new relationship, one about to connect me to this land-locked desert nation more than I could have imagined.

Chris was twelve when his older brother left to serve in Peace Corps Niger. Mark had been so anxious to know whether Peace Corps accepted him that he handed the letter to his little brother to open and read to him. It was 1985 when Mark left for Niger, where he completed his first three months of training. In the middle of a February night, he boarded a bus for the northern town of Arlit where he was to spend two years as a medical technician. About six hours outside of the capital city, the bus was hit by a truck—the driver is rumored to have been drinking.

In the basement of Chris's house, over twenty years after the accident, we found a box of Mark's things: group photos from training, a copy of his last journal entry, and signatures of those who attended his memorial at the embassy in Niamey where Volunteers planted a baobab tree and marked it with a plaque bearing his name.

After getting settled in Niger, I visited the Peace Corps office and mentioned Mark's name, knowing that many of the mechanics, drivers, and guards spend decades in service to the Peace Corps. A man in a khaki suit approached. He spoke very little French, and his thin body told the story of so many Nigeriens—one of poverty, hunger, and sickness. He seemed unsurprised that someone connected to the family would be now sitting in front of him, twenty-some years later. "I went to get his body that day." We stared at each other in silence before he continued, "For years I passed the site of the accident—the gnarled metal left at the side of the road haunted me." He was now an old man, sick and tired, but he remembered vividly.

Several months later, Chris traveled for the first time to Africa. He arrived to see me, but also to pay tribute to his older brother, to make a journey that fate forbade years before. The bus carried us north for fifteen hours, and I imagine the road has not improved since the 1980s. Large buses barrel down the eroding pavement, unable to stop should a goat, cow, or child be so unfortunate as to cross their path. Large trucks pass the buses so closely that divine intervention alone must keep the side mirrors on the vehicles intact.

The site of the accident passed us so rapidly it hardly seems possible that something so tragic could happen so quickly. We quietly gazed out the window at the dust in the air that swirled around the mud huts and granaries.

Chris carried Mark's guitar and played it on our travels, its song lifted to the night sky in an oasis on the night we became engaged to be married. I now wore Mark's godparents' ring on my left hand. The guitar joined the celebration in duets with Taureg musicians and paused only at the cue of clinking tea glasses: as the tradition says, one for death, one for life, and one for love.

Before departing Niger, I stopped by the Embassy and said goodbye to the new seedling now flourishing under the over-attentive Embassy sprinkler system. The old baobab tree next to the plaque had long since died. Turning to leave, I almost ran into a man who had silently approached. He had a hoe thrown over his shoulder. His clothes were tattered and, although his face was aged, he still carried his youth in his chiseled muscles.

"Was it you who planted the tree? I have been asking for you. I was there when we planted the first one. I remember." We stood for a moment, our eyes locked. A shared nod broke the contact, and I turned again to leave.

In his last existing journal entry, Mark expressed hesitation about leaving his new Peace Corps friends and departing for his post. He compared the anticipation to riding a roller coaster and feeling the first dip. "It is going to be incredible out there, that first time out on my own. I am sure it's something that I'll never forget, and after several months of hot season I expect to be a seasoned, emaciated, Peace Corps marine." And he writes, "I've just got to keep in mind why I'm here: (1) adventure; (2) to learn about another culture; (3) to learn a language; (4) to help people here; (5) to be less materialistic; (6) to have something in life to look back on; (7) to demonstrate willpower and resourcefulness and skill; (8) to finish something I started."

For Mark and other Volunteers who live on through the
memories of so many people around the world.

*Stephanie Oppenheimer-Streb was a PCV in Senegal from 1999-
2001 where she became good friends with ameobae, which eventually
inspired her to pursue a career in public health. She currently lives in
Baltimore with Chris, where she strives to make the perfect crabcake.*

BETSY POLHEMUS

✴

Jaarga

Politeness, and respect, can make family as strong as intimacy.

As Nanaman Diamanka and I walked across the scorched sand behind our family compound, he turned and smiled warmly at me. With his smile came so many distinctive facial effects: the flash of a few resilient teeth, weathered and shrunken skin drawn up into thin creases around his mouth, and sunlight reflected off of the moisture in his bloodshot eyes. I had been living in his compound for five months, but on that day the affection in his smile convinced me of my place in his family.

In high school I felt incredibly confined. I found breathing room in college during road trips to Canada, Seattle, the Redwoods, and Mexico. Needing more distance still, I went with the Peace Corps halfway around the world to Saare Foode, a small Pulaar village in the Kolda region of Senegal.

Scores of people were raucously awaiting my arrival, their deep black bodies overflowing on blazing off-white sand. My compound for the next three years was marked by a baobab tree, a species revered culturally and religiously in Senegal.

This one had a crooked trunk, bent over at the waist, extending a branchy hand in welcome. I was breathless for my first appearance, pedaling my standard-issue bike through winding paths of loose sand. Stomach afloat, my first impression of the village left me numb, blank, dizzy, dry-mouthed, grinning uncontrollably.

The group rushed toward me, drawing me into a swirling tide. One by one I shook calloused palms with my right hand. Horrified children ran screaming from me in all directions, a few never having seen a white person before.

Young men huddled around a small teapot resting in coals, unimpressed by my arrival. Women leapt, danced and clapped to drum beats, bare feet thumping the earth, elbows tucked in tight at their sides. A little girl meticulously stripped feathers from a limp, headless chicken while kitchen-hut smoke swirled black behind her. A cast-iron pot, so large I could have stepped inside, boiled fiercely over burning wood. Goats bleated and left trails of round droppings among trampling feet; donkeys let loose with horrendously foul flatulence.

The children returned from fleeing, lime-colored mucus dribbling over their mouths and chins, and began to stroke my arms and legs with their rough and dusty hands.

I was shown into the largest hut of the compound, now bursting with bodies. When my eyes finally adjusted to the darkness, I allowed them to wander shamelessly between the faces of men, seated on a thin mat made of quilted rice sacks. Some wore battered beanie caps, long tattered robes and cheap silver rings; others wore aged slacks and stretched polo shirts. They did not return my glances. I knew instinctively that these men ruled Saare Foode. As I sat on the hut's rickety bed, a platformed foam mattress covered with a ghost of a sheet, the group began to pray. With hands cupped together in their laps and open palms facing up toward Allah, the men grunted in unison as the leader paused for breath.

It was only after their prayers were complete that they saw me, an awkward moment for all. Brown eyes rested on me. Stiff bodies shifted on the mat. I looked down at my feet, comparing my new rubber slippers with theirs, old and worn, some fused together again with heat. I looked up at the roof, lashed together with bamboo poles, the wedge-shaped spaces filled in with dried grasses.

One by one they acknowledged my presence, hoping for good things to come from my work. But what could a young American girl do to improve Saare Foode? Did the village need a millet machine, vegetable garden, bigger boutique? Fingers pointed; the discussion became heated. Men stood and raised their voices. What I had learned so far of the language did me no good; I was lost.

A stretch of silence followed the chaos. The group then exchanged nods and murmurs of approval. The meeting was over. One man began to stand slowly, slightly wobbly from the stiffness of age. His skeletal frame revealed a height of six feet or more; a shadow of graying hair covered his chin. I knew this must be my father, the chief.

As he made to leave, I cleared my throat and surprised even myself as I asked, *"Hono woni inde am?"* He stopped, turned to look at me, and replied that I would now be called Sona. I nodded and added my consent, *"Awa."*

After he named me, I addressed him as *jaarga*, or chief, in the Fulakunda dialect of the Pulaar language. He seemed to appreciate the respect, but the rest of his family laughed at the stuffiness. At my mother's advice, I tried using *baaba*, or father. He seemed just as content; however, knowing that the words for father and for donkey sound alike, I grew self-conscious about getting it wrong. In the end I settled for Na (pronounced with a Spanish tilde over the n), short for his first name, Nanaman, just like everyone else.

For three years, he and I exchanged greetings each morning from the doorways of our neighboring huts. First he performed ritual ablutions of his hands, feet, face, ears and mouth with a plastic kettle full of water while I scanned the compound for the broom made of bound palm fronds I used to sweep my entry. Then he'd turn my way and ask how I had woken, and if I was with peace. I replied that I was *jam tan*, with peace only, and asked the same of him. These greetings are central to Pulaar conversations; I experienced the same with numerous people each morning, but my first exchange of the day was usually with him.

Truth be told, I grew closer to the other members of Na's family than I ever did with him. His only wife, Wonto, quickly became another mother, tucking me under her thin little wings to guide me through her extraordinary world. My older brother, Wuura, exceedingly intelligent, understood better than anyone where I had come from. His wife, Wopa, and I had a turbulent relationship, culminating in mutual admiration: her first born was named after me, and I intend to do the same for her. Na's only daughter, Maimuna, who has since passed away, immediately fell into place as the only sister I have ever had, sharing snickers with me over bad hairdos and *saisai*, tricky men. My three younger brothers, Daoda, Djibby and Diao, took care of me in any way that they could, preparing hot tea or a rare treat of fried eggs, running errands, guiding explorations via cattle trails, taking me to soccer games. Na remained remote, perhaps hesitant to fully embrace my cause or abilities. Despite this distance between us, I respected him deeply.

I presented both Na and Wonto with *gooro*, or kola nuts, wrapped in strips of torn paper bags, on a regular basis. For many of the cultures in Senegal, kola nuts are a respectful gift, offered and received during traditional ceremonies and holidays. The price fluctuates regularly, but never too far from affordable, even during the close of a meager dry season. Men sell them on street corners in Kolda town, out of large burlap sacks set upright, the nuts split into layers of variegated pink and brown. Both Na and Wonto endured an addiction to the nut's caffeine, suffering through headaches when not chewing on the rubbery slices. I could count the number of teeth left in their mouths on one hand; what was left was stained yellowish-brown by their habit.

My mother tied her *gooro* into a top corner of her *saba*, or sarong, secured inconspicuously at her waist. I asked her where Na kept his, since his billowing pants and tank top left little room for secret stashes. She flashed me a gaping grin, and told me that Na buried his kola nuts under a young mango tree behind his hut. I responded with disbelief, laughing at the picture in my mind of Na digging a hole in the soundless night, shifty like a prisoner spooning his way to freedom.

A few days after she told me this, Wonto appeared in my doorway. Na had gone to the fields, she whispered, and we needed to hurry. Not knowing what she had in mind, I dutifully followed as she led me through his hut and out back. It only took her a few minutes to find his treasure, carefully wrapped in a scrap of worn material and secured with rope. She smiled at me, and with her fingers pantomimed sealing her mouth in secrecy, her version of zipping up two lips and throwing away the key. Then she reburied the package carefully, just as we had found it.

Saare Foode's chief lived with a stutter. He could pull off ceremonial events without a hitch, yet the presence of strangers seemed to block his speech. Great patience was required to hear the final details of his stories; rounded "o" sounds were especially challenging for him. Mean-spirited children teased him behind his back. Spiteful adults attributed his stutter to poor leadership skills and a lack of power. In truth, Na's traditional ways did frustrate those who wanted to incorporate modernity into Saare Foode. He spent free afternoons coiling rope fashioned by hand from baobab bark he had harvested and dried; he indulged in lazy gossip and card games at the boutique. He did not understand banking, books or batteries; he was uninterested in lessons. Decisions, which by cultural rule should have involved the chief, were sometimes made in his absence.

Wherever I went in Senegal, guests were always escorted out of the compound when leaving. We would accompany a guest from the *bumbaa,* or the women's hut, across the compound while making small-talk, and then down the short sand path where the main road began. If the person was especially respected, we might escort them further, the slower the better. The day before I was supposed to leave for good, rumor had it that the entire village was planning to accompany me a mile, into Kolda town. I did not wait to find out if they actually would.

I had learned of another Pulaar custom surrounding a person leaving for a very long time: it is acceptable to sneak out in the middle of the night. The evening before I left, I told only Na that I would be gone in the morning. I did not want anyone to worry for my safety, and felt he deserved a sincere thank you for allowing me to be a Diamanka. He told me my decision had brought him relief and happiness, and then he wished me peace.

These days, Wuura and I talk on our cell phones sporadically, always on a Sunday. He called once and I knew something was wrong from the hesitancy in his voice. I allowed the conversation to meander; finally Wuura told me that Na was sick, and in the Kolda hospital with heart problems. My thoughts returned to Na's smile, and his acceptance of me as another daughter. He slowly recovered, although he will never work alongside his sons in the family's millet fields again. Wuura will someday become chief of Saare Foode, and in his capable hands I imagine the village successfully blending tradition with technology.

In my dreams, I see Na seated on an old mossy-green rice sack, spread out in the shade of his hut's bamboo overhang. He's surrounded by the makings of his rope: strips of dried bark coiled in loose loops. His limber body allows him to lean forward, his arms reaching along the length of his long legs, stretched out in front of him. Na's hands deftly twist and turn the strips, anchored around his oddly shaped big toe. Heat sizzles the ground, Wonto brings him a plastic cup full of cool water, and his wizened eyes shift between his work, the road and the sky.

Wuura called. I was hoping for another routine Sunday chat, filled with the familiar exchanges of *jam tan*. Instead, his voice shaky, he told me that my village father, Nanaman Diamanka, had passed away. Wuura had put off the phone call for weeks, he explained apologetically, not wanting to upset me. I remembered with a shudder what death encompasses for the Pulaar: thick emotional mourning, tears heavy with grief, and oftentimes a very real physical reaction. Women wail out loud in gut-wrenching tones, their cries heard in neighboring villages, and sometimes roll on the ground, as if trying to shake the pain of anguish from their bodies. Preparations for the funeral of a chief would have been all encompassing. So I did not blame Wuura for not telling me right away.

Just before Na died, Wuura had rented a car, he explained carefully, and taken Na all the way to the capital city of Dakar, looking for better medical care. These new doctors echoed what the Kolda doctors had already said: Na was simply old, and his heart had decided to let go. There was nothing they could do.

It was Na's first time to the big city, an exhausting twelve-hour car ride away from the only home he had ever known. I cannot imagine what jarring pain the bumpy and dusty journey must have caused his worn and fragile body. On the other hand, I can imagine the amazement his still-sharp mind must have registered on entering the city, those eyes I remember so well taking in high rises, smoke-choked traffic and the manicured lawns of the Place de Indépendance.

Interestingly, Wuura also told me of his decision to defer his right as chief to an uncle I had never met. I remembered stories of Alasan: he lived richly in Nigeria, had travelled to Mecca, and was regarded as worldly and full of broad intelligence. Wuura assured me that the decision had been his alone, and expressed his strong intent to become chief when he felt ready to carry such responsibility. Had I been there in person, he would have read the disappointment on my face. Instead, I voiced my support of his decision, as a younger sister in his culture should.

Wuura was also the proud bearer of good news: Wopa gave birth to their third daughter, Sadjio, and my younger brother Daoda and his wife had their firstborn, a son named Aliou. Nowhere has the ever-occurring cycle of life and death been more evident to me, blunt and numbed with reality, than in Saare Foode.

Betsy Polhemus, a PCV in Senegal from 2001-03, lives in Hawaii with her husband, Johnny Dyer, RPCV Zimbabwe 2001, Senegal 2002-04. She is, for the most part, jam tan.

For Lack of a Quarter...

Death never lacks its ironies, especially avoidable death.

SHE WAS LYING, HALF PROPPED UP AGAINST HER HUSBAND, ON THE bench in the back of the Land Cruiser. It was the only transportation they had found since she had fallen ill two weeks ago. Tata Daniel had yielded to pressure to give them a ride when on an errand delivering a message.

All eyes were on Lusadusu, who had just examined the woman. "She is very ill," he explained to me, the PCV along on the trip. "She has a liver abscess from years of suffering from malarial and other parasites: It has made her extremely anemic.

"Mama Irene," he requested, "we have to transport this patient with us to the hospital. There is no medicine or equipment here. Can you sit in the front between the driver and me?"

I looked at the stricken woman: *She does not appear very old, maybe late twenties.* "But of course, no problem, I'll squeeze in the front with you and Tata Daniel." My mind wandered, remembering: *These trips are always dramatic. Last time we transported a woman who was in labor, and I thought she was going to*

have the baby right there in the back of the truck. I suppose we have
to bring this one, too, in spite of the rules.

"All packed up and ready," Tata Daniel, the driver assured
himself of this by looking in the rear-view mirror. He started
to back the truck up the narrow path and toward the dusty
road. He worried aloud: "I hope we make it all the way to
Kimpese without a hitch, or I'll get blamed again, since I took
it upon myself to accept this ailing woman passenger."

While still backing, there was shouting from the rear:
"Stop, stop, she is having a seizure!" Nurse Lusadusu got out
and walked around to to re-examine the patient. Lusadusu
now yelled for a blood pressure gauge, the most high-tech
item available. As usual, excitement caused him to stutter.
After a couple of minutes, he explained, "Irene, we cannot
take this woman to Kimpese to die." Then he turned to the
village nurse and commanded: "Send one of your helpers to
the Seventh Day Adventist clinic and see if they have an IV
and some fluid. It would be embarrassing to lose a patient with
the villagers watching."

Just then the woman had another convulsion. Lusadusu
asked the nurses' aides to carry her into the mud-brick Health
Center. Besides my co-workers—Nketani and Matumona
and me—a crowd of curious villagers had gathered. Just as
the aides were passing, carrying the woman by her feet and
shoulders, her body went limp, releasing her fluids. I looked
at the wet trail on the red earth. *Oh, my God, the poor woman*
just died, right in front of my eyes. She is so young. Life isn't fair!
These people suffer so much. Damn politics! Damn these people for
being so complacent. They die for lack of a quarter...the fare for a trip
to the hospital. Life is too cheap here, worth less than a quarter....

Lusadusu came out from the room where they had taken
the body. Apprehensive, he made an announcement. His
mind was busy looking for the right words, but there were

none. "Everybody must think I am incompetent. I must save face. How do they expect me to do this job—an IV could have stabilized her to get her to the hospital in Kimpese." He looked up and, instead of commenting on what had just happened, said to his crew: "Let's re-load the truck; we must get home."

Daniel, Matumona, and Nketani, were talking on the side of the path.

"Lusadusu, this wasn't your fault; it's the system. They should have tried to find a ride on a produce lorry two weeks ago to take her to the hospital. They didn't want to spend the money for the ride on the lorry. They waited too long to get help. There is nothing you could have done to saver her."

The woman's husband huddled in the dust beside the path, next to a neat little pile consisting of their cooking pots, reed mats, and other meager belongings. He covered his face with his large calloused hands, trying to hide the tears. "How will I get her body back to my village now?" he pondered. "She deserves a decent burial in the ancestral cemetery. How will I justify these additional expenses to my other wives? I should never have brought her here. I would not be faced with this dilemma now."

Irene Brammertz immigrated to the United States from Switzerland in 1964. After her children were grown, she served in the Peace Corps in Zaire (now Democratic Republic of Congo) in the Public Health Program from 1988-1990. Her service in the Peace Corps was the catalyst that inspired her to further her education. She holds a master's degree in Public Health, International Health Management, from the University of South Florida in Tampa.

MICHELLE STONER

Crazy Cat Lady

Bridging the gap on wounded paws.

AN IMPRESSIVELY SEALED PACKAGE ARRIVED AT MY HOUSE WITH the Peace Corps logo neatly printed in the upper left corner. The anticipation of finding out where I would spend the next two-odd years of my life had grown so high that I almost couldn't open it. My roommates and I rushed inside; as they huddled around me, I broke the seal.

Niger. Niger? Where on Earth is Niger? I had spent the last year studying Sub-Saharan Africa, starring at a map of the continent, wondering where I'd be going. Somehow I skipped over Niger. Puzzled, we discovered a landlocked country right in the heart of the Sahara Desert.

When I envisioned myself in Africa, I fantasized about living along the coast in an animist culture, dancing around fires next to the ocean, praying to the wind for rain, wealth, and fertility. I imagined staying up late at weddings and naming ceremonies, dancing with the women until our feet blistered and the sun came up.

When the plane landed in Niamey, I was mortified. This was an Africa I knew nothing about, a vast, endless sea of chalky rust-colored sand, speckled with low and pokey shrubs and twisted knobby trees. I could feel the temperature rise as the plane hit the ground, fearing the dreaded hot season, where temperatures reach 140 degrees Fahrenheit. The mystery of the desert and its boundlessness could swallow me whole.

Settling in, I saw my dreams of dancing barefoot with African women shift. After two months of intensive training, I was delivered to my assigned village. Kiota. Niger is 99 percent Muslim, and Kiota is the most religious town in the western part of the country. An influential Sheik, or Caliph, resides in the town. People make pilgrimages from all over West Africa and the world to be blessed by this Sheik, who soon became my "father," as he came to refer to me as his daughter, or *sheikizo*.

Making a home for myself in Kiota, I unknowingly dipped into a world I knew nothing about and actually feared as an American. Instead of being in an animist culture, I was amongst some of the most devout Muslims in Niger. The Sheik attracted Nigeriens from diverse ethnic groups, who then installed themselves in different sections of the town. The cultivating Zarmas, the Hausas. The nomadic Tuaregs migrated in and out of the town, bringing their camels to the bush during the planting season. The pastoralist Fulani lived on the outskirts with their animals in tiny round mud huts covered in straw. I loved watching the young Fulani men come to town on market day with their ghetto-blasters blaring muffled Nigerien music, their stylish top hats, colorful necklaces of red, yellow, and blue, and coveted plastic sandals that didn't quite fit.

I was torn out of sleep every morning at 5:15 A.M. for the first call to prayer from the loudspeaker at the mosque. The usual calling, "Allahu Akbar," was followed by the voice of a man, ancient enough to have seen Niger when it was covered in water, singing. I could hear the entire town awakening: the crow of roosters, the screaming of children on their way to school, the banging of pots and pans from women beginning the long process of making meals, the sound of men getting water to perform their morning ablutions, washing their feet, hands, arms, necks, and face to pray. I rolled over, feeling like an alien looking perplexedly in on this culture, wondering how it all revolved around a mosque in the center of town.

Who would have known that 80 percent of my job as a Peace Corps Volunteer would be socializing, which was more exhausting than it sounds? All of a sudden, I had celebrity status, making half of my village curious admirers and the other half criticizing paparazzi. I made routines for myself, circling the village from different directions, ducking into random households to greet people. I usually got stuck with the kids, was fed interesting food, and would end up sleeping or staring at people, exhausted from the heat and unable to converse in the language.

As time went by, I began feeling more comfortable and less like an outsider. There were times when I forgot I lived in a rural bush town in West Africa, until catastrophic events happened and I needed Western conveniences or concepts—such as a veterinarian.

One morning I awoke in a funk, frustrated at the slow progress I was making. I decided to release some steam on a bike ride. At six in the morning, before the sun had unleashed its flames, I rode the farthest I had ever gone, passing sleepy villages just on the verge of waking.

My senses swelled as I took in my surroundings. A rainbow of bright colors slowly appeared on the horizon, a moving line of yellow, blue, and red flags swaying lightly against a rust orange world. A band of women was making the early morning trek up to my village to sell crafts and food, calabashes atop their heads overflowing with guavas, milk, and millet stalks. As I approached, we exchanged greetings, they laughing at the white girl with a weird hat and pants on who could somehow speak their language, me admiring their vibrancy and the little babies attached to their backs, asleep through their mothers' laughter.

My favorite part of the ride was dashing through a eucalyptus grove, enveloped by the healing smell. As I rode, little frogs jumped from under my wheels, seeking refuge in a rainy season lake. The sound of the swish of my tires against their plopping in water made my inner child laugh aloud.

On my way home, I passed through a village I knew, trying not to be seen by anyone, avoiding engaging in a stream of greetings. Nigeriens take greeting very seriously; one can get stuck on anything from the weather to being single and sleeping alone. One of my favorite greetings was "*Matte ndunya gorey*," which literally translates "How is sitting in the world," or "How is existing?" Sometimes greeting could be a sport, each party firing off greetings and responses, but other times it was exhausting for me. It always seemed someone called out when I tried to rush on by on American time.

An elderly Fulani woman called at me, "Charifa!" and asked me to sit with her and her family. We chatted and she lavished me with blessings from God and begged me to take her daughter to America to receive an education. I left her house with an uplifted but equally heavy heart and six guinea-fowl eggs in my pocket. Glorious! I would go home and boil some eggs. I pedaled gleefully, swishing and splashing through puddles with eggs on my mind.

Excited and exhausted, I opened my house to find it covered in blood. Confused, I searched around only to find my cat, Percy, lying pathetically inside, bleeding profusely from his front and back paws. He was cut so deeply that I saw bone, his tendons and muscles pouring out of the wound. Gagging in disgust and panic, I wrapped him in a blanket and washed his cuts with warm water and salt. I bolted outside to consult the blacksmith, Afoulan, who had become a father, brother, and best friend in my year living next to him. He had always been terrified of my "huge" cat, but he was my confidante.

Most Nigeriens couldn't understand the concept of caring for pets. Some people can barely feed their households; having a pet is a luxury. Pets in Niger are kept for practical purposes; storeowners owns cat to rid their stores of mice.

I begged Afoulan to come see my cat, and he told me to stop freaking out, that Percy would lick himself better. Keeping his distance, Afoulan took one look at Percy and understood my panic. He told me about a man in the village who treated livestock for a living and who might be able to help Percy.

I hustled around my village, never an easy task considering the importance of stopping to greet people and the slow pace of life in the village. Hustle Charifa, hustle! Just don't make eye contact! First stop: cancel my Arabic lesson. I walked into my teacher's house, a studied, highly religious man from Chad who lived amongst a group of other single male teachers who came to Kiota to teach school. Hassimi was very modern for being so religious and he often had rap videos or explicit videos showing on his TV/DVD. I got pressured into watching the video, all the while my heart beating pounding with worry over my poor cat! It is custom to stay for three rounds of tea, but I excused myself after the first.

The livestock man was tall and kind-faced with a beard and a mustache, which is uncommon for Nigeriens. He looked like he belonged in the 1950s in his clean, navy blue pressed suit. He seemed peaceful and dignified and was holding an equally peaceful baby, who didn't make a sound. I told him all about my problem. He listened with a confused expression, and I wasn't surprised when it turned out he had never worked on a cat. He reluctantly agreed to meet me at my house to assess the situation.

I ran to the doctor's office to ask for some cotton to clean the cat's wounds. The women who worked at the hospital always joked with me. When I came rushing in hysterical, demanding medicine for my cat, it caused quite a riot. The women asked me for an exorbitant sum of money for the cotton balls and then told me to kill my cat and get a new one. I stomped out with tears of frustration in my eyes.

I bought some meat on the way home to feed to Percy. The livestock doctor came over. When he saw Percy's wounds, he said he definitely needed stitches and that his front paw might be broken. What happened to the cat? He said kids may have tortured it or, since it's so fat, maybe some other cat attacked it and it couldn't run away, which I thought highly unlikely. Should I put Percy on a bush taxi and travel two to twelve hours with him to get to a regional capital and see a real vet or should I let this livestock doctor operate on him?

We explored options and decided to go ahead with cat surgery in the village. The next obstacle was finding out how we would hold the cat down while the doctor stitched him up. It was decided I couldn't do it; I wasn't strong enough and "pitied the cat too much."

Afoulan refused, saying he'd have nightmares. We found one guy who seemed overly excited. He was pacing back and forth, yelling about how we'd tie Percy's four legs between two trees. He almost seemed mad and his aggression toward the cat was unsettling, but he was the only volunteer we had. He grabbed Percy's legs and tried tying them in rope, which didn't work. I held Percy, who was struggling and scratching me, delirious and exhausted. I finally recruited two strong young men to hold Percy down while the doctor stitched him with string. I didn't even know if I wanted to go through with this! What if Percy got infected or he died from pain? Did this guy really know what he was doing?

It was two in the afternoon. This had been going on for hours. Luckily there was a prayer call; everyone left my concession before I broke down. I started bawling and had a meltdown.

As I was crying, one of my little friends, Barham, entered my concession and looked at me in terror. Nigeriens don't cry, ever. In the face of suffering or misery, the mentality is, *Kala Suuru*, or "Have patience"; everything that happens was intended by God. Barham distracted me by asking about my mango tree and instructed me on how to water my other trees. He scolded me because I didn't add enough manure to my garden and I had to laugh at the fact that I was being schooled by a seven year old. I was humbled by his successful attempt at calming me.

After prayer, everyone came back and I decided it was time to stop discussing and stitch him up. We were already all exhausted from running back and fourth, recruiting people, and exploring options. I sterilized the doctor's equipment and fed everyone crystallized ginger so our stomach's wouldn't turn. The surgery was one of the most gruesome and brutal things I had ever witnessed, the three of us holding Percy down while he was crying and jerking.

In the end, Percy survived. I wrapped his feet every other day from my Peace Corps medical kit, and the doctor came to give him a shot for to avoid infection. Because of this experience, all of us grew close. Even Afoulan and the doctor took a fondness to Percy.

The whole village talked about the cat incident. People from surrounding villages would ask me about Percy's health.

I got made fun of but, for the most part, people recognized how important my cat was to me. When in the past, people ran away from my cat or didn't understand my affection toward him, now villagers would come to greet my ca and bring me dinner because they knew I was distressed.

After having witnessed me doctor Percy, mothers came knocking on my door accompanied by their children. The mom would announce that her child had a cut and ask for a bandage and some disinfectant. Even though I'd been trying to avoid using my Peace Corps medical kit, I surrendered and bandaged up every single one of those kids until my supplies ran out.

There is a fine line between cultural integration and cultural exchange; Percy bravely and admirably did his part to further mutual understanding. Through his suffering, he bridged a gap I had been perplexed by, and marked a poignant shift in how I existed in my village. Sure, there was laughter about the "cat incident," but the support the people of my village showed suggested that, although they may have not understood the concept of pet care and cat surgery, they cared enough about me to embrace and even nurture my neurotic and irrational behavior. That, to me, is love and acceptance.

Although I have moved back to America, Percy is still roaming free in the village, recognized and respected by all those he meets on his path.

Merci Percy.

Michelle Stoner, upon earning a degree in French and Geography, joined the Peace Corps and served as a community and youth educa- tion volunteer in Niger, West Africa from 2006-09. She extended her Peace Crops service to become the HIV/AIDS and Gender and Development Coordinator for Peace Corps Niger.

A A R O N   B A R L O W

Elephant Morning

Sometimes events get away from us…
or something allows us to get away.

SITTING UNDER A RESTAURANT VERANDA, AUGUST 2, 1990, IN
Dapaong, Togo, eating half of a grilled chicken, a bottle of
sparkling water beyond. Jean jacket draped over a chair. Below
me, on the street, my motorcycle rests safely on its kickstand,
the sun having long since dried the mud beneath it.

I pick. There isn't much taste to the chicken.

The sound of other dirt bikes draws my attention. Bikes.
Four round the corner, each topped by a rider in a yellow
full-faced helmet and goggles. They come to rest in a neat row
next to mine.

A normal occurrence: Dapaong is where we get our mail. I
move my jacket, tossing it onto the low cement wall. Helmets
now hanging from handlebars, gloves stuffed inside, jackets
coming off quickly in the heat, the riders come to my table,
pulling over a couple of chairs from the next.

"What happened to you this morning?"

"We heard the strangest story."

"In your village, they said you were hurt; you don't look hurt."

I reach up and feel the scratches on my scalp. "No, not much." They wait expectantly. I sigh, and start:

"I was drinking my coffee, under the *paiotte* outside my compound, by the bean field. Listening to the BBC."

"Did you hear the news?" I interrupt myself. "There's a war in the Mideast. Iraq invaded Kuwait." I speak in a monotone simply because I don't know what emotion to express. I'd been going over this for hours, but was no closer to any understanding. "The BBC began to tell about the war. But something caught my attention, moving towards me from out by Nassiett.

"From out in the bean field, an elephant was walking toward me."

"But you see elephants all the time!"

"That would be exciting for us posted where there are none. Not for you!"

"Yeah, but I've never gotten close." I pause again; this time, they wait. "So, I ducked back into my bedroom hut for my camera bag. As I ran back out, I scooped up the radio.

"That small hill behind my house, you know it?" They nod. "I thought I would be safe there, and could get a good picture, for it was headed right by my house, on its way back to the *Fosse aux lions* across the road." Again, they nod. They had passed through the game park on the road to Dapaong.

"Further on from my house, on the other side of the bean field, a group of people also watched as the elephant lumbered toward me. Damage to crops was already done; the elephant was heading home. So we all just watched, waited.

"I had two cameras, one you look down into. I did. Then I lifted my little rangefinder and snapped again.

"I felt great, excited; never had I been so close. But the elephant, without warning, without ear-flapping or trunk-raising, turned toward me and charged—straight up my little hill." I stop there. One of the things that had been bothering me was that no one was going to believe this. These four, however, had already heard some of the story. So, I knew I could continue, but slowly, deliberately. I did.

"It moved fast, shaking the ground, steps roaring as I turned and ran.

"I lost my sandals as I dashed down the other side of the hill and sprinted into the bean field, cameras and paraphernalia flapping, radio in hand blaring about Kuwait," I laugh; it does seem strange, "elephant right behind me. I remember deciding to scream, but it came out an odd, low moan as scary as the elephant, so I clipped it off.

"I remembered hearing that elephants don't corner too well. I might be able to circle around behind the elephant and back up the hill and over to the safety of my house. But I slipped on the moist earth as I turned, and I fell.

"Fell flat." How to tell what happened? I look in the faces of my fellow PCVs for a moment before continuing:

"I felt hopeless, sliding, about to hit the ground." How could anyone understand this? "As I went down, I twisted to look at the elephant and wondered what its foot was going to feel like on my head. I wondered if I would survive and doubted I would."

Remembering, I feel I'm not really even sitting here, but am only watching.

"Oddly—yes, it was odd and I can't explain it—but looking back at the elephant seemed better than imagining it behind me. Yes, I really did feel less panic as I fell. Before, I had no idea how close it was, no idea if it were about to crush me right then. Now I would, at least, see my end.

"The elephant was slowing. It knew I was trapped. It seemed to take so long for me to hit the ground.

"I decided to stay down. Scrambling about in a panic would do no good.

Staying still, I felt a weird sensation. Face it: this may be very painful, but there's nothing you can do about it. Let it happen. Maybe it won't be so bad. The mud may cushion the blows.

"Stupid thoughts, I know.

"The elephant, even walking now, could have been on top of me.

"Instead, it halted about three meters from me.

"We watched each other. I've been sitting here for hours, remembering. Running it through, again and again.

"First, it looked at me out of its right eye. Then it swung its head for its left. I stared at its trunk, at the massive furrows between its eyes. It moved its head back and looked at me once more out of the right eye. The radio, still on, speaker facing the mud, babbled." Now, I lean forward over the table, closer to the others.

"The elephant's ears had a series of healed gashes along their edges, and holes torn clear through in places. Perhaps it was old. It had no tusks, none at all. Just emptiness where they should protrude. It swung its head, for the other eye to see me, and then again. I looked at its skin, rough and dirty, wrinkled and gray, with occasional thick hairs upon it.

"'It's your move.' I stared back, concentrating on its eye. 'I'm at your mercy. But please make it soon, whatever you do; this lying here waiting will kill me if you do not. Imagining what it might feel like if you do me in: I do not like these thoughts.'

"The elephant swung its head, looking at me from one eye and then the other.

"I hadn't moved, hadn't done anything but look back. Now, slowly, I slid the straps attached to my cameras, bag, and meter from around my neck. If given the chance, I'd decided, I would run once more. This time unencumbered.

"The elephant was giving me hope. I wasn't going to let that die. If it only wanted to crush me, it would have already done so.

"It continued its slow swinging contemplation for a moment more, then turned slowly to its left, to face the *Fosse*, turning its head back to watch me, still. It had its tail, now, towards that group of villagers who had been watching when I first came out of my compound—who had witnessed the chase and fall in absolute silence, completely unable to come to my aid.

"'Are you offering me a chance, elephant? If so, I'm going to take it.'

"Scrambling, then, I was up, dashing madly toward the watchers, who were yelling now, 'run' and 'hurry,' though I hardly needed encouragement. *They* didn't run away as I neared, and I couldn't hear the thundering that had pursued me earlier. I stopped when I reached them and turned to watch the elephant. I was completely out of breath and beginning to shake, but curious as to why it had let me go and why it had chased me in the first place.

"It had turned back to where I'd lain, had stepped over to the equipment I'd dropped. One piece at a time, it lifted the radio, my light meter, and each camera to its mouth with its trunk, tasting and dropping each in its turn." I stop again and look at each of them. This part had seemed unreal even as it happened. I didn't know if I believed it, even though I'd seen it. "Then it took my camera bag by its strap, lifted it high over its head, and twirled the bag through the air. Film canisters, filters, and odds and ends of paper flew from it before the elephant let go, sending the bag on an arcing course out over the field. The elephant turned away from us, then, walked a few meters on, and looked back. Slowly, it reached down with its trunk and snatched up a clump of grass. Slowly, it ate the grass. Then, it headed back to the park."

No one says anything for a moment. Then I continue:

"I walked back to where my cameras, radio, and bag lay, gathered up as many of my things as I could, and carried them home. As far as I could tell, neither of my cameras was broken—the ground, after all, was soft. The radio was still playing.

"At home, I examined myself in a mirror, finding I was bleeding from a couple of scrapes by my hairline. My right side was a solid streak of mud down arm, trunk and leg.

"A couple of the villagers, guys I know fairly well, accompanied me home, and kids were now running up, presenting me with bits and pieces of my belongings, including my sandals. I thanked them, took a bucket shower, put water on for more coffee, and stepped inside to find fresh clothes.

"The clock by my bed said it was now twenty-five minutes before seven, just a bit more than half an hour since I'd sat down before. I mixed more coffee, walked back outside, sat down, wiped the dirt from the radio, adjusted the dial back to the BBC, and tried to prepare for the day once more. Now I could focus on the more important news, the conquest of Kuwait."

No one says anything. I pick up my knife and fork and try to eat the chicken.

Aaron Barlow, a PCV in Togo from 1998-90, is the author of a number of books in the cultural-studies field, including The Rise of the Blogosphere *and* The DVD Revolution: Movies, Culture, and Technology. *He teaches at New York City College of Technology. His most recent book is* Quentin Tarantino: Life at the Extremes. *He is the editor of this volume.*

JACK MEYERS

At Night the Bushes Whisper

Learning to see the world through other eyes at a cattle station in Somalia, though too late to save the other and barely in time to save himself, Meyers confronted the bush—and a lion.

SOMALIA IS HARSH. A LAND OF SEMI-ARID SAVANNA WITH A FEW fertile areas along the two main rivers, its predominant vegetation is flat-top acacia sprouting from red soil, intermixed with thorn bush. It is hot and dry inland and hot and humid on the coast, broken only by the two rainy seasons tempering the heat with added humidity.

I was to be acting veterinarian on a 20,000-acre cattle holding ground in the southern part of the country, about forty kilometers west of the southern port city of Kismayu. I had only the barest of information about the place and knew very little other than I would be sharing a bungalow with an Indian veterinarian by the name of Dr. K.K. George.

The place looked exactly as I pictured a compound in the heart of Africa would. There was a small clearing cut from the brush and cleared of all vegetation. One large building stood on one side of the compound and across from it were two huts closely packed together. They were made of mud and wattle, painted white and topped with thick grass roofs. The

425

contrast of whitewashed buildings on red sand was spectacular, and the overall appearance was one of an oasis of comfort and hospitality.

A thin, very dark man of East Indian features emerged from the one of the huts as I arrived. He approached with a wide smile and extended a bony hand that appeared to be all knuckles.

"Afternoon, sir," he said around a mouthful of brilliant white teeth, "I'm being Dr. K.K. George." He then added, "No doubt."

I shook a hand, rather limp and much frailer than it looked, and told him my name and expressed pleasure meeting him.

Dr. George had no time for sentiment; he grabbed my duffle bag and started toward a green door to one of the huts, "This vere you being placed. Very nice accommodations," he said, and then added, "no doubt."

The room was spartan indeed. A thin sagging mattress was laid on a rusted spring bed. Next to the bed was a rough wooden nightstand with a kerosene lantern and a candle. An oval, woven rush mat lay on the floor to complete the furnishings. As I walked into the room I saw a lone light bulb hanging from a crossbeam. At least I could expect light, but then why the lantern and candle? I hauled my footlocker into the room and Dr. George deposited the duffel bag on the bed.

"Being just like home, most likely," he chirped. "I'm showing you around."

We started with the hut next door; this was the eating room and was open and screened. Next was the outhouse, about thirty feet behind the huts.

He then stopped at a tiny dollhouse sitting atop a five foot post from which dangled a rope. Out popped a little monkey that immediately began to chatter and make all manner of noise. It jumped onto Dr. George's shoulder and began to groom his hair as Dr. George made the same chattering noises back, the two carrying on a conversation for some time before remembering I was standing there.

"This being Monk. He is black faced vervet monkey and being here vhen I arrived although being in much finer fiddle now." He placed the monkey back in the house and beckoned me to follow to a small building similar to the huts but with a metal roof. This was the laboratory. Dr. George took out an impressive ring full of keys, searched for some time, then produced one that he inserted into the massive lock hanging on the door. He opened it and motioned me in. Inside was a well-stocked and clean laboratory complete with everything needed to diagnose and treat cattle maladies.

"Dinner at seven, vater for vashing in cook hut, generator starting at six and running to nine." With that Dr. K.K George walked off to chatter with Monk some more.

Dinner usually consisted of onions sautéed in ghee with tomato paste and some meat, sometimes goat, but mostly you didn't want to know. This was poured over a glob of mushy noodles. Drink was either watery lime juice or sweet tea. Dr. George loved the stuff and made little mewing sounds as he ate. I, on the other hand, lasted about three days before cooking for myself.

After dinner that first evening, Dr. George became expansive and wanted to talk. However, I first asked him if it was O.K. to drop the Dr. George business. What could I call him?

"K vould being alright."

"O.K. K...," I began.

He interrupted me, "Vhich vone?"

"Which one what?" I asked.

"Vhich K first or middle?"

"Beats the hell out of me. Let's try the first K," I said.

"That being vrong. I using middle K," he said with smile and a little wiggle of his head. Dr. George was full of odd mannerisms, each one meaning something different. Wiggling his head on his shoulders like one of those bobbing dolls on the dashboard of a car could mean a number of things. It was up to me to figure them out.

"Alright, so middle K, I wanted to ask you…"

"Actually ve Indians don't usually use given names, my surname vill sufficing. George being fine… just George." Again the head bobbed, but this time he also cracked his knuckles. This meant that he was pleased with himself for making a jolly good joke.

Over the next few weeks, I was to learn a lot about and from Dr. George. To say he was one of the oddest and at the same time one of the most intriguing people I have ever met is not an exaggeration. For starters, Dr. George practiced Ayurvedic medicine. This is an ancient practice perfected in India and, in many cases, running contrary to modern Western medicine; in some cases it supersedes it. Basically Ayurvedic medicine uses herbs, poultices and infusions as its main means of treatment.

My first introduction to Ayurvedic medicine came after I was on the holding ground about a week. Dr. George and I were in the laboratory examining some slides under the microscope for trypanosomiasis when a voice yelled out from over by the cattle dip, "*Hodi, Hodi. Ngombe na mahaaradi.*" Neither one of us knew what it was saying, but rushed to the door to find out what the clamor was about. One of the herdsmen was standing next to a large white bull sporting the largest set of lyre-shaped horns I had ever seen. The man was pointing to the right leg of the bull and which was swollen below the knee and seeping blood and serum. He kept talking but, again, neither of us had the slightest idea of what he was saying until another herdsman approached and translated for us, in a mixture of Somali, Italian, and broken English, that a twig had stabbed the bull's leg a few days before and it had become infected. I was intrigued by the strange language of the herdsmen and was later to learn it was Swahili, a lyrical language and the linga franca of East Africa.

Dr. George examined the wound then went into the laboratory returning with a scalpel, gauze, and several pharmaceutical bottles. He bent down and quickly made a deep incision below and on the opposite side of the leg from the wound. He then mixed a combination of herbs and ointments and applied them to both sites, wrapping the gauze around the leg. He stood up and cracked his knuckles in appreciation of the fine surgery he just accomplished. I asked him about antibiotics. He said that herbs and the ointment of the nemantha tree were sufficient along with the natural abilities of the animal to heal itself. The problem with Western medicine, he explained, was that it presupposed that the body had no ability to heal itself. Eventually the body came to rely on antibacterial intervention and virtually shut down its own inherent homeostasis. I had to admit this was a novel and thought provoking approach.

Dr. George had a habit of challenging me to expand my knowledge into other areas. As it turned out, however, the leg got worse, infected at both wounds now. I gave the bull a large dose of ampicillin and dosed the wounds with gresiofulvisin. It made remarkable progress after that. Dr. George seemed unaffected by my application of Western medicine saying, "Vell it being apparent the herbs and ointments prepared the beast for your antibiotics. I must say they vorked vell together." That summed up our relationship, different cultures, different training; but we worked well together.

I was feeling particularly bored and depressed when George knocked on my door one night and asked if I would like to take a walk with him. This was unusual, as it was after dark and there were unfriendly animals lurking in the bush. It was a full moon, a hunting moon and I had rather strong trepidations about venturing outside the compound. But he persisted, and I grabbed an old shotgun and the only three shells we had.

The night was silent except for the occasional cackle of a guinea fowl or the low of the cattle in the night *bomas*. The sand was soft and warm from the day and the air was beginning to cool. The moon was up about 45 degrees and cast a bright glow on the bush, throwing shadows across our trail. George walked on for some time without saying anything. We had gone a little more than a mile, and I was beginning to feel more at ease when he abruptly stopped and cocked his head to the side, listening. He walked over to a large thorn bush and leaned over, touching his ear to the feathery leaves, "What…" I started to ask, but he held up a hand for silence. He turned to me and said, "There being danger about. Ve must returning to the compound."

He turned and jogged off the way we had come. Not about to be left behind even if I didn't know what the danger was, I overtook George and left him behind as I ran back to the compound. I was waiting at the cook hut as George staggered up and sat down.

"What was the danger?" I asked. "And how did you know?"

It took a few moments for him to catch his breath. "The bush telling me."

"What do you mean the bush told you? Bushes don't talk." I was starting to feel that George was playing a prank, an East Indian version of the mythical snipe hunt.

"No," he said. "Everything talks. You just having to listen. Animals, trees, brush, the vind. All having story. Trick being learning to listen. Brush talks best at night vhen the rest of the world stops to rest. It recalls the events of the day and comments about vhat happened. How many and vhat kind of bird rested in its branches, the antelope that foraged on its leaves, the ant that tickled its bark as it scampered up and down, the hated termite that ate its flesh. It talks of the sun and the vind and the rain and the aches and pains of getting old. Just like us. No different," he then added, "no doubt."

I still didn't believe a word of it, "You mean that bush actually talked to you? What language? Hindi or English or maybe bushes have their own language."

My sarcasm was lost on him, "No language. They talking into your head. I telling, you have to learn to listen. The ancients learned to listen. Modern man losing the art. Too many distractions; radio, TV, yelling."

"So what did that bush tell you?" I asked.

"It telling lion vas about." He was bobbing his head now, and I knew he was pulling my leg and it pissed me off, so I told him good night and went to my hut to read.

The next morning, while we were at breakfast, a herder came running up the yelling, "*Calli, calli daxxo. Nin wa demadi.*" My Somali was good enough by now to know that he was saying come quickly, a man was dead. We followed him at a run. About quarter of a mile into the bush we came on a small circle of herders standing around a pile of bloody rags. They parted as we approached. My stomach instantly turned and I lost my breakfast onto a small termite mound. There wasn't much left of the man. He had been torn apart from the chest down and his entrails and ribs were exposed and gleaming in the early morning sun. Ironically his face was untouched and appeared relaxed and composed as if asleep.

"What happened?" I asked in a raspy voice.

One of the men answered, "*Libah.* Lion."

I looked at George and the hair stood up on the back of my neck, and I had the strangest sensation that I had witnessed something beyond my ability to process. This was unnatural, strange, and scary. I looked at George; he just stood there with his hands clasped together, slowly bobbing his head.

There was the sound of cloth rustling and footsteps. A rush of bodies pressed us. The women from the village had been informed of the death and were descending on us. One strode forward and stood staring at the body, and then began a high-pitched keening. The other women joined in. A man stepped forward and covered the remains with a white sheet and several others stooped to pick up what was left of the body. They took him off to the village to prepare for the funeral, which by Muslim practice must occur before sundown. As George and I walked back to the compound I asked, "They really did tell you of the lion, didn't they? But how?"

He didn't answer for the longest time, finally saying, "Vhen I first obtained vet degree I vas assigned to game preserve in Rahjastan. It being most isolated and remote of areas. Dry, desolate, hot and unfriendly. I vas from Karala State, rainy, green, and having large family and very large populations of peoples. Now I vas all alone. No vone, just me and the animals and the bush. Not even much food and the vater vas terrible. I vas about to quit and going home vhen an old Fakir vandered into camp vone day."

"A what? " I asked.

"Fakir, a holy man," he answered. "For four days he sitting in shade under tree. I ask him, vanting food or vater? He saying nothings. Then finally he spoke. 'It is time for me to eat and drink, for what you give me, I will teach you many things.' He stay for three years, talk little, eat little; but I learn many things."

"How long did you stay at the preserve?" I asked.

"I staying twelve years." He answered. "Until the var and the soldiers coming and kill everything and there vas nothing left for me to take care of."

"He taught you to listen to the bushes?"

"Vell not exactly. He teaching me to opening my mind and seeing the vorld through other eyes. Vonce you seeing vorld from other eyes, you having different perspective. He telling me that vhat ve seeing not always being vhat is really. There being complete other vorld vere all things being equal and all things able to being talking to each others."

At the edge of the compound he stopped and continued his tale, "I trying for many, many years to free mind and see other vorld. Vone day I staring into a small pool from recent rain and seeing my reflection. Then reflection disappearing, and I seeing something else and then I looking from reflection at myself. I seeing from other eyes. From that day on I look, see and hearing different. And I able to listen."

My skepticism had been withering for some time. It was being replaced with a sort of reverence for this thin, quiet man who was so completely self-composed and so completely at peace that he could shed physical confines and enter into an ethereal universe.

"You keep saying that you're able to listen. Can you talk to other entities also?"

"Listening is most important. First listen. Listen, learn, feel. My opinion not vorth much until I learn. I being apprentice for many years. Finally vhen I listen enough, learn enough then I able to communicate."

He fell silent. I could tell the death of the herder had a strong effect on him. It affected me also, but more so as a shock at seeing a human body so brutalized. Before George entered his room he turned and said, "Lion liking human meat now. Ve must be very careful."

I could hear the lion roaring deep into the night. It was close to the compound, and I can truly say that the roar of a lion, loose, close and ready to do harm is the most terrifying of sounds. My bladder was close to bursting before first light gave me enough confidence to run to the outhouse, clutching the shotgun tightly with one hand while undoing my belt with the other.

Three nights later, the lion made another kill, a young girl who was carrying a jar of water on her head and was only fifty feet from her hut. It happened so fast that she uttered not a cry and then she was gone into the descending darkness. They came to my hut and asked me to help them search for her. I had a flashlight and the shotgun. I asked George to come along and, although very frightened, he agreed. We started tracking at the point she was taken. The Somalis were the best trackers and took the lead, although it was one of the Bantu girls, Tatu, who had been taken. They carried torches held high in one hand and spears or machetes in the other. They were silent, following the faint tracks in the sand or the tiny drops of blood that were sprinkled so carelessly along the trail. The silence was ominous; success would give no rewards. The silence was ominous because we all knew that death would be a visitor again this night. The silence was ominous because each of us knew what had to be done.

We stopped for no apparent reason. It was George who spoke in a whisper, "The bush being afraid. This lion is evil creature. It kill not for food. It kill young girl for fun. Not natural. Not natural making scare bush and all creatures. All animals run away, the hyena even. Birds fly away, small animals burrow. Bush saying be very careful. Saying must drive evil spirit away. Tonight!"

The men couldn't understand George's words, but they understood his tone. They were closer to the earth than I and sensed George's talent. The men accepted and revered George as a soothsayer and took seriously his fear. We looked at each other as fellow travelers on a trail of death then took up the chase again.

An old Turkana named Faro led at a fast trot. How he could read signs in the dark, on the run, was a mystery, yet he followed the spoor. We had gone less than a mile and had entered into heavy brush when a loud roar erupted just off the trail. Immediately a scream followed as the lion tore at a man's midsection then bolted off into the darkness. It happened so fast that no one could react, only the the man who was writhing on the ground, one side laid open chest to mid thigh, blood already soaking the sand. George and I stopped to administer to him and the rest ran after the lion. I was really scared, shaking scared. My upbringing and experience had not prepared me for this. Here at my feet was a man silently suffering a horrible wound endured from a beast whose power, ferocity and cunning were beyond us. George tore off his shirt and stuffed it into the most gaping wound, trying to stem the blood. I started to help, but saw a white object lying behind a thorn bush several feet away. I cautiously walked towards it. It was the little girl, Tatu. She was dead, but the lion had had no time to start in on her. She was intact except for an broken neck and long gashes along her body.

George got up and walked over to where I stood, "Not being much we doing for dead girl, needing help with living man." He tugged me back to the injured herdsman, and I took off my shirt to help bandage him. We were so engrossed that we didn't notice the tawny shape watching from under the spread of a thorn tree not twenty feet away. Suddenly George looked up with a start. He touched my arm for attention, "Lion being here. Bush all around frantic. That devil give shake to herdsmen and double back. It being close, getting shotgun. Now!"

I reached behind me, picked the shotgun up and turned. And looked dead into the eyes of pure, unabated evil, its hot, fetid breath washing over me. I jerked the barrel up instinctively and pulled the trigger. Nothing, a dud shell. The lion bowled me over, knocking the two other shells away. It was on George in a flash. Stunned I still was able to grab the shotgun by the barrel and swing it as hard as I could down on the lion's back. I swung again and again, cursing and swearing to try and close out the sound of George's screams.

Then it was quiet and the lion turned its eyes on me. It stared at me with the most malevolent look I had ever seen, as if to say, I'm leaving you for another time. It gave a last swipe at George's inert form and vanished into the brush.

I dropped the gun and knelt at George's side. His eyes were open and a look of bemusement was on his face. I was afraid to look at his body; I had seen the dead herdsman and couldn't face that mutilation again. Instead I cradled his head in my arms and held one of his long, bony hands until he gave a gasp and his hand fell limp in mine. I gazed into his sightless eyes, remembering all this kind and gentle man had said to me over the short time I had known him.

It surprised me to see his face glisten in the moonlight as if awash until I realized that my tears were freely flowing. I could hear the footfall of many shoeless men running towards us and then a circle of light cast over us from the burning torches. The men fell silent as they saw the body in my arms, then they gathered around in a circle as one by one they knelt to touch George's cheek and say a brief prayer. I held my friend like this until I knew it was time. I motioned for one of the men to take George then stood up, shaky. They knew what was next; one of the men handed me the shotgun. I told them the shells had been knocked out of my hand and we all searched the brush until they were found. I loaded one and clutched the other between my fingers. I dropped to one knee to touch George once more and asked for his protection and guidance. Faro nudged my arm and I followed him into the darkness.

He went fast as usual, following the spoor at a trot, ignoring the pull and tear of the wait-a-bit thorns grabbing at our bare arms and legs. Suddenly, he stopped and stared at a clump of dense brush, then walked slowly forward.

He was five feet from the brush when it exploded. The lion burst forward with blinding speed and ran straight into Faro, knocking him down and with a great roar was about to tear his throat out when it suddenly turned its head and looked at me with a mixture of hate and disdain. It dropped Faro like a rag doll and took two steps toward me. I raised the shotgun and was about to fire when the lion jumped to the side and disappeared into the bush. I rushed to Faro who didn't appear to be seriously hurt, but was in no way able to continue the chase.

I plunged into the bush after the lion. I had no clue as to where it was or where I was. I did know two things: that I wanted to kill that beast worse than I had wanted anything before and that lion would find me.

I stopped running and started thinking about George and his teachings. Something of him entered into me; a great peace came into my soul and hatred was pushed out.

Now I didn't want to kill the lion, all I wanted to do was return to the compound and prepare Dr. K.K. George, my friend, for burial. And to mourn him as befit the departure of a pure soul from this tarnished earth.

I turned and was following my tracks in the sand, dragging the shotgun by the barrel and remembering the days and evenings spent with him when suddenly I heard sounds all around. Soft sounds, high-pitched sounds, wheezing and soughing and the sounds of ancient voices, raspy and dry. I looked around and tried to pinpoint them, but they came from all directions and seemed mostly to come from...within. I didn't really hear them, they were simply present, and they didn't come from anywhere specifically. I listened, but in a different way. I listened from another source, another sense, and then I was able to understand individual sounds, not as words but as ideas. I listened as George had said, not with my ears, but with my body. I tried to become one with my surroundings, a part of everything. The bush was within me and it too mourned George. It also warned me that the lion was stalking and that that I should continue walking just as I was and that the bush would guide me and protect me.

It couldn't protect George, evil incarnate wanted his soul as it did all souls that were pure and good, and so the ancients had sent this abomination. But I was neither pure nor particularly good and the ancients really didn't care, so the abomination could do with me as it wished, but the bush was not about to abandon me. Fear left and I felt comforted and ready.

Now! The acacia, the thorn, the wait-a-bit and the tall grass all crowded into my head. *Turn and fire*! Without hesitation I swung around, threw up the gun and fired into the darkness. A flash of flame illuminated the lion not five feet behind me and springing. The blast caught the creature full in the face and smashed it to the ground. It was again quiet and dark.

I started to panic, fearing that the lion was still alive, when the sounds again entered my mind.

This devil is dead they said. But there will be more. Maybe not here but elsewhere in your life, far from here or maybe even in your own heart. Strive for purity in all that you do. When the devil comes forth, come to us and listen. For you must fight him. We'll be there and so will be another.

I swore I then heard a short chirp, the sound of knuckles popping and a faint voice saying, "No doubt."

Jack Meyers (Somalia, 1968-69; Kenya, 1969-70) became a resource economist. His last career position was Director of International Programs for Resource Management International before moving into consulting and writing (currently he has two completed novels and two in progress).

PART FIVE

SUSTAINABLE
PEACE

MICHAEL TOSO

Children of the Rains

Context and culture: Africa was much before the coming of the
Europeans, and continues to be Africa, for all the outside influence.

WE ARE IN ANZA'S GARDEN, WATCHING A HARMATTAN SUN SINK
over a mangled screw palm and what's left of the season's
millet harvest. Thieves broke into Anza's granary and, while
they didn't take everything, he is disheartened. Conversation
has taken an unusually somber tone. Abdou says that what he
wants in life, to feel secure, is a zinc roof over his head.

Most Djerma use braided grass and reeds for roofing. Some
of the upwardly mobile have begun to buy sheets of zinc, a
widely popular and sought after commodity because they do
not leak during our short rainy season. Anza stares out into his
garden and says that stored away millet is what gives his mind
rest. When you have a sack of millet in the corner, he says,
your wife and kids sleep soundly at night. You sleep soundly
because they sleep soundly. As we watch the last rays of sun
through broken millet stalks, Anza speaks in a quiet, measured
tone, *Nda wayno go ga kun ni ga, wa tun ga di, a go ga tun windi*
kulu bon. "You think the sun sets on your compound alone?

Stand up and see how it falls on the entire village." A succinct Djerma proverb.

I have seldom been accused of coming up short on words. Learning Djerma didn't change that, but has taught me the value of spoken word. Discovering, memorizing, and learning to call upon just the right proverb, at just the instant, changed my life in Falmey.

These age-old sayings encompass much of what makes seemingly threadbare Djerma such a poignant language. As with a proverb, there are few words; each and every one has multiple meanings. This is the power of a living, spoken language, the power of a proverb; should you draw upon conventional wisdom, no one will argue with you; with the right words, you can silence your enemies, embrace your loved ones, and tell a fanciful story to toddlers—in the same breath.

Before the French came to unite the Djerma, Hausa, Fulani, Toureg, Beri-Beri, and Gourmanche inside arbitrary lines on a piece of paper and began imposing head taxes, there were the Fulani Jihads of the eighteenth century. Before the Fulani spread across the Sahel to purify Islamic practices, there was the Songhai empire. Before the Songhai controlled the salt caravans, Touregs navigated the desert seas by starlight, marking each secret oasis town with a distinct silver cross.

Yes, long before white Peace Corps Volunteers arrived in Niger, people have been uprooted, supplanted, forced to migrate, learned to thrive in whatever place must now be called home.

The Land Rover dropped me off in the village in late October. Falmey was teaming with youth; the harvest was about to begin. Had I been dropped off in March, I would have met women, children, and old men. There is no economy to speak of in Niger and, with desertification growing worse each year, most young men travel south to Cotonou,

Accra, Lagos, Kano to find work. They work until clouds
gather above the Sahel, and then they follow these clouds
home to begin the harvest. These are the *kurmizey*, *taabusizey*,
children of the rain. They are the diaspora of this age.

Truly there is nothing new under the sun.

Kurmizey are the sons of Djerma farmers who travel across
the Sahel, down through the Savannahs to the sea coast in
search of work, only to return for the season of rains and harvest each year. *Taabusizey* are children born in a foreign land,
they are the fruits of a prodigal son's harvest sent home to be
claimed by their family. French-speaking Djermas named this
diaspora, this scattering of youth, Exode. A Djerma folk hip-
hop poet, the late Moussa Poussi, sang a song, *"Taabusizey."*
Moussa wove old farmers' songs of longing for their children's
return with the rebellious songs of youth ready to seek greener
pastures.

Every young traveler in my age-set knows this call-and-
response. When you travel to a foreign place, when the bright
city lights hit you for the first time, when you first taste Coca-
Cola, when you learn to eat foods other than millet, baobab
leaves and peanut sauce, and you don't know a soul in the
world because you can't speak the language, you begin to
whistle this song. You sing the song as you walk along, and
more likely than not, your song will find its companion.

Another Djerma youth's whistle will join yours and you are
no longer a stranger in a strange land: you have found someone to look after you and to look after.

My friend Yaye taught me this song shortly before I was to
begin my preparations for departure. He insisted that I learn it,
that I know the words elders sing from their fields as clouds
gather on the horizon: *rain clouds gather and bring your children
home for the harvest.* Elders and children sing to one another from
across the Savannahs and cloud-filled skies the separate them.

*Children of the rains, prodigal children: give birth and send
    your children home.*
*We are leaving, until we come again. Father mustn't look
    for us: mother mustn't look for us.*
Those that searched for us were belittled.
The water of belittlement catches one in the eyes.
The automobile is leaving, mother is crying.
The guitar and its strings should never separate.
The old kokoroba-*made hoe leans against a* kokoroba *tree.*
*The sleeper and his millet spoon are sleeping underneath the
    granary.*
*Wild millet is waiting to become porridge, the family awaits
    its arrival.*
*And this millet drink left in the sun must speak of its place
    and look to the sun.*
*For if it ferments and turns to poison, it will be the family
    who dies.*

Yaye's mother is a Fulani herder, his father is a Djerma
farmer. He was born in Falmey; he often travels to Ghana to
find work. The year I came to the village, he married. The
week before I left, he and I slaughtered a sheep for his son's
naming ceremony. Yaye speaks the pigeon English spoken in
Accra, but we converse in Djerma. We had never related with
words.

He and I were friends because of the knowing stare I would
catch out of the corner of his eye, as some passer-by made
comments about my "foreignness." We connected because he
knew what that was like.

I packed to leave Falmey as the third season of rains fell
down around us. A Djerma proverb says life is like a mango,
just as it becomes ripe, if falls from the tree. Yaye taught me to
sing "*Taabusizey*," and as I sang it for my age-set before leaving, I realized that Yaye wasn't teaching me this song so that I

could find a Djerma friend in the United States: that was the fanciful story for the toddlers. Yaye was silencing those who had mocked him, who had mocked me, for being different, because some had never left themselves. Because some of them had never sung the song in a foreign land. Yaye's gift to me was a word to associate with a precious time in my life. He was wise enough to know that it isn't the spoken word that matters, but the layers of meaning you can fold beneath its sound.

Michael Tosso was a Community and Youth Educator in Niger from 2004-06. Since 2009 he has been a Preventative Health Educator with the Peace Corps responsible for improving rural environmental and nutrition outcomes through non-formal education and community action in Senagal.

Acknowledgements

WHEN JANE ALBRITTON ASKED ME TO EDIT THE AFRICA VOLUME of *Peace Corps @ 50*, I had no idea what I was getting into, no idea what a wonderful project this is or of the power of the essays that she had collected (though one of them was mine). Jane had a vision for this series that I only learned to appreciate as I worked on it, coming to understand something that I may have forgotten in the years since my own formative Peace Corps experience: Peace Corps changes lives, both of the Peace Corps Volunteers (PCVs) and those they interact with. Few development projects or organizations (if any) have had such a continual and personal impact as Peace Corps.

So, the first person I have to thank here is Jane. Though my name may be on the cover of the book with hers, this is really her project, a result of her vision. My hat goes off to her.

Then I have to thank the contributors. We have had an overwhelming response to Jane's call for submissions, and I have had the unfortunate task of winnowing them down to a still-unreasonable (but workable) size, sometimes cutting much of what these passionate Returned Peace Corps Volunteers (RPCVs) have written so that more of them can be included. They have reaffirmed the importance and power of the Peace Corps experience, but have pulled no punches, depicting the bad and the difficult as well as the good.

This volume owes a great deal to Production Director Susan Brady, who demands a higher level of work than I can provide, getting more from me (and from the stories) than would otherwise be possible. Any success this book has will come because she has made it welcoming and accessible.

Finally, I want to thank my wife, Jan Stern, who not only has assisted me, but who has been willing to accommodate the work into our already over-extended lives, finding ways for this project to be included even as it became more and more a labor of love and more and more consuming.

Story Acknowledgments

"Why I Joined the Peace Corps" by Robert Klein published with permission from the author. Copyright © 2011 by Robert Klein.

"There at the Beginning" by Tom Katus, George Johnson, Alex Veech, and L. Gilbert Griffis published with permission from the authors. Copyright © 2011 by Tom Katus, George Johnson, Alex Veech, and L. Gilbert Griffis.

"Learning to Speak" by Tom Weller published with permission from the author. Copyright © 2011 by Tom Weller.

"First and Last Days" by Bob Powers published with permission from the author. Copyright © 2011 by Bob Powers.

"*Hena Kisoa Kely* and Blue Nail Polish" by Amanda Wonson published with permission from the author. Copyright © 2011 by Amanda Wonson.

"Coming to Sierra Leone" by Sarah Moffett-Guice published with permission from the author. Copyright © 2011 by Sarah Moffett-Guice.

"Shattering and Using Book Learning" by Susan L. Schwartz published with permission from the author. Copyright © 2011 by Susan L. Schwartz.

"The Adventures Overseas" by Larry W. Harms published with permission from the author. Copyright © 2011 by Larry W. Harms.

"A Toubac in the Gloaming" by E. T. Stafne published with permission from the author. Copyright © 2011 by E. T. Stafne.

"Family Affair" by Arne Vanderburg published with permission from the author. Copyright © 2011 by Arne Vanderburg.

"Your Parents Visited You In Africa?" by Solveig Nilsen published with permission from the author. Copyright © 2011 by Solveig Nilsen.

"What I Tell My Students" by William G. Moseley published with permission from the author. Copyright © 2011 by William G. Moseley.

"Slash and Burn" by Kelly McCorkendale published with permission from the author. Copyright © 2011 by Kelly McCorkendale.

"Two Years Lasts a Lifetime" by Sally Cytron Gati published with permission from the author. Copyright © 2011 by Sally Cytron Gati.

"Sister Stella Seams Serene" by Starley Talbott Anderson published with permission from the author. Copyright © 2011 by Starley Talbott Anderson.

"Late Evening" by Lenore Waters published with permission from the author. Copyright © 2011 by Lenore Waters.

"The Forty-Eight Hour Rule" by Martin R. Ganzglass published with permission from the author. Copyright © 2011 by Martin R. Ganzglass.

"Full Circle" by Delfi Messinger published with permission from the author. Copyright © 2011 by Delfi Messinger.

"A Promise Kept" by Beth Duff-Brown published with permission from the author. Copyright © 2011 by Beth Duff-Brown.

"The Utopia of the Village" by Heather Corinne Cumming published with permission from the author. Copyright © 2011 by Heather Corinne Cumming.

"The Engine Catches" by Susanna Lewis published with permission from the author. Copyright © 2011 by Susanna Lewis.

"Yaka" by Kelly J. Morris published with permission from the author. Copyright © 2011 by .

"*Nous Sommes Ensemble*" by Anna Russo published with permission from the author. Copyright © 2011 by Anna Russo.

"The Sweetest Gift" by Jayne Bielecki published with permission from the author. Copyright © 2011 by Jayne Bielecki.

"The Conference" by Marcy L. Spaulding published with permission from the author. Copyright © 2011 by Marcy L. Spaulding .

"Girls' School" by Marsa Laird published with permission from the author. Copyright © 2011 by Marsa Laird.

"Testimony" by Stephanie Bane published with permission from the author. Copyright © 2011 by Stephanie Bane.

"African Woman" by Dorothea Hertzberg published with permission from the author. Copyright © 2011 by Dorothea Hertzberg.

"My Rice Crop" by Edmund Blair Bolles published with permission from the author. Copyright © 2011 by Edmund Blair Bolles.

"Gentle Winds of Change" by Donald Holm published with permission from the author. Copyright © 2011 by Donald Holm.

"La Supermarché" by Jennifer L. Giacomini published with permission from the author. Copyright © 2011 by Jennifer L. Giacomini.

"Mokhotlong" by Allison Scott Matlack published with permission from the author. Copyright © 2011 by Allison Scott Matlack.

"Changing School" by Sandra Echols Sharpe published with permission from the author. Copyright © 2011 by Sandra Echols Sharpe.

"The Season of *Omagongo*" by Alan Barstow published with permission from the author. Copyright © 2011 by Alan Barstow.

"Tapping" by Eric Stone published with permission from the author. Copyright © 2011 by Eric Stone.

"The Drums of Democracy" by Paul P. Pometto II published with permission from the author. Copyright © 2011 by Paul P. Pometto II.

"Boys & Girls" by Ryan N. Smith published with permission from the author. Copyright © 2011 by Ryan N. Smith.

"I'd Wanted to Go to Africa, But the Peace Corps Sent Me to Sierra Leone" by Bob Hixon Julyan published with permission from the author. Copyright © 2011 by Bob Hixon Julyan.

"Breakfast" by Jed Brody published with permission from the author. Copyright © 2011 by Jed Brody.

"Daily Life" by Kathleen Moore published with permission from the author. Copyright © 2011 by Kathleen Moore.

"*Watoto* of Tanzania" by Linda Chen See published with permission from the author. Copyright © 2011 by Linda Chen See.

"Begging Turned on Its Head" by Karen Hlynsky published with permission from the author. Copyright © 2011 by Karen Hlynsky.

"Time" by Patricia Owen published with permission from the author. Copyright © 2011 by Patricia Owen.

"Learning to Play the Game of Life" by Lawrence Grobel published with permission from the author. Copyright © 2011 by Lawrence Grobel.

"A First Real Job" by Joy Marburger published with permission from the author. Copyright © 2011 by Joy Marburger.

"It's Condom Day!" by Sera Arcaro published with permission from the author. Copyright © 2011 by Sera Arcaro.

"The Civilized Way" by Bryant Wieneke published with permission from the author. Copyright © 2011 by Bryant Wieneke.

"Who Controls the Doo-Doo?" by Jay Davidson published with permission from the author. Copyright © 2011 by Jay Davidson.

"The Ride Home" by Bina Dugan published with permission from the author. Copyright © 2011 by Bina Dugan.

"The Little Things" by Stephanie Gottlieb published with permission from the author. Copyright © 2011 by Stephanie Gottlieb.

"There Will Be Mud" by Bruce Kahn published with permission from the author. Copyright © 2011 by Bruce Kahn.

"The Hammam in Rabat" by Shauna Steadman published with permission from the author. Copyright © 2011 by Shauna Steadman.

"Straight Razors in Heaven" by Paul Negley, Jr. published with permission from the author. Copyright © 2011 by Paul Negley, Jr.

"Big Butts Are Beautiful!" by Janet Grace Riehl published with permission from the author. Copyright © 2011 by Janet Grace Riehl.

"Monsieur Robert Loves Rats " Bob Walker published with permission from the author. Copyright © 2011 by Bob Walker.

"Imani" by Daniel Franklin published with permission from the author. Copyright © 2011 by Daniel Franklin.

"Hail, Sinner! I Go to Church" by Floyd Sandford published with permission from the author. Copyright © 2011 by Floyd Sandford.

"A Visit From H.I.M." by Carol Beddo published with permission from the author. Copyright © 2011 by Carol Beddo.

"Moon Rocket" by Robert E. Gribbin published with permission from the author. Copyright © 2011 by Robert E. Gribbin.

"Bury My Shorts at Chamborro Gorge" by Thor Hanson published with permission from the author. Copyright © 2011 by Thor Hanson.

"Near Death in Africa" by Nancy Biller published with permission from the author. Copyright © 2011 by Nancy Biller.

"Boeuf Madagaskara" by Jacquelyn Z. Brooks published with permission from the author. Copyright © 2011 by Jacquelyn Z. Brooks.

"The Baobob Tree" by Kara Garbe published with permission from the author. Copyright © 2011 by Kara Garbe.

"The Sports Bar" by Leita Kaldi Davis published with permission from the author. Copyright © 2011 by Leita Kaldi Davis.

"One Last Party" by Paula Zoromski published with permission from the author. Copyright © 2011 by Paula Zoromski.

"The Peace Corps in a War Zone" by Tom Gallagher published with permission from the author. Copyright © 2011 by Tom Gallagher.

"Holding the Candle" by Suzanne Meagher Owen published with permission from the author. Copyright © 2011 by Suzanne Meagher Owen.

"A Morning" by Enid S. Abrahami published with permission from the author. Copyright © 2011 by Enid S. Abrahami.

"A Brother in Need" by Genevieve Murakami published with permission from the author. Copyright © 2011 by Genevieve Murakami.

"A Tree Grows in Niamey" by Stephanie Oppenheimer-Streb published with permission from the author. Copyright © 2011 by Stephanie Oppenheimer-Streb.

"Jaarga" by Betsy Polhemus published with permission from the author. Copyright © 2011 by Betsy Polhemus.

"For Lack of a Quarter..." by Irene G. Brammertz published with permission from the author. Copyright © 2011 by Irene G. Brammertz.

"Crazy Cat Lady" by Michelle Stoner published with permission from the author. Copyright © 2011 by Michelle Stoner.

"Elephant Morning" by Aaron Barlow published with permission from the author. Copyright © 2011 by Aaron Barlow.

"At Night the Bushes Whisper" by Jack Meyers published with permission from the author. Copyright © 2011 by Jack Meyers.

"Children of the Rains" by Michael Toso published with permission from the author. Copyright © 2011 by Michael Toso.

Special thanks to
The Jason and Lucy Greer Foundation
for the Arts for their generous support of
the Peace Corps@50 Project.

About the Editor

BEFORE JOINING THE PEACE CORPS AS AN AGRICULTURAL EXTEN-
sion agent for animal traction (plowing using oxen) in Togo,
Aaron Barlow spent two years teaching at the University of
Ouagadougou in Burkina Faso, where he was Senior Fulbright
Lecturer in American Studies. Fascinated by Africa, but realizing the city experience was far from the whole, he wanted to
live and work in a village.

Barlow's Ph.D. from the University of Iowa was capped by
a dissertation on the science-fiction writer Philip K. Dick and
completed in 1988. He did not become a full-time academic
in the United States, however, until 2004. In the meantime,
in addition to his Peace Corps experience, he co-founded
and ran a café/gift shop in Brooklyn, NY called Shakespeare's
Sister, dedicated to the idea that there is talent and art in every
individual.

Now a specialist in the intersection of technology and culture, Barlow has produced four books over the past six years,
two relating to film and two to new media and the blogosphere. He teaches at New York City College of Technology,
a part of the City University of New York where he enjoys
working with a student body representing over 100 different
languages and cultures, a diversity he learned to appreciate
while a Peace Corps Volunteer.